LANDSCAPES AND LANDMARKS OF CANADA

CULTURAL STUDIES SERIES

Cultural Studies is the multi- and inter-disciplinary study of culture, defined anthropologically as a "way of life," performatively as symbolic practice, and ideologically as the collective product of varied media and cultural industries. Although Cultural Studies is a relative newcomer to the humanities and social sciences, in less than half a century it has taken interdisciplinary scholarship to a new level of sophistication, reinvigorating the liberal arts curriculum with new theories, topics, and forms of intellectual partnership.

Wilfrid Laurier University Press invites submissions of manuscripts concerned with critical discussions on power relations concerning gender, class, sexual preference, ethnicity, and other macro and micro sites of political struggle.

For more information, please contact:

Siobhan McMenemy
Senior Editor
Wilfrid Laurier University Press
75 University Avenue West
Waterloo, ON N2L 3C5,
Canada

Phone: 519-884-0710 ext. 3782
Fax: 519-725-1399
Email: smcmenemy@wlu.ca

LANDSCAPES AND LANDMARKS
OF CANADA real, imagined, (re)viewed

Maeve Conrick, Munroe Eagles, Jane Koustas, Caitríona Ní Chasaide, editors

WILFRID LAURIER
UNIVERSITY PRESS

Wilfrid Laurier University Press acknowledges the support of the Canada Council for the Arts for our publishing program. We acknowledge the financial support of the Government of Canada through the Canada Book Fund for our publishing activities. This work was supported by the Research Support Fund.

The editors would like to acknowledge the financial assistance of the National University of Ireland and the Association of Canadian Studies in Ireland.

Library and Archives Canada Cataloguing in Publication

    Landscapes and landmarks of Canada : real, imagined, (re)viewed / Maeve Conrick, Munroe Eagles, Jane Koustas, and Caitríona Ní Chasaide, editors.

(Cultural studies series)
Includes bibliographical references and index.
Issued in print and electronic formats.
ISBN 978-1-77112-201-6 (paperback).—ISBN 978-1-77112-202-3 (pdf).—
ISBN 978-1-77112-203-0 (epub)

    1. Landscape assessment—Canada. 2. Cultural landscapes—Canada. 3. Human geography—Canada. 4. Historic sites—Canada. I. Koustas, Jane, 1954–, editor II. Eagles, Munroe, [date], editor III. Conrick, Maeve, editor IV. Ni Chasaide, Caitriona, 1974–, editor V. Series: Cultural studies series (Waterloo, Ont.)

GF91.C3L38 2016   304.20971   C2016-904836-5
                                                                                            C2016-904837-3

Cover image and page-viii image by Shawn Serfas: *Rise* (Plaything series, 2010; acrylic, oil, and mixed media on canvas; 152.4 cm x 121.9 cm), www.shawnserfas.com. Cover and text design by Lime Design Inc.

© 2017 Wilfrid Laurier University Press
Waterloo, Ontario, Canada
www.wlupress.wlu.ca

Every reasonable effort has been made to acquire permission for copyright material used in this text, and to acknowledge all such indebtedness accurately. Any errors and omissions called to the publisher's attention will be corrected in future printings.

No part of this publication may be reproduced, stored in a retrieval system, or transmitted, in any form or by any means, without the prior written consent of the publisher or a licence from the Canadian Copyright Licensing Agency (Access Copyright). For an Access Copyright licence, visit http://www.accesscopyright.ca or call toll free to 1-800-893-5777.

CONTENTS

INTRODUCTION
1 **Landscapes and Landmarks of Canada:**
Real, Imagined, (Re)Viewed

ONE
11 **Canada:** Islands, Landscapes, and Landmarks
Stephen A. Royle

TWO
27 **Science at Service of Sublime Landscapes:**
Scientific Ecology and the Preservation of Canada's
Wilderness Landmarks in 1970s Quebec
Olivier Craig-Dupont

THREE
47 **Patriotisms of the People:** Understanding the
"Highway of Heroes" as a Canadian National Landmark
Tracey Raney

FOUR
63 **Material Differences:** Ethnic Diversity and
the Power of Things in Greater Sudbury
Tim Nieguth

FIVE
77 **Our Home and Native Land:** Invocations of the Land
in the 2011 Canadian Federal Election
Shauna Wilton

SIX
91 **Memorializing an Imagined Past:**
Evangeline and the Acadian Deportation
Jane Moss

SEVEN
109 **Time and Space in the Nationalism
of Thomas D'Arcy McGee**
David A. Wilson

EIGHT
123 **Contesting Historical Space:** The Campaign to Have Grosse Île Designated a National Historic Site with the Irish Dimension as its Main Theme
Pádraig Breandán Ó Laighin

NINE
145 **Environmental Exposure:** Two films "de légitime défense": Richard Desjardins and Robert Monderie: *L'erreur boréale / Forest Alert* (1999) and *Trou Story / The Hole Story* (2011)
Rachel Killick

TEN
175 **Postcolonial Territorial Landmarks within Canada's Multiculturalism:** The Myth of Virility
Édith-Anne Pageot

ELEVEN
197 **Mapping the Migrant Mindscape in Gabrielle Roy:** A Macro Definition of *écriture migrante*
Julie Rodgers

TWELVE
217 **The Green Fields of Canada – Forgotten!** A Reappraisal of Irish Traditional Music History in Canada
Gearóid Ó hAllmhuráin

THIRTEEN
243 **The Contemporary Powwow in Eastern Canada:** A Practice of Gathering
Dalie Giroux and Amélie-Anne Mailhot

261 ABOUT THE AUTHORS
267 INDEX

LIST OF ILLUSTRATIONS

Frontispiece   *Rise*, by Shawn Serfas **/ viii**

Figure 6.1   Acadian population in 1750 **/ 93**

Figure 6.2   Acadian deportations 1755–57 **/ 94**

Figure 6.3   Acadian embarkation **/ 104**

Figure 8.1   Celtic cross on southwest peninsula **/ 126**

Figure 8.2   Portion of mass-grave cemetery of 1847 on southwest peninsula **/ 130**

Figure 8.3   Monument near the entrance to the Victoria Bridge, Montréal **/ 138**

Figure 8.4   Taschereau Monument, Québec City: detail **/ 139**

Map 13.1   Eastern powwow trail **/ 249**

INTRODUCTION

Landscapes and Landmarks of Canada: Real, Imagined, (Re)Viewed

n their influential article about memorialization on Canada's Parliament Hill, David Gordon and Brian Osborne reflect on the role of statues and other landmarks in creating, focusing, and sustaining national identity. They note:

> One of the principal strategies of nationalising in overcoming internal difference and plural imaginations is to construct a cohesive collective memory and associate the state with a national symbolic space. What has been [more] difficult however has been the sense of collective memory of the past and mission for the future.... In particular, the *idea* of the nation-state has to be nurtured through symbolic identification with an "imagined community," and collective memory through foundation myths and heroic narratives, and the identification with particular places.[1]

The concept of an "imagined community," based on Benedict Anderson's groundbreaking work,[2] and its relation to the creation of a national symbolic space concretized by the celebration and promotion of landscape and the building and veneration of landmarks, underpins the articles in this book. Like the contributors to *Land, Memory, and History*, the authors explore and assess "how perceptions of and values attached to landscape encode values and fix memories that become sites of historical identity."³ Canada's preoccupation with collective memory and its strategies to cope with such a concept in an officially multicultural environment must also be considered against the background of the nation's desire to project an image abroad, to the Other, or to a public outside of the "community," however diverse. Hans-Georg Gadamer in his discussion of "effective historical consciousness" reminds us that "the apprehension of the past is always framed by the interpreter's finite, partial, and fallible horizon of interpretation."⁴ He argues that interpretive dexterity is required to understand the past of other cultures. As Neatby and Hodgins note, referring to Gadamer: "Without marshalling the ethical and political courage to revise and reject aspects of those forms, codes, and media, we will continue to obscure our vision of the past or that of others."⁵ The present collection considers landmarks and landscapes from both within and outside the "imagined community" to which they belong.

The image of the "land" is an ongoing trope in both past and contemporary conceptions of Canada. From the national anthem to the flag, to the symbols on coins, the land and nature remain linked to the Canadian sense of belonging as well as to the image of the nation abroad. If earlier portrayals of the land focused on a rugged, unspoiled landscape, such as in the paintings of the Group of Seven, contemporary notions of identity, belonging, and citizenship are established, contested, and legitimized within sites and institutions of public culture, heritage, and representation that reflect integration, with the land transforming landscape into landmarks. Grosse Île, the Highway of Heroes, and the Irish Memorial National Historic Site in Quebec are examples of landmarks that transform landscape into a built environment that endeavours to respect the land while using it as a site to commemorate, celebrate, and promote Canadian identity. Similarly, in literature and the arts, the creation of the built environment and the interactions among those who share it is a recurrent theme.

This volume includes essays by Canadian, Irish, American, and other international scholars whose engagement with the theme stems from their disciplinary perspective as well as from their personal and professional experiences, which are rooted, at least in part, in their own sense of national identity and in their relationship to Canada. The famine memorial at Grosse Île, for example, takes on a different meaning for the Irish, whose personal and national history has become a space of memory and testimony on the Canadian landscape. This book focuses on research by historians, geographers, political scientists, other social scientists, scholars of literature and art, and folklorists. By bringing together a wide range of disciplinary perspectives from scholars of international origin and reputation, this collection offers Canadian and international readers new perspectives from which to consider the interactions of the land, landmarks, and landscapes and the communities engaged in their interpretation. Neatby and Hodgins count among sites of memory "monuments, art, various forms of cultural practices such as parades, as well as history textbooks, websites, historical fiction, and the past as represented in the moving image."[6] Landmarks, or sites of memory, defined by Pierre Nora as "any significant entity, where material or non-material in nature, which by dint of human will or the work of time has become a symbolic element of the memorial heritage of any community," can become contested spaces.[7] This collection, which considers monuments, film, literature, cultural practices, and history texts, shows how the natural landscape and the built environment are both products of, and actors in, the creation of sometimes divergent ideological notions of Canada.

Perceptions of boundaries may be moulded by political, collective, and individual perspectives so that landscape becomes a function or measure of space and place. As Stephen Royle's contribution to this book demonstrates, while geographical landscape may change slowly, its role in national identity is dynamic. Because Canada is demarcated geographically by island compass points (Cape Spear in Newfoundland, Boundary Peak 187 in the Yukon, Cape Columbia on Ellesmere Island, and Middle Island in Lake Erie), islands and coasts may be considered central, rather than peripheral, in articulations of the country. Indeed, from First Nations beliefs, such as the founding myth of Turtle Island, to the Europeans' (re)discovering of the continent, perceptions of islands have been significant in geographic and historical interpretations and definitions of Canada's space and place.

If "from sea to sea" ("A mare usque ad mare," Canada's motto) poetically evokes the island image, however large the land mass, "the true north strong and free," from the national anthem, suggests another equally resonant and familiar representation of Canadian space and place—namely, that of the wilderness. Parks Canada, charged with the mission to "protect and present nationally significant examples of Canada's natural and cultural heritage and foster public understanding, appreciation and enjoyment in ways that ensure their ecological and commemorative integrity for present and future generations," actively participates in the transformation of landscape into a key factor of identity.[8] As Olivier Craig-Dupont demonstrates in this volume, "wilderness" is paradoxically an idealization of nature free from human interference, but also a social concept, one in which the iconicity of wild and unspoiled landscape becomes a deeply political construct. If land mass is fixed geographically, identified and delineated politically and historically, the landscape can be moulded both physically and symbolically.

National parks, for example, are specifically designated, and tamed, "wilderness" spaces that achieve landmark status and hence become cultural products.

Similarly, if the "wilderness" can be defined as a nationally significant example of Canada's heritage, the built environment, itself a moulding of the landscape into an urban space, can achieve landmark status, thus joining "significant examples of Canada's cultural heritage" even though well beyond the sphere of the national park.[9] The Macdonald–Cartier Freeway, more commonly known as Highway 401, was, as its official name suggests, already emblematic of Canadian unity; stretching from Windsor to Montreal, it was built as a physical link between Ontario and Quebec and was named after two prominent Fathers of Confederation from those provinces. A stretch of this highway beginning at CFB Trenton became a landmark of patriotism. Tracey Raney considers the sociocultural phenomenon of the "Highway of Heroes," where people lined the highway from the military base to show solidarity with the families of Canadian soldiers killed in Afghanistan whose coffins were being transported to their respective regimental headquarters along this route. The display of national, provincial, and town flags along the highway conveyed the complexity of Canadian patriotism founded on the unity of many local identities. In lining the highway, people themselves became a feature of Canadian landscape.

If the presence—and, arguably, power—of people can transform a mere highway into a landmark of national patriotism and indeed mourning, then "things," material objects, as Tim Nieguth demonstrates, have a similar power to construct ethnic identity and diversity. He considers the urban landscape from a social constructivist perspective, highlighting the use of city-texts and public iconography to delimit the landscape in Greater Sudbury. It can successfully be argued that human communities, identities, and perceptions of reality are social constructs rather than natural givens, so it is important to recognize the role of objects such as street names, public signs, and public art in the social construction of collective identities and thus in the cultural landscape.

If the preservation and promotion of Canada's natural and cultural heritage is the purview of Parks Canada, and if the urban landscape can be transformed to perform a social function, invocations of the land can be used to promote a sense of Canadian identity and belonging—even, as Shauna Wilton demonstrates, during election campaigns. During the 2011 federal election, representations of the Canadian landscape, including the built environment, images of nature, and Canadian national symbols, were embedded in discourses about Canadian values and political priorities. As with the motto "from sea to sea" and the line "the true north strong and free" from the national anthem, political parties used the familiar symbolic image "our home and native land" to connect with voters—and especially television viewers—at a visceral level. In these political broadcasts, landscape was one tool used to frame voters' perceptions of Canada and of political candidates. In her analysis of these broadcasts, Wilton links the natural landscape, the media, and political ideologies. The political parties mined voters' attachment to place, space, and landscape for their potential to win elections.

Landmarks and landscapes are not merely physical spaces. Canada is very much a storied landscape lived and (re)interpreted through individual and collective memory and imagination; sites of memory become landmarks. As Neatby and Hodgins contend, memories can be both settling and unsettling, reliable and unreliable, forgotten or institutionalized, functional or dysfunctional, but they are consistently "usable" in creating an image of the nation:

> The notion of competing collective memories has in turn led scholars to think of them as "usable." Indeed, the study of remembering makes it apparent that "some memories once functional, become dysfunctional. Thinking of memories as usable has helped to account for the fact that some memories become dominant or institutionalized often in the form of an "official narrative of nation."[10]

Collective memories, woven into the tapestry of a nation's narrative, are expressed through literature, music, and visual arts and are frequently grounded in or interpreted through landscape. As Wylie notes: "landscape is not something we see, it is also a *way of seeing things*, a particular way of looking at and picturing the world around us. Landscapes are not just about *what* we see but about *how we look*. To landscape is to gaze in a particular fashion."[11]

Gazing in a particular fashion and rendering memories "usable" in the narrative of the nation, poets, film writers and directors, musicians, and visual artists create a storied landscape. But there conceivably exist numerous, even competing stories: "There is a growing recognition that every memory text or performance is the product of a series of complex negotiations between cultural producers, their patrons and communities."[12]

"Evangeline" is a striking example of the layering of historical fact, poetic fiction, physical landscape, and constructed landmarks. Jane Moss shows how the fictional character Evangeline was taken from the realm of the imagination and literature and given a place within the Canadian landscape. The legitimization of a romantic ideal through Evangeline facilitated the erasure of painful memories of the Acadian deportation, and the arts subsequently played a key role in the reappropriation of the unsettling collective memory of *Le Grand Dérangement* at the Grand Pré National Historic Site. While decidedly fictional, and hence unequivocally unreliable, the figure of Evangeline proved itself eminently usable in the official Acadian narrative.

According to Wylie, "nature plus culture equals landscape."[13] Implied in this equation is the notion of time and place, culture being rooted in both. In his examination of Ireland's influence on Canada, David Wilson shows how landscape moulds the "Other" in communities; he also looks at McGee's "efforts to overcome parochialism in space and parochialism in time" in both Ireland and Canada. For his part, Pádraig Breandán Ó Laighin studies the memorial to Irish immigrants at Grosse Île National Historic Site.

Wilson explores the influence of both geography and history on McGee's Canadian and Irish nationalism. He notes that throughout history, notions of communities and outsiders are often determined by perceptions of place. He considers the role of the land—be it the romanticized wilderness or the ghettos of big cities—in shaping communities. Ó Laighin also explores the link between Canada and Ireland. He looks at the campaign to have Grosse Île designated as a national park with the commemoration of the Irish who died there as its main theme. This memorial provides a focal point for the collective memory of Irish Canadians. Like Moss and Craig-Dupont, Ó Laighin examines the ways in which national parks are used to promote and denote aspects of Canadian history, thus linking concepts of identity, rooted in collective memory, to landscapes, which become sites of memory and landmarks.

As Wylie declares, the official narrative, the official "way of seeing things," may not be the only one: "Studying landscape involves thinking about how our gaze, our way of looking at the world, is always laden with particular cultural values, attitudes, ideologies and expectations."[14] *Trou story* (and the play on words through code switching is telling) and *L'erreur boréale / Forest Alert* (where the translation conveys a double meaning), documentaries produced and screened in Quebec, challenge the perception that Canada's wilderness is infinite and owned by the Canadian people. Here, Rachel Killick explores the disconnect between the big business view of landscape as an expendable source of raw materials and those of local residents and activists keen to ensure the preservation and long-term sustainability of Canada's natural environment. Different values produce a different gaze.

Visual art, too, can challenge the notion that there is one official narrative. The Group of Seven's iconic portrayal of Canada, firmly rooted in the intersection of space, place, and the wilderness, decidedly usable, can be reframed. Against the backdrop of these traditional artistic clichés of the Canadian landscape, Édith-Anne Pageot parodies the myths associated with the land and Canadian peoples.

The art studied here draws on stereotypes of race, gender, and landscape and aims to provoke the audience to reassess official and personal discourses of diversity and national unity.

Migration is typically viewed as movement from one area or country to another and as linked to the physical landscape. The notions of migration and *écriture migrante* are explored by Julie Rodgers through the works of Gabrielle Roy where characters feel "caught between two worlds" (Rogers, this volume). The "lands" explored in this chapter are social, geographical, and within the minds of the characters, revealing the discontinuity between community and place and between identity and a sense of belonging. Landscape and landmarks become the stuff of frequently unsettling memory.

Continuing the theme of immigrant influences, Gearóid Ó hAllmhuráin examines soundscapes in Canada from the perspective of both music and language, demonstrating their links to the landscape. He shows how the transplantation and adaptation of Irish traditional music significantly contributed to the construction of Canadian Irish identities, placing music on the landscape map and reminding us, as does Wylie, that "landscapes are human, cultural and creative domains as well as, or *even rather than,* natural or physical phenomena."[15] Ó hAllmhuráin looks at ways in which the movement of peoples is reflected in the soundscapes of Canada. The memory and continuation of the various peoples who live and lived in Canada can be heard in their music. The lack of travel between rural areas in Canada facilitated the maintenance of traditions of various groups, thus securing music's place in specific, often isolated, Canadian landscapes.

Several authors note how the First Nations are often ignored in official discourse, which emphasizes the role of the French and the British in Canadian history. Hence there is a need to focus on the relationship between the landscape and its first inhabitants. Dalie Giroux and Amélie-Anne Mailhot map the powwows of First Nations on the Canadian landscape, exploring how these celebrations are used to maintain and develop cultural aspects of different First Nation worlds. The authors look at the dynamic culture of First Nations in Canada, situating them as grounded in a history that encompasses past and future ideas of land and landmarks.

In his introduction to the collection titled *Landscape*, Wiley asks:

Does the word landscape describe the mutual embeddedness and interconnectivity of self, body, knowledge and land—landscape as the world we live in, a constantly changing emergent perceptual and material milieu? Or is landscape better conceived in artistic painterly terms as a specific cultural and historical genre, a set of visual strategies and devices for distancing and observing?[16]

The concept of landscape as both an ever-changing, dynamic factor in the identity equation and as, by contrast, a static, historically and culturally grounded symbol can be applied equally to landmarks. In their discussion of the memorialization of the Canadian "heroes" Madeleine de Verchères and Laura Secord, authors Colin Coates and Cecilia Morgan argue that collective memory is always in "permanent evolution." This constant dynamic is subject to the dialectic of remembering and forgetting, unconscious of the distortions to which it is subject, vulnerable in various ways to appropriation and manipulation, and capable of lying dormant for long periods only to be suddenly reawakened.[17]

This book demonstrates that if the role, interpretation, and exploitation of landscape (built *and* natural) and landmarks can be dynamic (as with the evolution of the "Highway of Heroes") *and* static (as with the "frame freezing" on Grosse Île), both are also subject to different interpretations from outside the "imagined community" by which and for which they were conceived.

This book offers readers an overview of landscape and landmarks in Canada from a rich variety of perspectives. Traditional notions of landscape are expanded to include urban centres, the imagination, the built environment, and publicly funded museums. Notions about how landscape and landmarks are delineated and perceived in Canada are continually challenged. Landscape is a focal point of testimony, of lore, and of imagined pasts. The landscape, however, is also an actor in shaping the lives of those who engage with it. This transdisciplinary collection invites the reader to literally and figuratively review Canadian landscapes and landmarks. In doing so it contributes to our understanding of the Canadian landscape and of those who engage with it. ■

NOTES

1. Gordon and Osborne, "Constructing National Identity," 620–21.
2. Anderson, *Imagined Communities*.
3. Stewart and Strathern, *Land, Memory and History*, 1.
4. Gadamer, "The Problem of Historical Consciousness."
5. Gadamer, quoted in Neatby and Hodgins, *Settling and Unsettling Memories*, 7.
6. Ibid., 6.
7. Nora, *Realms of Memory*, xvii.
8. Parks Canada.
9. Ibid.

10 Neatby and Hodgins, *Settling and Unsettling Memories*, 5.

11 Wylie, *Landscape*, 7

12 Neatby and Hodgins, *Settling and Unsettling Memories*, 6.

13 Wylie, *Landscape*. 7

14 Ibid., 7.

15 Wylie, *Landscape*, 8.

16 Ibid., 2.

17 Coates and Morgan, *Heroines and History*, 4–5.

WORKS CITED

Anderson, Benedict. *Imagined Communities: Reflections on the Origin and Spread of Nationalism*, rev. ed. London: Verso, 1991.

Coates, Colin, and Cecilia Morgan. *Heroines and History: Representations of Madeleine de Verchères and Laura Secord*. Toronto: University of Toronto Press, 2002.

Gadamer, Hans-Georg. "The Problem of Historical Consciousness." In *Interpretive Social Science: A Second Look*, ed. Paul Rabinow and William Sullivan. Berkeley: University of California Press, 1987.

Gordon, David, and Brian S. Osborne. "Constructing National Identity in Canada's Capital, 1900–2000: Confederation Square and the National War Memorial." *Journal of Historical Geography* 30 (2004): 618–42.

Kovacs, Jason F., and Brian S. Osborne. "Re-membering Dead Heroes: Quebec City's Monument to Short-Wallick." In *Settling and Unsettling Memories*, ed. Nicole Neatby and Peter Hodgins, 67–94. Toronto: University of Toronto Press, 2012.

Neatby, Nicole, and Peter Hodgins, eds. *Settling and Unsettling Memories*. Toronto: University of Toronto Press, 2012.

Nora, Pierre. *Realms of Memory: The Construction of the French Past*. Trans. Arthur Goldhammer. New York: Columbia University Press, 1996.

Parks Canada. http://www.pc.gc.ca/eng/agen/index.aspx

Stewart, Pamela, and Andrew Strathern (eds.). *Land, Memory, and History*. London: Pluto Press, 2003.

Wylie, John. *Landscape*. London and New York: Routledge, 2007.

ONE

Canada: Islands, Landscapes, and Landmarks

Stephen A. Royle

ISLANDS AND CONTINENT

A **famous geographical phrase** that undoubtedly applies to Canada is "from sea to shining sea," although the fact that it is found in the American patriotic song "America the Beautiful" rather handicaps its use in a Canadian context. Instead Canada, in the words of its national anthem in English, is "the true north strong and free." Both North American nations, then, associate their identity with their geography. These are mighty continental countries with large regions subject to what school geography books used to characterize as "continental" climates, as anybody who has experienced the associated considerable seasonal variations will be able to confirm. Yet Canada, less so the United States, is also a country of islands. It can be visualized as a massive archipelago, albeit one that surrounds a substantial continental land mass. Canada has by some estimates the largest number of islands in the world, depending on what threshold size for an island is used. Furthermore, three of its cardinal points are insular: Cape Spear, Newfoundland, to the east; Cape Columbia on Ellesmere Island, Nunavut, to the north; and an island in Lake Erie – Middle Island, Ontario – to the south. Visual inspection of maps of Canada based on the commonly used conical projection, which favours the bottom (usually south) and squeezes the top, have led some to assume that Haida Gwaii (formerly the Queen Charlotte Islands) is Canada's westernmost point. However, that is not the case; rather disappointingly, the Yukon–Alaska border along the 141 degree meridian is the western extremity of the nation.

Indeed, such is Canada's insular significance that the country has featured in *Island Studies Journal*. In an article there, subtitled *The Imagining of a Canadian Archipelago*, Phillip Vannini and four co-authors state:

> Traditional "continental" articulations of Canada seem inadequate to capture a fulsome sense of the country; indeed, they could be alternatively seen as deeply complicit in the process of relegating marine, insular, and littoral Canada to the margins of national, cultural, and political consciousness. As an alternative, we propose a recontinentalisation of Canada wherein what typically is conceived of as a continental land-mass is reconceptualised as a large peninsula inside an even larger archipelago—a dynamic assemblage of land, ice, and water whose spatiality is mobile and whose geophysicality is fluid. Within this new articulation, islands and coasts are central rather than peripheral.[1]

BEFORE THE "'CONTINENTAL' ARTICULATION"

Vannini and his colleagues make a case for reconceptualizing Canada away from its continental articulation. We will return to this, but it might be pointed out—as indeed it was by these writers—that what became continent-focused Canada had an earlier manifestation in insular, archipelagic terms. This was certainly a European view, but there are also First Nation considerations to be charted. For example, the confederated Aboriginal nations forming the Wendat saw themselves as "dwellers of the peninsula" or "island nations." It could be that their geographical references were a product of their local geography around Georgian Bay and Lake Simcoe on and near Lake Huron rather than being an early version of Vannini's Canadian peninsula, with their "island" being an area of land with lakes around it. However, one might also bring to bear the Wendat foundation myth, their creation story of Aataentsic. She lived in the sky but fell through a hole towards the then watery earth. A big turtle saw her falling and got the marine animals to scrape together material from beneath the water to pile onto his back. Aataentsic landed softly on this soil, which formed the land of the earth. One of her then unborn sons, Iouskeha, later created food for people to grow and found animals in a cave, which were released for them to hunt. Land was thus an island on the back of a turtle. Other Native American creation myths also feature such turtles with islands, land that become North America—to them, of course, the only land mass known.[2]

European visualizations of North America could also be insular. The Vinland Map of the world, purporting to be from the fifteenth century, locates an island west of Greenland, which sits where North America would be. It has two gulfs on its eastern side, which could be Hudson Bay and the St. Lawrence; a little beyond them the land mass ends in an imaginary west coast completing an island. However tempting it might be in this context, we should not necessarily claim this as definitive evidence that North America was seen as an island, given that the Vinland Map might well be a forgery. Other, genuine, European world maps from the late fifteenth century such as Behaim's Globe (1490–92) do not show North America; Columbus had yet to (re)"discover" it. After he had done so in 1492, and after other voyages of exploration, including circumnavigations starting with that of one of Magellan's ships (if not of their leader) from 1519 to 1522, long-distance navigation became reasonably commonplace, with the result that sixteenth-century European maps of North America sometimes show the west coast. Clearly, the continental scale of the land mass was known; North America was then not an island.

Such knowledge did not mean that the continent could not be regarded in insular or at least archipelagic terms. Sir John Franklin in 1845 and others earlier and later who searched for the Northwest Passage were concerned with the archipelago, not the continent, and their attempts to navigate through the northern Canadian islands to reach the splendours of Asia was hardly an endorsement of the attractions of the Canadian land mass itself. Regarding the continent as an island, one small-scale example comes from off the west coast of Ireland. This relates to Great Blasket Island, which is noted for having produced three great writers in the Irish language who penned autobiographies in the 1920s and 1930s. One of them, Maurice O'Sullivan, wrote of America, to where his fellow islanders were migrating in droves, as "New Island": "New Island was before me with its fine streets and great high houses."[3] Perhaps Blasket Islanders might almost be expected to conceive of land masses as islands, coming as they did from an island (Great Blasket) off an island (Ireland) off an island (Great Britain), especially as O'Sullivan and his contemporaries would have had the experience of living in the United Kingdom of Great Britain and Ireland, an all-insular polity that broke asunder, bloodily, in 1921.

ISLANDS IN CANADIAN COLONIZATION

Other Europeans may have developed, if not an insular conception of Canada and North America, then at least a disproportionate sense of the significance of the islands, given their role in colonization. The first significant European penetration into what became Canada—indeed into North America itself—was to an island; this was the short-lived Viking settlement at L'Anse aux Meadows in northern Newfoundland around 1000. In the sixteenth century, Basque whalers as well as cod fishers from England, France, Spain, and Portugal were working at some scale off Newfoundland, whose Eurocentric name relates to John Cabot's "discovery" in 1497. Some fishers were staying for part of the year on Newfoundland by about 1630, by which time other now-Canadian islands had been settled by Europeans: Charles Lee had established a Protestant settlement on the Îles de la Madeleine (Magdalen Islands) in the Gulf of St. Lawrence, now part of Quebec, in 1597; and the Marquis de la Roche had established a short-lived convict settlement on the unpromising sandy wastes that comprise Sable Island, Nova Scotia, in 1598.[4] Farther south, Europeans settled on American islands—thus, the lost colony of Roanoke on the island of that name in what is now North Carolina, founded in 1584, deserted by 1590; and Jamestown, Virginia, settled in 1607. Jamestown did not survive as a town; the oldest continually settled European town in the New World is on another island: St. George's, founded in 1612 on one of the islands of Bermuda.

The significance of islands might be ascribed to their location; ships coming from Europe might well encounter islands before they did the mainland. Another reason might be the characteristic of insularity: islands are bounded spaces and thus can offer at least the *appearance* of being controlled and defended easily, and so might be selected ahead of mainland areas for the initial small settlements of new colonial enterprises. An example of this is Manhattan. Here, from 1614, in its incarnation as New Amsterdam, capital of New Netherland, the southern tip of the island was taken so that it was protected by water on three sides, with the northern defence being a wall; hence, probably, the name of Wall Street. Other islands such as Governors Island were also utilized. Manhattan and the rest of New Netherland was traded by the Dutch to the British in 1667 as part of the complicated territorial readjustments under the Treaty of Breda. The Dutch received Pulo Run in what is now Indonesia, an island that produced nutmegs, then very valuable, but perhaps the British got the better bargain.

VANCOUVER ISLAND COLONY AND ISLAND GATEWAYS

Islands can also be stepping stones to the mainland or, to mix metaphors, they can be portals, gateways. An important example here is Vancouver Island. That this island is now part of British Columbia seems perfectly logical. However, the fact that the province's capital city is located on the island at Victoria rather than on the mainland at Vancouver seems less logical. In fact, Victoria being the provincial capital is only the most lasting manifestation of Vancouver Island's history, which was separate from that of mainland BC, for which the island was both a stepping stone and a sort of parent.

Canada, like the United States, received its European settlers initially from the east. This coast was much easier to reach from Europe than the west coast, a voyage to which took several months and required a terrifying rounding of Cape Horn on a sailing ship or the different but also taxing challenge of crossing the Isthmus of Panama. The division between British North America and the United States was also initially largely an eastern concern. The 49th Parallel, part of that border, was established in 1818 under the Anglo-American Convention, a complex arrangement that required much transfer of territory. The 1818 border did not extend west of the Rockies, where there was at that time limited European settlement, associated with the activities of the Hudson's Bay Company. Only in 1846 did the Oregon Treaty establish that the 49th Parallel should continue as the border to the Pacific Ocean. It does not deviate even where this seems illogical. Thus the few residents of Point Roberts, Washington, are American given that they live in an exclave of 12.65 square kilometres at the end of an otherwise British Columbian peninsula that drops just south of the 49th Parallel.

However, a little farther west the boundary does drop south to place the whole of Vancouver Island into what was then British North America. There is logic or at least tradition in not sundering an island; few islands are crossed by an international boundary.[5] Also there was the need to facilitate the recasting of the HBC enterprise from its Columbia District, which was placed in Oregon Territory. The company's people would have to move north to stay under British rule. The obvious place from which to manage affairs was their 1843 settlement at Fort Victoria to the south of Vancouver Island. Negotiations kept the island whole and British, and after 1849 Fort Victoria became the capital of Vancouver Island Colony, which was granted to the HBC to manage and rule in the name of Queen Victoria. There was a need to encourage settlement and formalize the administration of Vancouver Island to ensure that it was not taken by others, either the United States or—a real fear at the time—the Mormons. A number of colonization proposals were put to the British government, but the only body with an established local organization was the HBC, and the company was certainly willing to become engaged in the colonial endeavour, actually applying initially to be granted all territory west of the Rockies.

The HBC expected that their local official, James Douglas, would become Vancouver Island's colonial governor, but instead Her Majesty's Government selected one Richard Blanshard. Blanshard, whose appointment attracted no salary, arrived after a dreadful journey, including nights in a canoe crossing the Isthmus of Panama during which he seems to have contracted malaria. His grand notions of colonial governorship then had to be squared with the reality of being in only nominal charge of a trading post at the southern end of the island and, in its far north, a mining camp, Fort Rupert, destined never to produce marketable quantities of coal. The local First Nations Blanshard treated badly, especially after three deserting seamen were murdered by Indigenous people at Fort Rupert. He inflicted collective punishment on the group instead of just punishing the perpetrators. This was contrary to HBC practice, their "Indian Trades Policy," which was to maintain good relations with the always more numerous local groups among whom company people in the field lived. Blanshard's European "subjects" were HBC employees and already had a hierarchical system of rule, and this English solicitor who had been sent as colonial governor was redundant. Ill and disillusioned, Blanshard returned home and was replaced as governor by James Douglas, who then managed both company and colony.

Douglas's copious despatches reveal the difficulties of balancing these responsibilities with their sometimes-opposing priorities. He was successful in many ways, being able to keep Vancouver Island Colony from involvement in both the Crimean War (Russian America was to its north) and the United States' Puget Sound War with Indigenous groups just to the south, and also preventing rebellion among the First Nations on Vancouver Island. However, he and the HBC generally were not successful in establishing a sufficiently numerous European migrant population on Vancouver Island. During this period, in the 1850s, there were intervening opportunities for British and European migrants in the American West; especially off-putting was the fact that on Vancouver Island, land cost settlers the significant sum of £1 per acre. Not all who signed up to migrate to Vancouver Island settled there. Some just deserted after arrival. Even the HBC policy of forbidding migrant ships to touch land en route so that migrants could not escape did not always succeed in delivering settlers to Vancouver Island. In 1853, migrants taking passage on the *Colinda* mutinied off the coast of Chile. The ship had to put into Valdivia; after much brouhaha with many escaping, eventually *Colinda* delivered to Vancouver Island just seventeen of its original complement of more than 200 migrants.

After a Parliamentary Enquiry in 1857 into the HBC governance of Vancouver Island, at which one significant witness was the still-embittered Richard Blanshard, it was decided that the company's rule should not be renewed. Ironically, the following year after discovery of gold in New Caledonia (as the adjacent mainland was then called), Vancouver Island Colony was swamped with people using the island as a stepping stone to the mainland diggings. Douglas took it upon himself to impose some sort of order on the mainland until New Caledonia was transformed into a properly established colony called British Columbia; indeed, he added its governorship to his portfolio (although he did stop working for the HBC at that point). After Douglas was relieved of both governorships in 1863, Vancouver Island and British Columbia remained separate colonies with their own governors until the *British Columbia Act* of 1866 united them under the name British Columbia. There was then a considerable dispute as to where the capital should be, with Victoria eventually winning in 1868 over the mainland's New Westminster (an earlier settlement than Vancouver), given that Victoria was the more developed settlement. Thus, until the early 1860s Vancouver Island was the most significant part of Western Canada; the island overshadowed the mainland.[6]

Another Canadian island gateway is Grosse Île in the St. Lawrence. One history even has the term in its title: *Grosse Île, Gateway to Canada, 1832–1937*.[7] This island served for more than a century as a quarantine station for migrants entering Canada along the St. Lawrence. Its most notorious year of operation was 1847, at the height of *An Gorta Mór*, the Great Famine, in Ireland. That year, almost 100,000 migrants entered Canada at the port of Québec, of whom 8,691 were treated at Grosse Île, where 5,424 died.[8] The island is now designated as the Irish Memorial, an important landmark indeed. In the United States from 1892 to 1954, about 12 million migrants passed through the Immigration Inspection Station on Ellis Island in New York harbour. More than one million arrived in 1907 alone, and about 100 million Americans have ancestors who were processed through the island. Angel Island in San Francisco Bay, California, sometimes known as the Ellis Island of the West, was used as an immigration station from 1910 to 1940, and about one million Asian immigrants passed through it. Both islands are now protected as historic landmarks.

ATLANTIC CANADA

On Canada's east coast during early European involvement, islands enjoyed a significance out of proportion to their land area, resources, and certainly their current status. Newfoundland continued to look east, remaining a British colony, its protracted journey into Canadian Confederation ending only in 1949.[9] Cape Breton Island, southwest of Newfoundland, for many years was and indeed still is an economically troubled part of Canada's "Down East." Yet it was once of such relative importance that it was a separate colony of both Britain and France. Indeed, one book about Cape Breton cultural history has it as *The Centre of the World at the Edge of the Continent*.[10]

John Cabot is usually credited with "discovering" Cape Breton Island in European terms in 1497. The first European settlers were Portuguese fishers in the early sixteenth century. A century later there was a Scottish settlement, but the Scots were defeated by the French, who remained until the 1650s. The French returned in 1713 and began to develop the island, then named Île Royale, principally by building the fortified colonial trading settlement of Louisbourg, which also was a base from which they could manage their regional fishing interests. This was after the Treaty of Utrecht, under which France was granted Île Royale and its subsidiary territory Île St-Jean (now Prince Edward Island); however, it lost territory in Acadia (mainland Nova Scotia) and Newfoundland. Louisbourg was of such significance that the British captured it to protect their own interests, first in 1745 and again in 1758, after which it was demolished. Under the Treaty of Paris of 1763, Cape Breton Island, as it became called, was ceded to Britain and was joined to Nova Scotia (which at that time also included New Brunswick). In 1784 what was only a "frail link" between the island and the mainland was broken and Cape Breton became once again separate, with its capital at Sydney.[11] This situation pertained until 1820, by which time the island was being overwhelmed by Scottish migrants.[12] Proper representative government had become necessary, and "the British Colonial Office ... with an eye towards simplifying colonial management and saving money, decided that the Cape Bretoners get their assembly as part of Nova Scotia"[13]—an example of Vannini and colleagues' "continental articulation" of Canada, when the insularity of this part of the New World was subsumed in the development of the continent.

Prince Edward Island is another such case. That it was separately administered was important in its early European history. However, the island also had to join itself to the continent eventually. It was transferred from French to British control in 1763 under the Treaty of Paris; the first British governor was appointed in 1769, when the island was split from its initial attachment to Nova Scotia. Originally called St. John's Island, it was renamed Prince Edward Island in 1798. PEI at first struggled to attract migrants, despite a lottery for landholdings on the island in 1767, which created a set of proprietors, who were required to provide settlers for their holdings. One proprietor who acquired land shortly after 1767 was the lieutenant-governor, Thomas DesBrisay. In the press of his native Ireland in the early 1770s, he indulged in some overblown advertising of the island's charms, including its healthy climate and potential for agriculture, fish, and game. This was in spite of there being a regulation that settlers to PEI were not permitted to be recruited from the British Isles—a fact that came to the notice of the Board of Trade, which halted DesBrisay's practice in 1773.[14] Letters home from some of DesBrisay's tenants appeared in the press and gave the lie to his advertisements. One woman in 1772 thought PEI "not for any Christian to live in, as there are six months of a severe winter in it of frost and snow." Indeed, "I hope that if God spares us days we will go to Philadelphia or some other place about one year from this time. For God's sake do not send my dear babies here to starve with hunger."[15]

PEI developed reasonably well from this unpromising beginning. Indeed, Lucille Campey was able to use a positive quote from 1803 as the title of her book about the island's Scottish pioneers: *"A Very Fine Class of Immigrants."*[16] However, the fact that the lottery had burdened the island with absentee landlords—its "predominance of leasehold tenure was absolutely untypical of North America"—proved to be a disincentive to settlers, who could readily obtain freehold land elsewhere. The quote is from Ian Ross Robertson's book on the Tenant League of PEI, which explored the struggles of the island's tenants for land reform in the 1860s.[17] As Robertson noted, this period coincided with shifts towards Canadian Confederation. PEI is called the "Birthplace of Confederation," given that in 1864 its capital, Charlottetown, hosted the meeting from which the Dominion of Canada in 1867 can be traced. PEI itself did not enter Confederation immediately; rather, there were discussions about the island joining the United States—potential "continental articulation" indeed. In the end, Sir John A. Macdonald, concerned about possible American expansionism, offered the island's leaders an arrangement where in return for joining Canada, the national government would assume the debts of the island's railway and also buy out the last of the absentee proprietors. In addition—pertinently to the theme of this article—there was the following clause in the 1873 confederation agreement:

> The Dominion Government shall assume and defray all charges for the following services, viz: ... efficient steam service for the conveyance of mails and passengers to be established and maintained between the island and the mainland of the Dominion, winter and summer, thus placing the island in continuous communication with the Intercolonial Railway and the railway system of the Dominion.[18]

Thus PEI was brought into Confederation with a deal that emphasised efforts to overcome its insular problems of accessibility by linking it as effectively as possible to the mainland, a concern that continued until the building of the Confederation Bridge in 1997 transformed the island functionally, if not in the emotions of most of its people, into a peninsula.

CONTINENTALIZATION

Confederation was an important part of the continentalization of Canada, with political power at the federal level emanating from Ottawa deep into the continental land mass. Except for Newfoundland, which held out until after the Second World War, the other once-island colonies were fixed within the continental web before PEI: Cape Breton joined Confederation as part of Nova Scotia in 1867 as one of the original members, and Vancouver Island joined as part of British Columbia in 1871. That Vancouver Island had by then begun to lose its domination of western Canada is evident in the 1865 comment made by the governor of British Columbia (at that time not yet united with Vancouver Island) to the Secretary of State for the Colonies that he did not wish his territory to become "the dependency of an outlying island."[19] Far from being "centres of the world," Canada's islands were now "outlying." This would remain the case for many decades, and increasingly so as Canada stitched itself together through its utility lines and transport links. The Canadian Pacific Railway stretched from the Atlantic to the Pacific by 1885; Canadian National Railways was organized in 1919 as an amalgam of several other companies and operated in every province. The early roots of Air Canada can be traced to 1937 with the founding of Trans-Canada Air Lines as a Crown corporation, the mission of which was to provide a transcontinental airline service within the borders of Canada rather than to connect Canada with the rest of the world. Initially the airline was part of the state-owned CNR. Then in 1971 the Trans-Canada Highway was finished, its extremes linking to ferry routes from Vancouver Island and Newfoundland to the continent; another loop stitched Prince Edward Island to the mainland.

Canada had become a continental country, its geography summed up by the subtitle of Larry McCann's 1982 book, *Heartland and Hinterland*. The "hinterland" included much of rural Canada outside southern Ontario and Quebec and certainly the peripheral islands. The hinterland was characterized by "an emphasis on primary resource production, scattered population and weakly integrated urban systems, limited innovative capacity; and restricted political prowess."[20] Only St. John's and Victoria were picked out as "regional metropolitan centres" on McCann's figure illustrating heartlands and hinterlands, Victoria in association with the much larger mainland city of Vancouver.

As to what was happening to the northern islands, one example comes from what was once called King William Island. This island had experienced interactions with the wider world in 1903 as the Norwegian explorer Roald Amundsen wintered there in his ship *Gjøa* during his attempt to navigate the Northwest Passage; earlier, some of Franklin's men had died there. Amundsen remained for almost two years, interacting with the local people and honing his skills in exploring and traversing high-latitude environments—proficiencies that stood him in good stead when he beat Robert Falcon Scott to the South Pole in 1911. The Hudson's Bay Company reached this remote place in the mid-1920s, and the site of their post became that of the island's first permanent settlement at Gjøa Haven, where Amundsen had stayed. In the fashion of the HBC, company officials left records of the trading post's activities. The daily reports are usually three or four lines in an exercise book, the handwriting of which changes regularly. It seems that company officials were rotated quickly through this extremely remote environment. The log details trading and weather reports, mostly connected with snow, with occasional temperature measurements. There are details of boats, fishing, local journeys, and occasional expeditions. Now and again there are nuggets of information about local island life. The tone of these comments is usually negative.

In these logs, the Indigenous people, the Nestsilik Inuit, are seen in a poor light. There is no appreciation of the postcolonial role of the HBC post and its contribution, however unwitting, to the development of a sedentary settlement for people who in Amundsen's day and for generations before had lived nomadic lives exploiting caribou and seals seasonally. Contact with the government and missionaries as well as the opportunities offered by the HBC to trade items such as fox pelts, with the returns being used to acquire imported goods, was transforming northern life, perhaps to material benefit but at a social cost. One wonders at the story in April 1928 behind the tragedy of a local man who killed his three children before committing suicide. In June of that year, the anonymous, but certainly white, Canadian HBC official wrote in the post journal: "Several natives arrived, visiting with their families. They would be better employed hunting seals which are plentiful on the ice. About 16 families again camped." This lack of interest in traditional prey was seen again a year later when a different HBC man, presumably unconsciously, depicted a society under stress and change as modern, continental Canada reached out to this northern island:

> Now that all the furs have been traded, the hangers on will just wait for an opportunity to bum. The worst offenders in this respect are the Canalaska people who are just lying around doing nothing. They are all so poorly outfitted that they are continually bumming, rebuffs have no effect, they believe in the old proverb. Constant nagging wears away one's patience and they firmly believe in keeping at it.[21]

This is early evidence of changing postcolonial circumstances for the Indigenous peoples of the North with their growing and often sad involvement with modernized Canada: the development of sedentary lifestyles and the development of the now-scorned residential school system, which removed children from their families and their culture. The Inuit of the northern reaches and islands certainly became people on the "margins of national, cultural, and political consciousness," as Vannini and colleagues had it.

"THE TRUE NORTH"

Today King William Island is Qikiqtaq, its Inuit name, which is used in acknowledgement of the significance to its story of its Indigenous people rather than Britain's King William IV after whom it was called before. Gjøa Haven is Uqsuqtuq, but at least the *Gjøa* was part of the island's narrative, unlike the distant monarch. In a similar vein, one can point to the foundation of Canada's newest territory, Nunavut, in 1999, as a withdrawal from the hegemony of white continental Canada, granting what in effect is home rule to the Inuit of the North and its islands. Another provincial capital, Iqaluit (not now known as Frobisher Bay) is located on an island, in this case on the mighty Qikiqtaaluk (Baffin Island), the fifth largest island in the world. These changes should not simply be regarded as a new articulation of Canada; they also reflect an acknowledgement of wrongs done to Indigenous peoples. Elsewhere, including on Vancouver Island and in other parts of British Columbia, the First Nations have protested for their rights.

The author has a photograph of the statue of Captain Cook in Victoria with the map roll under his left arm used during a First Nations demonstration as a hook from which to hang a banner reading "No Justice! No Peace!"

Global warming is another issue that has turned the Canadian gaze to the North. The softening of the harsh climate could make it simpler to extract minerals, including oil, from the northern reaches, and this could set off a new resource boom. Also "crucial" for the "archipelagic vision of Canada—centred on the North, rather than the Southern border with the United States—is the Northwest Passage" and its potential.[22] Unlike Martin Frobisher in the 1570s and all other explorers who attempted to find the Northwest Passage, Roald Amundsen was able to make his way through the islands of northern Canada. That this took him three years was hardly an encouragement for commercial use of the route. However, the rise in temperature in the Arctic and the lessening of ice cover associated with global warming has made navigation in these waters much less difficult. Thus, of greater potential significance than *Gjøa* making its transit between 1903 and 1906 was the twenty-five-day passage of the 48,500 ton floating residential community *The World*, from Nome, Alaska, to Nuuk, Greenland, in August and September 2012. Rather than navigational problems, even for large vessels, the issue with the Northwest Passage now is its political status. Many countries, crucially including the United States, regard the Northwest Passage as an international strait, meaning that all ships may traverse it freely. By contrast, Canada regards much of the passage as internal waters over which it has complete control; thus, Canada could close the passage to ships that it declared unsafe or to all shipping entirely if it so desired. There have already been a number of incidents between Canada and the United States in this regard; one involved a tanker, SS *Manhattan*, in 1969; another, the US Coast Guard icebreaker *Polar Sea*, which navigated the passage without requesting permission from Canada in 1985. The sovereignty of the passage was an issue in the 2006 Canadian election, and major military manoeuvres by Canadian forces took place that year in the Arctic "for the first time in more than a generation," as the CBC report put it.[23]

Canada seems then to be progressing some way towards being recast as an "archipelagic assemblage of land, islands, ice, and water ... atuned with its Northern coast and islands"[24]—"the true north" indeed. ∎

NOTES

1 Vannini et al., "Reterritorialising Canada," 125.
2 See Trigger, *The Children of Aataentsic*.
3 Ó Suilleabhain, *Fiche Blian ag Fás*, 235.
4 Armstrong, *Sable Island*.
5 Baldacchino, *The Political Economy*.
6 Royle, *Company, Crown, and Colony*.
7 O'Gallagher, *Grosse Île*.
8 O'Gallagher and Dompierre, *Eyewitness Grosse Île 1847*, 395.
9 Blake, *Canadians at Last*.
10 Corbin and Rolls, *The Centre of the World*.
11 Morgan, "Separatism in Cape Breton, 1820–1845," 41.
12 Hornsby, "Scottish Emigration and Settlement," 49–70.
13 Morgan, "Separatism in Cape Breton, 1820–1845," 41.
14 Royle and Ní Laoire, "DesBrisay's Settlers."
15 Royle and Ní Laoire, "'Do Not Send My Dear Babies Here to Starve."
16 Campey, *"A Very Fine Class of Immigrants."*
17 Robertson, *The Tenant League of Prince Edward Island*, 4.
18 Prince Edward Island Terms of Union (Order of Her Majesty in Council Admitting Prince Edward Island into the Union) At the Court at Windsor, the 26th day of June, 1873. See, for example, www.canadahistory.com/sections/documents/documents.html.
19 Frederick Seymour to Edward Cardwell, 21 March 1865, *Papers relating to the proposed union of British Columbia and Vancouver Island*, British Parliamentary Papers, 1866, xlix, 119. See also Chapter 8 of Royle, *Company, Crown, and Colony*.
20 McCann, *A Geography of Canada*, 4.
21 The three quotes are from the HBC post journal for Gjøa Haven held both in the Hudson's Bay Company Archives in Winnipeg (B.427/a/1) and in the British National Archives at Kew (BH1/3155). Entries are 11 April 1928, 11 June 1928, and 10 June 1929.
22 Vannini et al., "Reterritorialising Canada," 128.
23 CBC News "Northwest Passage: The Arctic Grail" (2006), http://www.cbc.ca/news/background/northwest-passage.
24 Vannini et al., "Reterritorialising Canada," 128.

WORKS CITED

Armstrong, Bruce. *Sable Island*. Toronto: Doubleday, 1981.

Baldacchino, Godfrey, ed. *The Political Economy of Divided Islands*. London: Palgrave Macmillan, 2013.

Blake, Raymond B. *Canadians at Last: Canada Integrates Newfoundland as a Province*. Toronto: University of Toronto Press, 2004.

Campey, Lucille H. *"A Very Fine Class of Immigrants": Prince Edward Island's Scottish Pioneers, 1770–1850*. Toronto: Natural Heritage Books, 2001.

Corbin, Carol, and Judith Rolls. *The Centre of the World at the Edge of a Continent*. Sydney: University College of Cape Breton Press, 1996.

Hornsby, Stephen. "Scottish Emigration and Settlement in Early Nineteenth Century Cape Breton." In *New Perspectives on Cape Breton History, 1713–1990*, ed. K. Donovan. Fredericton: Acadiensis Press, 1990.

McCann, L.D. *A Geography of Canada: Heartland and Hinterland*, Scarborough: Prentice Hall, 1982.

Morgan, Robert. "Separatism in Cape Breton, 1820–1845." In *Cape Breton at 200: Historical Essays in Honour of the Island's Bicentennial, 1785–1985*, ed. K. Donovan. Sydney: University College of Cape Breton Press, 1985.

O'Gallagher, Marianna. *Grosse Île: Gateway to Canada, 1832–1937*. Sainte Foy: Carraig Books, 1984.

O'Gallagher, Marianna, and Rose Masson Dompierre. *Eyewitness Grosse Île 1847*. Sainte Foy: Carraig Books, 1995.

Ó Suilleabhain, Muiris. *Fiche Blian ag Fás*. Dublin: Clólucht an Talbóidigh, 1933. (Published in English as Maurice O'Sullivan, *Twenty Years a-Growing*, London: Chatto and Windus 1933.)

Robertson, Ian Ross. *The Tenant League of Prince Edward Island, 1864–1867: Leasehold Tenure in the New World*. Toronto: University of Toronto Press.

Royle, Stephen A. *Company, Crown, and Colony: The Hudson's Bay Company and Territorial Endeavour in Western Canada*. London: IB Tauris, 2011.

Royle, Stephen A., and Caitriona Ní Laoire. "DesBrisay's Settlers." *Island Magazine* 51 (2002): 19–23.

———. "'Do Not Send My Dear Babies Here to Starve': St. John's Island in 1772." *Island Magazine* 53 (2003): 12–15.

Trigger, Bruce. *The Children of Aataentsic: A History of the Huron People to 1660*. Montreal and Kingston: McGill–Queen's University Press, 1976.

Vannini, P., G. Baldacchino, L. Guay, S.A. Royle, and P. Stein. "Reterritorialising Canada: Arctic Ice's Liquid Modernity and the Imagining of a Canadian Archipelago." *Island Studies Journal* 4, no. 2 (2009): 121–38.

TWO

Science at Service of Sublime Landmarks: Scientific Ecology and the Preservation of Canada's Wilderness Landmarks in 1970s Quebec

Olivier Craig-Dupont

Science provided nineteenth-century colonists, both English Canadians and some French-Canadians, with not only the practical means to dominate their physical surroundings but also an ideological framework within which to comprehend the experience of doing so.... In particular, science gave credence and respectability to the very idea of a transcontinental Canadian nation, and to the conviction that, with science, the idea would become reality.[1]

As with the first geological surveys of the eighteenth century (analyzed by historian Suzanne Zeller), government agencies often used science as a means to define and confirm the idea of the nation-state.[2] Even while enabling a rational framing of the natural environment, science emphasizes the very notion of the nation over that of the land, especially through the inventories and mapping activities conducted by government bodies responsible for exploiting and preserving natural resources.[3] As it examines the history of the founding of La Mauricie National Park in Quebec by Parks Canada, this chapter explores these dynamics of nation-building through science. In particular, it shows how scientific ecology permitted a new interpretation of the Mauricie vernacular territoriality in accordance with Parks Canada's long-held ideal of a transnational preserved "wilderness."

This idea that wild magnificence represents Canada's national spirit (as well as that of the United States) has deep roots. Many historians, in fact, share the conviction held by the government agencies they study—that national parks, with their great unspoiled wilderness, protect a fundamental dimension of North American history. These scholars embrace the seminal claims of American historian Roderick Nash, who argued in 1970 that parks "reflect some of the central values and experiences in American culture."[4] From the Sierra Nevada to the Canadian Rockies, wilderness has been the pride of North American political, intellectual, and artistic elites. In the late nineteenth century, the famous naturalist John Muir (1838–1914) and the twenty-sixth president of the United States, Theodore Roosevelt (1858–1919), both campaigned for the creation of the first national parks; the transcendentalist poets Henry David Thoreau (1817–1862) and Ralph Waldo Emerson (1803–1882) philosophized about the moral and spiritual virtues of wilderness; and Canada's Group of Seven painted the magnificent landscapes of Canada. All were sensitive to the sublime beauty of the North American wilderness. Their masterworks, such as Muir's Yellowstone Park, Thoreau's *Walden*, and Tom Thomson's (1877–1917) *The Jack Pine*, have all helped shape the notion that wilderness is a fundamental component of North American culture and national history.[5]

But environmental historians have recently criticized this concept of wilderness, especially when it comes to national parks. More and more American and Canadian historians have been demonstrating that national park wilderness is in fact a powerful *cultural* product. In the wake of William Cronon's myth-demolishing essay "The Trouble with Wilderness," they have shown how national parks served state initiatives to deprive Native peoples of their lands,[6] and to transform inhabited landscapes into human-free, "pristine" wilderness, with the end goal of strengthening the grip of Canadian political and economical elites over the land, *a mari usque ad mare*.[7] While growing in number, these voices are still too few to overcome the image long sanctioned by Parks Canada for the public imagination. The wilderness ideal is still deeply embedded in many representations of national parks. Since the creation of Canada's first national parks (Banff and Jasper, in 1885 and 1907 respectively), Parks Canada has often used this idealized representation of wilderness to promote its work. Even today, its website tells us that national parks "celebrate the beauty and infinite variety of our country. Protected and preserved for all Canadians and for the world, each is a sanctuary in which nature is allowed to evolve in its own way, as it has done since the dawn of time. Each provides a haven, not only for plants and animals, but also for the human spirit."[8] Parks Canada's *Guiding Principles* clearly stipulate that the national parks of Canada exist to "protect for all time representative natural areas of Canadian significance in a system of national parks, and to encourage public understanding, appreciation, and enjoyment of this natural heritage so as to leave it unimpaired for future generations."[9]

This mandate may seem self-evident today, but throughout its history Parks Canada has used a number of discourses—scientific, economic, political, and touristic—to promote its national parks. At various times, it has promoted its parks as resource reserves, as celebrations of Canada's beauty, and as areas protecting Canada's natural ecosystems.

This evolution in mandates is evident in the history of Canada's national parks. Canada created its first national parks (Banff and Jasper) as a means to protect resources for eventual commercial use. The government of John A. Macdonald permitted the exploitation of park resources such as timber, minerals, and grazing lands even while encouraging the development of tourism in them.[10] Not until the late 1920s did some civil servants begin questioning this approach. The first commissioner of the Dominion Parks Branch, James B. Harkin, helped change the parks' commercial mandate. In 1927 he argued that "areas deemed suitable for a National Park must possess scenic beauty and recreational qualities of a character so outstanding and unusual as to be properly classified national rather than merely local."[11] It was during Harkin's administration, which lasted from 1911 to 1936, that "scenic beauty" became essential in justifying the protection of the already established parks, as well as in the selection of the sites of future national parks.[12]

This transformation of the parks' mandate suggests that their "wilderness" state is, in fact, a profoundly social construct.[13] The protected environment of a national park is an amalgam of its natural environment's material dimensions and the multitude of social representations that have been layered over it. The various stakeholders, such as Parks Canada, industries, Aboriginal populations, and local inhabitants who use the territory for recreational purposes, articulate very different representations, and all have their own views regarding the territory being made into a park. The construction of this material and symbolic "double nature" requires a certain abstraction of the object being debated.[14] Just as Cambrosio, Limoges, and Pronovost suggest in their analysis of biotechnological policy in Quebec, this sort of institutional object is "a locus where representations of scientific and technological practices are translated into yet other, more abstract representations of these same practices, while being at the same time associated with representations of other domains (for instance financial, economic or social needs)."[15] Creating a national park is a territorial and national project that goes well beyond the heterogeneous aspects of local discourse and practices.[16] Science, be it ecology, geology, or biology, has this power of abstraction.

La Mauricie National Park, perhaps more than any other park in eastern Canada, inspired this reworking of the land through science. Completed in 1977, it was one of the first in Canada to preserve marsh ecosystems and other types of wetlands. The great sub-boreal forests of the Canadian Shield, which make up the largest ecosystem in this park, had supported industrial activity for centuries in the Mauricie region—especially forestry, a pillar of the local economy.[17] This industrial presence also opened up the territory to hunters and fishermen, who began exploiting its game and fish resources in the early twentieth century.[18] Although they were dying out by the end of the 1950s, these industrial and recreational activities were still well established on the Mauricie's landscape at the time the national park was being established.[19]

Considering that Mauricie's landscape had been modified by humans long before it became a park, this chapter analyzes how Parks Canada succeeded in creating here "a representative natural area of Canadian interest" where, according to the park's official history, the visitor could find an "atmosphere of primitive wilderness ... much as it was when discovered by the early travellers and native Indians so many years ago."[20] To justify a national park in the hybrid landscape of the Mauricie, Parks Canada would have to transform local territorialities, with all their industrial and recreational imprints, so that they corresponded to this wilderness ideal. To achieve this, the agency presented the natural and cultural history of the territory through concepts taken from the science of ecology, while at the same time erasing any contradictory human dimensions present on the landscape. Instead of being a socially neutral space preserved by a legal and scientific framework, La Mauricie National Park will thus serve as a tool for structuring landscapes and for transforming local territorial characteristics in accordance with Parks Canada's wilderness ideal.

THE "NATURAL BEAUTIES" OF CANADA AND THE PROJECT OF A PARK IN THE MAURICIE

The idea of a park in the Mauricie arose during a time of profound change for this region. In the early 1970s, the Mauricie, like other resource-based regions of Quebec such as the Gaspé and the Lower St. Lawrence,[21] was having difficulty adapting an economy long based on resources and manufacturing (i.e., on mines, timber, and textiles) to one based on services.[22] Early on, the federal and provincial governments recognized outdoor tourism as an activity likely to stimulate economic recovery in these regions.[23] An increase in outdoor activities in the 1960s,[24] and interventions by the expanding Canadian welfare state, led to the creation of a multitude of federal and provincial programs aimed at developing recreation and tourism in these parts of Quebec.[25] For example, the Bureau d'aménagement de l'Est-du-Québec (BAEQ) supported a series of touristic initiatives in eastern Quebec,[26] notably the creation in 1971 of Quebec's first national park, at Forillon on the Gaspé Peninsula.[27] Established by the province's Liberal government in 1963, BAEQ attracted significant funds from federal programs, such as the Canada Land Inventory (1961), the Fund for Rural Economic Development (FRED, 1966), and the Agricultural Rehabilitation and Development Act (ARDA, 1966), whose mandate was to introduce economic diversification into single-industry peripheral regions.[28]

The federal and provincial governments realized that national parks were enjoying soaring popularity.[29] So in 1966, the Pearson government created a new Department of Indian Affairs and Northern Development to govern the management of "Indian affairs, Eskimo affairs, the Northwest Territories, the Yukon Territory, the national parks, the national battlegrounds, the historical sites and monuments, the migratory bird and wildlife."[30] In July 1968 the federal government entrusted this broad mandate to a young minister from Shawinigan, who also happened to be the MP for the riding of Saint-Maurice-Laflèche: Jean Chrétien. From the start, Chrétien declared himself a fervent supporter of national parks. During the *Canadian National Parks: Today and Tomorrow* conference held in Calgary in October 1968, he outlined how he intended to improve and promote the Canadian park system. Like many at the conference, he saw the popularity of the parks as a potential curse: when too many people visited too few parks, it threatened the "natural heritage" the parks represented.[31] So he proposed creating more national parks throughout Canada—at least one in each province. In his estimation, "to achieve an adequate representation of Canada's heritage at suitable scale, we would require forty to sixty new national parks in a complete system."[32]

Having received a public commitment (formalized a year later in the Parks Policy of 1969), and equipped with a sizeable budget, he suggested the creation of a second national park for the province of Quebec, in the Mauricie. He believed strongly that the landscape of the Mauricie was especially suited to such a project. In a speech to the committee for the national park there, he confirmed that

> in a splendid region such as this one, I don't need to convince you of the merits of conservation and of the joys of outdoor recreation. The Mauricie has just as many picturesque landscapes than the most beautiful national parks that I have visited. There is no need also to insist on the economic advantages that the whole Mauricie region would gain from the creation of a national park, as well as from its association with the system of Canadian National Parks.... As in the case of Kootenay, Kejimkujik, Yoho, Banff, Jasper and all the others, your national park will celebrate the beauty and grandeur of our country.[33]

Banff and Jasper were picturesque, and lucrative; surely the "natural beauties" of the proposed new park could have the same economic impact on the Mauricie. In the 1960s, Banff National Park was the flagship of the Canadian parks system.[34] Economists at Parks Canada referred heavily to its example when estimating that 1 million visitors per year would visit the new park in the Mauricie.[35] According to Parks Canada's Planning Division, tourist spending in the region, based on a projected 1.5 million visitors per year, could reach "a conservative estimate of $5.4 million."[36] As a result, park committees in the Mauricie organized many field trips to Banff and other iconic parks between 1969 and 1971 in order to promote the project of a national park to the local population.

However, the National Parks Branch still faced the challenge of making a picturesque park out of an industrial landscape. This would be a substantial and complex undertaking in a place that still bore the imprint of timber harvesting and fish and game exploitation. It was precisely these human dimensions that the branch would try to erase from La Mauricie National Park as it attempted to turn a sow's ear into a "wild" silk purse.

HUNTING AND TIMBER HARVESTING: THE INDUSTRIAL AND RECREATIONAL IMPRINT IN THE MAURICIE

Within the proposed park's boundaries, industry and recreation were both still flourishing in 1970. This was especially the case with timber harvesting, which had been a pillar of the regional economy ever since the first logging camp was established there in 1830 by Edward Grieve.[37] One forest company in particular, Consolidated-Bathurst, had exploited various forest concessions and private lands, which together made up almost the entirety of the site of the future park—until the late 1960s.[38] In addition to concessions of Crown lands under provincial jurisdiction and a territory of 26 square kilometres obtained from the federal government, this company also managed an experimental forest of 15 square kilometres, created in 1918 by the Canadian Forest Service,[39] and a spruce plantation established by La Laurentide pulp and paper company in 1915.[40] Consolidated-Bathurst also used sections of the Mattawin and Saint-Maurice rivers (which were to form part of the park's northeastern boundary) for stream-driving logs and had built dams to regulate the water level of certain lakes.[41] Meanwhile, another forest company, Domtar, was exploiting a forest concession in the southern part of the watershed of Lake Wapizagonke.

Signs of this forest exploitation were still plain to see in the Mauricie at the end of the 1960s. Indeed, the first master plan of the Mauricie National Park cautioned in 1971 that "visitors strolling through paths might have the impression that the forest is considerably disturbed, even dilapidated, for they will have access only to the areas more recently affected by logging."[42] The imprint left by forest harvesting was especially apparent because a vast network of logging roads ensured access to the territory. The local people used these roads to reach the interior of the forest to fish and hunt with the permission of the logging companies.

Fishing and hunting were popular activities in the Mauricie. Ever since 1883, when the Shawinigan Club was established, a large number of private hunting and fishing clubs had occupied vast stretches of territory.[43] These were owned mainly by wealthy Canadian and American businessmen, but the locals also frequented some of the smaller clubs. Of the 450 private clubs active in the region by the end of the 1960s, sixteen held lands designated for the future park.[44] Erasing the presence of these private clubs was complicated because they had constructed numerous buildings and other facilities throughout the future park. Park superintendents' weekly reports indicate that ongoing cleanup work was aimed specifically at eliminating these structures. According to one of these reports, it was not until 1973 that garbage was removed and the debris of an old saw mill were removed and burnt, and the dump sites of old clubs were cleaned up. In the Wapizagonke sector, the dump of the Shawinigan Club, where garbage had been accumulated for more than fifty years, has been completely emptied.... At Lake Wapizagonke, all the camps of the Shawinigan Club were demolished and burnt, except for one garage.... The five camps of the Désaulniers Club were demolished and burnt.... The camps at the western end of Lake Maréchal are demolished and burnt, and at Lake Waber, all that is left of the Consolidated-Bathurst camps is the section used for the construction site office.[45]

The clubs had also undertaken substantial "improvements" to the local ecosystem to support their hunting and fishing activities.[46] In 1960, for example, the Woco Club had a dam built at the outlet of Lake Bouchard to block access by white suckers (*Catostomus commersonii*).[47] As early as 1910, the Shawinigan Club introduced Atlantic salmon to the region; other clubs experimented with speckled trout (*Salvelinus fontinalis*) and lake trout (*Salvelinus namaycush*);[48] eventually these clubs introduced fish into more than twenty lakes within the future park. The Laurentian Club went so far as to fertilize two of its lakes in 1947 with seven tons of phosphate fertilizer in order to increase fish size. The same club tried planting wild rice (*Zizania aquatica*) in three of its lakes to improve waterfowl production.[49]

In summary, a variety of local users had occupied and modified the territory of the future national park. Many of them, whether as employees, tourists, or residents, knew the Mauricie region and its resources well. To erase this industrial and recreational past and reinvent it as wilderness, the Parks Branch would have to reinterpret the region's natural and cultural history. Science would prove helpful in this.

THE SCIENTIFIC REINTERPRETATION OF THE MAURICIE'S LANDSCAPES

Science played a key role in the creation of the national park in the Mauricie region. By focusing on the natural environment—using data collected during inventories of its geology, fauna, and flora—federal scientists were able to construct a new and authoritative "natural history" for La Mauricie National Park. This official portrait of the park as wilderness erased certain dimensions of its industrial and recreational past. Maps of bioclimatic domains and ecosystem-based zoning plans portrayed the landscapes within the park boundaries in an abstract and non-human way, simplifying their socio-historical complexity.[50]

In the 1970s, the biological and ecological sciences held an ambiguous status in the management of national parks in both Canada and the United States.[51] Scientists working for the Canadian government and the US National Park Service had to address the traditional mandate of tourism development while producing new knowledge in scientific ecology.[52] In the case of La Mauricie, scientific findings were used specifically *for* touristic imperatives instead of as "pure" research for the advancement of knowledge. For example, when the head of the Department of Chemistry and Biology of the Université du Québec à Trois-Rivières wrote to Chrétien in October 1970 to propose "the establishment of a biology station on or near the territory of the park, for purposes of monitoring, teaching and research,"[53] Chrétien referred to the parks policy of 1969 as a reason not to grant permission, arguing that "it goes without saying that national parks are not established mainly for scientific research."[54] Research in the national parks, he continued, was to be limited to "the observation of natural conditions, without taking any specimens and without any manipulation of the environment."[55] Indeed, the 1969 policy specified that "the main goal of a national park is to resemble a museum or an art gallery."[56] Thus, the fauna inventory work compiled by the interpretation service at La Mauricie National Park confirms the Parks Branch's interest in using scientific findings to promote "spectacular" aspects of nature for tourism. In an internal memo in 1971, the park's head of natural resources, Pierre Desmeules, tellingly notified the Ottawa head office that "consideration should be given to attempting to re-establish populations of fur-bearers such as marten, otter and fisher." These species, he specified, "have decreased markedly and their re-establishment could be beneficial, although they are not as spectacular from a publicity point of view."[57]

This subordination of ecology to the agency's traditional mandate of highlighting the "natural beauty" of the country is especially noticeable in the master plans produced at the time the park was being established. These were meant to serve as a framework for the park's development and to ensure its harmonious integration with the national parks system. They also served to render official and operational representations of nature—and representations of the park *as* natural. In particular, the master plans provided a scientific reinterpretation of the Mauricie's landscape by characterizing the new national park as "the Laurentian Heritage."

From 5 to 15 June 1971, an "interpretive specialist" from the Branch, R.C. Gray, visited the territory of the future park with a working copy of the preliminary master plan drafted by the Société d'exploitation des ressources éducatives du Québec (SEREQ). SEREQ relied on the predominant landscape architecture practices, which were based primarily on the ecological planning approaches developed by Scottish American landscape architect Ian McHarg. Using McHarg's system of transparent plastic-coloured maps, SEREQ proposed a layered cartography of the multiple biogeographical and human dimensions of the future park. With this proto-GIS cartography, SEREQ established different zones of activities (i.e., "Special Preservation Areas," "Wilderness Areas," "Natural Environment Areas," and "Outdoor Recreational Areas") based on the "ecological values" of the land.[58] These four zones provided the basis of the future park's infrastructure, such as camping sites, roads, picnic areas, a boating complex, and trails.

With this first plan in hand, Gray was to evaluate its quality with regard to the "interpretive possibilities" of the Mauricie territory. Although generally satisfied with SEREQ's work, he contended that the authors had not recognized "the primary values inherent to this landscape." He added that "La Mauricie National Park is, at present, almost completely unspoiled in terms of prime wilderness lake and forest land located very near industrial centres of the lower St. Maurice Valley." He argued that

> although there were forest areas that had been logged and areas where logging had only recently ceased and sites of major logging camps remained (Consolidated Bathurst) the Park nonetheless included clear, unpolluted lakes of varied dimensions, wide zones of mixed forests, pure stands of hardwood, swamps, fresh-water marshes, streams, cascades, waterfalls, beaches, bogs, valleys and rivers; all the components of the natural wilderness of the Laurentian Shield.[59]

Gray defined more clearly what he believed the authors of the SEREQ document have failed to recognize in this landscape. In his estimation,

> the outstanding feature of La Mauricie National Park is not its lakes and forests, or streams or waterfalls, considered as separate landforms. The sum of these parts is more than their separate entities. It is the <u>wilderness</u> that makes La Mauricie National Park a vital addition to the system of National Parks in Canada. It is the wilderness that dictates the value system we must use when assessing priorities in this new National Park territory. [emphasis Gray's]

He concluded that "La Mauricie National Park is nothing less than a true 'Laurentian Wilderness,'"[60] confirming eloquently the Parks Branch's mission of recognizing true wild nature and promoting its value. Gray disliked the overly utilitarian emphasis of the draft master plan, particularly its zoning arrangements. He proposed "radically" reducing the zones dedicated to intensive activities or moving them to more "appropriate" areas. For example, he suggested that campground development be clustered near the old Grand-Mère plantation in the southeastern part of the park, "since this is a completely artificial plant community."[61] He also recommended changing the zoning of lakes Maréchal, Weber, and Atikamac, in the western part of the park, from Type III, a "Natural Environment Area" (a sort of buffer zone between areas of intensive recreational activities and the "back country") to Type II, a "Wilderness Area" (which permitted only activities without significant impacts on the environment, such as hiking, canoeing, or camping). According to Gray, "only then will the lake country of the south-western portion of the Park be true wilderness and officially considered as such."[62] Parks Canada incorporated Gray's recommendations into its second draft master plan in 1975.[63] But further work had to be done to complete the establishment of La Mauricie National Park's scientific wilderness.

FINAL INCLUSION OF THE MAURICIE INTO PARKS CANADA'S TRANSNATIONAL ECOSYSTEM GRID

Gray's comments give us some indication of the process whereby a "true Laurentian Wilderness" was constructed in La Mauricie National Park. For visitors to be able to recognize the wilderness expected in national parks, official zoning plans had to initially circumscribe and label it as such. As a tool for structuring the territory, the zoning plan served to materialize the abstract representations of the national park's scientific nature.

Gray's new zoning representing the "wild" backcountry of La Mauricie National Park was only the first step in reconstructing the Mauricie's historic landscapes. Under a new system introduced in 1970, the branch integrated La Mauricie National Park into a management plan laid out by the 1972 National Parks System's Planning Manual. This manual, largely inspired by a similar plan developed by the US National Parks Service, aimed at "formulating a plan ensuring the creation of a network of National Parks that would be a judicious sample of the landscapes and natural attractions of Canada."[64] According to the manual, it was important that this plan "be objective and use criteria that all those interested can accept and understand"—and thus be "based on the natural sciences and be free of all political or social impediments."[65] This manual, then, was meant to integrate all of Canada's national parks into a scientific grid of land management and land categorization that largely excluded local cultural practices. To free it of "all political or social impediments," the Parks Branch adopted the maturing discourse of scientific ecology. The 1972 manual proposed a nationwide territorial classification based on "natural regions" and "natural history themes worthy of representation."[66] These themes were to be the "primary imperatives" in choosing the site of future national parks—*together with* the "outdoor recreation needs" of a given region. The same manual identified which geological and ecological features best conveyed "the essence of the natural regions."[67] The Systems Plan thus defined thirty-nine "natural regions" covering all of Canada's territory; these regions are still in use in the national parks system.

Because it was a new park, the Mauricie was ideally positioned to exemplify this new approach to park planning. First, the 1972 Planning Manual designated La Mauricie National Park as part of the "Canadian Shield" region, also identified as "19 b — Centre of the Precambrian Region of the St. Lawrence and the Great Lakes." Then, it identified themes such as "The Precambrian," "The Age of Primitive Invertebrates," and the ecosystems typical of the "Great Lakes–St. Lawrence Forest Region, Section 4a, Laurentians."[68] Finally, in a stance that clearly showed the Parks Branch's new commitment to nation-building through science, the manual specified which "natural values worthy of being represented" would best illustrate these themes. For the Mauricie, this was the presence of the Canadian Shield; chains of lakes and rivers; the Great Lakes–St. Lawrence forest; and the "steep point of contact with the centre of the St. Lawrence lowlands."[69]

In short, the manual clearly presented the "natural values" of the landscape as being the primary interest of national parks. It contained no mention at all of local land use or of the social and cultural history of the landscape that was being transformed into parks. In the case of the Mauricie, forest and fish and game exploitation was nowhere mentioned, although as noted earlier, such activities had played an important role in shaping the region. By applying concepts taken from geology and ecology, as well as maps that rendered these new scientific representations of the land concrete, Parks Canada succeeded in re-creating its wilderness ideal on this territory.[70] In such an ideal wilderness, human activity would, by definition, be absent.[71] The agency recognized the traces of a past human presence in La Mauricie National Park; however, the humanized characteristics of the newly protected ecosystems became at best artifacts of the "museum" of natural history that national parks were supposed to be.[72] An internal memo from the director of the Parks Branch in Ottawa illustrates very well this effacement of the social and cultural dimensions of the Mauricie landscape. This memo outlined choices by the head office regarding the materials to be presented at the official opening of the park's interpretation centre on 4 August 1972.[73] After a visit to Ottawa by Gilles Ouellette, who was in charge of the park's interpretation service, branch director John I. Nicol decided that the park's "natural history" should be divided into four thematic sections: "Laurentian Uplands," "Diversity of Forest Types," "Aquatic Environment," and "Human History."[74]

Nicol then selected the objects that were to be characteristic of each theme: samples of gneiss and photos of taluses and eskers to represent "Uplands"; around thirty samples of nuts, insects, and stuffed animals for "Wildlife Mosaic"; and about twenty photos of fish and specimens of aquatic insects for "Aquatic Web." As for the last theme, "Human History," out of the ten or so objects proposed by the regional director, such as axes, logger cant hooks, and sculptures of a trapper and a logger, he retained only three photographs—of a canoe, a logging camp, and stream driving—along with a few Aboriginal artifacts.[75] The Mauricie's human history was thus limited to a "folklorized" presence marked by the use of Aboriginal artifacts[76] and by photos of industrial and recreational activities that the branch considered ended in this part of the Mauricie. Albeit without the scale and grandeur of the mountain parks, the agency had (re)created, through scientific representations, a significant wilderness in the Mauricie.

This "scientification" of the landscape is eloquently portrayed in a further publication by the agency. In 1975, Parks Canada presented a temporary master plan for the La Mauricie National Park that stressed that

> an overview of the territory of the park allows one to observe a great homogeneity of the elements composing the biophysical environment. We observe a uniform distribution of interesting sites that can be retained as having potential for interpretation. This uniformity is also found at the level of the comparisons and evaluation among the components. The absence of large disparities among the elements composing this potential brings us to pay a particular attention to natural groupings that can occur at certain sites. Taken from a more general perspective, several isolated phenomena of moderate importance can create, in a given sector, as a set, a high interpretative potential.[77]

This encapsulates several elements of the present analysis. The search for "interesting sites that can be retained as having potential for interpretation" reveals the traditional sensitivity of Parks Canada to the picturesque in Canadian nature.

The first Canadian parks established in the Rocky Mountains at the end of the nineteenth century, with their "large disparities" in geology, were the reference for deciding what was "interesting" in the Canadian landscape. The plan asserted that the Mauricie was devoid of such "large disparities." Taken separately, the biophysical characteristics of La Mauricie National Park, such as the marshes and the great coniferous forests, were considered phenomena of only "moderate importance." Accordingly, and seeking new arguments to justify the presence of a park in such a landscape, Parks Canada used the science and mapping of ecology to create a landscape that was scientifically significant, thus transforming the Mauricie territory into a new "representative natural area of Canadian interest."[78] The key moment in this scientific reinterpretation was the integration of the park into the 1972 planning manual's classification system, which was to be "based solely on natural sciences and thus detached from any political or social considerations."[79] At that point, the park became a scientific object, completely detached from the social and cultural history that had shaped its former landscapes.

CONCLUSION

Far from being a natural area composed of biogeographical dimensions, La Mauricie National Park appears as an object laden with interpretations of what wilderness, according to Parks Canada, *should* be. In this regard, parks are "frontier-objects" that in their forms and functions encompass many discourses and practices.[80] As we have seen, for such an institutional object to superimpose the heterogeneity of local territorialities, these very territorialities must be rendered abstract. Science has allowed this spatial manipulation, especially through the new series of plans and charts that define the park's physical—and symbolic—representation. As demonstrated by Cambrosio, Limoges, and Pronovost in their analysis of the institutional trajectories of scientific policies in Quebec, governmental science projects "appear to be, first and foremost, *representational practices* grounded in particular kinds of *literary activities* characterized by an extended *intertextual web*."[81] The creation of La Mauricie National Park followed one of these "intertextual webs," where scientific inventories, maps, and unpublished reports of the land's touristic potential served to document, frame, and materialize Parks Canada's project for a park in the Mauricie.

Our history leads to two conclusions. In considering the natural and cultural history of landscapes, we can first compare national parks to historiographical productions.[82] Indeed, in establishing La Mauricie National Park, Parks Canada joined an important current of environmental thought that contrasts the wild frontier of the North American West with the industrial landscapes of the East.[83] Parks Canada long ago institutionalized this representation of wilderness, beginning with its iconic parks in the Canadian Rockies; it later sought to transpose that representation onto the Mauricie territory. The area transformed into a park thus bears the cultural stamp of the creator agency, in the same way that it bore the industrial and recreational territorial marks of the Mauricie's past human presence.

Second, our analysis shows how scientific rationality, like the environment, is never neutral. Scientific discourse, especially that of ecology, has the power to "naturalize" the institutional culture of agencies in charge of national parks. When Parks Canada presents its ideals of wilderness through scientific discourses, and with material support such as maps and master plans, these ideals become a tangible reality. The materialized representations of the environment that are the national parks can then transform the territory and its uses in relation to the political, economic, scientific, or cultural objectives of the institutions that promote the parks. The map of the thirty-nine "natural regions" of the 1972 Planning Manual speaks volumes in this respect. Through concepts taken from biology and geology, the federal agency presented Canada as a totally integrated geographical unit, where provincial political boundaries—as well as their associated social issues—disappear under the scientific lens. As Suzanne Zeller has noted, scientific discourse in La Mauricie National Park helped, in its own way, to materialize federal governance over the nation-state's provinces,[84] thus continuing Canada's long nation-building endeavour, although, this time, through the pursuit of the scientific sublime. ■

NOTES

1   Zeller, *Inventing Canada*, 6.

2   Kaufmann, "'Naturalizing the Nation,'" 666.

3   Scott, *Seeing Like a State*, 11.

4   Nash, "The American Invention of National Parks," 726.

5   Cronon, "The Trouble with Wilderness," 13.

6   Sandlos, *Hunters at the Margin*, 7.

7   MacEachern, *Natural Selections*, 6.

8   Parks Canada (2014), *Parcs nationaux du Canada: Réseau des parcs nationaux*, http://www.pc.gc.ca/progs/np-pn/pr-sp/index_e.asp.

9   Parks Canada (2008), *Guiding Principles*, http://www.pc.gc.ca/eng/docs/pc/poli/princip/sec2/part2a/part2a2.aspx.

10 Foster, *Working for Wildlife*, 64–66.

11 Taylor, "Legislating Nature," 125–37.

12 Ibid., 5.

13 Micoud, *Des hauts lieux*, 53.

14 Macchabée, *La double nature de la nature*, 26.

15 Cambrosio, Limoges, and Pronovost, "Representing Biotechnology," 196.

16 Olwig, "Reinventing Common Nature."

17 Hardy, «Exploitation forestière et environnement au Québec, 1850–1920», 63.

18 Bouin, *Aménagement et exploitation faunique*, 7.

19 Hardy and Séguin, *Histoire de la Mauricie*, 837.

20 Lothian, *A Brief History of Canada's National Parks*, 144.

21 Moquay, «La référence régionale au Québec».

22 Hardy and Séguin, *Histoire de la Mauricie*, 837.

23 Searle and Brayley, *Leisure Service in Canada*, 22.

24 Martin, *La chasse au Québec*.

25 Bellefleur, *L'évolution du loisir au Québec*.

26 Jean, «La "ruralité" bas-laurentienne».

27 Thibeault, *La création d'un premier parc national au Québec*, 1–142.

28 Brown, "Federal-Rural Development Programs," 239.

29 MacEachern, *Natural Selections*, 37.

30 Lothian, *A Brief History of Canada's National Parks*, 25.

31 Nelson and Scace, *The Canadian National Parks*, 10.

32 Ibid., 10.

33 Parks Canada, centre de services du Québec. *L'aménagement d'un parc en Mauricie*, 24 mars 1971, 5.

34 Taylor, "Banff in the 1960s," 133.

35 LAC, *Prévisions sur l'effet économique d'un parc en Mauricie*, 1970 LAC, RG22, 1229, 321-1, 3, *Prévisions sur l'effet économique d'un parc en Mauricie*, 26 février 1970.

36 Parks Canada, *Economic Aspects of the Proposed St. Maurice National Park March 1970*, 1. PC-centre de services du Québec, *Economic Aspects of the Proposed St. Maurice National Park, March 1970*, p. 1.

37 Parks Canada, *L'aménagement d'un parc en Mauricie*, 24 mars 1971, 141.

38 Consolidated-Bathurst ltée. *Exploitations et tenures*, 1.
39 Lothian, *A Brief History of Canada's National Parks*, 142.
40 Ibid., 135.
41 Ibid., 136.
42 SEREQ, *La Mauricie National Park*, 137.
43 Pringault, *Le parc national de la Mauricie*, 67.
44 Bouin, *Aménagement et exploitation faunique*, 7.
45 LAC, *Rapports semi-annuels des surintendants*, RG 84, 2344, C-1445-101/L1, 24 May 1973, 3.
46 Pringault, *Le parc national de la Mauricie*, 67.
47 Bouin, *Aménagement et exploitation faunique*, 47.
48 Ibid., 36.
49 Ibid., 47.
50 West, Ingoe, and Brockington, "Parks and Peoples," 260.
51 Dunlap, "Wildlife," 187.
52 Sellars, *Preserving Nature in the National Parks*, 49.
53 LAC, Lefebvre à Chrétien, RG 22, 998, 321-10, Lefebvre à Chrétien, 7 October 1970, 1.
54 Canada, Direction des parcs nationaux et des lieux historiques, *Politique des parcs nationaux* (Ottawa: Affaires indiennes et du Nord, 1969), 4.
55 LAC, Chrétien à Lefebvre, RG 22, 998, 321-10, 4 November 1970, 1.
56 Supra note 54.
57 Parks Canada, Office national, Bureau central de classement, C-98103L1, *Desmeules à Lesaux*, 26 January 1971.
58 Parks Canada, Office national, Bureau central de classement, N-BCC, C-8320/L1, *La Mauricie National Park—Visit of the Interpretive Specialist R.C. Gray, 9 to 15 June 1971*, 9.
59 Ibid., 9.
60 Ibid., 9.
61 Ibid., 10.
62 Ibid., 10.
63 Parks Canada, centre de services du Québec. *Plan directeur provisoire: parc national de la Mauricie*, 1975, 53.
64 Parks Canada, centre de services du Québec, *Manuel de planification du réseau des parcs nationaux*, 1972, 3.
65 Ibid. 3.
66 Ibid., 4.

67 Ibid., 48.
68 Ibid., 107.
69 Ibid., 115.
70 Parks Canada, *Rapport annuel: Année financière 1971/1972*, 1972, 9.
71 Cronon, "The Trouble with Wilderness."
72 MacEachern, *Natural Selections* 3–4.
73 Pronovost, «Au parc national de la Mauricie».
74 Parks Canada, Office national, Bureau central de classement, Nicol au directeur régional (région du centre), C-8333/L1, February 1972.
75 Ibid.
76 Jasen, *Wild Things*, 13.
77 Parks Canada, centre de services du Québec, *Plan directeur provisoire: parc national de la Mauricie*, 1975, 31.
78 Parks Canada. *Parks Canada Guiding Principles and Operational Policies*, http://www.pc.gc.ca/eng/docs/pc/poli/princip/sec2/part2a/part2a2.aspx.
79 Parks Canada, centre de services du Québec *Manuel de planification du réseau des parcs nationaux*, 3.
80 Cambrosio, Limoges, and Pronovost, "Representing Biotechnology," 206.
81 Ibid., 196.
82 White, "From Wilderness to Hybrid Landscapes," 557.
83 Judd, «Approches en histoire environnementale», 68.
84 Zeller, *Inventing Canada*, 269.

WORKS CITED

Archives nationales du Canada. RG 84, 2344, C-1445-101/L1, 3. *Rapports semi-annuels des surintendants*, May 24, 1973.

Bellefleur, Michel. *L'évolution du loisir au Québec : essai sociohistorique*. Québec: Presses de l'Université du Québec, 1997.

Bouin, Thierry. *Aménagement et exploitation faunique antérieurs à la création du parc national de la Mauricie (1970)*. Parks Canada, Service de la conservation et des ressources naturelles, 1979.

Brown, C.S. "Federal–Rural Development Programs and Recreation Resources." In *Canadian Parks in Perspective*, ed. James Gordon Nelson and Robert C. Scace. Montreal: Harvest House, 1970.

Cambrosio, Alberto, Camille Limoges, and Denyse Pronovost. "Representing Biotechnology: An Ethnography of Quebec Science Policy." *Social Studies of Science* 20, no. 2 (1990) : 195–227.

Canada, Direction des parcs nationaux et des lieux historiques. *Politique des parcs nationaux.* Ottawa: Affaires indiennes et du Nord, 1969.

Consolidated-Bathurst ltée. *Exploitations et tenures des terres avant 1972 sur le territoire du parc national de la Mauricie, 1959-1972.* Trois-Rivières: Université du Québec à Trois-Rivières, cartothèque, +615.43GCRKIN (Q) CaQTU.

Cronon, William. "The Trouble with Wilderness: Or, Getting Back to the Wrong Nature." *Environmental History* 1, no. 1 (1996): 7–28.

Dunlap, Thomas R. "Wildlife, Science, and the National Parks, 1920–1940." *Pacific Historical Review*, 59, no. 2 (1990): 187–202.

Foster, Janet. *Working for Wildlife: The Beginning of Preservation in Canada.* Toronto: University of Toronto Press, 1978.

Hardy, René. «Exploitation forestière et environnement au Québec, 1850–1920». *Zeitchrift Für Kanada-Studien* 27, no. 1 (1995): 63–78.

Hardy, René, and Normand Séguin, eds. *Histoire de la Mauricie.* Québec: Institut québécois de recherche sur la culture, 2004.

Jasen, Patricia Jane. *Wild Things: Nature, Culture, and Tourism in Ontario, 1790–1914.* Toronto: University of Toronto Press, 1995.

Jean, Bruno. «La "ruralité" bas-laurentienne : développement agricole et sous-développement rural». *Recherches sociographiques* 29, no. 2 (1998): 239–63.

Judd, Richard W. «Approches en histoire environnementale : le cas de la Nouvelle-Angleterre et du Québec». *Globe. Revue internationale d'études québécoises* 9, no. 1 (2006): 67–92.

Kaufmann, Eric. "'Naturalizing the Nation': The Rise of Naturalistic Nationalism in the United States and Canada." *Comparative Studies in Society and History* 40, no. 4 (1998): 666–95.

Lothian, W.F. *A Brief History of Canada's National Parks.* Ottawa: Parks Canada, 1987.

MacEachern, Alan. *Natural Selections: National Parks in Atlantic Canada, 1935–1970.* Montreal and Kingston: McGill–Queen's University Press, 2001.

Macchabée, Louis, *La double nature de la nature : une analyse sociologique de la naturalisation des espaces verts en milieu urbain.* PhD diss., Université du Québec à Montréal, 2002.

Martin, Paul-Louis. *La chasse au Québec.* Montréal: Les Éditions du Boréal, 1990.

McNamee, Kevin. "From Wild Places to Endangered Places: A History of Canada's National Parks." In *Parks and Protected Areas in Canada: Planning and Management*, 2nd ed. Philip Dearden and Rick Rollins. New York: Oxford University Press, 2002.

Micoud, André. *Des hauts lieux : la construction sociale de l'exemplarité.* Paris: Éditions du Centre national de la recherche scientifique, 1991.

Moquay, Patrick. «La référence régionale au Québec. Les visions étatiques de la région et leurs incarnations». In *L'institutionnalisation du territoire au Canada*, ed. Jean-Pierre Augustin. Québec: Les Presses de l'Université Laval, 1996.

Nash, Roderick. "The American Invention of National Parks." *American Quarterly* 22, no. 3 (1970): 726–35.

Nelson, James Gordon, and Robert C. Scace. *The Canadian National Parks: Today and Tomorrow.* Proceedings of a conference organized by the National and Provincial parks Association of Canada and the University of Calgary, 9–15 October 1968. University of Calgary, 1968.

Olwig, Kenneth. "Reinventing Common Nature: Yosemite and Mount Rushmore—A Meandering Tale of a Double Nature." In *Uncommon Ground: Toward Reinventing Nature*, ed. William Cronon. New York: W.W. Norton, 1995.

Parks Canada, Office national, Bureau central de classement, C-98103L1. Desmeules à Lesaux, 26 January 1971.

Parks Canada, Office national, Bureau central de classement, N-BCC, C-8320/L1. *La Mauricie National Park—Visit of the Interpretive Specialist R.C. Gray, 9 to 15 June 1971.*

Parks Canada, Office national, Bureau central de classement, C-8333/L1, Nicol au directeur régional (région du centre), February 1972.

Parks Canada. *Parcs nationaux du Canada : Réseau des parcs nationaux*, http://www.pc.gc.ca/progs/np-pn/pr-sp/index_e.asp.

Pringault, Jérémy. *Le parc national de la Mauricie : mise en valeur d'un espace protégé dans la perspective du développement durable.* MA thesis, Université de Caen, 1994.

Pronovost, Carole. «Au parc national de la Mauricie : Inauguration d'un centre d'interprétation de la nature». *Le Nouvelliste*, 5 August 1972.

Sandlos, John K., *Hunters at the Margin: Native People and Wildlife Conservation in the Northwest Territories.* Vancouver: UBC Press, 2007.

Scott, James C. *Seeing Like a State: How Certain Schemes to Improve the Human Condition Have Failed.* New Haven: Yale University Press, 1998.

Searle, M.S., and R.E. Brayley. *Leisure Service in Canada: An Introduction.* Edmonton: Venture Publishing, 2000.

Sellars, R.W. *Preserving Nature in the National Parks: A History.* New Haven: Yale University Press, 1997.

SEREQ, *La Mauricie National Park.* Montreal: S.L. SEREQ, 1971.

Taylor, C.J. "Legislating Nature: The National Parks Act of 1930." *Canadian Issues* 13 (1991): 125–37.

Taylor, C.J. "Banff in the 1960s: Divergent Views of the National Park Ideal." In *A Century of Parks Canada, 1911–2011*, ed. Claire Campbell, 133–52. Calgary: University of Calgary Press, 2011.

Thibeault, J.-M. *La création d'un premier parc national au Québec: le parc Forillon, 1969–1970.* MA thesis, Université de Sherbrooke, 1991.

West, Paige, James Ingoe, and Dan Brockington. "Parks and Peoples: The Social Impact of Protected Areas." *Annual Review of Anthropology* 35 (2006): 251–77.

White, Richard. "From Wilderness to Hybrid Landscapes: The Cultural Turn in Environmental History." *Historian* 66, no. 3 (2004): 557–64.

Wright, R.G., and D.J. Mattson. "The Origins and Purpose of National Parks and Protected Areas." In R.G. Wright and John Lemons (ed.), *National Parks and Protected Areas: Their Role in Environmental Protection.* Hoboken: Blackwell Science, 1996.

Zeller, Suzanne. *Inventing Canada: Early Victorian Science and the Idea of a Transcontinental Nation.* Toronto: University of Toronto Press, 1988.

THREE

Patriotisms of the People:
Understanding the "Highway of Heroes" as a Canadian National Landmark

Tracey Raney

In February 2002, Canadian prime minister Jean Chrétien sent 850 troops from the Princess Patricia's Canadian Light infantry to Afghanistan as part of "Operation Enduring Freedom." Between 2002 and 2011, 158 Canadian soldiers died in Afghanistan during this mission. In addition to the grief experienced by the fallen soldiers' families and the nation as a whole, these deaths have influenced how Canadians think about their nation and its place in the world. One possible reason for this heightened national awareness is the media's coverage of the repatriation ceremonies. The first repatriation ceremony in April 2002 was broadcast live, when Canadians bore witness to the fact that Afghanistan was not a mission of "peacekeeping," but rather a mission of war, and that more Canadian soldiers were likely to die. These ceremonies, and the images of caskets and grieving soldiers' families, permitted Canadians to see up close the grief and loss of war for the first time in Canada's modern history.

Here I focus on the Canadian public's response to the official repatriation ceremonies, which on Canadian soil begin when a fallen soldier's remains are flown from the combat zone to Trenton Air Force Base (CFB Trenton), around two hours east of Toronto, Ontario. Beginning in 2002, many Canadians gathered along the bridges and overpasses of a busy multi-lane highway as the remains of the fallen soldiers and their loved ones left CFB Trenton on their way to the

Ontario Coroner's Office in downtown Toronto. What is particularly intriguing about these events is the public outpouring of patriotism, something previously quite uncommon in Canada outside Quebec.

In this chapter I try to understand Canada's "Highway of Heroes" as a distinctly Canadian phenomenon not seen to the same extent in other countries involved in the war in Afghanistan. I do so by explaining patriotism not as a state commodity but rather as a phenomenon located in the social and cultural practices and public rituals of the national collective. I suggest that these kinds of patriotic expressions—what I call "grassroots patriotisms"—constitute important cultural events during which representations of the nation are contested, performed, and possibly rearticulated beyond the formal boundaries of the state. I offer Canada's Highway of Heroes as an important site of this grassroots patriotism, and I argue that this national landmark represents a departure from—and challenge to—official state discourses of patriotism that have dominated Canada outside Quebec for more than half a century. Importantly, this version of patriotism has now been embraced by the Canadian state through its recognition of the Highway of Heroes as an official national landmark.

This chapter unfolds as follows. First, I review the research on patriotism and identify an oversight in the literature regarding the need to bridge state/institutional and individual/socio-cultural explanations of patriotism. Using the Highway of Heroes as a case study, I then consider the factors that drew participants to the overpasses; a phenomenon that is rather unique in Canada given accounts of Canadians as a quiet and unpatriotic people. Next, I explain how this grassroots patriotism challenges Canada's official patriotism. Finally, I marshal evidence that demonstrates that the Highway of Heroes has influenced the Canadian state's discourses of patriotism and as well as the collective national identity.

PATRIOTISM RESEARCH

Most political research on patriotism views it as a state resource used for the purposes of nation-building, whereby states produce and draw upon national group attachments to construct a cohesive national political community in the hearts and minds of its citizens. Viroli traces the historical uses of patriotism by political leaders and more recently by national states as a means to "strengthen or invoke love of the political institutions and the way of life that sustains the common liberty of a people, that is love of the republic."[1] As social constructions, nations and national identities require citizens to think or feel connected in some way to a wider national group. Strongly felt emotions, such as loyalty, love, and pride, have great power to induce individuals to act in ways that may not always be perceived as in their personal best interests, but that *are* in the interest of the larger national collective (examples include paying one's taxes, voting, or joining the military).

To instill citizens' patriotic attachments to the nation, states have at their disposal a variety of symbolic resources, including cultural traditions, stories, symbols, and mythologies that connect the past to the present. These resources provide states with discursive and symbolic tools to help individual members view the nation as "beyond the self"—as an enduring, living, concrete entity that transcends time and space.[2] As Hobsbawm suggests, national traditions like anthems and flags were invented precisely to "inculcate certain values and norms of behaviour."[3] In heterogeneous societies, wars are especially good at helping define the national in-group, for they draw clean lines between "us" and "them."[4]

State-sponsored civic rituals provide states with the opportunity to regulate and legitimate "acceptable" modes of patriotic sentiments and actions. State-endorsed public events instruct citizens on the importance of the nation to their lives by transforming their everyday routines into special moments or days of national celebration or remembrance. As Hayday observes, "Canada Day (July 1st) celebrations provide historical opportunities for the Canadian state to create and cement a sense of national identity and belonging in the Canadian citizenry."[5] A nation's civic rituals also help clarify the actions, subjects, and ideas available for communication and consideration about "the nation" to the broader national community.[6]

Patriotism can also be thought of as a socio-cultural phenomenon. Social psychological studies emphasize that individuals' patriotic attachments to the national group can be characterized by a variety of individual emotional sentiments, including a sense of love, pride, commitment, or loyalty. As an individual-level variable, patriotism can take different forms. In social psychology research, attitudes towards the nation are generally divided into two categories: patriotism and nationalism.[7] Patriotism (or "constructive" patriotism) is defined as a generalized sense of attachment to one's country, or a sense of belonging, pride, or love, whereas nationalism (sometimes referred to as "blind patriotism") includes feelings of superiority, dominance, or hostility toward other countries.[8] Although studies indicate that the two are positively correlated, they are usually treated as separate constructs. Generally, patriotic attitudes and beliefs provide individuals with a wider sense of community, one that fulfills certain human needs, such as to the need to belong.

Various studies have explored patriotism as a state/institutional-level variable (and its effects on individuals), or as an individual-level variable. Considerably less attention has been paid to how citizens' patriotic beliefs and practices might inform state patriotisms. For example, patriotism may not always be a top-down process; it is conceivable that individuals' patriotisms could influence the larger, collective identity, from the bottom up. Social psychological research has begun to consider this possibility. David and Bar-Tal suggest that "the collective identity is sculpted by means of individuals' identification with the macro-level collective."[9] In other words, the processes of national identity construction require us to consider the ways in which individual group members conceive of, enact, and inhabit patriotism in their everyday lives, and how and under what conditions these "unofficial" patriotisms might either challenge or reflect the dominant patriotic views of the state.

There are a number of ways in which patriotisms can emerge beyond the state. One signpost of a citizen-led (or grassroots-style) patriotism is that it is organized *by and for citizens* in a public place, so that patriotic cues and practices emerge from citizen-to-citizen interactions in the absence of state actors (e.g., politicians or government agencies) or spaces (e.g., state buildings or public squares). Arguably, since these events are voluntary, they are especially well suited in explaining how members of a collective define their national identity outside state narratives. In liberal democracies, the media can play an especially important role in the transference of individual/grassroots patriotisms to the broader public discourses of the nation.

Grassroots patriotisms can appear anywhere in civil society: in people's backyards, in their homes, or in neighbourhood streets or sports arenas. Billig has drawn our attention to the mundane routines of daily life, or what he calls "banal nationalism."[10] He presses upon us the notion that national identity is to be encountered not just in the actions of states or in the individual psychologies of citizens but, importantly, in people's everyday actions.[11] One overlooked consideration is how and when the seemingly everyday, patriotic routines of citizens are transformed into shared cultural and public performances of patriotism by citizens themselves. Civic rituals organized by and for citizens are potentially vital sites of national identity construction because they signify the transference of patriotic expression from a single act to the larger group, which then collectively practises and performs patriotism. Civic rituals also serve to develop public discourses and public spaces that emphasize national unity among citizens. This may be especially helpful to the national group in times of struggle or crisis.[12] To explore these ideas further, I turn to the phenomenon of Canada's Highway of Heroes.

A GRASSROOTS PATRIOTISM: CANADA'S HIGHWAY OF HEROES

Canada's first repatriation ceremony during the Afghanistan war occurred in April 2002 after four Canadian soldiers were killed in a "friendly fire" incident by an American F-16 fighter jet. Notably, these were the first war deaths Canada had suffered since the Korean War (1950–53). The repatriation ceremonies of all Canadian soldiers killed in combat generally follow the same protocol: on returning from Afghanistan, the aircraft lands at 8 Wing/CFB Trenton, where an official repatriation (or "ramp" ceremony) is performed by a Canadian Forces chaplain. The chaplain offers a silent prayer while an Honour Guard removes the remains of the fallen soldier from the aircraft.[13] If the soldier was killed in action, a minister of the government or a representative must be present, and the remains must undergo an autopsy at the Ontario Coroner's Office in Toronto, Ontario, around 170 kilometres away. Families may choose to accompany the hearse on this route. For several of the repatriation ceremonies, official government dignitaries have been in attendance, including the Governor General and the defence minister.

It is after the repatriation ceremonies, while the remains of the fallen soldiers and their families are travelling down the highway, that the grassroots patriotism occurs. Although the number of participants was initially quite small, it is clear that those who lined the bridges were motivated not only by a desire to express their grief and gratitude to the fallen soldiers and their families, but also by their patriotism. Many who stood on the bridges wore Canada's official colours (red and white), and the bridges were often covered in a sea of Canadian flags. By 2006, the number of those participating in this national vigil had grown and many more Canadians were arriving to stand on one of the fifty-nine overpasses along the route.[14] The increasing crowds were synchronistic with the growing number of Canadian soldiers killed in Afghanistan, and with Canada's changing role as it moved its troops into the more volatile Kandahar region. Although official numbers are not known, Fletcher and Hove offer a conservative estimate that by 2011 the number of participants was approximately 3,000 people per repatriation.[15]

Canadians were drawn to the highway for various reasons, but an underlying factor seems to have been the desire or need to feel a sense of belonging to the national group in a time of national crisis. This phenomenon is grounded in research: for example, Tajfel and colleagues suggest that individuals may be drawn to identify with and feel attached to social groups that provide emotional significance and meaning to them as a member of that group.[16] In his study of the "Support the Troops" campaign in the United States, Huiskamp argues that citizens may be more likely to feel a need to belong to the national group during times of national crisis, such as wartime.[17] Appeals to a united sense of shared grief and sorrow through patriotism may be one way in which some Canadians have come to terms with the sacrifices Canadians have made in this war.

The repatriation ceremonies also provided opportunities for Canadians to express their patriotism in ways that transcended some of the boundaries of difference in Canada. Repatriation procession participants waved not only Canadian flags but also the flags of the provinces and towns that the deceased and their families were from. When two soldiers from Quebec were killed, one participant on a bridge waved the Fleur-de-Lis (the flag of Quebec), and stated: "I'm holding it up because you just don't see them around here. I want the families to see just how much we respect the boys for doing their job.... I know the support is low in Quebec and that's why I'm here.... I'm trying to show the families that we all care."[18] Given Canada's vast geography and its highly decentralized federal system, the waving of flags from provinces other than Ontario—and especially from the province of Quebec—offered Canadians a moment of national "oneness" and solidarity with one another as a national family grieving its losses.

One of the most common reasons participants came to the bridges was an overriding sense of obligation to pay respect to the fallen soldiers and to share the grief with their families.[19] When asked why she came to the bridge to watch the procession below, a seventy-one-year-old woman said: "I believe it's the least we can do."[20] Another woman described her experience on a bridge in 2008 as follows: "Within a few minutes, the cavalcade approached. My knees buckled; I held the rail as I looked down at the hearses passing beneath us. I choked up as a family member waved up at us out a window."[21] In a sense, the highway bridges became spaces upon which Canadians could collectively grieve the war losses of the "Canadian" national family in a way not seen before in Canadian history.

THE HIGHWAY OF HEROES: CHALLENGING CANADA'S OFFICIAL STATE PATRIOTISM

The significance of the Highway of Heroes extends beyond the immediate participants to the wider Canadian political community through the national and international media. As the crowds grew along the highway, local and provincial media began to take more of an interest not only in the repatriation ceremonies themselves, but also in the public displays of support and patriotism during the repatriation processions. The many images of the bridges lined with Canadians wearing red and waving Canadian flags were broadcast around the country through news media outlets, and reached into Canadian popular culture in the form of two popular books and two songs available on iTunes.

The Highway of Heroes also grabbed the international spotlight when a major American network (NBC) ran a feature during its November 2008 evening newscast about the outpouring of Canadian support along the Highway of Heroes, commending Canadians on their support for their soldiers.[22] The media in the United Kingdom also covered Canada's Highway of Heroes, with several editorials commenting on the shameful treatment of British fallen soldiers, where "the hearses are denied outriders and go unremarked" compared to Canada, where "there is a police escort and crowds line the route."[23] Writing in *Maclean's*, Stephen Marche observed: "Over the course of the long and unsatisfying war in Afghanistan, the Highway of Heroes has become the primary ritual in Canadian life for comprehending the cost of the conflict. It has also grown into something more, a statement of our collective hopes and fears, an essential demonstration of Canadianness."[24]

The Highway of Heroes offered Canadians a physical space to collectively express their "Canadianness," and through the media, it signalled to others (both within and beyond Canada) the kinds of symbols and values deemed important to their definition of what it means to be Canadian. To quote David Miller, these ritualistic performances entailed a rebuilding of a "common public culture," which, among other things, constituted a "set of understandings of how a group of people is to conduct its life together."[25] A new Canadian ritual to pay respects to the fallen Canadian soldiers in a public and spontaneous way had emerged along this highway.

This new "set of understandings" challenges several aspects of Canada's state-crafted national identity outside Quebec. Since at least the postwar era, Canada has been defined by the state through its promotion of pluralistic, universal values and goals such as democracy, multiculturalism, the rule of law, and peacekeeping. State-sanctioned national symbols (e.g., the Maple Leaf and the beaver), constitutional documents (e.g., the Canadian Charter of Rights and Freedoms [1982]), social programs (e.g., Medicare and equalization), and public policies (e.g., official bilingualism, multiculturalism, and multilateralism), have all sought to promote an image of Canada as a compassionate, caring, sharing society. Canada's postwar identity has also been constructed through its foreign policies, which would have it that Canada is a multilateral or "peacekeeping" nation (in contrast to the unilateral, war-prone United States). Indeed, the term "peacekeeping" emerged during the post–Cold War era to reflect the belief that the best way to safeguard Canadian security was by promoting multilateralism.[26]

The Highway of Heroes reveals that for some Canadians, the postwar consensus of Canada's national identity outside Quebec—founded on democratic values like multiculturalism and diversity—may now also include (or perhaps even challenge) another version of national identity that is more strongly tied to its military, war involvement, and war heroes. Note here that not all bridge participants were supporters of the war in Afghanistan. In fact, when asked by reporters, several participants indicated that they were either ambivalent or opposed to Canada's involvement in the war.[27] At the same time, those who stood on the bridges (and those who watched these images from home on television, in the papers, and on the Internet) were also bearing witness to their country's involvement in war. This reality challenged a dominant national myth about Canada as a peacekeeping nation.

To be certain, the bridge participants did not reflect the only (or perhaps even dominant) narrative of patriotism in Canada outside Quebec. Indeed, Canadian public opinion polls at the time showed that support for the war ebbed and flowed over its duration (although many Canadians remained committed to it as a means to fight global terror), with Quebec respondents consistently less supportive than the rest of Canada. At the same time, the Highway of Heroes made clear that the public's response to Canadian military war deaths in Afghanistan was deeply connected to a sense of national pride, identity, and belonging to the Canadian nation outside Quebec.

One possible reason why this spontaneous grassroots patriotism emerged may lie in structural changes to the Canadian state over the past several decades. Previous research has demonstrated that the Canadian state's postwar national policy tools (e.g., Medicare, multiculturalism, and foreign policy) had given way to an increasingly neoliberal and securitized Canadian state.[28] A withdrawal of the Canadian state in areas of social and foreign policy traditionally tied to Canadian nationhood, combined with heightened concerns about global security and terrorism, may have provided a context out of which a reinvigorated Canadian national identity would appear, given the right set of events (such as a war). Certainly, the spaces from which claims of patriotism are made have shifted in Canada: instead of relying on old state policies to knit together a "sharing, caring" society from the top down, many Canadians chose to recognize the sacrifices of fallen Canadian soldiers as central to their sense of national identity, and they did so through the reclamation of a seemingly benign public space—overpasses along a highway—that had previously not held national importance.

POLITICAL RESPONSES TO THE HIGHWAY OF HEROES

The grassroots patriotism that emerged along the Highway of Heroes is significant not only because it signalled a departure from official state discourses of nationalism, but also because of how the Canadian state chose to respond to it. The name Highway of Heroes was coined by a newspaper columnist in 2007; shortly after that, a petition emerged with more than 20,000 signatures requesting the name change.[29] In response to public pressure, in 2007 the Ontario provincial government renamed this section of the highway to officially recognize this title; in the process, it secured the space as an official cultural landmark. Today, the highway is marked with "Highway of Heroes" signs that include a red poppy, Canada's official symbol of remembrance. With its official renaming in August 2007, Canada became the only country in the world at that time to honour its fallen soldiers in Afghanistan in this way.

In 2011 the Ontario government announced that it would be placing twenty-six bronze plaques along the Highway of Heroes to commemorate Canada's fallen soldiers in Afghanistan.[30] The coins and bronze plaques legitimize the highway as an important cultural landmark for future generations. Several other provinces (British Columbia, Saskatchewan, Manitoba, and New Brunswick so far) have also adopted their own highways to honour their fallen soldiers. In November 2015 the Ontario government announced that it would be partnering with two organizations, Forest Ontario and Highway of Heroes Tribute, to plant one tree for every fallen Canadian soldier along the "Highway of Heroes," totalling 117,100 trees. These events signal the state's willingness to bring this grassroots patriotism into official discourses of Canadian nationalism.

At the federal level, Canadians' overwhelming support of their fallen soldiers contributed to a public policy change in 2006, when a new Conservative prime minister, Stephen Harper, attempted to ban the media from repatriation ceremonies and ordered a halt to the flying of the Canadian flag at half-mast when a Canadian soldier died. Many Canadians and newspaper columnists decried this sudden policy change, likening it to George H.W. Bush's 1991 media ban that prevented news organizations from photographing or recording flag-draped coffins of American soldiers as they were brought back to the United States during the first Gulf War (a ban that was finally lifted in 2009).[31] After considerable public outcry (including from a fallen soldier's family and from the Canadian military itself), the Canadian government changed its course and permitted the Canadian media to record the repatriation ceremonies, with the permission of the families.

The Canadian government also approved the minting of a Highway of Heroes memorial coin, which was unveiled in 2011. The coin features an overpass along the Highway of Heroes lined with draping Canadian flags as viewed from the perspective of the fallen soldier's family travelling along the route. On its website, the Royal Canadian Mint highlights the grassroots element of the highway: "The people on the bridge come from every walk of life. Grandparents, firefighters, students, soldiers, business people, police officers. Nobody told them to be here. Their assembly is spontaneous and many of them carry Canadian flags. This is the spirit of the Highway of Heroes."[32]

A more concerted focus on Canada's military and war efforts further dovetailed with Prime Minister Harper's (2006–15) conservative brand of Canadian national identity.[33] Although the Canadian state had already withdrawn itself considerably from social policies that had formed the pillars of the country's national identity for half a century (e.g., health care spending), Harper often used the symbolic resources of the Canadian state to signal the importance of Canadian military history to Canadian identity. For example, in the summer of 2011, the government offered the military a new Canadian identity by reinserting the word "Royal" in the names of Canada's air force and navy. And in March 2012 the Harper government announced an investment of $5 million to celebrate and promote education about and awareness about the centennial anniversary of Canada's involvement in the War of 1812.[34]

An emphasis on the Canadian military—and the government's embracement of the Highway of Heroes as an important national site—likely facilitated the Conservative government's efforts to challenge some of the foundational policies and myths tied to Canada's postwar identity (e.g., multiculturalism and peacekeeping), many of which find their origins in the Liberal Party. The 2015 election of a new Liberal government under Prime Minister Justin Trudeau may signal an end to the Conservatives' refashioning of Canada's national identity, although at the time of writing it is yet too early to tell. In the midst of this changing political landscape, the Highway of Heroes remains as a somewhat rare glimpse of how Canadians define and express their own sense of identity. As an official landmark, this grassroots patriotism has been cemented as an important marker of Canadian identity for generations to come.

CONCLUSION

Canada's formal combat role in Afghanistan ended in 2011, yet the cultural and political significance of the war reached beyond the mission itself. The phenomenon of Canada's Highway of Heroes provided space for a new patriotism to emerge, founded on national values and symbols that depart from the previously held postwar consensus. Understanding the conditions that gave rise to the groundswell of patriotic support for the fallen troops along Canada's Highway of Heroes is critical to understanding the processes of national identity formation, central to which was a shared public space from which a new cultural landmark emerged. Examination of this phenomenon reveals a new, grassroots patriotism in Canada that has influenced and will continue to influence how the nation views itself. Importantly, the Highway of Heroes also demonstrates how unofficial acts of patriotism can shape the formal state discourses of patriotism. It draws our attention to the possibility that patriotism—conceived of as a socio-cultural phenomenon—is not always the exclusive purview of states and state actors, but can be reproduced by citizens themselves. A "patriotism of the people" is not one that has been readily accepted or broadly understood in the Canadian context, and requires future study. ∎

NOTES

A previous version of this paper was published in French in the journal *Critique international* as "Le 'patriotisme par le bas' au Canada : reconstruire l'identité nationale sur l'Autoroute des héros,' vol. 58 (janvier–mars 2013): 19–34.

1. Viroli, *For Love of Country*.
2. Kong and Yeoh, "The Construction of National Identity."
3. Hobsbawm, "Introduction."
4. Shahzad, "Forging the Nation."
5. Hayday, "Fireworks," 290.
6. Davis, *Parades and Power*.
7. Kosterman and Feshbach, "Toward a Measure of Patriotic and Nationalistic Attitudes"; Bar-Tal, "Patriotism as Fundamental Beliefs of Group Members."
8. Bar-Tal and Staub, *Patriotism in the Lives of Individuals and Nations*; Schatz and Staub, "Manifestations of Blind and Constructive Patriotism."

9   David and Bar-Tal, "A Sociopsychological Conception," 358.
10 Billig, *Banal Nationalism*, 66–67.
11 Ibid., 66–67.
12 David and Bar-Tal, "A Sociopsychological Conception," 356.
13 National Defence and the Canadian Forces, "*Backgrounder.*"
14 Fletcher and Hove, "Emotional Determinants," 53.
15 Ibid., 36.
16 Tajfel et al., "Social Categorization."
17 Huiskamp, "'Support the Troops!'" 285.
18 Dalrymple, "Two Fallen Soldiers Return Home."
19 Fletcher and Jennifer Hove, "Emotional Determinants."
20 Boswell, "Grief, Support Greet War Dead."
21 McKeown-Robertson, "Remembering Canadian Soldiers."
22 Burnett, "U.S. Media Pays Tribute."
23 Almond, "Pictures That Should Shame Us All."
24 Marche, "The Return of Private Todd."
25 Miller, *On Nationality*, 26.
26 Wagner, "The Peaceable Kingdom?"
27 Hartley, "These Boys Fought with Honour."
28 Brodie, "On Being Canadian"; Nimijean, "Articulating the 'Canadian Way'"; Lennox, "From Golden Straightjacket to Kevlar Vest"; Raney and Berdahl, "Shifting Sands?"
29 Warmington, "Our Own Trail of Tears."
30 Hume, "Bronze Plaques."
31 Bumiller, "U.S. Lifts Photo Ban."
32 Royal Canadian Mint, "Honouring the Highway of Heroes."
33 Nieguth and Raney, "Guarding the Nation."
34 Government of Canada, "Harper Government Boosts Tourism."

WORKS CITED

Almond, Peter. "Pictures that should shame us all reveal the shabby way British treats its fallen soldiers." *Daily Mail* April 2008. Web. 9 Sept. 2012.

Bannerji, Himani. *The Dark Side of the Nation: Essays on Multiculturalism, Nationalism and Gender.* Toronto: Canadian Scholars' Press, 2000. Print.

Balthazar, Louis. "The Faces of Québec Nationalism." *Québec: State and Society*. Ed. Alain-G Gagnon, Ontario: Nelson Canada, 1993. 2–17. Print.

Bar-Tal, Daniel. "Patriotism as Fundamental Beliefs of Group Members." *Politics and the Individual* 3.2 (1993): 45–62. *Academic Search Premier*. Web. 27 Feb. 2007.

Bar-Tal, Daniel and Ervin Staub. *Patriotism in the lives of individuals and nations*. Chicago: Nelson-Hall, 1997. Print.

Billig, Michael. *Banal Nationalism*. London UK: Sage Publications, 2004. Print.

Boswell, Randy. "Grief, support greet war dead; Four fallen soldiers, journalist return home." *Windsor Star* 4 Jan. 2010: A1. Web. 4 Jan 2010.

Brodie, Janine. "On Being Canadian." *Reinventing Canada—Politics of the 21st Century*. Ed. Janine Brodie and Linda Trimble. Toronto: Prentice Hall, 2003. 8–29. Print.

Bumiller, Elisabeth. "U.S. lifts photo ban on military coffins." *New York Times* 7 Dec. 2007. Web. 6 Sept. 2012.

Burnett, Thane."U.S. media pays tribute to 'Highway of Heroes.'" *Toronto Sun* 11 Nov. 2008. Web. 12 March 2012.

Dalrymple, Tobin. "Two fallen soldiers return home; Supporters line road for duo from Quebec." *Vancouver Sun* 27 Aug. 2007. Web. 12 March 2012.

David, Ohad and Daniel Bar-Tal. "A Sociopsychological Conception of Collective Identity: The Case of National Identity as an Example." *Personality and Social Psychology Review* 13.4 (2009): 354–79. *Academic Search Premier*. Web. 12 March 2012.

Davis, Susan G. *Parades and Power: Street Theatre in Nineteenth Century Philadelphia*, Philadelphia, PA: Temple University Press, 1986. Print.

Fisher, Pete. *Highway of Heroes—True Patriot Love*. Toronto: Dundern, 2011. Print.

Fossum, John Erik. "On the Prospects for a Viable Constitutional Patriotism in Complex Multinational Entities: Canada and the European Union Compared," Paper presented at the Annual Conference of the Canadian Political Science Association, Saskatoon Saskatchewan, Canada, 2007. Web. 12 March 2012.

Fletcher, Joseph F., and Jennifer Hove. "Emotional Determinants of Support for the Canadian Mission in Afghanistan: A View from the Bridge." *Canadian Journal of Political Science* 45.1 (2012): 33–62. Print.

Government of Canada, "Harper Government Boosts Tourism by Investing in War of 1812 Commemorations across Canada." Web. 12 March 2012.

Hartley, Matt. "These boys fought with honour; From Trenton to Toronto, thousands come out to line overpasses to pay their respects to the six soldiers killed in Afghanistan." *Globe and Mail* 9 July 2007: A8. Web. 12 March 2012.

Hayday, Matthew. "Fireworks, Folk-dancing, and Fostering a National Identity: The Politics of Canada Day." *Canadian Historical Review* 91.2 (2010): 287–314. *Academic Search Premier*. Web. 12 July 2012.

Hobsbawm, Eric. "Introduction: inventing traditions." *The Invention of Tradition*. Ed. Eric Hobsbawm and Terence O. Ranger. Cambridge: Cambridge University Press. 1983, 1–14. Print.

Huiskamp, Gerard. "'Support the Troops!': The Social and Political Currency of Patriotism in the United States." *New Political Science* 33.3 (2011): 285–310. *Academic Search Premier.* Web. 27 January 2012.

Hume, Jennifer. "Bronze plaques to line Ontario's 'Highway of Heroes.'" *National Post* 2011 (August 19). Web. 7 Sept. 2012.

Kirton, John. (with Jenilee Guebert). "Two Solitudes, One War: Public Opinion, National Unity and Canada's War in Afghanistan." Conference Proceeding on "Quebec and War," Université de Québec à Montréal, Montreal, 5–6 October 2007. Web. 12 July 2012.

Kong, Lily and Brenda S.A. Yeoh. "The Construction of national identity through the production of ritual and spectacle—An Analysis of National Day parades in Singapore." *Political Geography* 16.3 (1997): 213–39. *Academic Search Premier.* Web. 12 March 2012.

Kosterman, Rick and Seymour Feshbach. "Toward a measure of patriotic and nationalistic attitudes." *Political Psychology* 10.2 (1989): 257–74. *Academic Search Premier.* Web. 27 Feb. 2007.

Kemmelmeier, Markus and David G. Winter, "Sowing Patriotism, but Reaping Nationalism? Consequences of Exposure to the American Flag." *Political Psychology* 29.6 (2008): 859–79. *Academic Search Premier.* Web. 6 April 2012.

Lennox, Patrick. "From Golden Straightjacket to Kevlar Vest: Canada's Transformation to a Security State." *Canadian Journal of Political Science.* 40.4 (2007): 1017–38. Print.

Mathieu, Genevieve. *Qui est Quebecois? Synthese du debat sur laredefinition de la nation*, 2001, Montreal: VLB. Print.

McKeown-Robertson, Ruth. "Remembering Canadian Soldiers." *Hamilton Spectator* 2008: WR06. Web. 13 Dec. 2008.

Marche, Stephen. "The Return of Private Todd. Other wars saw tributes to the Unknown Soldier. In this war, the crowd along the Highway of Heroes knows each name." *Maclean's Magazine* 5 May 2010. Web. 19 Feb. 2012.

Miller, David. *On Nationality.* New York: Oxford University Press, 1995. Print.

National Defence and the Canadian Forces. "*Backgrounder: Repatriation of Fallen Canadian Soldiers Personnel. BG-09.012.*" 2009. Web. 14 March 2012.

Nieguth, Tim, and Tracey Raney. "Guarding the Nation: Reconfiguring Canada in an Era of Neo-Conservatism." Canada: The State of the Federation 2012: Regions, Resources and Resiliency. Ed. Loleen Berdahl, Carolyn Tuohy, and Andre Juneau, 189–210. Kingston: Queen's University Institute of Intergovernmental Relations; Montréal-Kingston: McGill-Queen's University Press. 2015, 189–210.

Nimijean, Richard. "Articulating the 'Canadian Way': and the Political Manipulation of the Canadian Identity." *British Journal of Canadian Studies* 18.2 (2005): 26–52. *Academic Search Premier.* Web. 12 March 2012.

Raney, Tracey, and Loleen Berdahl. "Shifting Sands? Citizens' National Identities and Pride in Social Security in Canada." *American Review of Canadian Studies* 41.3 (2011): 259–73. Print.

Royal Canadian Mint. "Honouring the Highway of Heroes." Web. 7 Sept. 2012.

Schatz, Robert, and Ervin Staub. "Manifestations of blind and constructive patriotism: Personality correlates and individual-group relations." *Patriotism in the lives of individuals.* Ed. Daniel Bar-Tal and Ervin Staub. Chicago: Nelson-Hall Publishers, 1997. 229–45. Print.

Shahzad, Farhat. "Forging the Nation as imagined community." *Nations and Nationalism* 18(1) (2012): 21–38. *Academic Search Premier.* Web. 12 March 2012.

Tajfel, Henri, Michael Billig, Robert Bundy, and Claude Flament, "Social categorization and inter-group behavior." *European Journal of Social Psychology* 1.2 (1971): 149–78. *Academic Search Premier.* Web. 12 March 2012.

Viroli, Maurizio. *For Love of Country: An Essay on Patriotism and Nationalism.* Oxford UK: Oxford University Press, 2nd edition, 2003. Print.

Wagner, Eric, "The Peaceable Kingdom? The National Myth of Canadian Peacekeeping and the Cold War," *Canadian Military Journal.* 2006/2007, 45–54. Web. 12 March 2012.

Warmington, Joe. "Our own Trail of Tears." *Toronto Sun,* 2007 (June 23), p. 3. Web. 6 April 2012.

FOUR

Material Differences:
Ethnic Diversity and the Power of Things in Greater Sudbury

Tim Nieguth

It has become commonplace in the social sciences to suggest that human communities, identities, and perceptions of reality are social constructs rather than natural givens. To mention just one example among many others, Benedict Anderson's oft-cited definition of the nation insists that nations are "imagined communities"—that is, mental constructs.[1] In many ways, the language of social constructivism has become firmly entrenched in the mainstream of political science, sociology, anthropology, and related disciplines. According to some observers, the spread of constructivism may have come at a price: precisely because constructivism has become so widely accepted in the past few decades, they argue, its ability to generate critical insights into social realities may have suffered. As Rogers Brubaker suggests somewhat provocatively, "the constructivist idiom has grown 'weary, stale, flat, and unprofitable.' ... It is not that the notion of social construction is wrong; it is rather that it is today too obviously right, too familiar, too readily taken for granted, to generate the friction, force, and freshness needed to push arguments further and generate new insights."[2]

This chapter will argue that one way to respond to Brubaker's challenge—and to push constructivist analysis towards new insights—is to engage with an emerging literature that can loosely be labelled "new materialisms." While this literature is extremely diverse, one of its basic tenets is that material objects matter. From a social science perspective, they matter in particular because they shape social realities—including collective identities, possible ranges of action, and the nature of power relations. In order to support its argument, the chapter will first point to some of the ways in which collective identities and differences are socially constructed. In doing so, it will pay particular attention to changing notions of what counts as "diverse," drawing on Canadian historical developments as an example. The chapter will then draw our attention to the potential contributions of new materialisms to our understanding of ethnicity. In particular, it will emphasize the power of things—material objects—in the construction of ethnic identity and diversity. The chapter will illustrate the importance of material objects by exploring the role of selected *actants* (to borrow a term from one of the new materialisms) in transmitting, transforming, and challenging notions of ethnic or national diversity in the city of Greater Sudbury. More specifically, the chapter will focus on the significance of city-texts and public iconography in this context.

CONSTRUCTING ETHNIC DIVERSITY

Considered over the long term, collective identities are curiously malleable phenomena. The same is true of any particular notion of difference and diversity. The declining importance of Canada's Protestant–Catholic cleavage is a case in point. In the nineteenth century, this cleavage constituted one of the central fault lines in Canadian society, sparking several profound political crises. In 1888, for example, Quebec's legislature passed the *Jesuit Estates Act*. Outside Quebec, responses to the act varied widely: while many Canadians had no objections to it, some (including several Members of Parliament) described it as an act of profound national humiliation, an attack on the people's fundamental rights and freedoms, an attempt to allow foreign potentates to meddle in Canadian affairs, and a threat to Canada's character as a British country. Thus, William Edward O'Brien, MP for Muskoka and Parry Sound, asserted in the House of Commons that the "Act violate[d] the Constitution ... [and] interfere[d] with the rights and privileges of the people."[3] What had provoked this kind of response?

The *Jesuit Estates Act* was intended to provide compensation for lands the Jesuit Order had lost to the Crown over a hundred years before, when the Order had (temporarily) been dissolved by the Pope. According to the act, Quebec was to pay $400,000 to Catholic institutions and organizations. The distribution of funds between the various Catholic organizations and institutions was to be determined by the Pope. The province also granted $60,000 to the Protestant Committee of

Public Instruction, and in consequence, Quebec's provincial legislature passed the *Jesuit Estates Act* with the unanimous support of its Protestant members. Nevertheless, many Anglo-Protestants outside Quebec strongly objected to the fact that the Pope would be playing a role in settling what they perceived to be internal Canadian affairs. Their ranks included some of the leading political figures of the day, the most prominent being Dalton McCarthy—MP, Orangeman, powerful orator, and president of Ontario's Conservative Party. McCarthy and other parliamentarians called on John A. Macdonald's federal government to disallow the *Jesuit Estates Act*, but after some debate, it declined to do so.

While McCarthy and his allies were defeated in this particular instance, their views on the nature of Canada and the threat posed by French Catholic nationalism were widely shared. Many Anglo-Protestants felt that the *Jesuit Estates Act* fit a troubling pattern: supposedly, French-Catholics were aggressively expanding their power and, in doing so, undermining Canadian unity and equality. These sentiments played out in various battles over the nature of Canada and the accommodation of French Catholic minorities. From the vantage point of the early twenty-first century, these battles may appear both strange and familiar: strange, because few Canadians would today regard the division between Catholics and Protestants as a key dimension of Canadian diversity; familiar, because religious affiliation is clearly regarded as a key source of diversity in post-9/11 Canada (e.g., Islam is often portrayed as an "Other" to Canada's supposedly secular tradition). In addition, the distinction between anglophones and francophones is still a key element in Canada's self-portrayal as a "diverse" society.

The fact that some fault lines have become less important in Canadian society over time while others have retained their significance is perhaps not particularly surprising, especially in light of the insights generated by social constructivism. Taking these insights seriously requires social scientists to treat groups as an *explanandum* rather than an *explanans*. Brubaker, for example, emphasizes the need to abandon the notion of ethnic groups in trying to explain ethnicity. Ethnic groups cannot help us understand the dynamics of ethnic identity, ethnic relations, or ethnic conflict, since they are themselves part of those dynamics. Letting go of groups as part of our analytical apparatus consequently allows us to better understand the processes involved in fashioning ethnic groups.[4]

There are myriad actors at play in these processes. Much of the existing literature focuses on one of the most powerful among these actors, the state. The state plays a crucial role in identity construction; it does so through a wide range of policy fields (including immigration, education, and cultural policies) and with an equally wide variety of tools. James Scott's *Seeing Like a State* shows convincingly that a key feature of the modern state is its attempt to manage state populations by systematically dividing them into discrete categories.[5] This is not simply an act of describing or reflecting pre-existing divisions; rather, states actively shape their populations through the ways they choose to categorize them. In Scott's words, "the builders of the modern nation-state do not merely describe, observe, and map; they strive to shape a people and landscape that will fit these techniques of observation."[6]

While the state clearly is an important actor in fashioning collective identities and notions of difference, it is far from the only one. Brubaker forcefully reminds us that ethnic identities and "groupness" are constructed, not just by social and political elites, but by everyday citizens: "Ethnicity is embodied and expressed not only in political projects and nationalist rhetoric but in everyday encounters, practical categories, commonsense knowledge, cultural idioms, cognitive schemas, interactional cues, discursive frames, organizational routines, social networks, and institutional forms."[7]

In other words, ethnic identities—and notions of ethnic difference—emerge through ongoing, often routine encounters with a wide variety of actors, institutions, and texts. This includes governmental agencies, but also the media, arts, popular culture, municipalities, and community organizations, to name just a few. For example, the Group of Seven has long been considered critical to the construction of Canadian identity,[8] hip hop serves as an important site of articulating Aboriginal identity,[9] and the town council of Hérouxville recently touched off a heated debate about the accommodation of ethnic diversity in Quebec.[10]

None of these actors operate in isolation. Rather, they constantly interact, affecting one another's aspirations, resources, and opportunities. This is true even in undertakings one might think of as the exclusive preserve of the state, such as the preparation and implementation of official censuses. As Bruce Curtis has observed,

> census making is commonly an object of political struggle and contest. The contending and conflicting social imaginaries sustained by social classes, groups, and political parties produce antagonistic or competing representations of social relations as population. Struggles over census making are to be found with respect to the legitimacy of representations of population as such, and also with respect to the legitimacy of the policy measures that result from those representations.[11]

Overall, ethnic identities, ethnic difference, and ethnic relations are products of a complex (and constantly changing) web of interactions among a multitude of actors with sometimes conflicting, sometimes complementary agendas.

THE POWER OF THINGS

Interestingly, there is one class of actors that has received fairly little attention in the literature on ethnicity: things. This reflects the state of affairs in the social sciences more generally. Inanimate objects, if they are considered at all, are typically treated as facilitators of or restraints on human action. Scholars have paid much less attention to the ways in which things may be involved in constituting groups, identities, or perceptions of reality. In part, this is because the impact of material objects on such mental constructs is difficult to trace. However, this does not mean they are insignificant. For example, "recent empirical work has demonstrated an array of unconscious effects of exposure to national symbols . . . including increased implicit national identification, an automatic orientation toward group unity, and the automatic activation of concepts associated with one's nation."[12]

In addition to the methodological difficulties inherent in attempting to measure the impact of material objects on human consciousness, there may be a second reason for the relative neglect of things: unlike human actors, inanimate objects lack agendas—at least in any understanding of the term that would be applicable to the domain of human action. Things matter, nonetheless, because they display agency in the sense that they "modify a state of affairs by making a difference."[13] Arguably, attempts to understand why and how objects matter stand to benefit from engaging with recent theoretical and philosophical approaches that challenge the analytical divide between humans and non-humans. This includes such approaches as speculative realism, actor-network theory, and vital materialism.[14] These approaches are sometimes grouped together under the loose label of "new materialism." While there are significant differences between them, they share a central concern with the power of objects. In various ways, the new materialisms emphasize that things matter and must be taken seriously as actors in their own right. Latour's notion of an *actant* is especially useful in this context, since it insists that agency does not require intentionality:

> *Actant* ... is Bruno Latour's term for a source of action; an actant can be human or not, or, most likely, a combination of both. Latour defines it as "something that acts or to which activity is granted by others. It implies no special motivation of human individual actors, nor of humans in general." An actant is neither an object nor a subject but an "intervener," akin to the Deleuzean "quasi-causal operator." An operator is that which, by virtue of its particular location in an assemblage and the fortuity of being in the right place at the right time, makes the difference, makes things happen, becomes the decisive force catalyzing an event.[15]

Clearly, things routinely make a difference to human society. For example, there is an extensive literature attesting to the political significance of murals in Belfast during the so-called "Troubles": these murals often served as border demarcations, signs of communal difference, means of claiming space, and expressions of political cleavages.[16] More generally, both private and public spaces are suffused with signs and symbols that affect how humans perceive social reality, how they think of themselves, how they see others, and how they interact with one another. Many of these objects appear perfectly unremarkable; they are part of our daily surroundings but tend not to be noticed explicitly. Street names, for example, typically only register as routine parts of our everyday lives. However, their ordinariness does not mean that they exercise no power; as Azaryahu reminds us,

> commemorative street names (like other place names) conflate history and geography and merge the past they commemorate into ordinary settings of human life. Embedded into language, they are active participants in the construction and perception of social reality. The merit of street names is their ability to incorporate an official version of history into such spheres of human activity that seem to be entirely devoid of direct political manipulation. This transforms history into a feature of the "natural order of things" and conceals its contrived character.[17]

Street names, then, reflect the views of groups or individuals who are sufficiently powerful to control the naming of urban spaces; they provide a glimpse into the history of social power relations; they point to the traditions, values, or events that powerful groups or individuals considered worth commemorating; and they shape our sense of social reality. It is worth mentioning that street names can transmit political meaning even if they do not commemorate specific events or individuals, or if residents are unaware of the fact. For instance, in multiethnic and multilingual societies, street signs often involve a choice between languages, scripts, and symbolic repertoires.[18] In consequence, street names point to the differential access of linguistic groups to the definition of public space. If most street names are drawn from a specific language or linguistic tradition, this both reflects and entrenches the dominant role of a particular linguistic group. Likewise, if there are few street names in another language, that language and its speakers are marked as marginal.

To put these points in a Canadian context, the country's history as a British colony and its continued adherence to British political traditions is evident not just in many practices and institutions of the Canadian state; it is also flagged by the preponderance of place and street names that emphasize Canada's British heritage. This includes the names of several provinces (British Columbia, Alberta, and Prince Edward Island, for example), and cities (Halifax, Kingston, London, Regina, New Westminster, and Victoria, among others), as well as common street names (such as King, Queen, and Regent). Walking through the city centre of Greater Sudbury, for example, pedestrians might take Elm, Elgin, or Brady Street; they might cross Notre Dame Avenue, Paris Street, or Brebeuf Avenue; and they might stroll along Larch, Cedar, or Durham Street.[19] In other words, they will encounter street names that signal the dominance of British (primarily) and French (to a much lesser degree) cultural traditions.

More generally, Sudbury's inventory of street names reflects the country's two official languages. Few street names in the city point to a non-British, non-French heritage. This is especially true when considering the city's major roadways. There is a Ghandi Lane, an Antwerp Avenue, and a Madrid Lane, but names such as these are rare and typically assigned to minor streets. As a whole, downtown Sudbury street names erase the significant historical and contemporary presence of Aboriginal peoples in the area. For the most part, they also exclude several ethnic minorities that represent a large share of the city's population (such as German, Finnish, and Italian Canadians). Overall, then, Sudbury street names reflect the historical dominance of Canada's two so-called charter groups. At the same time, and in doing so, they draw particular attention to the distinction between the British and French, flagging this distinction as a key element of "diversity."

Similar observations apply to some of the other public signs that form part of the visual landscape in downtown Sudbury. This is especially true of signs identifying public buildings, which employ both of Canada's official languages. For example, a sign affixed to Sudbury's central public transport hub informs visitors in English and French that they have reached the *Transit Centre* or *Centre de transport*.[20] Likewise, the *Main Branch* of Sudbury's *Public Library* is simultaneously identified as the *Branch Centrale* of the *Bibliothèque publique*.[21] These bilingual signs reflect and amplify the presence of two dominant linguistic communities in Greater Sudbury. In contrast, another category of public signs—traffic signs—downplays the city's linguistic diversity. Like street names and signs on public buildings, many traffic signs involve a choice between linguistic repertoires. In downtown Sudbury, these choices systematically favour the English language; as such, they reflect (and constantly signal) the dominant status of English—both in the city and in the province of Ontario as a whole. A stop sign at the intersection of Beech and Durham streets, next to downtown Sudbury's shopping mall, can serve as a fairly straightforward example here: the sign communicates the command to bring one's vehicle to a complete halt exclusively in English, rather than in any other language or in several languages.[22]

Sudbury's street names, building signs, and traffic signs suggest overall that discourses on ethnic diversity within the city are produced under conditions that are closely aligned with biculturalism and bilingualism. These conditions may favour definitions of diversity that hinge on the British/French divide, and do so to a much much greater degree than in other regions of the country, where that divide may be perceived as less relevant in everyday life. However, street names and traffic signs represent only some of the ways in which particular notions of ethnic identity and difference are embedded in public space. Other elements, such as the iconography of public space (including flags, murals, and monuments), are equally important in this regard. For example, a mural located at the intersection of Elgin Street and Ste. Anne Road celebrates the fiftieth anniversary of *Le Carrefour Francophone*, a French community organization. It displays a variety of Franco-Ontarian symbols and traditions, such as the Franco-Ontarian flag (which was designed at Sudbury's Laurentian University in the 1960s). The mural effectively signals the presence of a sizable francophone community within the city, and serves to remind passersby of the fact.[23] Not unlike Sudbury's city-text, this mural reflects and reinforces an understanding of ethnic diversity that centres on British/French dualism.

This emphasis on dualism contrasts noticeably with the content of another mural, this one located in close proximity to the first, but inside downtown Sudbury's shopping mall. The second mural depicts important facets of the city's historical development, landmarks, and community life, such as the mining industry and the railway. One part of this mural shows several miners drilling, collecting, and transporting ore. In the background, one miner is running towards his co-workers, clearly trying to alert them to an unspecified threat.[24] Of course, the mural as a whole is neither accurate nor comprehensive in a strictly historical sense; it likely is not intended to be. For present purposes, it is nonetheless interesting to consider which ethnic groups seem to be included in the mural, how these groups are portrayed, and which groups appear to be absent. For instance, the mural only hints at the presence of Franco-Ontarians (in the guise of a Catholic priest). In addition, the only scene depicting individuals who can fairly confidently be identified as Aboriginal shows them as Europeanized and appears to emphasize their harmonious coexistence with various representatives of settler society, thus erasing the historical reality of colonialism and racism. The same scene offers a striking and deeply problematic depiction of an individual who appears to be of East Asian extraction: his skin is literally rendered with yellow paint, he wears a conical straw hat, and he sports a long, thin moustache and chin beard. This imagery thus strongly resonates with a number of tropes and stereotypes historically associated with racist, Orientalist discourses.[25]

Notions of diversity are further complicated by several other elements in Sudbury's public iconography. In 2007, for example, the city changed the name of the Paris Street Bridge—one of the major arteries for traffic flowing in and out of downtown—to Bridge of Nations. The bridge is lined by the flags of various states, nations, and cultural groups, literally flagging the diverse origins of the city's population. Among the ethnic and national groups whose flags are flown above the bridge are the Anishnabek, Métis, Franco-Ontarian, English, Scottish, Northern Irish, and Welsh—in other words, local Aboriginal nations and various fragments of the two charter groups of European settlers.[26] The flags are a highly visible reminder of the city's multicultural and multiethnic nature. In consequence, they help engender a notion of ethnic diversity that runs counter to the predominantly bicultural, bilingual reading of diversity conveyed by the street names, public signs, and murals discussed above. However, it is interesting to note that, while the country flags flying above the Bridge of Nations represent states from all regions of the globe, their numbers noticeably tilt towards Europe and the Western hemisphere. Thus, Africa accounts for 28 percent of UN member-states, but only 11 percent of the country flags flown at the Bridge of Nations represent African states. Conversely, while Europe, North America, and Australia comprise 26 percent of UN member states, these world regions are significantly overrepresented at the bridge, accounting for nearly half of all country flags (Table 4.1). This suggests a reading of multiculturalism and ethnic diversity that heavily favours specific areas of the globe.

Table 4.1. Countries by world region

World region	Percentage of countries represented at the Bridge of Nations	Percentage of UN member-states
Africa	11	28
Asia–Pacific	16	29
Europe–North America–Australia	48	26
Latin America and the Caribbean	25	17
Total	**100**	**100**

Source: Author's calculations.
Note: World regions are defined on the basis of regional groups within the UN, with two exceptions: Turkey, Israel, and Kiribati are included with the Asia–Pacific region; and Europe–North America–Australia includes the Eastern European Group, Western European, and Others Group, and the United States.

CONCLUSION

It has become commonplace to argue that collective identities, group relations, and perceptions of social reality are not simply natural givens, but are the result of complex social processes. These processes involve a multitude of actors, such as the state, municipalities, corporations, the media, voluntary associations, and families. The literature on ethnicity has scrutinized many of these actors in great detail. However, as with the social sciences and humanities in general, it has paid little attention to the power of objects. This chapter argued that our understanding of "ethnic diversity" stands to benefit from considering a group of theoretical and philosophical approaches sometimes described as new materialism. Whatever their (substantial) differences, all of these approaches argue that things matter.

From the perspective of the social sciences, things matter specifically because they make a difference to the world we inhabit.

To support this argument, the chapter began by discussing the social construction of collective identities, linking the concerns of constructivists such as Rogers Brubaker to the new materialist literature. It then turned its attention to street names, public signs, and public iconography in the city of Greater Sudbury. In doing so, it illustrated the extent to which these objects are involved in promoting certain notions of ethnic diversity. Sometimes, these notions are complementary; sometimes, they conflict. For example, Sudbury's street signs reflect and entrench an understanding of ethnic diversity that privileges the British/French divide and erases other ethnic groups. In contrast, some elements of Sudbury's public iconography emphasize the city's multicultural, multiethnic, and multilingual heritage. ∎

NOTES

1. Anderson, *Imagined Communities*.
2. Brubaker, *Ethnicity Without Groups*, 3.
3. House of Commons, *Edited Hansard*, 812.
4. Brubaker, *Ethnicity Without Groups*, 7–27.
5. Scott, *Seeing Like a State*.
6. Ibid., 82.
7. Brubaker, *Ethnicity Without Groups*, 2.
8. Dawn, *National Visions*.
9. Morgan and Warren, "Aboriginal Youth."
10. Nieguth and Lacassagne, "Contesting the Nation."
11. Curtis, *The Politics of Population*. See also, among others, Abu-Laban and Stasiulis, "Constructing 'Ethnic Canadians'"; Howard-Hassmann, "Canadian as an Ethnic Category"; Kukutai and Didham, "Re-making the Majority?"; and Thompson, "Making (Mixed-)Race."
12. Butz, "National Symbols."
13. Latour, *Reassembling the Social*, 71.
14. See, for instance, Harman, *Towards Speculative Realism*; Latour, *Reassembling the Social*; and Bennett, *Vibrant Matter*.
15. Bennett, *Vibrant Matter*, 9.

16 See, among others, Brown and Macginty, "Public Attitudes"; Jarman, "Painting Landscapes"; Kuusisto, "Territoriality"; and McAtackney, "Peace Maintenance."
17 Azaryahu, "German Reunification," 481.
18 Ibid., 481.
19 City of Greater Sudbury, No title [Map].
20 Tim Nieguth, "Transit Centre," https://drive.google.com/open?id=0B3XJZ4IO3W0INVlSRnZpRFFGd1U.
21 Tim Nieguth, "Public Library," https://drive.google.com/open?id=0B3XJZ4IO3W0ISHNwUmVuaWFLUGc.
22 Tim Nieguth, "Traffic Sign," https://drive.google.com/open?id=0B3XJZ4IO3W0lYVlhbmxiZ1cxWFU.
23 Tim Nieguth, "Carrefour Francophone Mural, Detail," https://drive.google.com/open?id=0B3XJZ4IO3W0ldmpHTFBXblpRZ00.
24 Tim Nieguth, "Rainbow Centre Mural, Detail 1," https://drive.google.com/open?id=0B3XJZ4IO3W0IT2FpVlFZd2Z2NEk.
25 Tim Nieguth, "Rainbow Centre Mural, Detail 2," https://drive.google.com/open?id=0B3XJZ4IO3W0lVjRscFR2dlZ1MXM.
26 City of Greater Sudbury, "Bridge of Nations," http://www.greatersudbury.ca/cms/index.cfm?app=div_leisureservices&lang=en&currID=10656.

WORKS CITED

Abu-Laban, Yasmeen, and Daiva Stasiulis. "Constructing 'Ethnic Canadians': The Implications for Public Policy and Inclusive Citizenship: Rejoinder to Rhoda Howard-Hassmann." *Canadian Public Policy* 26, no. 4 (2000): 477–87.

Anderson, Benedict. *Imagined Communities: Reflections on the Origin and Spread of Nationalism.* London: Verso, 1983.

Azaryahu, Maoz. "German Reunification and the Politics of Street Names: The Case of East Berlin." *Political Geography* 16, no. 6 (1997): 479–93.

Bennett, Jane. *Vibrant Matter: A Political Ecology of Things.* Durham: Duke University Press, 2010.

Brown, Kris, and Roger Macginty. "Public Attitudes toward Partisan and Neutral Symbols in Post-Agreement Northern Ireland." *Identities: Global Studies in Culture and Power* 10, no. 1 (2003): 83–108.

Brubaker, Rogers. *Ethnicity Without Groups.* Cambridge, MA: Harvard University Press, 2004.

Butz, David A. "National Symbols as Agents of Psychological and Social Change." *Political Psychology* 30, no. 5 (2009): 779–804.

City of Greater Sudbury. No title [Map]. N.d. http://maps.greatersudbury.ca

Curtis, Bruce. *The Politics of Population: State Formation, Statistics, and the Census of Canada, 1840–1875*. Toronto: University of Toronto Press, 2001.

Dawn, Leslie. *National Visions, National Blindness: Canadian Art and Identities in the 1920s*. Vancouver: UBC Press, 2006.

Harman, Graham. *Towards Speculative Realism: Essays and Lectures*. Ropley: Zero Books, 2010.

House of Commons, Canada. *Edited Hansard*. 6th Parl., 3rd sess. Ottawa: B. Chamberlin, 1889. http://eco.canadiana.ca/view/oocihm.9_07186_7_2

Howard-Hassmann, Rhoda E. "Canadian as an Ethnic Category: Implications for Multiculturalism and National Unity." *Canadian Public Policy* 25, no. 4 (1999): 523–37.

Jarman, Neil. "Painting Landscapes: The Place of Murals in the Symbolic Construction of Urban Space." In *Symbols in Northern Ireland*, ed. Anthony Buckley, 81–98. Belfast: Institute of Irish Studies, 1998.

Kukutai, Tahu, and Robert Didham. "Re-making the Majority? Ethnic New Zealanders in the 2006 Census." *Ethnic and Racial Studies* 35, no. 8 (2012): 1427–46.

Kuusisto, Anna-Kaisa. "Territoriality, Symbolism, and the Challenge." *Peace Review* 13, no. 1 (2001): 59–66.

Latour, Bruno. *Reassembling the Social: An Introduction to Actor-Network-Theory*. Oxford: Oxford University Press, 2005.

McAtackney, Laura. "Peace Maintenance and Political Messages: The Significance of Walls During and After the Northern Irish 'Troubles.'" *Journal of Social Archaeology* 11, no. 1 (2011): 77–98.

Morgan, George, and Andrew Warren. "Aboriginal Youth, Hip Hop, and the Politics of Identification." *Ethnic and Racial Studies* 34, no. 6 (2011): 925–47.

Nieguth, Tim, and Aurélie Lacassagne. "Contesting the Nation: Reasonable Accommodation in Rural Quebec." *Canadian Political Science Review* 3, no. 1 (2009): 1–16.

Scott, James C. *Seeing Like a State: How Certain Schemes to Improve the Human Condition Have Failed*. New Haven: Yale University Press, 1998.

Thompson, Debra. "Making (Mixed-)Race: Census Politics and the Emergence of Multiracial Multiculturalism in the United States, Great Britain, and Canada." *Ethnic and Racial Studies* 35, no. 8 (2012): 1409–26.

FIVE

Our Home and Native Land:
Invocations of the Land in the 2011 Canadian Federal Election

Shauna Wilton

INTRODUCTION

The land is closely connected to national identity and nationalism. Images of the land remind citizens of who they are and where they belong. Territorial borders demarcate the land that belongs to the people and create a clear division between us and them. People fight and die to protect the land and its people, values, and culture. Within a country such as Canada—a multinational, multicultural, and bilingual state—the land takes on increased importance as a source of national identity and unity. The existing literature on Canadian identity and the theoretical literature on nationalism both recognize the importance of land, territory, and landscapes. The common themes of taming, civilizing, and surviving the Canadian landscapes inundate Canadian history and literature, whether it be the stories of homesteading and hardship told by our grandparents, the novels of Margaret Atwood and W.O. Mitchell, or the art of the Group of Seven. Thus, in a country as ethnoculturally diverse as Canada, land, territory, and landscapes are a powerful and neutral way to appeal to Canadians and to represent Canadian identity. As such, Canadian landscapes can be a powerful visual tool for political campaigns and advertisements, especially TV ads, which are generally designed to speak to a national audience. Somewhat surprisingly, an analysis of the television advertisements from the 2011 federal election in Canada reveals that the ads rarely include visuals representations of Canadian territory. The relative lack of emphasis on the land contrasts with the leader-centric and antagonistic nature of the ads. But when the ads do include images of the land, the Canadian landscape is used in both positive and negative ways and provides a powerful tool for connecting with Canadian voters.

This chapter asks how Canadian political parties invoke the land and landscapes in order to promote a sense of Canadian identity and belonging. Using a critical discourse and content analysis of the campaign materials from the 2011 Canadian federal election, I first examine the images of the Canadian landscape, including the built environment, images of nature, and Canadian national symbols, in order to explore the ways in which the land is connected to discourses surrounding Canadian values and political priorities. This research then analyzes the texts within the campaign materials and the ways in which they speak to the relationships between the Canadian people and the land, including the environment, as part of general campaign strategies and platforms.

LAND, NATION, AND THE SOCIAL CONSTRUCTION OF LANDSCAPES

Territory and land are key concepts in the study of nations and nationalism. Anthony Smith, for example, argues that national identity "suggests a definite social space, a fairly well demarcated and bounded territory, with which members identify and to which they feel they belong."[1] Others, such as Brieully and Gellner,[2] argue that the nation is inherently connected to a sovereign piece of territory or land. The relationship between nation and state in their work gives territory a central role. As well, in international law, territory has been connected to the rights of peoples to self-determination.[3]

Finally, Michael Billig argues that the images associated with the land—landmarks, statues, and so on—create the physical and human landscapes that surround us and are part of the banal reproduction of nationalism.[4] All of these major theorists of nationalism, albeit in different ways, view the land as an important component of national identity. This is most evident in the claims to land and territory that generally accompany nationalist movements, whether it is the claims of Quebec nationalists to sovereignty over Quebec or the claims of Aboriginal peoples, who use their historical governance of the land as proof of their nationhood and who claim that their status as nations entitles them to govern themselves and their historical territories.

Territory or land, however, has no social or political meaning other than what we give it. Landscapes, therefore, are socially constructed and contested spaces. Sverker Sorlin, for example, argues that "landscape has provided the raw material for images and projections of territorial entities, be they empires, nations, regions or localities, and these landscapes have been culturally reproduced and mediated. The end product of these cultural processes are diverse, they are landscapes of honour and virtue, of bountiful resources and future wealth, of touristic marvel, and, most commonly, they are landscapes of distinction."[5]

Similarly, Brian Osborne writes that the material world becomes loaded with symbolic importance, creating an "a-where-ness" among people regarding the relationship between territory and identity.[6] This shared sense of belonging and of connection to a particular piece of nationalized land is learned. As Sorlin states, they "learned the characteristics of their territory and they have had them imprinted in their minds because there has been a long process of imprinting, partly organic and spontaneous, partly conscious, in some instances even with elements of manipulation."[7] This chapter engages with the idea that Canadian landscapes are imbued with historical meanings that connect the land to the process of settling Canada and the creation of a unique Canadian identity. At the same time, it explores the manipulation of the connection between land and national identity through election campaigning.

So we need to recognize that our ideas about the land, its history, and our relationship with it are socially constructed and variable in time and space. The role of political elites in the process, combined those of artists, authors, and others, is worthy of study. Historically, the land has played a significant role in Canadian nation-building. For example, the Group of Seven, with their paintings of stark wilderness of Ontario, constructed a particular vision of the Canadian landscape that came to be associated with Canadian identity. Erin Manning suggests that the Group of Seven "sought, through art, to create a vision of Canada that would be a departure from their colonial (British) roots, claiming that it was only through a relationship to the land that Canadians could become acquainted with their 'true' nature."[8] Yet this landscape reflects only part of the country. Also, as Canadians become more urban and "farther from the farm," the typical images of nature in Canada—the Canadian Shield, prairie wheatfields—become further removed from collective memory, challenging the idea that we could find our "true nature" in our relationship to the land.

Although it is central to Canadian identity, the land continues to be a contentious element in Canadian history and politics. Whether we are re-examining the mythology behind the settlement of the "terra nullius" of Canada, discussing

Arctic sovereignty and Ottawa's relations with the Inuit and the North, or dealing with the political fallout resulting from different understandings of the land (e.g., with regard to Aboriginal land claims or the Keystone pipeline), the land that is Canada continues to be reimagined, reworked, and contested.

Considering the importance of land and images of landscapes to Canadian history and national identity, one would expect the land to appear in Canadian politics and political advertising in a variety of ways. First, issues of territorial sovereignty—for example, with regard to the Canadian Arctic or Aboriginal lands—play a prominent role in Canadian politics and receive regular media coverage. Second, the environment is a prominent political issue facing governments today. Obviously, how Canadians use (and misuse) their land is an environmental issue. Canada's recent withdrawal from the Kyoto Accord and its failure to meet even the weakest targets for reducing carbon emissions make this issue a pressing one for Canadian politicians. The emergence of the Green Party in Canada has brought further attention to this topic. Third, Canada's economy is strongly resource-based (oil and gas, fisheries, agriculture, mining, and so on), and this speaks to the dominance and control of the land by Canadians as well as to the idea that the land is the source of future Canadian prosperity. As the health of the economy continues to dominate political debate, the relationship between the land and the economy remains pivotal. Finally, the symbolism of the land has long been used to unite Canadians and to inspire a sense of belonging and identity. This is one of the most obvious uses for the Canadian landscape, whether it is the North being depicted, or the Canadian Shield, the vast prairies, the Rocky Mountains, or Peggy's Cove. Canada has many landscapes that speak differently to people in different parts of the country, but all of these images are fairly representative of the "natural" landscape of Canada. Also included in this category are "man-made" landscapes such as grain elevators, oil rigs, and fishing dories.

METHODS

The quantitative part of the analysis was conducted using content analysis. Content analysis is a systematic method for analyzing content in communications.[9] The content analysis of the television advertisements was done using the coding guidelines provided through the Comparative Manifesto Coding Database (Manifesto Project). In addition to the fields of analysis provided through the Manifesto guidelines—which include external relations, freedom and democracy, welfare and quality of life, fabric of society, and social groups—two additional categories related to this specific project were added: representation of land and landscapes, and representation of the "other."

A content analysis of the campaign materials only tells part of the story; it does, however, provide a foundation on which to engage in broader critical discourse analysis (CDA). CDA attempts to create linkages between discourses, text, language, and social context; it suggests that language is not merely a tool for conveying discourse but also a site of struggle in itself. Discourses are important because they carry social meanings that are politicized by the power concepts embedded in them.[10] CDA helps provide the context for the content analysis, enabling a deeper understanding of the use of the images in the advertisements. The questions regarding how the ads represent the relationship between the land and the nation require the use of CDA to identify the ways in which images and text (both spoken and written) reflect, challenge, or participate in the social construction of the Canadian landscape.

The use of mixed methods draws on the strengths of each. This in turn allows for both a qualitative and quantitative analysis of the texts, one that enables the researcher to uncover the values embedded in these documents and that provides ways to replicate the research and findings.[11] This approach also adds depth to the analysis. Images remain the primary focus of the analysis; however, as Thornham points out, it is also essential to probe the predominant and resistant discourses within which the images are embedded, the contradictions and absences within the texts, and the counter-discourses that emerge.[12] In particular, CDA creates room for agency and social transformation by revealing counter-discourses and contradictions in the ads. This CDA of the campaign materials focuses on discourses surrounding the land that appear in the advertisements, especially those related to (1) the environment, (2) the resource economy, (3) territory and sovereignty, and (4) the symbolic use of landscapes. This culminates in an analysis of the differences and similarities between the ads and the political parties.

Ultimately, this research seeks to understand how these campaign materials promote competing, potentially partisan, discourses about the relationship between the Canadian people and the land, including the environment, as part of a general campaign strategy and platform. Campaign materials are central to contemporary political campaigns but are rarely the focus of political studies.[13] The few academic articles that do examine campaign materials point to the multilayered meanings contained in these "simple" forms of political communication, which are often the only contact voters have with political parties. As such, they are rich sources for exploring how group identity and power structures are constructed and disseminated. Once we understand how the major political parties represent the nation, we can better understand the relationship between land and identity as well as the competing discourses presented by the major political parties. Osborne argues that "people live in places and identify with them, or are alienated by them. But space, like time, is metaphysically neutral. There is no inherent identity to places. It is the actions of humans at specific locations that turn objective space into subjective places constructed by human behaviour."[14] How, then, does campaign literature contribute to this process of turning objective space into a Canadian national space?

ELECTION 2011

The goal of this chapter, then, is to explore how politicians and the major political parties use the land and landscapes in their federal election ads. The dominant parties in the 2011 federal election were the governing Conservatives, the Liberals, the New Democrats (NDP), the Bloc Québécois (BQ), and the Green Party. Although the Greens were less successful than the other parties during the election (they won only one seat), we include them in this study because they did capture a significant portion of the popular vote and because they are the only major party with a female leader. The materials were collected during the campaign; through follow-up contact with the political parties (both the local candidates and campaign managers and the national party headquarters); and from the Internet (party websites and their YouTube channels). Overall, 5 ads

Table 5.1 Campaign spending by political party, 2011

Political party	Radio/TV advertising ($)	Total election expenses	Ads as % of total spending
Conservative	10,408,914.15	19,519,994.87	53%
NDP	9,511,705.12	20,372,231.49	47%
Liberal	8,276,033.15	19,507,745.82	42%
BQ	2,952,810.52	5,343,060.89	55%
Green	999,088.13	1,924,478.05	52%

Source: Elections.ca financial reports.

from the BQ, 12 from the Conservative Party, 8 from the Green Party, 20 from the Liberal Party, and 14 from the NDP were collected.

Television ads are important in election campaigns. In the 2011 federal election, all of the major federal parties spent millions of dollars on television and radio ads—indeed, such ads accounted for around 50 percent of all election spending during the campaign. (See Table 5.1.)

In the television ads we analyzed, land played only a marginal role. The primary focus of the ads was on the party leaders, who appeared in almost every ad. The second most common feature of the sample was the use of attack ads as a campaign strategy. Attacks ads are defined here as ads in which at least 50 percent of the ad focuses on the other parties or leaders in a critical manner. Generally speaking, an attack ad is personal attack on another political party or candidate, often as part of negative campaigning. Such ads may unfairly criticize the opponent's faults or use innuendo to influence voters. An large majority of the TV ads from the major parties were attack ads: over 83 percent of the Conservatives', 75 percent of the Liberals', 64 percent of the NDP's, and 40 percent of the Bloc Québécois's ads focused on opposing parties. The Greens, by contrast, ran only one ad that qualified as an attack ad, and that one attacked the other parties for using attack ads, arguing that "It doesn't have to be like this" (13).

Figure 5.1 Attack ads as a proportion of total ads, 2011

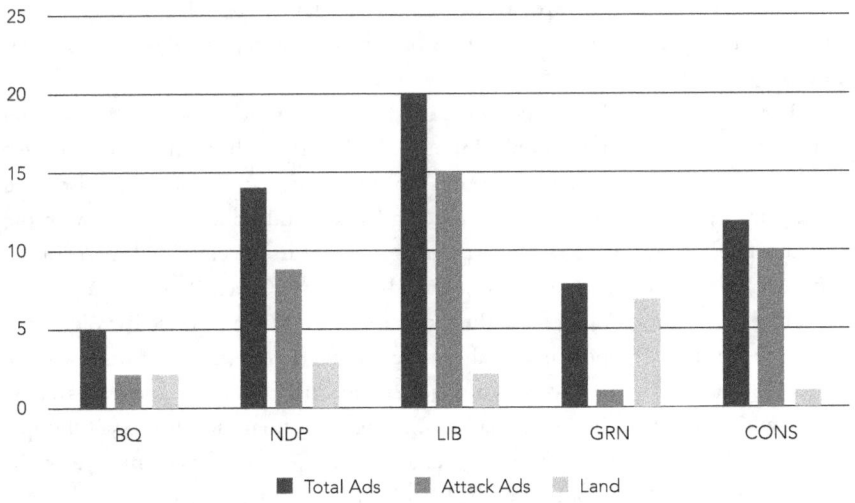

Landscapes were utilized to convey negative messages in the ads. In a Liberal ad attacking the Conservative government's corporate tax cuts, we were presented with an image of Prime Minister Harper in front of a grey and ominous cityscape, with green dollar signs falling around him (27). Here the urban environment was portrayed darkly and negatively, and the dollar signs resembled rain or falling leaves. In two attack ads, the NDP also used the Canadian landscape to convey their message. The first of these, on the environment (52), began with Stephen Harper in front of the Canadian Rockies—one of Canada's iconic landscapes, and the one closest to his political roots—and then shifted to show drawn-in oil rigs (another image closely associated with Harper's political base) polluting an environment of mountains, lakes, and fields. The ad closed with a city skyline billowing pollution into the atmosphere and a girl with an inhaler. This ad, quite obviously, was connecting the policies of the Harper government and his ties to the oil and gas industry to environmental degradation and the resulting health consequences for Canadians. The second NDP ad (53) began with an image of Jack Layton, the party leader, against a Canadian flag and then segued to him standing in front of an idyllic winter rural landscape while he commented that his party would look after Canadians, not corporations, and reduce heating costs for homes. The first NDP ad, then, used negative images to convey a negative political message about Stephen Harper and the Conservative government, while the second used a positive image to convey both a negative message about the Conservatives and a positive message about the NDP. This suggests that images of the landscapes with which Canadians identify can be used both to create a connection with voters by presenting them with a landscape with which they can identify, and to create fear in the minds of voters by presenting dystopian images of those landscapes.

In the attack ads, landscapes were used to generate fear and mistrust among voters, as a means to raise doubts about whether the other parties and leaders were concerned about Canada's natural environment. Landscapes were also used to convey a positive message by associating leaders and political parties with the environment of their voters. This was most apparent in the election trailers of the Conservatives (2) and BQ (25) and in the ads from the Green Party (14–20).

The one-minute trailer from the Conservative Party (2) featured a voice-over of Prime Minister Harper talking about the virtues, strengths, and mission of the Canadian nation, while showing images of various Canadian landscapes combined with images of diverse Canadians, along with images of hockey, Olympic athletes, soldiers and the Snowbirds (Canada's famous aerobatics team)—all well-recognized images and sources of pride in Canada. While this ad did not convey much information about the actual policies or platform of the party, it did suggest strongly that Harper was a "courageous warrior and a compassionate neighbour," that is, a paragon of Canadians as a whole. Here, the Canadian landscape was being used to speak explicitly to Canadian nationalism and pride.

The Bloc Québécois also successfully used images of the land to speak to the nation, albeit, in this case, a different nation. In one long BQ ad (1m 39s), Gilles Duceppe, the party leader, was shown speaking both *to* and *for* the Quebec nation. This ad began with images of Quebec landscapes, both urban and rural, taken from the window of a bus. These were landscapes that Quebecers would recognize and associate themselves with. However, the road Duceppe was travelling on in his bus was also a metaphor for the road travelled by the BQ and Quebec nationalists. He said: "Somewhere along the road, we lost each other. You stopped believing you could make a difference and you stopped asking yourselves questions. Why do we do all this? Why do *I* do all this?" (Quelque part sur le chemin, on s'est perdu de vue. Vous avez arrêté de croire que vous pouviez faire une différence et vous avez arrêté de vous poser des questions. Pourquoi est-ce qu'on fait tout ca? Pourquoi *je* fais tout ca?) (25). The answer: for the "country in his heart" (25). The ad ended with Duceppe, alone, staring out over a bleak winter landscape empty of buildings, people, trees, or animals, and encouraging Quebecers to make their voices heard—to unite their voices and make Canada listen. This ad effectively used the landscapes of Quebec to connect with voters; it also used the land a metaphor for the perhaps lonely or isolating struggle for sovereignty in Quebec and Quebec's proper position in Canada.

The Green Party ads were the most focused on the environment and used the most images of the environment to convey their message. Most often, this was done through the use of positive images and messaging. Three of Greens' six ads featured Canadians standing outside, either on beautiful, sunny urban streets, or in nature—for example, in front of a lake. They ended with Elizabeth May standing in front of a harbour encouraging Canadians to vote Green. It is no coincidence that the Green Party ads featured outdoor scenes and their leader in front of a harbour; in contrast, many of the other parties used images of the leader inside a building speaking to Canadians, or negative images of the other leaders, as the key images in their ads. One Green Party ad was probably the most effective and explicit at linking Canada's natural environment and landscapes to the Canadian identity. It began with a photo of the Rocky Mountains and declared, "This is our Canada"; it went on to show other natural Canadian "assets," suggesting that one way to keep Canada Green was to vote Green (14).

In other Green ads, the land was presented as at risk and the Green Party as the solution to a looming environmental crisis. One of these ads, for example, depicted a young girl in front of a dystopian environmental wasteland (19). Except for a text that invited Canadians to "Vote Green for her future," the ad used no words, relying completely on images to convey the party's message about the risk to Canada. It ended with this text: "It's time. Vote Green." This ad was not counted as an attack ad, for it did not mention any of the other parties; however, it did use landscape in a negative way to "scare" voters into choosing the Green Party.

CONCLUSION

Images of the Canadian landscape and symbols of Canada appeared only infrequently in the television ads from the 2011 federal election campaign. The overwhelming focus was on the party leaders, who were portrayed either positively (shaking hands, speaking to groups, etc.) or negatively (i.e., in attack ads). Over 50 percent of the ads studied projected a negative perspective on opposing parties instead of outlining party positions. Thus, when images of Canada did appear, they deviated from the norm. But even within the attack ads, landscapes were used to target or highlight problems with the opposition's policies, practices, or record. In the ads that did focus on images of Canada and the land, the overwhelming themes were (1) the land as representative of Canada, and (2) the land as something that needed to be taken care of or as something that was at risk. Clearly, representations of the land in the television ads were much more narrowly utilized than they could have been; the land was presented mainly in environmental or symbolic terms, and less often in reference to the economy (explicitly or implicitly—e.g., oil rigs). Territorial sovereignty was not raised as an issue in any of the ads studied. Also, except when it came to environmental concerns, the land as a source of conflict or as contested was absent.

Canada's landscapes seem to have the potential to connect viscerally with viewers (and voters). The ads studied, which focused on the environmental or natural surroundings of Canada, had the potential to move voters, yet they focused on policy even less than the other ads; instead they spoke in a broader, grander way about the Canadian people, our territory, and the aspirations of specific parties. The literature on nationalism and on the social construction of landscapes and identity in Canada suggests that the land is a prominent theme in Canadian national identity. The land can be a powerful campaigning tool; yet the emphasis on the land in the ads discussed here was minimal. This leads us to wonder why the political parties do not take advantage of this potentially useful tool in their campaigning, especially in their national television ads. That observation raises an interesting avenue for further analysis. ■

APPENDIX

LIST OF TELEVISION ADVERTISEMENTS

1 "American Democrat," Conservative Party of Canada, 2011. 0:30
2 "Election Trailer," Conservative Party of Canada, 2011. 1:00
3 "Economy," Conservative Party of Canada, 2011. 0:30
4 "Hidden Agenda," Conservative Party of Canada, 2011. 0:30
5 "Human Smuggling," Conservative Party of Canada, 2011. 0:30
6 "Ignatieff Liberals," Conservative Party of Canada, 2011. 0:30
7 "Ignatieff's Election," Conservative Party of Canada 2011. 0:30
8 "Illegal Immigration," Conservative Party of Canada, 2011. 1:00
9 "Arrogance," Conservative Party of Canada, 2011. 0:30
10 "Yes, Yes, Yes," Conservative Party of Canada, 2011. 0:30 (pulled from the air)
11 "Tax Hike," Conservative Party of Canada, 2011. 0:30
12 "Taxes," Conservative Party of Canada, 2011. 0:30
13 "Change the Channel," Green Party of Canada, 2011. 0:30
14 "Environment," Green Party of Canada, 2011. 0:30
15 "Join One Million Green Voters," Green Party of Canada, 2011. 0:30
16 "Make History, Green the Hill," Green Party of Canada, 2011. 0:30
17 "May in Your House," Green Party of Canada, 2011. 0:30
18 "New Green Economy," Green Party of Canada, 2011. 0:30
19 "Vote Green for Her Future," Green Party of Canada, 2011. 0:30
20 "Your Greens, Your Neighbours," Green Party of Canada, 2011. 0:30
21 "Parlons égalité," Bloc Québécois, 2011. 0:30
22 "Parlons régions," Bloc Québécois, 2011. 0:30
23 "Parlons solidarité," Bloc Québécois, 2011. 0:30
24 "Parlons vérité," Bloc Québécois, 2011. 0:30
25 "Pour quon nous entende," Bloc Québécois, 2011. 1:39
26 "Abuse of Power," Liberal Party of Canada, 2011. 0:30

27 "Corporate Tax Cuts," Liberal Party of Canada, 2011. 0:30
28 "Economy," Liberal Party of Canada, 2011. 0:30
29 "Fighter Jets," Liberal Party of Canada, 2011. 0:30
30 "Harper and Layton," Liberal Party of Canada, 2011. 0:30
31 "Harper on Health Care," Liberal Party of Canada, 2011. 0:30
32 "Health Risk," Liberal Party of Canada, 2011. 0:30
33 "Hey Stephen Harper," Liberal Party of Canada, 2011. 0:30
34 "High Stakes," Liberal Party of Canada, 2011. 0:30
35 "Liberal Learning Passport," Liberal Party of Canada, 2011. 0:30
36 "Liberals Have a Better Plan," Liberal Party of Canada, 2011. 0:30
37 "A Canada We Can Be Proud Of," Liberal Party of Canada, 2011. 0:30
38 "Liberal Family Care Plan," Liberal Party of Canada, 2011. 0:30
39 "Michael Ignatieff on the Liberal Family Pack," Liberal Party of Canada, 2011. 0:30
40 "Reckless," Liberal Party of Canada, 2011. 0:30
41 "Stephen Harper Corruption," Liberal Party of Canada, 2011. 0:30
42 "The Liberal Family Pack," Liberal Party of Canada, 2011. 0:30
43 "Together," Liberal Party of Canada, 2011. 0:30
44 "Your Choice," Liberal Party of Canada, 2011. 0:30
45 "Your Family, Your Liberals," Liberal Party of Canada, 2011. 0:30
46 "Imagine a Leader," New Democratic Party of Canada, 2011. 0:30
47 "A New Kind of Strong," New Democratic Party of Canada, 2011. 0:30
48 "Chalk Talk: The Economy," New Democratic Party of Canada, 2011. 0:30
49 "Chalk Talk: Health Care," New Democratic Party of Canada, 2011. 0:30
50 "Strong on Health Care," New Democratic Party of Canada, 2011. 0:30
51 "Strong on the Economy," New Democratic Party of Canada, 2011. 0:30
52 "Strong on the Environment," New Democratic Party of Canada, 2011. 0:30
53 "NDP Home Heating Campaign," New Democratic Party of Canada, 2011. 0:30
54 "Together We Can Do This," New Democratic Party of Canada, 2011. 0:30
55 "HST BC," New Democratic Party of Canada, 2011. 0:30
56 "HST Ontario," New Democratic Party of Canada, 2011. 0:30
57 "What Is Canadian Leadership?" New Democratic Party of Canada, 2011. 0:30
58 "Where do we start?" New Democratic Party of Canada, 2011. 0:30
59 "You Have a Choice," New Democratic Party of Canada, 2011. 0:30

NOTES

1. Smith, "Civic and Ethnic Nationalism," 177.
2. Bruilly, "Nationalism and the State."
3. Moore, "On National Self-Determination."
4. Billig, *Banal Nationalism*.
5. Sorlin, "The Articulation of Territory," 103.
6. Osborne, "Landscapes."
7. Sorlin, "The Articulation of Territory," 109.
8. Manning, "I Am Canadian."
9. Burnham et al., *Research Methods in Politics*, 236.
10. Henry and Tator, "Critical Discourse Analysis," 25.
11. Fairclough et al., "Introduction."
12. Thornham, *Women, Feminism, and Media*.
13. For example, see Richardson, "Our England"; Richardson and Wodak, "The Impact of Visual Racism"; and Wall, "It Is and It Isn't."
14. Osborne, "Landscapes."

WORKS CITED

Billig, Michael. *Banal Nationalism*. Thousand Oaks: Sage, 1995.
Brueilly, John. "Nationalism and the State." In *Nations and Nationalism: A Reader*, edited by Philip Spencer and Howard Wollman, 61–73. New Brunswick: Rutgers University Press, 2005.
Burnham, Peter, Karin Gillard, Wyn Grant, and Zig Layton-Henry. *Research Methods in Politics*. New York: Palgrave Macmillan, 2004.
Elections Canada. 2012. "Breakdown of Paid Election Expenses by Expense Category and Registered Political Party—2011 General Election." http://www.elections.ca/content.aspx?section=fin&dir=pol/break&document=brk41ge&lang=e
Fairclough, Norman, Phil Graham, Jay Lemko, and Ruth Wodak. "Introduction." *Critical Discourse Studies* (2004): 1–7.
Gellner, Ernest. *Nations and Nationalism*. Oxford: Blackwell, 1983.
Henry, Frances, and Carol Tator. "Critical Discourse Analysis: A Powerful but Flawed Tool?" In *Race, Racialization, and Antiracism in Canada and Beyond*, edited by G.F. Johnson and R. Enomoto, 117–30. Toronto: University of Toronto Press, 2007.
Manifesto Project. "Manifesto Project Coding Database" (2011). https://manifestoproject.wzb.eu
Manning, Erin. "I AM CANADIAN: Identity, Territory, and the Canadian National Landscape." *Theory and Event* 4 (2000). *Project MUSE*, EBSCO*host*.

Moore, Margaret. "On National Self-Determination." In *Nations and Nationalism: A Reader*, edited by Philip Spencer and Howard Wollman, 221–36. New Brunswick: Rutgers University Press, 2005.

Osborne, Brian S. "Landscapes, Memory, Monuments, and Commemoration: Putting Identity in Its Place." *Canadian Ethnic Studies* 33, no. 3 (2001): 39–77.

Richardson, John. "'Our England': Discourses of 'Race' and Class in Party Election Leaflets." *Social Semiotics* 18, no. 3 (2008): 321–35.

Richardson, John E., and Ruth Wodak. "The Impact of Visual Racism: Visual Arguments in Political Leaflets of Austrian and British Far-Right Parties." *Controversia* 6, no. 2 (2009): 45–77.

Smith, Anthony D. "Civic and Ethnic Nationalism." In *Nations and Nationalism: A Reader*, edited by Philip Spencer and Howard Wollman, 177–83. New Brunswick: Rutgers University Press, 2005.

Sorlin, Sventer. "The Articulation of Territory: Landscape and the Constitution of Regional and National Identity." *Norsk Geografisk Tidsskrift—Norwegian Journal of Geography* 53, nos. 2–3 (1999): 103–12.

Thornham, Sue. *Women, Feminism, and Media*. Edinburgh: Edinburgh University Press, 2007.

Wall, David. "It Is and It Isn't: Stereotypes, Advertising, and Narrative." *Journal of Popular Culture*. 41, no. 6 (2008): 1033–50.

SIX

Memorializing an Imagined Past:
Evangeline and the Acadian Deportation

Jane Moss

One of the great ironies of Acadian history is that the communal tragedy of the 1755 Deportation was made known to the world by the American poet Henry Wadsworth Longfellow. Published in 1847, the bestselling long poem *Evangeline* relates the tragic story of two young Acadian lovers separated on their wedding day and exiled to different places. Faithful to her Acadian heritage and her lost fiancé Gabriel Lajeunesse, Evangeline Bellefontaine wanders all over America for years before finding her beloved on his deathbed in Philadelphia. As he dies in her arms, she thanks God for reuniting them. The final two stanzas tell us that the long separated lovers are buried together in a Philadelphia churchyard, while back in their Maritime homeland only a few Acadian peasants dwell among the new English Protestant proprietors of their confiscated land. Translated into many languages, reworked in historical novels, dramatized on stage and screen, depicted in paintings and statues, the story of *Evangeline* became the story of the Acadian dispersal even though it was invented by an American poet who had never visited either old Acadie in Nova Scotia or New Acadia in Louisiana. Ironically, Acadians in the Canadian Maritimes and Cadiens (Cajuns) in Louisiana adopted the poetic fiction of Evangeline and Gabriel and constructed monuments and tourist sites memorializing their versions of this imagined past at Grand Pré, Nova Scotia (a *lieu de fausse mémoire*) and St. Martinville, Louisiana (a *faux lieu de mémoire*). In this chapter, we examine the monuments and memorials at the sites associated with the *Evangeline* story and how they relate to evolving constructions of collective memory and national identity. We then look at more contemporary attempts to replace Longfellow's mythical past with more accurate representations of Acadian history.

The Acadian Deportation has much to offer historians, geographers, cultural critics, and literary scholars. It is an eighteenth-century example of ethnic cleansing, during which French-speaking Catholics were removed from their prosperous lands to make way for Anglo-American Protestant colonists from New England. It was justified by what the British viewed as political necessity: the need to remove the potential threat posed by the Acadians in the years preceding the Seven Years' War. After Acadie came under the control of Great Britain in 1710, the Acadians had refused to take the oath affirming their loyalty to the British Crown and promising to defend their new colonial masters against the French. They had tried to negotiate neutrality by promising to be loyal British subjects in exchange for the right to maintain their language, religion, and way of life. But their 1730 loyalty oath was conditioned on a refusal to take up arms against the French in the event of a renewal of armed conflict between the rival empires. The construction of French forts at Louisbourg on the Atlantic Coast of Cape Breton Island and Fort Beauséjour at the eastern end of the Bay of Fundy made this neutral stance difficult for the Acadians, who were pressured by Catholic clergymen (such as Abbé LeLoutre) and military leaders to leave their farms and assist their French brethren and Mi'kmaq allies in the fight against the English. There is no dispute that Acadian neutrality was compromised on several occasions. There is also no doubt that the deportation order of 1755 was motivated by greed, by the desire to confiscate the rich farmlands created by the Acadian network of dykes in the marshlands of the Bay of Fundy, and by anti-Catholic sentiments.

The details of the deportation were recorded by Lieutenant-Colonel John Winslow, the Massachusetts military man who had been tasked with informing the Acadians of Grand Pré of the removal order, rounding them up, loading them onto the ships that would transport them to various sites along the Atlantic Coast or back to Europe, and destroying their communities by burning homes, barns, crops, and churches. Despite promises to keep families together, many were separated in the chaos of the forced removal. Many other Acadians were killed or drowned, or they died of disease or starvation or escaped to the woods. Some men joined an armed resistance movement that briefly fought the British. There were other removal operations at Acadian communities between 1755 and 1763. It is

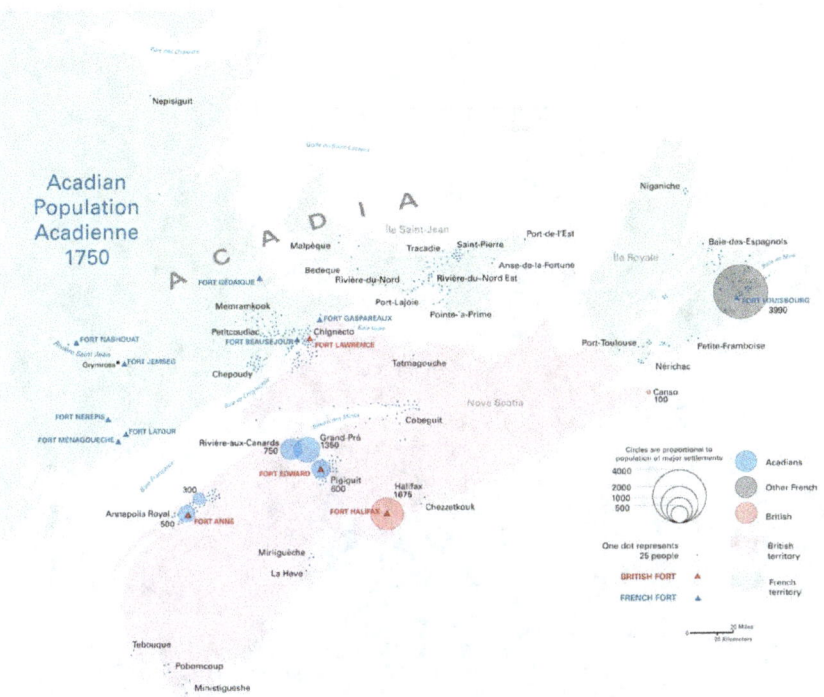

Figure 6.1. Acadian population in 1750
Reproduced with permission of the University of Maine Canadian–American Center.

estimated that between 10,000 and 11,000 (around 75 percent of the total Acadian population) were deported.

Although the French had been established there since the early seventeenth century, Acadie was primarily an agricultural colony, and the lack of urban centres or educational institutions meant that the Acadians left little in the way of historical or literary records, except for petitions to British colonial administrators. For their version of the deportation trauma, we must rely on these refugee petitions and on oral accounts passed down in families. The collective memory of the terrible years following the forced removal constituted an oral Acadian history for decades, until historians began publishing accounts of the events. The non-Acadian historians included Frenchman Abbé Raynal; French Canadians Abbé Casgrain and Lionel Groulx; English Nova Scotians Thomas C. Haliburton, Thomas Akins, Beamish Murdoch, Charles Roberts, and James Hannay; and

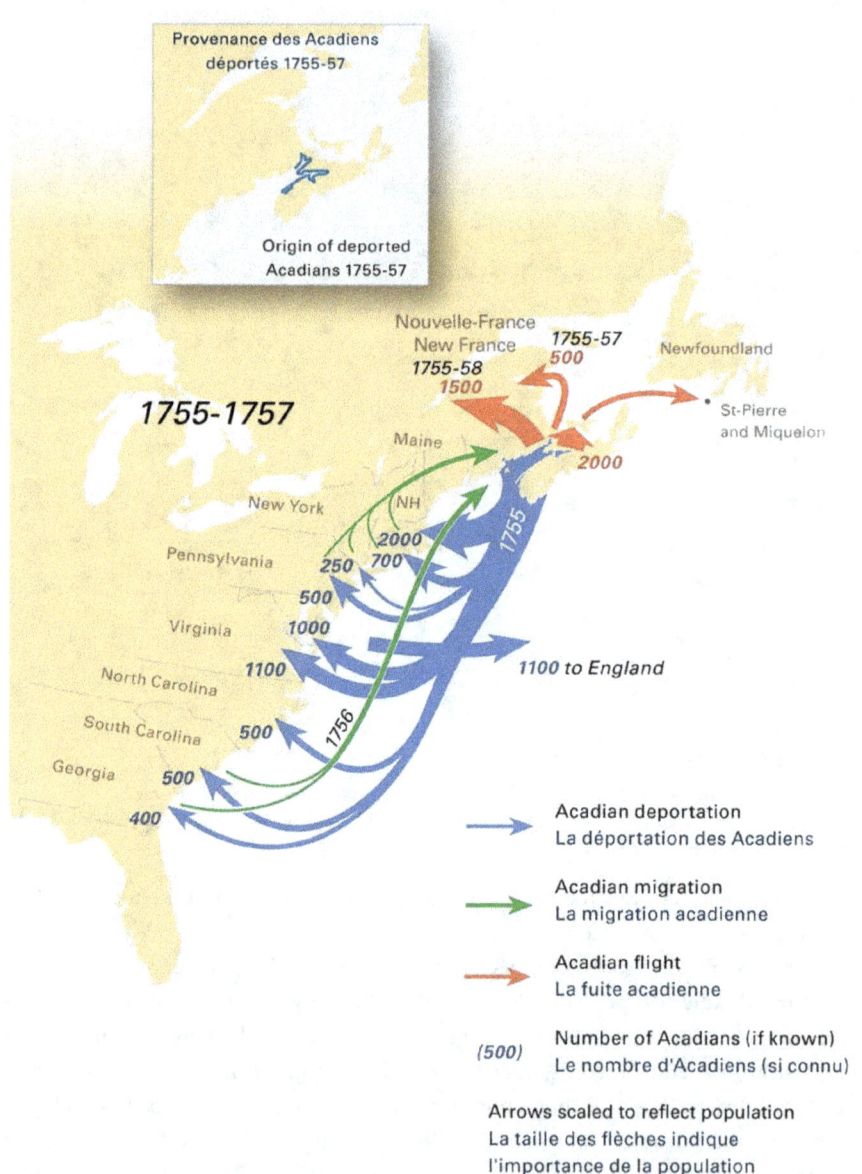

Figure 6.2. Acadian deportations, 1755–57

Reproduced with permission of the University of Maine Canadian–American Center.

American historians George Bancroft and Francis Parkman. Given the small size of the Acadian community, its remoteness from centres of power, and the broader context of the Anglo-French conflict, the Acadian story attracted little attention until the publication of Longfellow's *Evangeline* almost a century after the events. After 1847, many others created their own visions of Acadian history and identity, interpreting the deportation and its aftermath for their own ideological and commercial purposes.

Longfellow's Evangeline has become the ideal Romantic heroine, incarnating "the beauty and strength of a woman's devotion."[1] The poet is more interested in the pathos of the tale of two lovers separated on their wedding day because of events beyond their control than in the political causes of the deportation and the horrible suffering it produced. He seems to blame the British rather than the American colonists for the tragic events, and he absolves the Acadians of their refusal to swear unconditional loyalty. To make the victims even more sympathetic, he invents a scene in which the priest, Father Felician, exhorts the Acadians to forgive the enemy.[2] It should be noted that while historical accounts of the embarkation do record that the Acadians went to the ships praying and singing hymns, there were no priests left among them at the time to lead these demonstrations of pious submission to their fate. For their part, French Canadians, a conquered colonial people, transformed Longfellow's "Tale of Acadie" from a sentimental tragedy into an inspiring and uplifting story of fidelity to French heritage—that is language, religion, and communal customs. Under the influence of the ultramontane clerical nationalism of their political and intellectual leaders, French Canadians and Acadians came to see this historical event as a lesson on the providential mission and the survival of minority French Catholics in North America. As Longfellow's poem declares: "Man is unjust, but God is just; and finally justice triumphs."[3]

Different interpretations of the deportation underscore deep divisions between French and English Canadians. Quebecer Pamphile Lemay's French translation or adaptation of *Evangeline* (1870)[4] passes harsh judgment on the Anglo-Americans, who carried out the removal with great cruelty,[5] and presents the episode as a cautionary tale and an inspiration for French Canadian nationalism. Quebecer Napoléon Bourassa's historical novel *Jacques et Marie* (1866) recounts the heroic armed resistance of Acadians (like Joseph Broussard, dit Beausoleil), who escaped the deportation.[6] Bourassa shows the Acadians as angry rather than passively resigned to their fate. French Canadian clerico-nationalists like Henri-Raymond Casgrain and Lionel Groulx speak of the brutality and criminality of the deportation. Groulx said that upon seeing the Acadian ruins at Grand Pré, "j'ai su pourquoi nous portons tous au coeur de vieilles blessures inguérissables" (I knew why we all carry in our hearts old wounds that will not heal).[7]

Acadian oral literature tends to return to the pre-deportation period, as if trying to suppress the traumatic memories.[8] Beginning in the 1870s, a number of amateur plays dramatized the deportation, and some of these were based on the Evangeline story.[9] For example, we could cite Pascal Poirier's *Les Acadiens à Philadelphie suivi de Accordailles de Gabriel et d'Évangéline*.[10] The first historical novel by an Acadian, Antoine-J. Léger's 1940 *Elle et Lui: Tragique idylle du peuple acadien*, idealizes the Acadian past, stresses the loyalty of the "Neutral French," emphasizes British treachery, and presents with empathy the suffering and Christian resignation of the exiles. The lesson is always in keeping with the ideology of *survivance*, which preaches the messianic mission of the French in North America, along with fidelity to the French language and the Catholic faith.

English Canadian historians and writers of historical fiction emphasize the military necessity of the removals and often depict the Acadians as ignorant, dirty, quarrelsome, overly influenced by priests, and negatively affected by excessive intermarriage with the Mí'kmaq.[11]

Louisiana writers use the Evangeline material for their own purposes, often as a kind of foundational myth for the Cadien community since in their texts, the Acadian fiancés are permanently transplanted in Louisiana. Sidonie de la Houssaye, whose great-grandfather was an Acadian refugee, published her version *Pouponne et Balthazar* in 1888.[12] De la Houssaye vouches for the veracity of her story by claiming that she heard it from her grandmother, who heard it from her mother, but there is no reason to believe this claim, which was a conventional fictional strategy. In describing Acadie before 1755 in *Pouponne et Balthazar*, she speaks of the simplicity, honesty, piety, and sense of honour of Acadians, whose deportation she compares to the exile of the Trojans in the *Iliad*. But her characterization of Cadiens is less flattering: she portrays them as uneducated, vulgar, poor, and often involved in drunken brawls. De la Houssaye's narrative goes into detail about the Acadian resistance fighters, the battles leading to the fall of New France, and the fate of those Acadians who remained in Canada. While condemning the wanton brutality of the British commanders, she is equally harsh in blaming France for abandoning its North American colonies. Reunited and married in Louisiana, the Acadian lovers separated by the deportation become full members of French Creole society over time and American enough to support the revolutionary cause out of hatred for the British. In sum, her Acadian exiles are assimilated into American Louisiana.

Felix Voorhies's 1907 *Acadian Reminiscences: With the True Story of Evangeline*, is further evidence of the Americanization of Cadiens. Written in English, the book was presented as a "word painting of the life of the Acadians in the Teche country in the long ago."[13] Once again, the author assures readers of the narrative's authenticity by claiming to have heard it from his Nova Scotia–born grandmother. In fact, it was his great-grandmother who was an Acadian refugee, and he could not have heard the story from her because she died sixteen years before his birth.[14] After the description of Acadia as a pastoral utopia and an explanation of British–French conflict in the eighteenth century, Voorhies shows us the Acadians choosing exile: "We leave for Louisiana, where we shall be free to honor and reverence France, and to serve our God according to our belief."[15] Of course, the Acadians did not choose exile, nor did they have any inkling that many of them would end up in Louisiana when they were forcibly removed in 1755. Voorhies's Acadians are herded onto boats and deported to Maryland, where they remain for three years before finally making it to Louisiana, which they have been told "was a land of enchantment, where a perpetual Spring reigned."[16] In Chapter 8 of his text, Voorhies claims to be telling the true story of Evangeline and Gabriel, or rather Emmeline Labiche and Louis Arceneaux, their Louisiana avatars. Separated in the chaos of the deportation, they meet again by chance under a large oak tree at the Poste des Attakapas, present-day St. Martinville, Louisiana. On hearing that Louis has married another woman, poor Emmeline's sorrow turns to mental illness, and she dies soon after. She is buried near the St. Martin Church, near the oak tree where she spotted her faithless lover. This version of the Evangeline myth has been exploited by the Cadiens of St. Martinville to attract tourists to what can be called a false site of false memory.

Many cultural tourists make the pilgrimage to St. Martinville, where they may see the Evangeline Oak (the most visited tree in America, according to local guides), view the statue of Evangeline in the churchyard (a seated Evangeline modelled on Scottish artist Thomas Faëd's 1859 painting), and spend time in the Acadian Memorial, which lists the family names of the Acadian deportees. Tourists can also visit the Longfellow–Evangeline State Historic Site in St. Martinville and the recreated Acadian Village in nearby Lafayette.

The Cadien appropriation of Evangeline has been emphatic to the point that in 1928, French Ambassador Paul Claudel visited the supposed Evangeline sites in Louisiana, and in 1931, Nova Scotia Acadians demanded the return of her remains so that they could be reburied in the land of her birth.[17] The claim that Emmeline Labiche's remains were buried in the walls of the St. Martin de Tours Church was made by St. Martinville priests as far back as 1903 and repeated by local Evangeline booster Alfred Olivier during the filming of Edward Carewe's 1929 movie *Evangeline*.[18] We should also mention that the film's star, Dolores Del Rio, personally paid for the Evangeline statue that is a major tourist attraction in St. Martinville. More recently, there have been gestures towards honouring the true history of the Acadian exiles in Louisiana. Robert Dafford's mural depicting the arrival of the Acadians was added to the Acadian Memorial in the mid-1990s, and in June 2003 a replica of the Deportation Cross that marks the actual point of embarkation back in Nova Scotia was unveiled.

Further evidence that the history of the Acadian Expulsion and the myth of Evangeline have endured in the United States comes in the form of *Evangeline: The Novel*, published by Richard F. Mullins of Dixfield, Maine, in 2011.[19] Born and raised in Nova Scotia, Mullins had a long career as an English teacher in Maine. In an interview, he explained that he wrote his book because he had grown up with Maritime Acadians and had taught Mainers of Acadian descent, who had not only lost their connection with their francophone roots but seemed to know little or nothing about the traumatic history of their ancestors. He wanted to address that historical amnesia by rewriting Longfellow's romantic tale and expanding the historical narrative greatly with information about the French–English rivalry in North America. Mullins did a considerable amount of research for his book, and his footnotes, epilogue, bibliography, and acknowledgements page are evidence of the time he spent in libraries and archives.

The text is divided into three parts of unequal length (Part I has thirty-three chapters, Part II has thirteen, and Part III a mere six). Part I begins by describing the idyllic life of pre-Expulsion Acadia and the chaste but passionate love of Evangeline and Gabriel. In historically detailed chapters about the British–French rivalry in colonial North America, Mullins chronicles the growing tensions that led to the deportations in the fall of 1755 and the burning of most of the buildings at Grand Pré. The author presents these sad events with great sympathy, often depicting the British colonists as melodrama villains, the "Neutral French" as naive victims, and the Mi'kmaq allies as worried bystanders. The second section traces the fate of Acadian deportees shipped off to different ports on the Atlantic coast and the many years that Evangeline spent wandering across the American colonies and the Louisiana Territory in search of her beloved. At the end of Part II, she arrives in Philadelphia, where she will, as was the case in Longfellow's poem, devote herself to nursing the poor and indigent before being reunited with Gabriel on his deathbed, and dying of a broken heart. Part III of Mullins's version of the story makes Philadelphia another memory site for the Acadians. It is there that Evangeline and some of her ship companions had spent time in the immediate aftermath of the deportation, and it is there that many of her compatriots found permanent shelter. In fact, Mullins devotes several pages to one Acadian exile, Charles LeBlanc, who became a successful Philadelphia businessman.

Unlike other authors of fictionalized and poetic versions of the story, Mullins takes great pains to be historically accurate in representing the role of Abbé LeLoutre in betraying the interests of his Acadian parishioners. He also takes pains to create lively portraits of the British colonial administrators responsible for the decision to deport the Acadians and of the military officials who carried out their orders. While Nova Scotia governor Peregrine Hopson appears in a sympathetic light, New England colonial leaders Charles Lawrence, Jonathan Belcher, and John Winslow, and other British officials, come across as mean-spirited, self-interested, or cowardly functionaries. Mullins idealizes the Acadians of Grand Pré and gives a greater role to their Mi'kmaq allies than does Longfellow.

In this version, Evangeline does find her way to St. Martinville, Louisiana (erroneously identified as St. Martin), but her reunion with Basil Lajeunesse, the man who was to be her father-in-law, is a disappointment since he tells her that Gabriel was there but has since departed. Evangeline immediately leaves Louisiana in pursuit of her beloved, so we never hear about the transformation of the Maritime Acadians into the Bayou Cajuns. Mullins makes a point of telling the reader that Evangeline and her travelling companions found the tropical climate too uncomfortable for permanent settlement! Much of the second section of the narrative is devoted to Evangeline's Shawnee Indian friends, with whom she spends many years, sharing their nomadic wanderings through the Midwest. In this way, Mullins suggests a parallel between the dispossession of Native Americans and that of the Acadians. This Evangeline learns to speak the Shawnee language, learns about Native medicine, and encounters a number of other Midwestern peoples. In short, this is an Evangeline who has gone native and become Americanized.

As in Longfellow's poem, Gabriel and Evangeline are finally reunited in Philadelphia, where she finds him dying in the Almshouse of the Society of Friends. The actual site of the Quaker institution is today marked by a plaque that alludes to Longfellow's poem but makes no claim to historicity.

Even so, I would add Philadelphia to the list of dubious Acadian *lieux de mémoire*—dubious because, as Mullins makes clear, the Acadians become anglicized and Americanized in Philadelphia, and lose their identity in its urban American melting pot. In the end, Mullins seems to have erased the Canadian identity of his exiled Acadians.

The various literary, artistic, cinematic, theatrical, and musical versions of the Evangeline story (see Viau, Brasseaux, Leblanc) can also be counted as *lieux de mémoire*, to use Pierre Nora's term—that is, as forms of performative memorialization (to use Lisa Costello's term) that keep the memory of the *Grand Dérangement* alive.[20] As we have noted, Longfellow's poem created opportunities for "entrepreneurs de la mémoire," giving rise to tourist industries in Louisiana as well as Nova Scotia and New Brunswick.[21] Despite the absence of an actual Acadian presence at Grand Pré after 1755, Evangeline's supposed home became the primary site of Acadian memory and the geographic focus of what was called the Acadian Renaissance, a nationalist movement of the late nineteenth century. As Acadian documentary filmmaker Leonard Forest wrote, "nous savons enfin que les souvenirs ont besoin de lieux où habiter" (in a word, we know that memories need places to dwell).[22] Eventually, the Grand Pré site, a symbol of loss and displacement, evolved into a rallying point for a revised and historicized Acadian identity. It also became the focus of a politicized collective memory that deterritorialized *acadianité* by including diasporic communities and that demanded official recognition of the crime of *le Grand Dérangement*.

With the 1869 opening of a railway line from Annapolis (site of the first permanent Acadian settlement at Port Royal) to Grand Pré (site of the first deportations), the Beaubassin area became a destination for tourists and pilgrims. When various Nova Scotia railway lines were consolidated in 1895 as the Dominion Atlantic Railway, a major advertising campaign vaunted the "Land of Evangeline" for its beauty and its associations with the pastoral Acadie described by Longfellow. When the Canadian Pacific Railroad took over the line in 1911, the marketing of Evangeline continued.

As Monica MacDonald writes:

> The railway also generated ideas of authenticity by suggesting that Longfellow's story and the characters were real while diminishing and misinterpreting the significance of the actual Acadian experience. Though the overall aim of these strategies was to increase tourism, a certain vision of history was also endorsed—one that reinforced and validated the British legacy of the province over that of the Acadians, the very key to the railway's tourism activities.[23]

According to MacDonald, nineteenth-century Nova Scotian historians such as Thomas B. Akins and Beamish Murdoch blamed the priest Abbé LeLoutre and representatives from Quebec and France for manipulating the Acadians. They blamed the Acadians for not remaining truly neutral and for refusing the unconditional oath of allegiance to the British Crown. And finally, they blamed New Englanders for carrying out the deportation.[24] MacDonald tells us that this interpretation was also put forth in books published by the Dominion Atlantic Railway and written by James Hannay (*The Story of Acadia*, 1895) and Charles G.D. Roberts (*The Land of Evangeline and the Gateways Thither*, 1904), who rejected the notion that New Englanders coveted Acadian farmland and praised the United Empire Loyalists who bravely settled in Nova Scotia.[25] Subsequent retellings of the story aimed at glorifying British imperialism and promoting tourism tend to gloss over the unpleasant facts of the deportation and instead concentrate on the idyllic aspects of pre-1755 Acadian life. It was, after all, easier to market nostalgia for a premodern way of life. MacDonald characterizes this image of the Acadian past promoted by the Dominion Atlantic Railway as "constructed authenticity."[26] And she describes how the tourist guides written by Charles G.D. Roberts "manufactured authenticity" by identifying sites and artifacts in the Grand Pré area with Evangeline, as if she had been a real person.[27] Tourists could supposedly visit Evangeline's well and Basil's blacksmith shop, and admire willow and apple trees planted by the Acadians of yore. In these (mis)representations of Acadian sites of memory, actual Acadians were absent because they would have disrupted the poetic, mythical image of the "Land of Evangeline" that was being commodified.

It is worth noting that when the first steps towards creating a memorial site at Grand Pré were taken by an anglophone Acadian named John Frederic Herbin, the area was inhabited by English-speaking descendants of the Planters, who had taken over the lands cleared and drained by the Acadians, and also by the descendants of United Empire Loyalists, who had migrated to Canada after the American Revolution. Herbin purchased the Grand Pré property in 1907 and had a cross constructed using stones from the ruins of Acadian homes on the site of the Church of St-Charles-des-Mines.

Ten years later, Herbin proposed the construction of a more elaborate Acadian memorial. The first part of what would become a Canadian National Historic Site dedicated to the memory of the Acadian Deportation was a statue of Evangeline, unveiled in 1920. Sculpted by Henri Hébert using a design by Louis-Philippe Hébert, the statue was inspired by a line from the poem and shows Evangeline leaning on a stick, looking back tearfully as she leaves. It is hard to believe this, but not a single Acadian was invited or present when the statue was unveiled. Not only had the Acadians been forced out of Grand Pré, but it seems that their descendants were not welcome there.

The author of the most recent Evangeline novel, Richard Mullins, recounts that during a recent visit to Grand Pré, he checked the local phone book and did not find a single French name. At the Grand Pré National Historic Site, a young docent pointed to the beautiful weeping willows on the grounds and explained to Mullins that the early Acadians had planted them there with no conception that one day their sad, drooping appearance would be a symbol of their heartache. While this is a lovely image, of course there is no truth to the story. The docent did not seem to know that while creating the Grand Pré Historic Site in the 1920s, Canadian Pacific engineers had planted the willows to fight erosion problems, since willows have large, absorbent root systems and are perfect trees for marshy areas. Mullins also notes that at St. Paul's Anglican Church in downtown Halifax, the tombs of both Charles Lawrence and Jonathan Belcher are off limits to visitors—presumably because they want no reminders of the cruel events of 1755 and perhaps out of concern that Acadian nationalists might desecrate the tombs. Also, George's Island in Halifax Harbour, the site of the dungeon in which the Acadian delegates were imprisoned by Lawrence in the summer prior to the deportation, was declared a Parks Canada National Historic Site in 1968. Nearly four decades later, it is still closed to the public (phone interview with the author).

The intense debate that has raged in historical studies over the role of memory and its corollary, forgetting, is key to the discussion of how Acadians and Cadiens remember, commemorate, and memorialize the deportation. Because for many years there were no historians or writers capable of recording the experience in what was left of Acadie or in the scattered Acadian diasporic communities, there was no effective instrument to combat collective forgetting or the suppression of memory of bad acts except for oral testimony and a few petitions made on behalf of the deportees. Clearly, the new anglophone residents were not interested in writing a history of Nova Scotia that detailed how it was founded on acts of violent dispossession and appropriation. A completely accurate record of the deportation would have revealed an injustice that demanded recognition of moral claims, and perhaps compensation, reparations, public apology, or atonement, but the perpetrators were no longer available for punishment. By focusing the collective memory of the deportation on Grand Pré and by constructing a national identity from the starting point of the Evangeline myth of piety and fidelity, the Acadians kept the collective memory alive without dwelling on victimhood, resentment, and criminal responsibility. Grand Pré and Evangeline were *lieux de mémoire*, significant symbols for the Acadian community, but symbols that evoked an idealized past, a paradise lost, and a traumatic rupturing of a society.[28] It is very telling that the Grand Pré historical site originally consisted of a statue of the fictional Evangeline, a Memorial Church dedicated in 1922, a statue of Notre Dame de l'Assomption (the patron saint of Acadians) unveiled in 1923, and a cross dedicated in 1924 marking the nearby embarkation site (see below).

An Acadian Historical Museum was installed in the small Memorial Church in 1930, but it divided its space between the history of the French settlers and that of the British colonists who took over the region. On the occasion of the bicentenary in 1955, a new commemorative monument was unveiled: a bust of Henry Wadsworth Longfellow. Yet again, the history of the expulsion had been replaced by the false memory of Evangeline. If, as Christine Boyer claims (cited by Yilmaz), monuments and memorials are mnemonic devices erected to "stir one's memory," what does it say when the memory is imagined?[29]

As acts of memory, the creation of these monuments transformed trauma and tragedy into affirmations of virtues rather than signs of weakness. The virginal romantic heroine Evangeline and the Virgin of the Assumption have displaced the true victims of the expulsion. By focusing collective memory on survival and on the providential mission of French Canadians in North America, Grand Pré makes it possible for all Acadian descendants to celebrate their fictionalized and idealized history rather than mourn the historical past. We could argue that the memorial at Grand Pré also had the unintended consequence of commemorating dislocation and erasure because there were no longer any Acadians living in the area and only cellar holes remained of the once thriving community.

When Acadians in the Maritimes began creating more bonds with Louisiana Cadiens in the 1930s, the Grand Pré site began to take on new meanings. The revisionism had accelerated by the time the bicentenary celebrations were held in 1955; by then, Acadian intellectuals were rejecting the obsession with the past and the folklorization of their culture. In the late 1960s, a new generation of Acadian artists, writers, and politicians (inspired by Quebec's Quiet Revolution) began to call for a revised view of their history and identity, and it was decided to include the deportees in the Grand Pré memorial. Finally, in 1985, two stained glass windows designed by Terry Smith-Lamothe to depict the moment when the Grand Pré community was broken apart were installed in the church. In 1986 a series of six historical paintings by Claude Picard were added as part of the effort to represent the life of the Acadians before, during, and after the deportation. The scenes depict early Acadian life, the signing of the 1730 conditional loyalty oath, the reading of the deportation order in 1755, the burning of the settlements, the embarkation, and the return of some of the exiles. See Figure 6.3.

Also in 1986, two bas-reliefs by sculptor Claude Roussel were placed in the church—one representing the British soldiers and American militiamen who carried out the deportation order, the other showing the Acadians walking to the

Figure 6.3
This painting by Claude T. Picard (1932–2012), showing the Acadian embarkation, is part of a series owned by the Grand-Pré National Historic Site, Nova Scotia, that depicts the life of the Acadians prior to, during, and following the expulsion. Reproduced with permission.

ships that would carry them into exile. These works of art signal the Acadians' reappropriation of the Grand Pré site and serve as a truer commemoration of their history. Evangeline's statue and Longfellow's bust are still there, but the emphasis is now on the Acadians—their community, their dispersal, and their return.

Over the past few decades, more accurate historical accounts of the sad events have been published by English Canadian and Acadian historians Naomi Griffiths, Samuel Arsenault, Maurice Basque, and Barbara LeBlanc, and by American historians Carl Brasseaux, John Mack Faragher, and Christopher Hodson. Also, new historical dramas and novels about the deportation and its aftermath have corrected the historical record and valorized collective memories of the trauma. Acadian authors Antonine Maillet, Jules Boudreau, Herménégilde Chiasson, Rino Morin Rossignol, Melvin Gallant, and Claude LeBouthillier, the Cadien poet Jean Arceneaux (pen name of Barry Jean Ancelet), and musician Zachary Richard have worked hard to replace Longfellow's romantic heroine with works that memorialize the deportation from Acadian and Cadien perspectives. In addition, literary historians and critics such as Robert Viau, Zénon Chiasson, Hans Runte, Denise Merkle, and Denis Bourque, along with the sociologist Joseph-Yvon Thériault, have contributed to the process of demythifying literature about Acadian history.

This growing body of historical texts, literary works, and criticism helped foster demands for an official acknowledgement or apology. That apology finally came in December 2003: a Royal Proclamation by the Governor General of Canada acknowledged responsibility for the *Grand Dérangement* and its "tragic consequences, including the deaths of many thousands of Acadians—from disease, in shipwrecks, in their places of refuge and in prison camps."³⁰ The Royal Proclamation also designated July 28, the date on which the decision to deport the Acadians was taken in 1755, as "A Day of Commemoration of the Great Upheaval."³¹ In 2005, the 250th anniversary of the expulsion, two Acadian groups (la Commission de l'Odyssée acadienne and the Société nationale de l'Acadie) proposed that commemorative monuments be constructed at thirty-seven sites, places to which Acadians had been sent in Canada, the United States, Europe, and the Caribbean. The key features of these multiple memorials would be crosses, like the Croix de la Déportation erected in 1924 near Grand Pré, copies of the map drawn by Robert Leblanc detailing the geography of the dispersal, and historical plaques.³² Finally, the Acadians and their descendants are being commemorated in ways that remember and memorialize rather than idealize and obfuscate. ■

NOTES

1. Longfellow, "Evangeline," 30.
2. Ibid., 46–47.
3. Ibid., 41.
4. Lemay, *Évangéline*.
5. Viau, *Les Grands Dérangements*, 53.
6. Bourassa, *Jacques et Marie*.
7. Cited in Viau, *Les Grands Dérangements*, 95.
8. Ibid., 166–67.
9. Ibid., 172–73.
10. Poirier, *Les Acadiens à Philadelphie*.
11. Viau, *Les Grands Dérangements*, 190; Viau, *Grand Pré*, 66.
12. Houssaye, *Pouponne et Balthazar*.
13. Voorhies, *Acadian Reminiscences*, 9.
14. Brasseaux, *In Search of Evangeline*, 20.
15. Ibid., 57.
16. Ibid., 100.
17. Ibid., 45.
18. Carewe, *Evangeline* (1929).
19. Mullins, *Evangeline: The Novel*, 2011.
20. Belkhodja, "Savoir habiter le lieu de la mémoire," 281.

21 Ibid., 272.
22 Cited in ibid., 271.
23 MacDonald, "Railway Tourism," 159.
24 Ibid., 161,
25 Ibid., 162–63.
26 Ibid., 173.
27 Ibid., 175.
28 Cubitt, History and Memory, 47–49.
29 In Yilmaz, "Memorialization."
30 Faragher, A Great and Noble Scheme, 479.
31 Ibid., 479.
32 Viau, Grand Pré, 98.

WORKS CITED

Akins, Thomas B., ed. *Selections from the Public Documents of the Province of Nova Scotia.* Halifax: Charles Annand, 1869.

Bancroft, George. "Exiles of Acadia." *The Token and Atlantic Souvenir, An Offering for Christmas and the New Year,* 279–89 passim. Boston: D.H. Williams, 1842.

Basque, Maurice. *Les Territoires de l'identité : Perspectives acadiennes et françaises, XVIIe–XXe siècles.* Moncton: Chaire d'études acadiennes, 2005.

Belkhodja, Chedly. "Savoir habiter le lieu de la mémoire : le cas d'Acadie." In *Entre lieux et mémoire. L'inscription de la francophonie canadienne dans la durée,* ed. Anne Gilbert, Michel Bock, and Joseph-Yvon Thériault, 271–92. Ottawa: University of Ottawa Press, 2009.

Boudreau, Jules. *Cochu et le soleil.* Moncton: Éditions d'Acadie, 1978.

Bourassa, Napoléon. *Jacques et Marie. Souvenir d'un peuple dispersé.* Montréal: Eusèbe Senécal, 1866. http://www.archive.org/stream/cihm_03809#page/n7/mode/2up

Bourque, Denis, et Denise Merkle. " De L'Évangéline à l'américaine à L'Évangéline à l'acadienne." In *Traduire depuis les marges / Translating from the Margins,* 121–45. Québec: Nota Bene, 2008.

Brasseaux, Carl A. *In Search of Evangeline: Birth and Evolution of the Evangeline Myth.* Thibodaux: Blue Heron Press, 1988.

——— . *Scattered to the Wind: Dispersal and Wanderings of the Acadians, 1755–1809.* Lafayette: Center for Louisiana Studies, University of Southwestern Louisiana, 1991.

Carewe, Edward. *Evangeline.* United Artists, 1929.

Casgrain, Henri Raymond. *Un pèlerinage au pays d'Évangéline.* Québec: L.J. Demers & frère, 1887.

Chiasson, Herménégilde. "Évangéline, mythe ou réalité." 1982, unpublished.

———. "Oublier Acadie." In *Aspects de la francophonie*, ed. Simon Langlois and Jocelyn Létourneau, 147–63. Québec: Presses de l'Université Laval, 2004.
Chiasson, Zénon. "Théâtre, histoire, mémoire." In *Mélanges Marguerite Maillet*, ed. Raoul Boudreau et al., 119–31. Moncton: Éditions d'Acadie, 1996.
Cubitt, Geoffrey. *History and Memory*. Manchester: Manchester University Press, 2007.
Faragher, John Mack. *A Great and Noble Scheme: The Tragic Story of the Expulsion of the French Acadians from Their American Homeland*. New York: W.W. Norton, 2005.
Franchot, Jenny. *Roads to Rome: The Antebellum Protestant Encounter with Catholicism*. Berkeley: University of California Press, 1994.
Frigault, Jacques-A. *L'Acadie étoilée*. Tracadie-Sheila: La Grande Marée, 2004.
Gallant, Melvin. *Le Complexe d'Évangéline*. Lévis: Éditions de la francophonie, 2005.
Griffiths, Naomi. *The Acadian Deportation: Deliberate Perfidy or Cruel Necessity?* Toronto: Copp Clark, 1969.
———. "Longfellow's Evangeline: The Birth and Acceptance of a Legend." *Acadiensis: Journal of the History of the Atlantic Region* 11, no. 2 (1982): 28-41.
Groulx, Lionel A. *Au Cap Blomidon*. Montreal: Granger frères, 1932.
Halliburton, Thomas Chandler. *An Historical and Statistical Account of Nova-Scotia*. 2 vols. Halifax: Joseph Howe, 1829.
Hannay, James H. *History of Acadia, From Its First Discovery to the Surrender to England, by the Treaty of Paris*. Saint John: J. & A. McMillan, 1879.
Hawthorne, Manning, and Henry Wadworth Longfellow Dana. *The Origin and Development of Longfellow's Evangeline*. Portland: Anthensen Press, 1947.
Hodson, Christopher. *The Acadian Diaspora: An Eighteenth-Century History*. New York: Oxford University Press, 2012.
Holl, Shelley. "Past Meets Present in St. Martinville." *Times Picayune*, 18 October 1996.
Houssaye, Sidonie de la. *Pouponne et Balthazar. Nouvelle acadienne*. Nouvelle Orléans: Librairie de l'Opinion, 1888.
Jégo, Jean-Baptiste. *Le Drame du peuple acadien*. Paris: Oberthur, 1932.
LeBlanc, Barbara. *Postcards from Acadie*. Kentville: Gaspereau Press, 2003.
Le Bouthillier, Claude. *Le Feu du mauvais temps*. Montréal: Éditions XYZ, 2004.
———. *Les Marées du Grand Dérangement*. Montréal: Éditions XYZ, 2008.
Lemay, Pamphile. Évangéline. *Traduction du poème acadien de Longfellow*. Québec: P.G. Delisle, 1870.
Longfellow, Henry Wadsworth. "Evangeline." In *Evangeline and other poems*, ed. C.L. Bennet. New York: Airmont, 1965.
MacDonald, Monica. "Railway Tourism in the 'Land of Evangeline,' 1882–1946." *Acadiensis: Journal of the History of the Atlantic Region* 35, no. 1 (2005): 158–80.
Maillet, Antonine. Évangéline *Deusse*. Montréal: Leméac, 1975.
———. *Pélagie-la-charette*. Paris: Grasset, 1979.
Maillet, Marguerite. *Histoire de la littérature acadienne. De rêve en rêve*. Moncton: Editions d'Acadie, 1983.

Massicotte, Julien. "La tragi-comédie acadienne: différentes perceptions de 1755." *Argument. Politique, société, histoire* 8, no. 1 (automne 2005–hiver 2006).

Morin Rossignol, Rino. *Le Pique-nique*. Moncton: Éditions Perce-Neige, 2001 [1982].

Moss, Jane. "Les Théâtres francophones en Amérique du Nord." In *Des cultures en contact. Visions de l'Amérique du Nord francophone*, ed. Jean Morency, Hélène Destrempes, Denise Merkle, and Martin Pâquet, 393–409. Québec: Éditions Nota Bene, 2005. 393–409.

Mullins, Richard F. *Evangeline: The Novel*. Bloomington: Trafford Publishing, 2011.

Murdoch, Beamish. *A History of Nova-Scotia, or Acadie*. 3 vols. Halifax: James Barnes, 1865.

Neatby, Nicole, and Peter Hodgins, eds. *Settling and Unsettling Memories: Essays in Canadian Public History*. Toronto: University of Toronto Press, 2012.

Nova Scotia Legislature. "Evangeline" (homepage). http://legcat.gov.ns.ca/search/ftlist%5Ebib 21%2C1%2C0%2C22/mode=2

Parkman, Francis. *France and England in North America. A Half-Century of Conflict*. Boston: Little, Brown & Company, 1892.

Pelchat, André. "Evangeline: A Myth of Acadie." *The Beaver* (August–September 2004), 42–43.

Pellerin, Ginette. *Evangeline's Quest*. National Film Board of Canada, 1996.

Poirier, Pascal. *Les Acadiens à Philadelphie suivi de Accordailles de Gabriel et d'Évangéline*, ed. Judith Perron. Moncton: Éditions d'Acadie, 1998.

Raynal, Guillaume-Thomas-François. *Histoire philosophique et politique des établissements et du commerce des Européens dans les deux Indes*. Amsterdam: n.p., 1970.

Roberts, Charles G.D. *A History of Canada*. Boston: Page Company, 1897.

Robertson, Berton. "Grand Pre of the Acadians." *Canadian Geography Journal* 11, no. 2 (1935): 77–84.

Runte, Hans R. *Writing Acadia: The Emergence of Acadian Literature, 1970–1990*. Amsterdam: Rodopi, 1997.

Segura, Chris. "Unraveling the Myth of Evangeline." *Times Picayune*, 7 April 2002.

Société Promotion de Grand Pré. http://www.grand-pre.com/en/history-of-grand-pre-and-the-arts.html

Thériault, Joseph-Yvon. *Évangéline. Contes d'Amérique*. Montréal: Québec-Amérique, 2013.

Treash, Linda. "Creole vs. Cajun: St. Martinville Historical Site Sorts It Out." *Times Picayune*, 22 October 1999.

Viau, Robert. *Grand Pré: lieu de memoire – lieu d'appartenance*. Beauport: MNH, 2005.

———. *Les Grands Dérangements. La Déportation des Acadiens en littérature acadienne, québécoise et française*. Beauport: MNH, 1997.

Voorhies, Felix. *Acadian Reminiscences: With the True Story of Evangeline*. Boston: Palmer, 1907.

Yilmaz, Ahenk. "Memorialization as the Art of Memory: A Method to Analyse Memorials." *METU Journal of the Faculty of Architecture* (2010): 267–80.

SEVEN

Time and Space in the Nationalism of Thomas D'Arcy McGee

David A. Wilson

On **May 2, 1860,** Thomas D'Arcy McGee gave the most memorable speech of his Canadian political career. The politicians and journalists listening in the Legislative Assembly responded with "loud and general applause," and even McGee's political enemies praised his oratory.[1] During the twentieth century, the centrepiece of his speech was reprinted in school textbooks, recited by schoolchildren, quoted by Canadian nationalists, and reproduced in radio and TV documentaries:

> I see in the not remote distance, one great nationality bound, like the shield of Achilles, by the blue rim of ocean—I see it quartered into many communities—each disposing of its internal affairs—but all bound together by free institutions, free intercourse, and free commerce; I see within the round of that shield, the peaks of the Western mountains and the crests of the Eastern waves—the winding Assiniboine, the five-fold lakes, the St. Lawrence, the Ottawa, the Saguenay, the St. John, and the Basin of Minas—by all these flowing waters, in all the valleys they fertilise, in all the cities they visit in their courses, I see a generation of industrious, contented, moral men, free in name and in fact,—men capable of maintaining, in peace and in war, a Constitution worthy of such a country.[2]

It is a striking passage in many respects. In a debate on George Brown's resolutions about a federal union of Canada West and Canada East, McGee had expanded the picture to incorporate British North America from the Rockies to the Maritimes. The "one great nationality" that would emerge within this vast expanse of nature would embrace diversity and unity. Each component part, whether French, English, Irish, or Scottish, would bring out the best in itself and the others, retaining yet transcending its distinct cultural characteristics in an emerging synthesis of national identity. Each community—and there would be many of them, in McGee's vision—would combine local control with a wider sense of belonging to a common Canada. People who lived thousands of miles apart would be brought together by mutual commercial interests, by the transportation revolution, and by institutions that guaranteed real liberty through constitutional order. In the United States, he believed, men were free in name only; in Canada, they would be free in fact. Hard work would be rewarded, religious faith would instill true morality, and a virtuous people would not shrink from defending their country in time of war.

Yet the most moving part of McGee's speech was its evocation of landscape—the arresting images of majestic scenery, culminating in the call to make "a Constitution worthy of such a country." In the course of his career, McGee made many speeches outlining the case for Confederation, but nothing quite caught the imagination like this one. Mountains, lakes, rivers, and the sea gave the country a sense of grandeur beyond the quotidian. An enlarged landscape would produce enlarged horizons, and enlarged horizons would produce enlarged minds. A North British nationality, he had written five years earlier, "would give imperial importance to provincial politics, and the dignity of history to provincial life."[3]

This is not to view McGee as a geographical determinist; it was the interaction of different peoples with their environment that would produce a "new northern nationality," within the framework of British constitutional traditions. An admirer of Edmund Burke, McGee believed that traditions, time, and circumstances would produce organic change. His "one great nationality" was not a fixed entity to which newcomers should subscribe and adjust, but rather an ever-evolving work in progress. As a Burkean, McGee put great stock in "the dignity of history." But the trouble was that Canada, in his view, lacked the history that invested time-honoured traditions with a sense of respect, affection, and legitimacy. In a less-quoted section of his "Shield of Achilles" speech, he criticized the current constitutional arrangement in Canada as something that had been improvised by imperial politicians after the Rebellions of 1837–38. "There is no sanctity of age about this Constitution of ours," he said. "We cannot invoke its provisions as 'the wisdom of our ancestors!'" To make matters worse, these constitutional arrangements had been designed with the express purpose of "swamping the French," and as such were "wholly indefensible."[4]

McGee's support for Confederation was obviously intended to remedy the defects of the Constitution of 1840. But if the wisdom of ancestors were conspicuously lacking, and the "dignity of history" were found wanting, what might invest the new constitutional arrangement with a sense of reverential awe? To argue that Confederation was justified because it would break with recent history was not entirely comfortable territory for a Burkean. New traditions, based on the best of the old, must be created. To address the deficit of history, McGee turned to geography—specifically, to his reading of geopolitical realities, and more generally to his romantic image of the northern landscape.

In McGee's view, the geographical location of Canada meant that it was uniquely placed to avoid British colonial domination and American continental imperialism. British politicians knew that they had to tread carefully with Canada, or risk losing the country to the United States—a loss, McGee remarked, that would drive him to Australia.[5] At the same time, American annexationists also had to tread carefully—something they had not done elsewhere on the continent. As McGee put it during his speech in the Confederation debates of 1865: "They coveted Florida, and seized it; they coveted Louisiana, and purchased it; they coveted Texas, and stole it; and then they picked a quarrel with Mexico, which ended by their getting California. They sometimes pretend to despise these [Canadian] colonies as prizes beneath their ambition; but had we not had the strong arm of England over us we should not now have a separate existence."[6]

But the arm of England was three thousand miles away, and that of the United States was next door. Under these circumstances, McGee looked for ways to strengthen the connection with Britain as a bulwark against the rising American empire. His answer: to invite a member of the British Royal Family, such as the Prince of Wales, to found a British North American branch of the monarchy. This would not only strengthen the ties with Britain, but also provide an aura of majesty for authority in Canada. As such, it would function as a counterweight to American imperialism and to American democratic values that were seeping in from across the border.[7] The United States was not just a predatory power, in McGee's view; it was an out-of-control democracy. Without sufficient checks from above, democracy in America was producing a plethora of social and moral ills—rampant corruption, the breakup of families, a culture of sensationalism, crime on the streets, the elevation of individualism over communal values, endemic urban poverty.

That, indeed, was why he had come to Canada in the first place, after spending eight years as a journalist in New York, Boston, and Buffalo—to escape from the moral quagmire of democracy and from the nativism that was pressing down on his fellow Irish Catholics. It is significant, in the light of his rural romanticism, that his response to democratic dissolution and nativist intolerance had been to initiate a colonization program that was intended to take anywhere between 50,000 and 200,000 Irish Catholic immigrants out of urban ghettoes and into the countryside, where they could be inoculated against the contamination of Protestantism and revolutionary republicanism.

The idea was to establish self-governing communities in the American west or in Canada, where Irish Catholic immigrants would become respectable, independent farmers rather than exploited wage labourers. Catholics would marry Catholics, bring their children up in the faith, and be "morally certain of moulding the minds of their children." McGee's ideal image of Ireland would be redrawn on the blank slate of new territory in North America. The colonization project, McGee announced, should be launched under the name of "Shin Fane," which he translated as "Ourselves for Ourselves." He pushed it so hard that he became known as "Moses McGee."[8]

Although the project failed, it played a major role in focusing his attention on Canada, where he came to believe that Irish Catholics were much better off than in the United States. "Our rural numbers," he wrote after he moved to the country, "are almost in the inverse ratio to the urban to what the same classes are to each other in the United States.... If not quite three-fourths, certainly the large majority of our emigrants here, live by land, and own land."[9] In British North America, he argued, the Irish were dispersed throughout the countryside, rather than being crammed into cities; they enjoyed freedom of religion and their own separate schools; and their leaders were generally gentlemen rather than ward bosses. "The British flag does indeed fly here," he wrote, "but it casts no shadow."[10]

If the rural character of Canadian life was a major attraction for McGee, so was the entrenched position of the Catholic Church, with its power base in Canada East and its extensions in the Maritimes and Canada West. This was inscribed onto not only the rural landscape, but the town and cities of French Canada as well. Approaching Montreal on a visit from New York in 1854, McGee marvelled at "the glitter of a hundred crosses crowning the tin-covered domes and spires, which glisten like silver in the sun." "Within the city everything is in harmony with this first impression," he wrote. "The high-walled and deep-gated nunneries, the clergy, secular and regular, walking abroad in their proper habits, the courtesy of the laity, even of Protestants, who lift their hats whenever a priest passes—all things and signs speak the Christian city."[11]

At this point, the temptation is to categorize McGee as a rural and religious romantic, and there is indeed much truth in that. As a convert to ultramontanism in the United States, he projected his romanticism onto an imagined pre-Reformation golden age, and argued that the only meaningful kind of "progress" lay in the recognition that "all Truth has been already discovered; that God's Church is its depository and interpreter to man; that the true elevation of our species, is to begin by bringing it down upon its knees before God's altar."[12] Yet such views coexisted, sometimes uneasily, sometimes contradictorily, with an equally romantic faith in the civilizing potential of "progress" as the word is more commonly understood, in terms of technological and economic improvement.

Technology and commerce, McGee believed, had the capacity to counter parochialism, to bring together people who lived apart. Earlier in life, he had applied this logic to Ireland, arguing that railway development could contribute to national unity. "Four dislocated Provinces are not 'a country,' nor four estranged rural multitudes 'a people,'" he wrote. "A thorough system of internal railways ... will do much to unite Ireland." Not only that, but it could transform the character of the people: "The railroad has banished the fairies from Ireland, it has waked [sic] up the intellectual facilities of the agricultural classes, [and] introduced among them habits of punctuality and industry."[13]

McGee applied the same logic, fairies aside, to British North America. Railways would connect the Atlantic with the west, transforming dislocated provinces into a country and turning estranged communities into a people. Hence his strong support for an Intercolonial Railway when he became a cabinet minister in Sandfield Macdonald's administration in 1862–63; hence his close friendship with Edward Watkin, the president of the Grand Trunk; and hence the enthusiasm with which he chaired the Intercolonial Conference in 1862. When opponents of Confederation argued that British North America was too large for one government, McGee replied that east–west railway connections would bring people together and foster a consciousness of commonality.

Such railway connections would also facilitate British North American commerce and counterbalance the economic pull of the United States. A selective tariff would encourage domestic industry and provide the protection for a well-balanced economic system based on the reciprocal exchange of British North America's vast and varied resources. The telegraph, and especially the transatlantic cable laid in 1858, would further strengthen east–west ties and help keep Canada within the orbit of the British Empire.[14]

All this fitted closely with McGee's idea of establishing a branch of the monarchy on British North American soil. Like Confederation, technology, and commerce, a Canadian monarchy would serve as a centripetal political force that would check the centrifugal force of geographical expansion. But while his arguments for Confederation, technology, and commerce carried the day, his position on monarchy went nowhere, and has been almost completely forgotten. As his critics pointed out at the time, his proposal would have divided Canadians and driven many of them into the arms of the United States.[15]

If Canadians could not cohere around a putatively protective monarchy, and if they lacked the deep-rooted historical traditions that might sustain a sense of nationality, they could draw on other resources that could give life and meaning to the new constitutional arrangements—and this is where the literature of landscape came in. "Literature is the vital atmosphere of nationality," McGee wrote in 1857. "Without that all-pervading, indefinite, exquisite element, national life—public life—must perish and rot. No literature—no national life—this is an irreversible law." A central task of nation-building, then, was the creation of a distinct Canadian literature, "neither British nor French, nor Yankeeish, but the offspring and heir of the soil, borrowing lessons from all lands, but asserting its title throughout all!"[16] It must be wholesome, morally elevating (he was scathing in his criticism of "sensational and sensual books, many of them written by women, who are the disgrace of their sex"), and big-hearted. "When nationalism stunts the growth, and embitters the generous spirit which alone can produce generous and enduring fruits of literature," he wrote, "then it becomes a curse rather than a gain to the people among whom it may find favour, and to every other people who may have relations with such a bigoted, one-sided nationality."[17]

A poet as well as a politician, McGee made his own contribution to an emerging Canadian literature. The first book he published after he arrived in the country was *Canadian Ballads and Occasional Verses*, in 1858, written to show the younger generation and aspiring poets that they could "find many worthy themes ... without quitting their own country."[18] Among these "worthy themes," none was more important than landscape. "There is a glorious field upon which to work for the formation of our National Literature," McGee wrote:

> It must assume the gorgeous coloring and the gloomy grandeur of the forest. It must partake of the grave mysticism of the Red man, and the wild vivacity of the hunter of western prairies. Its lyrics must possess the ringing cadences of waterfall, and its epics be as solemn and beautiful as our great rivers. We have the materials;—northern latitudes like these have ever been famed for the

strength, variety and beauty of their literature; all we demand is, that free scope be allowed to the talent and enterprise of the country, instead of allowing an unhealthy foreign substitute to be presented to our people.[19]

In his Canadian poems, McGee followed his own prescription. Although he reached back into French Canadian history, writing on the explorers and missionaries who brought civilization to the wilderness and who converted the natives to Christianity, nature and landscape took centre stage. His most popular ballad, "Jacques Cartier," focused on the land he encountered—the majestic river and its equally majestic cliffs—and on the "Algonkin braves" and the changing seasons: "How the magic wand of Summer clad the landscape to his eyes, / Like the dry bones of the just, when they wake in Paradise."[20] In other historical poems, such as "Sebastian Cabot to his Lady," the sea, sky, sun, moon, and wind set the atmosphere. The struggle to survive in the "Arctic frosts" is a common theme, along with the mystery of the forest and the mysticism of its inhabitants. "On the round Canadian cedars," he wrote in "Arm and Rise," "Legends high await but readers."[21]

Another of the poems focused on Thomas Moore, who had always been one of his literary heroes, and who had composed his "Canadian Boat Song" while travelling through the country in 1804. In McGee's view, the "Canadian Boat Song" was a perfect example of the way that Canadian literature could draw inspiration from the wilderness. As he wrote in "Thomas Moore at St. Anne's":

> He came a stranger summer bird,
> And quickly passed; but as he flew
> Our river's glorious song he heard,
> His tongue was loos'd—he warbled too.
>
> And, mark the moral, ye who dream
> To be the Poets of the land:
> He nowhere found a noble theme
> Than you, ye favor'd, have at hand.
>
> Not in the storied summer Isles,
> Not 'mid the classic Cyclades,
> Not where the Persian Sun-God smiles,
> Found he more fitting theme than these.

> So, while our boat glides swift along,
> Behold! from shore there looketh forth
> The tree that bears the fruit of song –
> The Laurel tree that loves the North.[22]

Moore's Canadian poems, McGee noted, "must certainly be included in any future Canadian Anthology"[23]

Yet, interestingly, no further Canadian anthologies were forthcoming from McGee, despite his apology in the Preface for the inadequacy of his efforts and his promise to do "something better" in the future.[24] Even in his *Canadian Ballads and Occasional Verses*, the "Occasional Verses," where Celtic themes loomed large, outnumbered his Canadian ballads. The Canadian landscape could not supply enough material for his muse. "You can hardly imagine, the interest I now take in this Country, and all that belongs to it," he subsequently told Mary Ann Sadlier. "But it does not, and never can supply, the field for mental labor, and affectionate inspiration, which Ireland would have been."[25]

It is not surprising, then, that McGee's "affectionate inspiration" reverted to familiar Irish channels, or that the dominant theme in his Irish poems was historical rather than geographical. Although they are largely ignored today, McGee's Irish historical poems were central to his reputation as a poet. Samuel Ferguson maintained that McGee was the "greatest poet" the Young Ireland movement produced. Charles Gavan Duffy commented that no one surpassed McGee's poems for the "subtle charm" with which they brought Irish history back to life. And Mary Ann Sadlier herself believed that "the noblest of his poems are undoubtedly the historical" and that "his love for Ireland inspired Mr. McGee beyond all doubt with some of very best and sweetest of his poems."[26]

This preoccupation with Irish history reached back to his early years. A good example comes from the summer of 1845, when a twenty-year-old McGee joined Gavan Duffy on a fortnight's walking tour of Wicklow, following a route that had been suggested by Thomas Davis. Visiting historical sites such as the round tower of Glendalough and the Arklow battlefield from the Rising of 1798, their thoughts turned from the past to the present and future. Young Ireland, they agreed, was the current incarnation of the timeless spirit of the Irish nation—the spirit that lay behind the heroic battles of the past and that was destined to culminate in Irish freedom. McGee subsequently expressed these views in poems such as "Time's Teachings," which presented Time as the messenger of God, travelling along a path full of struggle and sacrifice that led to liberty and prosperity, and singing that "Reckoning delay'd will come at last."[27]

In fact, hard realities lay immediately ahead—the potato failure, the Great Famine, coffin ships (the name may have come from McGee's description of them as "sailing coffins"),[28] and the ignominious defeat of the Rising of 1848. Under these circumstances, McGee gradually and reluctantly came to the position that revolution was impossible and that Irish patriots would have to settle for reform within the Union. His Irish nationalism was still pervaded by a sense of destiny—and this would be true for his Canadian nationalism as well—but the historical dimensions of that destiny changed. Instead of pointing towards an Ireland completely free from British rule, McGee reimagined Irish history as a long march to religious freedom. His most famous historical work, the *Popular History of Ireland*, written in Canada between 1858 and 1862, chose as its closing date not the Famine or the failure of Young Ireland, but rather the triumph of Catholic Emancipation in 1829.[29] He emphasized the heroism of those who stood up for faith and fatherland, and produced a grand narrative of an Irish Golden Age, the fall (first with the Vikings, and then the Normans), suffering, struggle, and redemption, culminating in the victory of conscience over coercion.

Here, above all, history provided Irish Catholics with a source of pride in the face of both British rule and American nativism. The nature of his imagined magnificent Celtic past could and did change in the course of his career. When he was a republican, his Irish Golden Age was peopled by freedom-loving Celts who resisted monarchical and aggressive Anglo-Saxons.[30] When he was an ultramontane, he happily reinvented the Celts as ultramontane Catholics.[31] (The same approach characterized McGee's identification of "popular fallacies" in Irish history, which always happened to be ones that contradicted his own political position.)[32] But the common denominator is really what mattered: McGee was attempting to provide his countrymen with a serviceable myth that would counter nativist prejudice that associated Irish Catholicism with superstition, ignorance, drink, and poverty.

As well as countering attacks from without, history could instill a sense of self-worth and prevent the internalization of external nativist stereotypes. When Irishmen and Irishwomen realized and remembered that they were part of a great Celtic civilization, they would stop seeing themselves as passive victims and become active and engaged citizens—or active and engaged subjects, in the case of Canada. Nothing appalled McGee more than the Irish being saddled with, or saddling themselves with, a sense of victimhood. The notion that the Irish were the Most Oppressed People Ever (to coin Liam Kennedy's phrase) was utterly anathema to McGee.[33] Rather than being a trap, Irish history for McGee was a key to freedom. He wrote in his *Popular History*:

> If we go to the oracles of the past in a sincere spirit of enquiry, we shall never fail of instruction. But we shall find there, precisely what we seek for: if we consult History in a spirit of Hatred we shall find there poisonous and deadly weapons enough; but if, in a sincere desire to know and to hold fast by the truth, we seek that source of political wisdom, we can never come away empty or disappointed.[34]

While McGee certainly attempted to approach history in a "sincere spirit of enquiry," there is also no doubt that he found there exactly what he sought—not only a counter-narrative to victimhood and to nativism, but also, in his early Young Ireland constitutional writings, an antidote to revolutionary nationalism.

Towards the end of 1847, when the moderates in Young Ireland were resisting the revolutionary impulses of John Mitchel and his followers, McGee convinced himself, and tried to convince others, that the pivotal moment in Irish history was 1541, when Henry VIII became king of Ireland. According to McGee, this was the product of a compact between Henry and the Celtic and Norman chiefs; this compact, and not conquest, formed the true basis of the "Crown Connexion." But the compact had been betrayed and undermined by the "odious innovations" of power-hungry English ministers; had it not been for their "heartless & false conduct," particularly during the Famine, Ireland would have been the most "loyal Nation on the Earth." By interpreting 1541 as a compact that had been violated by an aggressive and rapacious ministry, McGee had provided a convenient historical justification for his pre-existing position that equal but distinct Irish and British legislatures should share a common allegiance to the Crown.[35]

McGee's views on "the golden link of the crown" made as little headway in Ireland as did his later monarchical views in Canada. But what is particularly interesting, apart from the similarity between his Irish and his Canadian constitutional nationalism, is the difference between his Irish and his Canadian route to monarchism. In Ireland, he reached his destination through an analysis of history; in Canada, he arrived at the same position through his analysis of geopolitical realities. The contrast is revealing. In Canada, McGee's nationalism put geography ahead of history; in Ireland, it put history ahead of geography. When McGee wrote about time in Canada, his thoughts immediately turned to space; when he wrote about space in Ireland, his thoughts immediately turned to time.

Time and space not only provided different routes to McGee's monarchism; they also had the common goal of opening up the mind, of producing a broad, tolerant, pluralistic polity characterized by generosity of spirit and benevolence of purpose. In Ireland, an ennobling history would instill national pride; in Canada, the grandeur of geography would fulfill the same function.

Beyond this, McGee's understanding of Irish history and of Canadian geography played a central role in the fight against Fenianism that preoccupied him during the mid-1860s, and that culminated in his assassination in 1868. In his view, Fenianism was very much the product of parochialism in time and space. Locked into a sense of victimhood, the Fenians consulted history in a spirit of hatred, he believed, and found there weapons poisonous and deadly enough to be employed against anyone who crossed or contradicted them. From this perspective, the Fenians inhabited the narrow ground of ethno-religious conflict, and of cramped American cities that reproduced in urban form the worst elements of pre-Famine Irish rural society—exploitative landlords, subletting, and subdivision—without any of its redeeming features. An impoverished, ghettoized, and alienated Irish American population, McGee wrote, produced the perfect breeding ground for the Fenian "disease." Everything about the movement was closed-minded, reflecting the environment from which it emerged.[36]

In Ireland, history was one of the main fronts in McGee's battle against the Fenian Brotherhood. "This sect is altogether novel in Irish history," he wrote, "and it is not to be put down, by half-apologetic pleadings of 'good intentions.'"[37] But in Canada, the sense of space, the rural diffusion of the Irish Catholic population, and the widespread ownership of land formed important arguments against the movement. Here, he wrote, the "great healthful mass of the Irish farmers ... breathing pure air and living pure lives," were untouched by Fenian infection. "And these are the people," he exclaimed, "their own flesh and blood (though not of the same spirit) the New York 'bloody sixth ward boys,' are coming here to invade, or they call it, 'to liberate.'"[38]

There were, of course, Fenians in Canada. But McGee dismissed them as "a few characterless desperadoes among the floating population of our principal cities"—precisely those people who occupied the slivers of narrow ground that existed in the country.[39] Most of them had brought their beliefs with them on the boat, and must be challenged at every turn. "If we will carefully convey across the Atlantic half-extinguished embers of strife in order that we may by them light up the flames of our inflammable forests," McGee wrote, "—if each neighbour will try not only to nurse up old animosities, but to invent new grounds of hostility to his neighbour—then ... we shall return to what Hobbes considered the state of Nature—I mean a state of war."[40]

The best way to prevent this from happening, to protect the inflammable forests, was to show that Canada worked—that an open, rural environment with religious freedom, just laws, and civil rights engendered an economically enterprising, politically conservative and loyal Irish Catholic population, and that a country where Irishmen were not fighting for limited resources could produce amicable relations between most Irish Catholics and most Irish Protestants. Canadian environmental conditions were obviously not transposable to Ireland, but there were lessons here, nonetheless. If the polity that arose in these conditions could demonstrate that when Irish Catholics enjoyed modest prosperity and religious equality, they would become loyal subjects of the Crown, then British statesmen should take note. "Let us put that weapon into the hands of the friends of Ireland at home," McGee said, "and it will be worth all the revolvers that ever were stolen from a Cork gunshop, and all the Republican chemicals that were ever smuggled out of New York."[41] The northern land of Canada might help open up the narrow ground of Ireland; Canadian geography could rewrite Irish history. ∎

NOTES

1 McGee, *Speeches and Addresses*, 176. See also *Canadian Freeman*, 11 May 1860.

2 McGee, *Speeches and Addresses*, 175–76.

3 *American Celt*, 16 August 1856.

4 McGee, *Speeches and Addresses*, 161, 164, 165–66.

5 *Gazette* (Montreal), 3 July 1863; *Morning Freeman* (Saint John), 30 July 1863.

6 McGee, "Speech on Motion for an Address to Her Majesty in Favour of Confederation," *Speeches and Addresses*, 278.

7 *New Era*, 1 June 1857, 19 January 1858, 16 February 1858.

8 Wilson, *Thomas D'Arcy McGee*, vol. 1, 341–42.

9 McGee, "The Irish Position in British and in Republican North America," *Gazette* (Montreal), 6 March 1866.

10 *American Celt*, 9 December 1854.

11 *American Celt*, 16 December 1854.

12 *American Celt*, 11 December 1852.

13 *American Celt*, 27 October 1855.

14 *New Era*, 25 May 1857, 18 August 1857.

15 See, for example, the comments of Timothy Warren Anglin in *Morning Freeman* (Saint John), 11 August 1863.

16 *New Era*, 17 June 1857.

17 *Gazette* (Montreal), 5 November 1867 (delivered 4 November 1867); see also McGee, "The Mental Outfit of the New Dominion," in Murphy, *D'Arcy McGee*, 1–21.

18 McGee, *Canadian Ballads and Occasional Verses*, vii.
19 *New Era*, 24 April 1858.
20 McGee, *Canadian Ballads*, 13.
21 Ibid., 42.
22 Ibid., 42–43.
23 Ibid., 63.
24 Ibid., vii–viii.
25 Library and Archives Canada (LAC), MG 24-C16, James Sadlier Fonds, McGee to Mary Ann Sadlier, 8 January 1864.
26 Lady Ferguson, *Sir Samuel Ferguson*, vol. 1, 139; Duffy, *My Life in Two Hemispheres*, vol. 1, 128n; Sadlier, *Poems of Thomas D'Arcy McGee*, 43–44, 47–48.
27 *Boston Pilot*, 18 October 1845; Duffy, *My Life in Two Hemispheres*, vol. 1, 121, vol. 2, 24; *Nation*, 22 January 1848; Sadlier, *Poems of Thomas D'Arcy McGee*, 142–43; Lambkin, "Moving Titles," 103–11.
28 *Nation*, 18 March 1848.
29 McGee, *Popular History of Ireland*.
30 *Boston Pilot*, 8 March 1845.
31 *American Celt*, 17 May 1851.
32 *Nation*, 9 January 1847.
33 Kennedy, *Colonialism*, 217.
34 *Canadian Freeman*, 3 December 1863.
35 Urquhart Papers, Balliol College, Oxford University, I/J6, McGee to David Urquhart, 2 September and 8 September 1847.
36 See, for example, his Wexford speech, as reported in *Dublin Evening Mail*, 16 May 1865; and his "The Irish Position."
37 LAC, Moylan Fonds, MG29-D15, vol. 1, McGee to James Moylan, 27 October 1865.
38 McGee, "The Irish Position."
39 LAC, Charles Murphy Fonds, MG27-IIIB8, folio 21586, McGee to the Earl of Mayo, 4 April 1868.
40 McGee, "The Policy of Conciliation," *Speeches and Addresses*, 6–7.
41 *Ottawa Times*, 18 March 1868.

WORKS CITED

Duffy, Sir Charles Gavan. *My Life in Two Hemispheres*. 2 vols. London: T. Fisher Unwin, 1898.

[Lady] Ferguson. *Sir Samuel Ferguson in the Ireland of his Day*, vol. 1. Edinburgh and London: William Blackwood and Sons, 1896.

Kennedy, Liam. *Colonialism, Religion, and Nationalism*. Belfast: Institute of Irish Studies, Queen's University of Belfast, 1996.

Lambkin, Brian. "Moving Titles of a Young Ireland Text: Davis, Duffy, and McGee and the Origins of Tiocfaidh Ar Lá." In *Ireland: Space, Text, Time*, ed. Liam Harte, 103–11. Manchester: Manchester University Press, 2005.

McGee, D'Arcy. *Canadian Ballads and Occasional Verses*. Montreal: Lovell, 1858.

———. "The Mental Outfit of the New Dominion." In *D'Arcy McGee: A Collection of Speeches and Addresses*, ed. Charles Murphy, 1–21. Toronto: Macmillan, 1937.

———. *Popular History of Ireland: From the Earliest Period to the Emancipation of the Catholics*. Montreal: D. & J. Sadlier, 1863.

———. *Speeches and Addresses, Chiefly on the Subject of British-American Union*. London: Chapman and Hall, 1865.

Murphy, Charles, ed. *D'Arcy McGee: A Collection of Speeches and Addresses*. Toronto: Macmillan, 1937.

Sadlier, J. *The Poems of Thomas D'Arcy McGee*. New York: D. & J. Sadlier, 1869.

Wilson, David A. *Thomas D'Arcy McGee*, vol. 1: *Passion, Reason, and Politics, 1825–1857*. Montreal and Kingston: McGill–Queen's University Press, 2008.

EIGHT

Contesting Historical Space:
The Campaign to Have Grosse Île Designated a National Historic Site with the Irish Dimension as Its Main Theme

Pádraig Breandán Ó Laighin

The proposal to develop Grosse Île as a National Historic Site dedicated primarily to the theme of immigration to Canada generated a unique contest over the control and management of historical space. Grounded in contemporary political contexts and in a conservative canon of Canadian history, the development concept posed a challenge not only to the collective memory of Irish Canadians but also to a whole body of historical evidence that transcended immigration matters. The epistemological bases of the historical and strategic positions of those leading the social movement to have the Irish dimension adopted as the main development theme require explanation, especially in the context of subsequent critiques.

BACKGROUND AND CONTEXT OF THEMATIC APPROACH

The Historic Sites and Monuments Board of Canada (HSMBC) is a statutory body whose mandate is to advise the Government of Canada, through the minister responsible for Parks Canada, on the commemoration of nationally significant historic sites, events, or persons. Members are drawn from the provinces and territories and from Library and Archives Canada, the Canadian Museum of Civilization, and

Parks Canada. Understandably, membership is usually predominated by historians, and this was the case for the period under study here.

Having declared the Quarantine Station at Grosse Île to be of historical significance in 1974, and immigration to be one of the most important themes in Canadian history in 1983, the HSMBC linked the two in 1984 and recommended the development of a national historic park at Grosse Île, "in light of the number and quality of the *in situ* resources on Grosse Île related to the theme of immigration." At the same time, the board explicitly recommended that interpretation on the island "should not focus solely on the experience of the Irish ... but should deal with the theme of national significance—Immigration."[1] This latter recommendation was not publicized at the time, and its role as provenance of the later approach to placing the Irish story in context only became public knowledge ten years later, after the emergence of a social movement responding to proposals published by Parks Canada. The 1984 recommendations were accepted by the minister.

In March 1992, Parks Canada, then temporarily known as the Parks Service and situated within the Department of the Environment, published development proposals for Grosse Île as a National Historic Site. As a general theme it proposed "Canada: Land of Welcome and Hope." This theme was to be expressed through "Immigration to Canada via Quebec City (1800–1839)" as a main theme, with "Grosse Île quarantine station (1832–1937)" as a secondary theme.[2]

There is a political dimension to the work of the HSMBC. Historic sites and monuments provide a framework within which historical memory and political affinities can be constructed and consolidated. That capacity to influence the Canadian national agenda was reflected in the selected themes. Grosse Île, in the very heart of Quebec, with appropriate themes, could be used to demonstrate and promote an appreciation of the central role played by Quebec in the development of Canada. The Parti Québécois, dedicated to the separation of Quebec from Canada, was in power in Quebec, and while a referendum on sovereignty in 1980 had been defeated by a substantial margin, a second referendum had been promised. And crucially, the federal government had retained ownership of the entire island of Grosse Île. In the broader Canadian context, mass immigration, especially from Asia, in the 1980s and 1990s, involved concerns about integration and shifting cultural balance, and these were being addressed by the federal government in a variety of ways, including thematic interpretation.

PROMOTIONAL ORIENTATION OF THE DEVELOPMENT CONCEPT

A key element of the proposed development from the perspective of Irish Canadians was a promotional orientation that Parks Canada expressed as follows: "It is also felt that there should not be too much emphasis on the tragic aspects of the history of Grosse Île. On the contrary, the painful events of 1832 and 1847, which have been overemphasized in the past, need to be put back into perspective, without robbing them of their importance."[3] The development concept document itself reflected the marginalization of Irish associations with Grosse Île: it referred to the Irish as part of a "British contingent"; it failed to give any account of the events of 1832, 1834, and 1847 on the island, except to describe them as "tragic years"; and it offered no discussion of the mass graves from 1847 and the Celtic cross erected in 1909 in memory of those who died there (see Figure 8.1).[4]

This promotional orientation struck the Irish Canadian community like a bolt from the blue. They were unaware, and were not informed by the document, that this orientation had been presaged in the in camera deliberations of the HSMBC eight years earlier. Consequently, Parks Canada, as messenger and implementation agency of the orientation, was the focus of the Irish community's response.

While Irish Canadians may have been astonished by the development proposals for Grosse Île, these were consistent with a traditional conservative Canadian historical canon whose main focus was on broad constitutional developments, especially those involving French and English political leaders and movements. Concerning the historical importance of Grosse Île, there was a serious disjunction between that canon and the collective memory of Irish Canadians. The canonical side of this disjunction is perhaps best expressed by descriptive passages from textbooks that were in use in introductory history courses in high schools and universities across English Canada at the time. The only reference to tragic circumstances surrounding the arrival of Irish immigrants in the nineteenth century in J.M.S. Careless's book of 449 pages is as follows:

> Between 1815 and 1850 more people came to the British North American colonies from Britain than there had been in all these provinces at the earlier date.... On the whole those who came proved themselves hardy and self-reliant. Many, however, had scraped together their last funds for passage-money for themselves and family. They arrived almost penniless, to tax the limited resources of the colonies. The Irish famine-immigrants of the late 1840's were perhaps the worst case of this sort. Starvation and disease carried them off in hundreds in the "emigrant sheds" on their arrival.[5]

Figure 8.1. Celtic cross on southwestern peninsula
Source: Pádraig Ó Laighin.

In similar vein, Desmond Morton states: "As the Irish Famine of the 1840s dumped shiploads of penniless, starving people in Canadian ports, the triumph of free trade in Britain wiped out Canada's only real export market."[6]

The collective memory of Irish Canadians, the other side of the disjunction, had its origins in historical events surrounding the arrival of the Irish immigrants in the Canadian colonies in the 1830s, and especially during the Irish famine of 1846–52—events that had found little or no place in the Canadian historical canon. The publication of the development proposals for Grosse Île brought this disjunction into focus and gave rise to a significant social campaign.

IRISH IMMIGRANTS AT GROSSE ÎLE QUARANTINE STATION, 1832–34

Following a survey conducted by the British navy, Grosse Île, in the upper St. Lawrence estuary, 48 kilometres downstream from Quebec City, was selected in February 1832 as the location for a quarantine station—an anchorage for all arriving vessels and onshore accommodation for the sick. The governing authorities of Lower Canada had resolved to implement an effective system of quarantine in order to prevent the introduction of cholera to the colony.[7] The disease had spread across Europe and become epidemic in Ireland. An unusually large number of immigrants—more than 50,000, the majority of whom were Irish—had arrived in Quebec City in 1831, and a similar number was expected during the shipping season of 1832.

A total of 51,746 immigrants arrived at the quarantine station in 1832.[8] Again, the great majority were Irish and were arriving from Irish and British ports. Due to misdiagnosis on the part of examining physicians who had no experience with cholera cases, some vessels carrying the disease were cleared at the quarantine station to proceed to Quebec City. Deaths from cholera at the Emigrant Hospital there were acknowledged on 8 June. Within a few days the disease had spread from the immigrants to the city's inhabitants and a cholera epidemic began to take hold. From there the disease spread to Montreal and Upper Canada as immigrants travelled west by steamboat. For the following month, an epidemic raged throughout the Canadas, leaving thousands dead—3,451 in Quebec City, according to the health board there, a greater number in Montreal, and perhaps a thousand elsewhere.

The quarantine system had proved ineffective in the first season of its operation. Part of the problem was that all aspects of the functioning of the quarantine station, including medical inspection, were under strict military control. Modifications were made to the regime the following year that extended more autonomy to the physicians, but the station remained under exclusive military command until 1840. It appears that no returns were made available by the military authorities regarding the number of deaths at the quarantine station in 1832.[9] Alexander Carlisle Buchanan, the Chief Agent for Immigration, estimated that 2,350 of the immigrants had died from cholera in Lower and Upper Canada during that year.[10] Most of them were Irish, and some were buried in the main cemetery in the west of Grosse Île, just south of an inlet which has since been known as Cholera Bay.

A further serious outbreak of cholera occurred in 1834. The majority of the almost 31,000 immigrants who arrived at Grosse Île that year were Irish. Buchanan reported that 800 of the immigrants died in Lower and Upper Canada.[11] Detailed returns provided by the quarantine station for the year indicate that a total of 264 immigrants died and were buried on the island. Almost all of them were Irish. We have their names, as well as their travel and illness details. The most frequent cause of death was cholera.[12]

"SUMMER OF SORROW" AT GROSSE ÎLE, 1847

From 1834 to 1845, the numbers of people dying on the island annually ranged from six to fifty-eight. In 1845, there were thirty deaths. In 1846, sixty-nine passengers, all Irish, died at the quarantine station. With stories of famine and mass emigration from Ireland reaching Canada, Dr. George Mellis Douglas, Medical Superintendent and Medical Boarding Officer of the quarantine station, expected that the approaching 1847 season would be characterized "by a greater amount of sickness and mortality."[13]

The first vessel of the season, the *Syria*, arrived on 15 May. It had fever on board, and there had been nine deaths on the passage. On the same day, the first of the immigrants died in the quarantine hospital: Ellen Keane, aged four years and three months, the daughter of Bridget McNally and her husband John Keane, a weaver, from Kilmore, County Mayo. She was recorded as having died "of fever," and was buried in the presence of her mother.[14]

Within a week, thousands of passengers had arrived. Dr. Douglas wrote that he had "never contemplated the possibility of every vessel arriving with fever, as they now do."[15] The quarantine system was soon overwhelmed. Healthy passengers were being kept on board in contravention of quarantine law. Most of the 12,450 passengers of thirty-six vessels in quarantine at Grosse Île on 28 May were still on board. Many were ill. There had been more than six hundred deaths on board these vessels on the voyage.¹⁶ On 2 June the Governor General, on the recommendation of a committee of the Executive Council, established a Medical Commission to examine the functioning of the quarantine station at Grosse Île, and to propose such regulations or measures as might be necessary.

The medical commissioners proceeded to Grosse Île without delay. They estimated that 25,398 immigrants had arrived by the morning of 6 June and that 1,097 had died at sea and 900 at Grosse Île by that time, including 200 who had died there during the previous twenty-four hours. They reported that there were 1,150 sick in the quarantine hospital, and 1,550 sick on board ships. They understood that about 45,000 immigrants had set sail for Quebec up to 19 May. The commissioners ordered the landing of all healthy passengers, the erection of tents, the appointment of additional medical doctors, and the forwarding of the healthy passengers by steamer to Quebec and Montreal, without necessarily complying with the full term of quarantine statutorily required.¹⁷

Despite extraordinary effort and sacrifice, mortality continued: it spread to Quebec City and onwards to Montréal, where thousands died, and thence to Kingston and Toronto and other places in Canada West. By the end of the season, according to emigration documentation, 4,092 passengers had died on board during the passage, 1,190 on board at quarantine, and 3,389 in the quarantine hospital, for a total of 8,671.¹⁸ In his report, Dr. Douglas gave 3,238 as the number who died at the quarantine hospital.¹⁹ Subtracting this from his total of 5,424 burials under quarantine auspices, one can extrapolate that in his estimation 2,186 passengers died while on ships during quarantine (see Figure 8.2). In addition, four Catholic priests, two Anglican ministers, four medical doctors, twenty-two nurses, orderlies, and cooks, three police officers, two carters, and four service employees died of fever contracted at Grosse Île. One of the doctors who died was Dr. Benson from Dublin, who arrived on board the *Wandsworth* on 19 May, offered his services in the quarantine hospital, contracted typhus, and died on 30 May.

Beyond Grosse Île, Buchanan reported the deaths of 712 immigrants at the Emigrant Hospital in Quebec City, 3,330 at the Montreal Emigrant Hospital, 201 elsewhere in Quebec, 863 at the Emigrant Hospital in Toronto, and 3,048 under various health boards in Ontario. The total for those who died on land in the province of Canada was 11,543. Adding those who died on board vessels prior to landing brings an officially estimated total number of deaths among the passengers to the province to 16,825.²⁰ Other official estimates were higher in some cases. John Joseph, for example, of the Committee of the Executive Council, gave 3,579 as the number of deaths at the Montreal Emigrant Hospital. Elsewhere in

Figure 8.2. Portion of mass-grave cemetery of 1847 on southwestern peninsula
Source: Pádraig Ó Laighin.

British North America, especially New Brunswick, there was also high mortality among the Irish arrivals.[21]

The extent of the mortality, especially in the province of Canada—comprising the present-day provinces of Quebec and Ontario—was a matter of public deliberation in the years immediately following 1847. For instance, a guide book to Quebec City, published in 1851, summarizes the situation at Grosse Île and beyond succinctly as follows:

> At the Lazaretto here five thousand emigrants died of ship-fever in 1847. In connection with this statement it is lamentable to be recorded, that about four thousand emigrants perished at Montreal, and that about twenty thousand, chiefly Irish, perished either at sea or in the Government sheds of this Province in 1847. Several medical men and clergymen, who caught the infection during the discharge of their perilous duty, fell victims.[22]

Over 86 percent of the 87,308 emigrants who sailed from Irish, English, or Scottish ports to Quebec during the year 1847 were Irish.[23] Almost all of the emigrants who died, on passage or after arrival, in the province of Canada or elsewhere in British North America, were Irish. The events of 1847 gave Grosse Île an iconic status in the collective historical memory of Irish Canadians. This status was enhanced by the monuments erected there, including the monument to the medical doctors erected by Dr. Douglas before the end of 1847, on which he had inscribed the following words: "In this secluded spot lie the mortal remains of 5424 persons who flying from Pestilence and Famine in Ireland in the year 1847 found in America but a Grave."

PARKS CANADA'S INITIAL ROUND OF CONSULTATION, MARCH–MAY 1992

The development proposals for Grosse Île were made public on 5 March 1992. A two-stage consultation program was announced, with information sessions to be held in Montmagny, Quebec City, L'Isle-aux-Grues, Saint-Malachie, and Montreal, with formal public hearings to follow in Montmagny, Quebec City, and Montreal.

Subsequent to the information session held in Montreal on 8 April, a meeting was called for 27 April to address the issues raised by Parks Canada's proposals. It brought together twenty organizations from across Quebec, and also from across a broad ideological and socio-economic spectrum; these included St. Patrick's Society, the Irish Protestant Benevolent Society, the United Irish Societies, the Ancient Order of Hibernians, and Comité Québec–Irlande. The organizations present agreed unanimously to form an umbrella organization—the General Assembly of Irish Organizations / Assemblée générale des associations irlandaises / Comhdháil na nEagras Éireannach. I was unanimously elected Chairperson of the new organization, and I continued in that role during all of the events described in this chapter. A further eleven organizations joined soon afterwards.

The General Assembly resolved to mobilize support, especially in Quebec and across Canada, for the Irish dimension to be the main theme of any development at Grosse Île, with participation in the public hearing in Montreal to be the immediate focus. Strategically, the concept as proposed would need to be challenged; policy-makers, especially the relevant department and the Government of Canada, would need to be convinced; and it would be necessary to demonstrate popular support and a historical basis for an Irish Canadian alternative to Parks Canada's project.

PUBLIC HEARING IN MONTREAL, 20 MAY 1992

Twenty-five submissions were presented orally at the public hearings in Montreal. Most of the member organizations of the General Assembly presented, as well as three organizations from Ontario, a representative of Action from Ireland (AfrI)—invited under the auspices of St. Patrick's Society—and several individuals.

As a director of St. Patrick's Society, I presented a submission on its behalf.[24] As a general critique, I argued that the main theme of immigration could be pursued more appropriately elsewhere—that Quebec City, and not Grosse Île, was the landing place for immigrants in 1847. We agreed that quarantine was most appropriate as a secondary theme for Grosse Île. The failure to present the Irish dimension of "l'Île des Irlandais, the Irish Island" was unacceptable to us and to the Irish Canadian community generally. I asserted that Grosse Île without an Irish central theme would be like Louisbourg without a French one. Acknowledging the Irishness of the site would imply respect for the spirit of the place, would encourage particular forms of sustainable tourism, and would reflect the Irish dimension of Quebec society, including the memory of the thousand or so Irish orphans who were adopted by French Canadians but retained their Irish names. The extraordinary omission of two of the island's most significant features—the Celtic cross and the mass grave cemetery—from the development proposal was criticized not only on historic grounds but also on the pragmatic grounds that these features, along with the 1847 hospital, had been the principal sites on the itinerary, not just of Irish Canadians, but of all visitors attracted there in recent years by local tour organizers. There were plenty of alternatives elsewhere for projected boating and yachting developments. I made additional specific recommendations regarding trilingual signage on the island, the restoration of the 1847 hospital, then in need of immediate repair, and the provision of modest facilities for visitors. The document's terminology was criticized—for example, the Irish were described as "British," and references were made to the "Potato Famine" as well as to "Britain" as the "mother country" of Irish immigrants. In conclusion, while acknowledging the excellent work of Parks Canada at other historic sites, I alleged that the development document constituted a rewriting of the history of Grosse Île.

Radio, TV, and newspaper reporters were present at the Montreal hearing, and the story was carried on local and national news across Canada. Dozens of TV, radio, and newspaper interviews followed, and then there were documentaries, films, and art exhibitions—all exploring and supportive of the selection of the Irish dimension as the main theme of a national historic site at Grosse Île.

Throughout Canada, and internationally, a social movement began to coalesce around the issue.

Parks Canada's *Report on the Public Consultation Program*, published in March 1994, describes the public hearing held in Montreal as follows:

> The Montréal meeting was to have been the conclusion of the public consultation. However, that meeting was attended by 200 members of the Irish-Canadian community who demanded that other public hearings be held outside Québec to allow other people across Canada to present their views on the concept. Participants also expressed the opinion that Parks Canada's project did not do justice or was otherwise deficient with respect to the "Irish dimension" of the site.[25]

As requested, further public hearings were held across Canada during the spring of 1993, in Vancouver, Fredericton, Charlottetown, and Toronto. Overwhelmingly, the submissions at these hearings asserted that the main historic significance of Grosse Île was as the Irish island, as cemetery and sanctuary, and as a garden of remembrance, and that these orientations should constitute the main thematic focus of the national historic site.

FURTHER CAMPAIGNING AND OFFICIAL DEVELOPMENTS

Following the Montreal hearing, the General Assembly sent detailed factual explanations of its position on the development of Grosse Île, outlining pragmatic reasons as well as evidence-based historical reasons as to why the Irish dimension should be central, to the Prime Minister of Canada, Brian Mulroney, to federal ministers concerned with the matter, and to other elected representatives. Dialogue with the Irish ambassador in Ottawa was initiated. Appeals were made to the Quebec government to intervene. Mayoral candidates in the Montreal municipal elections found it appropriate to publicly support the Irish Canadian position. Other ethnic groups and First Nations gave their unqualified support. The General Assembly in Quebec and AfrI in Ireland organized campaigns in which postcards with photographs of Grosse Île monuments were sent to Prime Minister Mulroney, urging him to intervene personally in the matter.

Independently, Action Grosse Île, based in Toronto, organized protests and presented petitions signed by more than 5,000 people. Also in Toronto, Petition Grosse Île collected more than 18,000 signatures. From across Canada, 228 briefs were submitted to Parks Canada, which also received more than 1,000 letters, almost all of which dealt with the "Irish dimension" of the project.[26]

I met with Jean Charest, Minister of the Environment, on 12 February 1993, and shortly thereafter he forwarded a supplement to the development proposals that described the cemeteries and Irish-related monuments.[27] Prime Minister Mulroney responded to my letter on 19 February 1993, and assured the General Assembly "that the place of Grosse Île in Irish Canadian consciousness cannot, and will not, be understated"; he indicated that further hearings were to be held at his direction, and stated that he was forwarding copies of our exchange of correspondence to the Minister of the Environment, Jean Charest. These and other similar communications and interventions kept the request for an Irish dimension on the agenda of the Government of Canada.

Parks Canada's public report of March 1994 on the public consultation synthesized the overwhelming support from across Canada that existed for the Irish dimension. Parks Canada implied that this report would inform the HSMBC in its deliberations.[28] Privately, however, a detailed secret report had been prepared and presented formally at a meeting of the HSMBC in November 1993. That report proposed two distinct options, both of which assumed the retention of the original and contentious commemorative themes of immigration and quarantine. First, the unlikely possibility of relocating the immigration theme to Quebec City was mooted, while the focus remained on the quarantine theme, albeit with an "Irish dimension," at Grosse Île. Second, Parks Canada reiterated its support for the original commemorative themes at the island site, while giving greater emphasis to the "Irish dimension."[29]

Unaware of this discrepancy between the private and public positions of Parks Canada, the General Assembly also made representations to the HSMBC, as well as to Minister Michel Dupuy of Canadian Heritage, the department to whose jurisdiction Parks Canada had been transferred. The board recommended that the primary commemorative intent of Grosse Île should be to tell the story of the immigrant experience, but added that the Irish experience "should become a particular focus of the commemoration." Minister Dupuy approved these HSMBC recommendations in August 1994 and established an Advisory Panel to advise him on implementation.

VISIT OF PRESIDENT MARY ROBINSON TO GROSSE ÎLE, AUGUST 1994

The visit of Irish President Mary Robinson to Grosse Île, on 21 August 1994, was of great symbolic importance and had a transformative effect on deliberations concerning the future of Grosse Île. The Irish Embassy in Ottawa had discussed her proposed visit with the General Assembly, and it was invited to participate in the organization of a day of commemoration on the island to coincide with her visit.

President Robinson opened her address on Grosse Île as follows:

> Islands possess their own particular beauty, and Grosse Île is no exception. But Grosse Île—Oileán na nGael—l'Île des Irlandais—is special. I believe that even those coming to this beautiful island knowing nothing of the tragedy which occurred here, would sense its difference. I am certain that no one knowing the story could remain unaffected. This is a hallowed place.[30]

Speaking also in Irish and French, she commemorated those who died there, paying tribute on behalf of the people of Ireland to those who cared for the sick there and gave homes to the orphans, and emphasizing the transformational potential of the island's symbolism in a world of hunger and famine.

Her visit to Grosse Île received extensive coverage in Canada and Ireland and worldwide. In February of the following year, addressing a joint session of the Houses of the Oireachtas (the national Parliament) in Dublin, she spoke of "being struck by the sheer power of commemoration" on Grosse Île.

FINAL APPEALS AND SATISFACTORY OUTCOME FOR IRISH CANADIANS

The visit of President Robinson set the scene for the final discussions on the future of Grosse Île. The General Assembly and representatives of St. Patrick's Society met with Dr. Larkin Kerwin, Chair of the Advisory Panel, in Quebec City in April 1995, and, as spokesperson, I insisted once again on the centrality of the Irish dimension in the naming and theme of the national historic site of Grosse Île. In June 1995, a summary of the historical background and an appraisal of the current status of development proposals for the island, which I had prepared, were presented by the General Assembly, through access arranged by St. Patrick's Society, to Finance and Economic Development Minister Paul Martin, who was known to have an influential voice in government. That summary pointed out the democratic deficit inherent in the discrepancies between the public reports issued by Parks Canada and its private document placed before the HSMBC, which was released to the General Assembly at my request only after Minister Dupuy's decision of August 1994. Further appeals seeking government support and intervention were made in August 1995 in anticipation of the submission of the Advisory Panel report to the heritage minister. The panel had told us that their mandate precluded them from recommending change to the immigration theme. The General Assembly again requested that the Irish associations of site be the dominant theme, and suggested that this could be achieved by naming the site "Grosse Île—l'Île des Irlandais—the Irish Island—National Historic Site."

Finally, in Quebec City on 17 March 1996, Deputy Prime Minister and Minister of Canadian Heritage Sheila Copps made the following announcement to invited members of the Irish Canadian community and the media:

> The story of Grosse-Île is an indelible part of the history of Canada and Ireland. Today, in recognition of the importance of Grosse-Île, and to mark the upcoming 150th anniversary of the island's greatest tragedy and greatest display of human decency, I am honoured to announce that this important national historic site will be known as "Grosse-Île and the Irish Memorial—Grosse-Île-et-le-Mémorial-des-Irlandais."[31]

Minister Copps was joined, by video, by Mary Robinson, President of Ireland. The General Assembly of Irish Organizations and Action Grosse Île issued a joint press release welcoming the decision.

THE ROLE OF COLLECTIVE MEMORY AND HISTORICAL EVIDENCE IN THE CAMPAIGN

Referring to the "Keegan diary" and Robert Whyte's *The Ocean Plague* in an article titled "Famine, Facts and Fabrication," Canadian historian Mark McGowan asserts that these "diaries proved as useful to the nineteenth-century Irish nationalists as to contemporary Irish Canadians fighting the initial conceptual plan for Grosse Île."[32] Towards the end of the article, he states the following: "Keegan's journal touched a nerve within those who feared cover-up of the Famine Memory in the proposed Parks Canada development of Grosse Île. In the end their intervention in the planning stage forced the Government of Canada to specify the Irish tragedy as integral to the Historic Site and National Park."[33]

These diaries played no role in the campaign approach of the General Assembly of Irish Organizations. The true origins of the "Keegan diary" and the false claims about its suppression had been exposed as early as 1988, when I informed Robert O'Driscoll, an editor of *The Untold Story: The Irish in Canada*,[34] prior to its publication, that not only had Robert Sellar's work not been suppressed, but that I had had no difficulty in finding a copy of *The Summer of Sorrow, Abner's Device, and Other Stories* in the McGill University Library, or in purchasing a copy of the single-volume 1895 version of *Gleaner Tales* at a second-hand bookshop.[35] Controversy concerning that "diary" may have damaged—rather than assisted—the campaign. Collective historical memory had been sustained in Quebec by monuments, commemorations, and personal testimonies, as well as by unassailable empirical evidence. There was no need for "fabrication."

As early as 1897, on the fiftieth anniversary of the Great Famine, Irish Canadians and Irish Americans had gathered for a day of commemoration on Grosse Île. On that occasion they initiated planning for a permanent monument on the island. On 15 August 1909, these plans came to fruition with the unveiling by the Ancient Order of Hibernians of a large Celtic cross on the top of the cliff-face on the southwestern peninsula, which holds the mass grave cemetery, facing the shipping channel for all to see.

There are commemorative texts in English, French, and Irish on the pedestal of the cross. The Irish text reads as follows:

> *Cailleadh Clann na nGaedheal ina míltibh ar an Oileán so ar dteicheadh dhóibh ó dlighthibh na dtíoránach ngallda agus ó ghorta tréasach isna bliadhantaibh 1847-48. Beannacht dílis Dé orra. Bíodh an leacht so i gcomhartha garma agus onóra dhóibh ó Ghaedhealaibh Ameriocá. Go saoraigh Dia Éire.*

> (Literal translation by author: "Thousands of the children of the Gael died on this island having fled from the laws of foreign tyrants and from a treasonous famine in the years 1847-48. God's own blessing upon them. Let this monument be a sign of praise and honour to them from the Gaels of America. May God free Ireland!")

On closure of the quarantine station in 1937, the Department of Defence resumed full control of the island, and it was declared "a prohibited place" under the *Official Secrets Act*. Bacteriological warfare research was conducted there between 1937 and 1945, and animal virus disease research between 1952 and 1965. The island was a quarantine station for imported livestock from 1965 to 1988.

Figure 8.3. Monument near the entrance to the Victoria Bridge, Montreal
Source: Pádraig Ó Laighin.

Despite its legal status as a "forbidden" site, an Irish Canadian commemorative visit to Grosse Île was permitted under licence in 1982, and annual commemorations there resumed from 1988 onwards with the ending of animal quarantine and the relaxation of restrictions—well before the announcement or publication of development plans. These commemorations involved visits to the three main cemeteries on the island, to the 1847 hospital and other heritage buildings, to the monument dedicated to the medical doctors, and to the Celtic cross where wreaths were laid.

Near the entrance to the Victoria Bridge in Montreal is a monument whose central feature is a large black rock—called "the Stone"—with its own story engraved on its front side in large lettering, as follows: "To preserve from desecration the remains of 6,000 immigrants who died of ship fever, A.D. 1847-8. This stone is erected by the workmen of Messrs Peto. Brassey & Betts, employed in the construction of the Victoria Bridge, A.D. 1859." This monument, on the site of the mass graves of the Montreal Emigrant Hospital of 1847, sustains collective memory not just because of its visibility on a busy thoroughfare, or the trilingual interpretation on-site, but also because of walks and commemorations that have been held there by the Irish community on an annual basis since 1885 (see Figure 8.3).

Figure 8.4. Taschereau Monument (detail), Quebec City
Source: Pádraig Ó Laighin.

In 1994, Montreal City Council had proposed naming a new road through the original site of the hospital buildings nearby "Rue de Village-aux-Oies," but voted unanimously and without hesitation to apply the name "Rue des Irlandais" instead when asked to do so by myself, as chairperson of the General Assembly, in a formal presentation.

The Taschereau Monument in Quebec City is a further example of the commitment of not just the Irish community, but of the people of Quebec in general, to keeping the memory of the events at Grosse Île in 1847 alive in the popular memory. A relief on the base of the monument, erected in 1923, shows the young Elzéar-Alexandre Taschereau, later to become Archbishop of Quebec City, ministering to the sick on Grosse Île (see Figure 8.4).

EVIDENTIAL BASIS OF IDEOLOGICAL SUPPORT FOR IRISH DIMENSION

The Irish Canadian collective memory of the famine was an important factor in resisting Parks Canada's plans. Continually reinforced by monuments and commemorations, and by the family memories of those whose descendants had come through Grosse Île, that collective memory was informed also from time to time by published historical accounts and literary versions of events. Sellar's *The Summer of Sorrow*, apart from the stage Irish introduction, is an impressive literary production.[36] Robert Whyte's powerful diary, published in 1848, which appears, like most diaries published as books, to have been recollected or reconstructed after the fact, may have been influential at the time of its publication. Claims made by James Mangan in his published versions about the 1847 provenance and suppression of Sellar's *The Summer of Sorrow* had been unambiguously dismissed by Jim Jackson in 1991 and 1992, and by Jacqueline Kornblum in early 1992, before the publication of Parks Canada's proposals or the Irish community's response.[37]

While respecting the collective memory of Irish Canadians in all its dimensions, the strategic informational approach of the General Assembly was based on empirical evidence of the events of 1847 drawn from undisputed historical documents. The contemporary evidence is, in fact, much more compelling and graphically phantasmagoric than anything to be found in the diaries. This evidence includes Dr. Douglas's own accounts of ships inspected, and his annual report, as well as the evidence of the Medical Commissioners, the reports of the Emigrant Commissioners, the report of the Land and Emigration Commissioners, the report of the Montreal Immigrant Committee, the British Parliamentary Reports on the Colonies and Emigration for 1847, Adam Ferrie's pamphlet of 1847, Terence De Vere's voyage account, voluminous documentation in the contemporary press, and, most graphically, the extensive evidence presented and recorded at formal hearings of the Legislative Assembly's Special Committee of Inquiry in Montréal in 1847.[38]

Dr. Douglas, for example, wrote of his inspection of the *Virginius* at the end of July, 1847, as follows:

> The "Virginius" sailed from Liverpool, May 28, with 476 passengers. Fever and dysentery cases came on board this vessel in Liverpool, and deaths occurred before leaving the Mersey. On mustering the passengers for inspection yesterday, it was found that 106 were ill of fever, including nine of the crew, and the large number of 158 had died on the passage, including the first and second officers and seven of the crew, and the master and the steward dying, the few that were able to come on deck were ghastly yellow looking spectres, unshaven and hollow cheeked, and, without exception, the worst looking passengers I have ever seen; not more than six or eight were really healthy and able to exert themselves.[39]

While Dr. Douglas's prose is normally objective and formal, it is difficult in examples such as this one to see implications, or long-term historical consequences, any less tragic than those arising from less restrained accounts such as the 1847 report of the Montreal Immigrant Committee.

A NEW MONUMENT, AND A MORE EXPANSIVE VERSION OF CANADIAN HISTORY

The Department of Canadian Heritage commissioned a commemorative work to mark the 150th anniversary of the Great Famine and the tragedy at Grosse Île. The monument was unveiled in August 1998, and contains—engraved on glass overlooking the mass graves—the names of 6,008 people buried there, almost all Irish, and symbols for 1,545 others known to be buried there but whose names went unrecorded.

The naming of the site as Grosse Île and the Irish Memorial National Historic Site, and the commemoration there of the suffering and death of the arriving Irish immigrants and the heroism of the Canadians who assisted them, brought a dignified end to a contest over historical space, a contest that is now itself part of a more expansive version of Canadian history. ∎

NOTES

1. Historic Sites and Monuments Board of Canada, "Recommendations," 13, 18–19.
2. Canada, Environment Canada, Parks Service, *Grosse Île: Development Concept*, 47.
3. Canada, Environment Canada, Parks Service, *Grosse Île: Development Concept*, 62.
4. Canada, Environment Canada, Parks Service, *Grosse Île: Development Concept*, 11, 47.
5. Careless, *Canada: A Story of Challenge*, 147.
6. Morton, *A Short History of Canada*, 45.
7. Lower Canada, *Journals*, 464–90.
8. British Parliamentary Papers [hereafter BPP], Emigration to North America and Australia.
9. BPP, Emigration Papers Relative to Emigration to the North American Colonies, 39.
10. Supra note 7.
11. BPP, Correspondence Respecting Emigration.
12. Library and Archives Canada, "Dr. Poole's Report."

13 Province of Canada [hereafter POC], *Journals of the Legislative Assembly*, "Letter from G.M. Douglas," 19 February 1847.

14 POC, "Weekly Return of the Sick"; Archives nationales du Québec, "Registre de l'Église Catholique."

15 POC, "Letter from G.M. Douglas," 21 May 1847.

16 POC, "Letter from A.C. Buchanan"; POC, "Letter from G.M Douglas," 29 May 1847.

17 POC, "Reports from Medical Commissioners."

18 BPP, Emigration: Papers Relative to Emigration to the British Provinces, 13, 21.

19 BPP, August 1848, "Annual Report," 10.

20 BPP, Emigration: Papers Relative to Emigration to the British Provinces, 23.

21 BPP, April 1848, "Extract," 5.

22 *New Guide to Quebec and Its Environs*, 66.

23 Supra note 20, 15.

24 Canada, Environment Canada, Parks Service, Mémoires Présentés à Montréal.

25 Canada, Canadian Heritage, Parks Canada, *Report on the Public Consultation Program*, 9.

26 Ibid., 9–10.

27 Canada, Environment Canada, Parks Service, *Grosse Île: Development Concept, Information Supplement*.

28 Supra note 25, 55.

29 Canada, Environment Canada, Parks Canada, "Grosse-Île National Historic Site."

30 President of Ireland, "Address."

31 Canada, Canadian Heritage, "Copps dedicates."

32 McGowan, "Famine, Facts and Fabrication," 48.

33 Ibid., 54.

34 O'Driscoll and Reynolds, *The Untold Story*.

35 Sellar, *Gleaner Tales*.

36 Sellar, *The Summer of Sorrow*.

37 Mangan, *The Voyage of the Naparima*; Mangan, *Gerald Keegan's Famine Diary*; Jackson, "'Famine Diary,'" 27; Jackson, "The Making of a Best Sellar"; Kornblum, "Mixing Fact and Fiction."

38 POC, "Reports of the Emigrant Commissioners"; POC, Session 1848, Appendix (W.); Montréal Immigrant Committee, "Report"; BPP, April 1848, "Copy of a Despatch," 35; BPP, "Emigration: First, Second, and Third Reports"; POC, Appendix (R.R.R.), "Report."

39 Supra note 21.

WORKS CITED

Archives nationales du Québec. "Registre de l'Église Catholique de Saint-Luc-de-Grosse-Île." 4M00 0303A.

British Parliamentary Papers. April 1848. "Copy of a Despatch from Earl Grey to Governor-General, the Earl of Elgin." London: Stationery Office, 1848.

———. April 1848. "Extract from a Report of a Committee of the Executive Council on Matters of State, dated 7th December, 1847." London: Stationery Office, 1848.

———. August 1848. "Annual Report of the Medical Superintendent of the Quarantine Establishment for the year 1847." London: Stationery Office, 1848.

———. Correspondence Respecting Emigration. March 1835. "Mr. Buchanan's Report on Emigration to Upper and Lower Canada for 1834." London: House of Commons, 1835.

———. Emigration: First, Second, and Third Reports from the Select Committee on Colonization from Ireland, with Minutes of Evidence, Appendix, and Index. "Passage of Stephen E. De Vere to Province of Canada, dated November 30, 1847." 9 March 1848. London: House of Commons, 1848.

———. Emigration: Papers Relative to Emigration to the British Provinces of North America. June 1848. "Annual Report of the Chief Emigration Agent for 1847." London: Stationery Office, 1848.

———. Emigration: Papers Relative to Emigration to the North American Colonies. "Annual Report of the Chief Agent for Emigration, 1851." London: Stationery Office, 1852.

———. Emigration to North America and Australia. April 1833. "Report of the Chief Agent for the Superintendence of Emigrants to Upper and Lower Canada, on Emigration to the Canadas, for the year 1832." London: House of Commons, 1833.

Canada. Canadian Heritage, Parks Canada. *Report on the Public Consultation Program*. March 1994.

———. Canadian Heritage. "Copps dedicates 'Grosse-Île and the Irish Memorial.'" March 1996. News Release P-03/96-47 CC950797.

———. Environment Canada. Parks Service. *Grosse Île: Development Concept*. March 1992.

———. Environment Canada, Parks Service. Mémoires Présentés à Montréal, le 20 mai 1992. Briefs Presented in Montréal, May 20, 1992. "Grosse-Île: The Irish Island." 1992.

———. Environment Canada. Parks Service. *Grosse Île: Development Concept: Information Supplement*. 1992.

———. Environment Canada, Parks Canada. "Grosse-Île National Historic Site: Presentation to the Historic Sites and Monuments Board of Canada." November 1993.

Careless, J.M.S. *Canada: A Story of Challenge*. Toronto: Macmillan, 1974.

Historic Sites and Monuments Board of Canada. "Recommendations of the Historic Sites and Monuments Board of Canada." November 1993.

Jackson, Jim. "'Famine Diary'—Fact or Fiction." *Irish Times*, 14 September 1991, 27.

———. "The Making of a Best Sellar." *Irish Review* 11 (Winter 1991–92): 1–8.

Kornblum, Jacqueline. "Mixing Fact and Fiction." Rev. of *Famine Diary: Journey to a New World*, by Gerald Keegan. *Irish Literary Supplement* (Spring 1992): 10.

Library and Archives Canada. "Dr. Poole's Report on Grosse-Isle, 1834." Asiatic Cholera Returns. RG7, G 18, vol. 17.

Lower Canada. *Journals of the House of Assembly of Lower-Canada.* Session 1831–32. Quebec City: House of Assembly, 1832.

Mangan, James J. *Gerald Keegan's Famine Diary: Journey to a New World.* Dublin: Wolfhound, 1991.

———. *The Voyage of the Naparima: A Story of Canada's Island Graveyard.* Quebec City: Carraig, 1982.

McGowan, Mark. "Famine, Facts, and Fabrication: An Examination of Diaries from the Irish Famine Migration to Canada." *Canadian Journal of Irish Studies* 33, no. 2 (2007): 48–55.

Montréal Immigrant Committee. "Report of the Montréal Immigrant Committee for 1847, January 13, 1848." *Montreal Transcript*, 22 January 1848.

Morton, Desmond. *A Short History of Canada.* Edmonton: Hurtig, 1983.

New Guide to Quebec and Its Environs. Quebec City: P. Sinclair, 1851.

O'Driscoll, Robert, and Lorna Reynolds, eds. *The Untold Story: The Irish in Canada.* Toronto: Celtic Arts, 1988.

President of Ireland. "Address by the President, Mary Robinson, at Grosse Ile on 21st August, 1994." Grosse Île. August 1994.

Province of Canada. Appendix (R.R.R.). "Report of the Special Committee appointed to inquire into the management of the *Quarantine Station* at Grosse Isle, 28 July 1847." Montreal: Legislative Assembly, 1847.

Province of Canada. *Journals of the Legislative Assembly of the Province of Canada.* Session 1847. Appendix (L.). "Letter from G.M. Douglas to Civil Secretary, 19 February 1847." Montréal: Legislative Assembly, 1847.

———. "Letter from A.C. Buchanan to Civil Secretary, 29 May 1847." Montreal: Legislative Assembly, 1847.

———. "Letter from G.M. Douglas to Civil Secretary, 29 May 1847." Montreal: Legislative Assembly, 1847.

———. "Letter from G.M. Douglas to Provincial Secretary, 21 May 1847." Montreal: Legislative Assembly, 1847.

———. "Reports from Medical Commissioners to Civil Secretary, 4, 5, and 7 June 1847." Montreal: Legislative Assembly, 1847.

———. "Reports of the Emigrant Commissioners." 26 July 1847. Montreal: Legislative Assembly, 1847.

———. Session 1848. Appendix (W.). "Report of the Colonial Land and Emigration Commissioners for 1847, 22 March 1848." Montreal: Legislative Assembly, 1848.

———. "Weekly Return of the Sick in the Quarantine Hospital, Grosse Isle, from the 8th to the 15th May, 1847." Montreal: Legislative Assembly, 1847. Print.

Sellar, Robert. *Gleaner Tales.* Huntingdon: Gleaner, 1895.

———. *The Summer of Sorrow, Abner's Device, and Other Stories.* Huntingdon: Gleaner, 1895.

NINE

Environmental Exposure:
Two films "de légitime défense": Richard Desjardins and Robert Monderie: *L'erreur boréale / Forest Alert* (1999) and *Trou Story / The Hole Story* (2011)

Rachel Killick

> Moi, je ne les crois plus [les hommes d'affaires et les hommes politiques] quand ils disent qu'ils font dans les normes et j'ai ... maintenant le sentiment [que j'ai] le droit d'entrer comme en légitime défense ... avec les armes qui sont les miennes.... C'est la guerre.[1]

INTRODUCTION

In **Montreal and Quebec City,** autumn 2011 was marked, as in other Western cities from London to San Francisco, by the occupation of public space by activists protesting against the excesses and failures of the capitalist system. In Montreal, the occupation of Victoria Square by "le Camp des Indignés" serendipitously coincided with the annual Montreal International Documentary Film Festival and the first showings in the city of several environmental documentaries. These included *Surviving Progress / Survivre au progrès* by Harold Crooks and Mathieu Roy, based on the global panoramic sketched out by Canadian Ronald Wright in *A Short History of Progress* (2004), and three films inspired by the activities of the Osisko mining corporation in Malartic, a small gold-mining town in the Abitibi region of Quebec. The three Québécois films were *Trou Story* / *The Hole Story* by singer/songwriter and environmental activist Richard Desjardins and his long-term documentary partner Robert Monderie; *L'or des autres* [*Other people's gold*] by Simon Plouffe; and *La règle d'or* [*The rule of gold*] by Nicholas Paquet. Each, in its own way, offers a critical examination of the environmental and social impacts of the Malartic mine,[2] but this chapter focuses on *Trou Story*, which sets Malartic within a broader context of mining in Ontario and Quebec. It also considers Desjardins and Monderie's other big documentary success, *L'erreur boréale* / *Forest Alert* (1999), exploring in both cases the creative contribution of the artist as "public intellectual," the media exposure that such a personality can harness to a cause, and the impact of Desjardin's celebrity profile in ensuring crucial publicity for his social and environmental activism and for his defence of the landscapes and ways of life of his home region of northern Quebec.

RICHARD DESJARDINS

From the start of his adult life in the 1970s, Richard Desjardins has always been a strong supporter of social and environmental causes, but his high-profile status dates only from the early 1990s. Born in 1948 in the company mining town of Rouyn-Noranda in Quebec's northwest Abitibi region, he regularly witnessed as a child the exhausted mineworkers returning home from their shifts.[3] His own father Yves was not, however, a miner but a "technicien forestier" in the other big local industry, the timber trade. Desjardins, rejecting both of these industrial employments, opted for an alternative odd-job and travelling lifestyle, while also beginning his musical career in local gigs with one of his older brothers. Slowly, over the 1970s and 1980s, he made his separate name as a solo singer/songwriter, often focusing on issues of politics and social justice, sometimes using a pithy, *joual*-like sociolect, sometimes a highly literary style, and providing his own accompaniment on guitar or piano. This combination did not, however, fit the formula of the mass appeal Québécois "pop" song à la Céline Dion, typical of the politically apathetic 1980s, and Desjardins's success at this point was limited to a small but committed alternative audience.[4]

The reigniting of the sovereigntist debate following the failure of the Meech Lake negotiations in 1989 and the Charlottetown Accord in 1992 transformed the musical environment, reactivating the legacy of the activist *chansonniers* of the 1970s but in a reactualized, updated mode that reflected the social and political context of the 1990s. Desjardins's polemical approach in his music and film work was now more closely aligned to broad public sentiment, and his profile an as artist and environmental activist grew accordingly.[5] His breakthrough to wider prominence was definitively achieved with his participation in Pierre Falardeau's film *Le Party* (1990), a gritty piece that portrayed the harsh realities of life in jail. Desjardins wrote the music for the film and had a minor role in it. As a tattooed, hard-bitten, foul-mouthed inmate, *"un bum-poète"* who echoes the events of Johnny Cash's 1968 visit to Folsom State Prison, he steps forward to vent the anger of the prisoners against their guards in a song ("Le Screw") with an even more violent lyric than that of Cash's "Folsom Prison Blues." His association with the high-profile polemicist Falardeau moved his career decisively forward, propelling him from "l'avant-garde bohême ... à l'avant-garde consacré" (*bohemian fringe ... to the official avant-garde*) and providing him with a stepping stone "pour ... sortir du sous-champ de la production restreinte et entrer doucement dans la grande production" (*from a small-scale niche audience to a mainstream commercial one*).[7] His status as a "poète intellectuel"[8] was considerably increased thereafter by the award of multiple prizes,[9] success in France, the 1991 publication of the words of some of his songs, *Paroles de chansons*, and by numerous interviews on TV and radio.

Desjardins's associations with documentary go back to his early career with *Comme des chiens en pacage* (1977),[10] which depicts the fiftieth-anniversary celebrations of Rouyn-Noranda, and *Mouche à feu (Firefly)* (1982), a portrait of the Métis guitarist Ken Wallingford, both made with Robert Monderie. They also include his musical scores for five other 1980s films, including, notably, *Noranda* (1984) by Robert Monderie and Daniel Corvec, which highlighted the arsenic and lead contamination produced by Noranda's mining operations in the Abitibi region. The earlier *Comme des chiens en pacage*, by contrast, covered not only the mining industry but also life in Rouyn-Noranda more broadly, including social and cultural activities, occupations other than mining, and small-town politics.[11] This first Desjardins–Monderie documentary offered a clear view of economic difficulties, privation, and exploitation, but though certainly critical of the mining employers, it was not yet as overtly polemical as their later productions would be.[12]

L'erreur boréale / Forest Alert (1999)

The lumber industry had been the subject of an important 1962 Québécois documentary, Arthur Lamothe's *Bûcherons de la Manouane (Lumberjacks of the Manouane River)*, which focused on the industry's harsh conditions in the remote winter logging camps and on the back-breaking exploitation of the workers, themes that

Desjardins also treats subsequently in his songs, monologues, and documentaries.[13] Lamothe's film does not, however, address the issues of sustainability and environmental degradation, central to the debates of the late twentieth and early twenty-first centuries.

L'erreur boréale, in contrast, has two main objectives: to expose the inadequate government regulation that allows the unbridled exploitation and destruction of publicly owned natural resources by greedy corporations; and to demolish the illusion that natural resources are inexhaustible, no matter how they are treated.[14] Europeans, Desjardins argues, long ago lost that illusion, but it has remained persistently present among Canadians and Quebecers, most of whom live in urban centres in the south, and whose thinking has been shaped by the myth of an endless northern "wilderness," which few people have ever experienced directly.[15] In contrast to this hazy, ill-informed view, *L'erreur boréale* insists that the northern forests need to be managed carefully to ensure their survival and that the health and well-being of the soils, lakes, and rivers, the flora and fauna, and the region's human inhabitants depend on sound environmental practices. What is happening instead is the desertification of inadequately protected public land. Huge, minimally regulated and monitored companies have moved in, clear-cut the forest, then moved on. The deforestation they leave behind has exposed poor soils to erosion, changed the ecological balance of the lakes, dramatically affected the variety of the region's plant and animal life, and opened the land and water to chemical pollution as pesticides are brought in to treat the few weakened and disease-prone tree species that remain.

In *L'erreur boréale*, Desjardins makes an urgent call for action. He recognizes the huge economic importance of the lumber industry for Canada and Quebec overall (C$10 billion of exports in 1999), and especially for towns like Trois-Rivières that are wholly reliant upon it, but he also points out that investment in forest management and regeneration remains minimal—a mere C$150 million, a massive imbalance that has gone unaddressed for fifty years, while the forests have shrunk by half, with the half that remains, most of it in the far north, now under aggressive attack.

Desjardins's message is a powerful one, but to convince the public and the politicians, his talents as writer and performer were crucial. In contrast to *Comme des chiens en pacage*, in which the various individuals are left to speak for themselves, it is Desjardin's charismatic voice and persona that provide shape and atmosphere for *L'erreur boréale*.[16] A narrative technique borrowed from his songs lends intimacy and credibility to his presentation. A striking example is the film's opening where the singer, reminiscing with his father outside the family's woodland "chalet," introduces viewers to the forest that was an enchanted part of his childhood. This initial conversation sets out the film's twofold agenda, not through ideological statement but through a characteristic blend of poetry and song. Desjardins establishes his anti-capitalist stance with a few lines from "La berceuse aux étoiles" (*Lullaby to the stars*), accompanied by the soft chords of his guitar: "Pendant que les heureux, les riches et les grands / Reposent dans la soie...";[17] he follows this with the lyrically expressed environmentalism of his father's recitation—in English—of some lines from (Alfred) Joyce Kilmer's 1913 poem "Trees":

> I think that I shall never see
> A poem so lovely as a tree
> A tree that may in summer wear
> A nest of robins in her hair
> A tree that looks at God all day
> And lifts her leafy arms to pray.[18]

The ensuing investigation of the lumber industry is shaped by a script that offers initial on-the-ground observation and discussion between Desjardins and his father; a view of the business environment through Desjardins's attendance at a Domtar annual general meeting in Montreal; a brief history of Quebec's lumber industry; and finally, a summary of the parlous state of the forest at the close of the 1990s and the political actions this demands. Desjardins serves throughout as anchorman, orchestrating a narrative that skilfully interweaves, in contrasting or complementary fashion, a multitude of divergent voices and opinions, featuring ineffectual politicians; eye-to-the-main-chance businessmen who know nothing about trees, only about profits; employees, qualified and casual, most of them expressing concern over the prospects of the forest and forestry; small local businesses and outfitters; a representative of the First Nations;[19] and scientists and academics. Highlights include the astonishing revelation by one government official that the Ministry of Natural Resources is empowered to look after lakes and campsites within the forest but not the forest itself; the glib business-speak of the Domtar company executives at the company AGM and their smoothly efficient smothering of Desjardins's awkward questions; the angry dismissal—"Question niaiseuse!" (*Tomfool question!*)—by one bristling shareholder when Desjardins asks whether he is concerned about the health of the forest; the prevarication and obfuscation of Gaston Day, the official Wood Companies PR representative, regarding the requirement to "inform" or to "consult" and what Day sees as the contentious issue of the "rights" of other users.[20] In counterpoint, a tourist pilot tells of the substantial detour he now must make to avoid showing his clients a deforested desert; and a First Nations trapper highlights, in his native Cree, the wanton destruction of a forest that had sustained the life of his ancestors from time immemorial.

Desjardins intervenes at carefully chosen intervals, sometimes speaking directly to the camera, sometimes in voice-over, to underscore the size of the forest and its problems with readily understandable statistics and analogies. For example, since the Quebec forest is a public forest, everyone in Quebec owns—in theory—twenty baseball diamonds worth of forest; in 1996, the Domtar shareholders met to divide up C$300 million in profits; accelerating production means that 1,000,000 lumber trucks are loaded per annum, a fleet that bumper to bumper would stretch halfway around the earth; and forty-two of the recognized fifty-five trapping territories of the Cree have been pillaged by lumber companies on the basis of their government-awarded forest management contracts (FMCS).

This ability to pinpoint and encapsulate translates also into mastery of the memorable one-liner: writing to the government, and receiving a reply from the lumber company, is "like writing to God and getting a reply from the Devil"; the Sylva software, used to model forestry resources long-term on scientifically unsound premises, "imposes a response, rather than posing a question"; the 1998 creation, by the Quebec Ministry of Natural Resources, of an agency to manage the forest that is entirely controlled by the lumber companies, is "like setting the fox to watch over the chickens," or, to rephrase this idea in business terms: "After privatising the natural resource, they have privatised the ministry." At the end of the film, speaking directly to the camera, Desjardins moves into clear attack mode with an incisive summary of key principles and consequential action points: (1) according to the law established in the nineteenth century, the Quebec forest is publicly owned; (2) the Quebec government, through the *Forest Act* (Law 150) of 1987, wrongfully conceded and guaranteed control of the entire forest to big business; (3) this law must be renegotiated publicly.

Supporting or contesting the spoken word, the visual image, in a multiplicity of modes, provides invaluable illustration and reinforcement of Desjardins' message. Factual visual aids—maps and clips from industrial and scientific government documents and documentaries—provide an objective accompaniment, sometimes in black and white, sometimes in faded 1950s colour, to his historical presentation of the lumber industry, from the colonial era, to the era of mechanical harvesting, to the large-scale exploitation of wood for the construction industry and for newsprint, to the chemical control of pests and disease in an increasingly monocultural forest. Supplementing this with poignant social commentary, black-and-white clips from Lamothe's *Bûcherons de la Manouane* highlight the backbreaking toil of men and horses in the snows of winter. Elsewhere, talking head shots visually establish an immediate impression of contrasting lifestyles and behaviours: the smooth, unlined faces of the businessmen; the deep wrinkles of the Cree trapper; thoughtful academics among their books; blue-collar lumbermen in open-necked shirts, or hard-hatted and protectively clothed among their destructive and dangerous machinery. Maintaining the dynamic of film, the camera slips rapidly between close-up and speech direct to camera, and wide-angle aerial shots with voice-over, that work in ironic counterpint with the remarks of the interviewees, or else as a tragic reinforcement of them. Thus, for example, the voice of Domtar's president and CEO is heard expatiating on the company's philosophy of sustainability as the camera roams across a landscape bare of any trees; the Cree trapper speaks of the devastation of Cree trapping grounds as aerial tracking shots reveal, first, the wide and apparently untroubled expanse of the Waswanipi River and its forested banks, and then, shockingly, the thinness of the stand of trees and the bare land beyond them; and Desjardins himself, against what appears to be an aerial view of dense woodland, speaks of a "superforest," which a change of camera shot reveals to be nothing more than a nursery of waist-high saplings.

Over and above all, Jacques Leduc's camerawork, assisted by a musical score that mingles plaintively isolated chords with snatches of relentlessly accelerating rhythm, brilliantly captures both the beauty of the forest and the traumatic impact of its mechanized destruction. Close-ups of the leafy splendour and the dappled sun and shade of the forest stand in stark and shocking contrast to panoramic aerial views of a devastated landscape, even as another telling visual contrast foregrounds each individual tree, in quasi-human terms, as a living presence, tragically destroyed in the briefest of instants by the monstrous teeth and unfeeling metal of industrial felling and debarking machinery.

L'erreur boréale: reception and impact

Desjardins ends his film with a question for the future posed through the reactions of a group of graduating forestry students at Université Laval, who, symptomatically, have not yet even visited the northern forest! Intercutting and superimposition of student discussion on the denuded boreal landscapes highlight their ignorance and also their shock, but skepticism is expressed—and not only by Desjardins—as to whether these emotions, under company pressure, will translate on the ground into any lasting commitment to accountability and responsibility. As to the implicit question, how will the Québécois public, and its government, react to the environmental loss and degradation revealed in Desjardins' film?, *L'erreur boréale* attracted strong praise in the media for both its poetic quality and its significance as an important topic of public interest.[21] More crucially, the film had a major public policy impact resulting in the establishing in autumn 2003 of the Coulombe Commission for the study of public forest management in Quebec. With continuing pressure from Desjardins and others, the recommendations of the Commission's 2004 report were implemented in the *Forest Act* of 2007.[22] The executive summary of *Forests: Building a Future for Québec* (2008) notes, however, that the new act's many positive changes have still "failed to generate either public confidence in the way the forests are managed or a consensus among stakeholders concerning priorities for the future" (3). These concerns played a significant part in the debate around the Plan Nord introduced by Jean Charest's Liberal government in 2011 and continue to preoccupy both the timber trade and the environmentalists.

Trou Story / The Hole Story (2011)

The huge success of *L'erreur boréale* ensured substantial media coverage for *Trou Story*, as well as strong interest from environmentalists, the Québécois general public, and, not least, the mining industry. Its well-publicized world premiere took place on Sunday afternoon, 30 October 2011, at the International Cinema Festival of Abitibi-Témiscamingue, a festival sponsored—ironically in this case—by the mining companies Noranda/Xstrata and Vale.[23] It was shown in Montreal one week later, first in French, then one week later again, in English. As a native of Rouyn-Noranda, Desjardins had been preoccupied throughout his career by the crudely exploitative behaviour of the mining industry, not only in his early films *Comme des chiens en pacage* and *Noranda*, but also in songs such as "16-03-48" (Desjardins's birth-date) and "Les Fros." The specific triggers for his renewed critique were, first, his involvement with the environmental protection group L'Action boréale and the constant obstacles posed to its work by the pre-emptive land claims of mining prospectors,[24] and second, the environmental and social debate around the renewed open-cast mining of gold—a largely useless metal in Desjardins's view[25]—by the Montreal-based company Osisko. Built originally as a gold-mining settlement and the subject of a repeated cycle of exploitation and abandonment, Malartic had seemed a town in terminal decline. Osisko's discovery of substantial new reserves beneath its southern section, coupled with a steep rise in world gold prices, had decisively reversed that trend, bringing, it would seem, a welcome boost to a dying local economy. Desjardins and Monderie's documentary does not contest the importance of local jobs; nevertheless, it uses the example of Malartic to underscore the environmental costs of mineral extraction—costs that mining companies have long preferred to ignore and for which they have regularly sought to abrogate responsibility.[26] As in *L'erreur boréale*, Desjardins and Monderie emphasize (1) the lack of effective government control over natural resources, which should by rights have the status of public assets; (2) the unacceptable disconnect between private corporations and their shareholders, and the human and environmental impacts of industrial activity on the ground; and (3) the unfairly skewed apportioning of profits and costs to the advantage of business and to the detriment of the local Québécois population and of Québécois taxpayers in general.

In addressing these points, *Trou Story* deploys a more strongly historical treatment than *L'erreur boréale*, in which the historical look at the lumber industry was neatly subsumed within the narrative body of the film. *Trou Story*, by contrast, has two parts. The first and substantially longer section is composed largely of fascinating archival material that vividly traces the successive establishment and despoiling, over the late nineteenth century and the first half of the twentieth, of the Ontario towns of Sudbury (copper and nickel), Cobalt (silver), Timmins (gold), and the Quebec town of Rouyn-Noranda (copper). The narrative relentlessly foregrounds the miserable and often lethal conditions of the unfortunate miners of the past, starkly contrasting their exhausting and dangerous work, dire living conditions, and lack of bargaining power with the ruthlessness of the employers and the uncaring ignorance of the fat-cat mining magnates of the Toronto Stock Exchange. Even respected politicians, notably Wilfrid Laurier, are brought to book for their unquestioning receipt of substantial mining dividends and their bland disregard of the miners' plight.[27]

Voice-over narration and comment are provided throughout this section by Desjardins. As previously in *L'erreur boréale*—and even more importantly here, given the emphasis on historical detail—his trademark gravelly voice, feel for the telling statistic, and succinct highlighting of uncomfortable paradoxes and tragic ironies are key to holding the attention of viewers and guiding them through a mass of unfamiliar information. The suppressed and tragic tale of subterranean secrets and eviscerated landscapes, suggested by the punning title, attracts a plethora of carefully selected details that insistently shape and punctuate the sorry catalogue of greed, exploitation, neglect, and misery. In the early twentieth century, life expectancy for miners was 45 years, and the maximum fine for company negligence was C$100; there was no rescue team on hand in Timmins for the Hollinger Mine fire of 1928, and help had to come from Pennsylvania, arriving 22 hours later. Thirty-nine men died in that disaster.

Pithy commentary and memorable ironies add further force to the narrative. The United States invaded Canada in the early twentieth century "not with arms but with cash"; Finns coming to Canada for three times their pay in rural Europe literally "dug their own graves" among the lung-clogging clouds of dust created by "widow-maker" drills; the 1898 Spanish–American War in Cuba and then in the Philippines was won by nickel from Sudbury, which was used to make the steel for American battleships, not one of which was lost in the fighting. During the First World War, the Germans killed Canadians with bullets made of Sudbury nickel, and the town, with all of its topsoil removed, looked, according to one returning soldier, just like a Great War battlefield.

Voices other than Desjardins's are rare in this first and longer section of the documentary. Only when the historical overview reaches the 1970s do talking heads take over the presentation. Former miners recall the harsh conditions of the past and the protracted struggle for unionization, but Desjardins also allows representatives of modern mining to speak. They are interviewed in their computerized environments above and below ground, or out in the field, disposing 'ecologically' of the mine slurry.[28] The new downside, as various miners point out, is that mechanization, while it has eased the physical demands of mining, has led to a loss of jobs and of hard-won bargaining power.[29] Meanwhile, pollution problems have not gone away; indeed, as Desjardins is at pains to illustrate, they may even have intensified. Copper mining in Rouyn-Noranda has ceased, but the company's smelter—shown in its overly close proximity to a residential area—is now recycling heavy metals from across North America, exposing the neighbourhood to high levels of chemical pollution. The choice is a stark one between employment and health. A local man carrying a small child speaks of welcome well-paid jobs for the sake of which he and others are apparently prepared to accept the environmental risks, including the risks to their children; the local doctor, meanwhile, equivocates over the possible short- and long-term health effects of environmental pollution versus the stress of unemployment. The defeated-looking mayor of Sudbury and his Val d'Or counterpart complete the gallery of talking heads and opinions, emphasizing the minimal contribution made by the mining companies to local taxes and infrastructure and the chronic inadequacy of vital municipal funding.

Mirroring the twists, turns and questionings of Desjardins' opening narrative and the subsequent comments of his interviewees, the visuals map and pinpoint both irrefutable realities and distortions of perception. Tracking shots in modern colour lead the eye of the viewer through the hole in the hillside into the mysterious world of the mine, and then deep within its tunnels and deep into the mining past of Ontario and Quebec. Archival photos and film footage then take over, confronting the modern spectator with the lost places and people of another age. The starkness of black and white both heightens and makes strange the portrayal of deprivation: the dangerously ramshackle mines and their cramped subterranean workings; the gauntness of the miners and the constricted environment of their harsh manual labour, their rickety poverty-stricken cabins and chaotic shanty towns. Conversely it gives an old-fashioned monumentality to the shot of an impressive American warship untouched by battle, and an aura of faded, outdated privilege to the spectacle of industrial barons at a luxurious stock exchange dinner. Regularly intercutting this succession of black and white and often static images, modern aerial views and travelling shots in startling sandy ochre or moonscape ashy white, set off by the blue of the sky or the green of distant trees, contrastively emphasize, by the striking impact of their visual effect, the overwhelming dereliction of degraded terrain, polluted ponds, and leaking arsenic deposits. Soundtrack arches across the years, mournful chords on strings or guitar and staccato or percussive passages, discreetly and evocatively linking the metallic clink of pick and drill on rock with the forlorn splash of dripping water and the hollow creaks and echoes of abandoned underground tunnels. The few departures from these plaintive modes include snatches of an accordion or brass band at company or municipal functions. Most telling and poignant, though, as an accompaniment to images of the hard-pressed miners, are the resolutely upbeat "Cobalt Song" (1928)[30] and a stirring modern equivalent, "War Down Below," from the album *Waiting for the Cage* (1996) by the group Grievous Angels.[31]

Osisko's reopening of gold mining in Malartic completes the documentary offering a brief textbook example of conflicting priorities and perceptions and a reprise in miniature of Desjardins's presentational approach. The opening shot—a festive parade through the town—is the backdrop for a voice-over summary by Desjardins of the boom-and-bust cycle of Malartic's mining past, the economic significance of Osisko's arrival, and the perhaps collusive association between business and government—a point repeated later through the juxtaposed shots of a public consultation on the project and Osisko's twilight moving of a house to a new location, following pre-emptive arrangements with local householders. A series of landscape shots then strikingly captures some of the environmental and human costs of the Osisko project: boarded-up homes along an empty road, which the filmmakers crosscut with one resident's account of the stupefying scale of the current Osisko mining operation;[32] an aerial panorama of the town, amputated on its southern flank by the barren terrain of the mine; and, finally, a zoom shot from above of the house of the last resister, its thin fringe of surrounding greenery sharp against the grey of the mining site—an image of displacement and loss, of the "little man" struggling in vain against a corporate monster, which became the emblematic and emotive poster for the film.[33] The presentation then reverts, as in the first section of the documentary, to contrasting interviews and talking heads. Two elderly couples, filmed in their homes adjacent to the mine, but not part of the company's relocation program, note the loss of amenity and value of their homes, which they now have little hope of ever selling. A woman, captured in back view, gazes through her window in the fading light at the earth wall of the mine that now forms her horizon. In contrast, André Vézeau, the mayor of Malartic, a thrusting forty-something, is resolutely bullish on the benefits of Osisko's presence, as well as cynical regarding the reasons for dissent; and a participant at the promotional fair for the Prospectors and Developers Association of Canada lauds the low-risk investment climate in Quebec and the hands-off approach of the Quebec government.

In a pattern similar to the ending of *L'erreur boréale*, the cue is thus provided for Desjardins's action points: increased environmental protection as a key priority for sustainable development; strong legislative measures to ensure Quebec's control over its natural resources; much tighter financial and regulatory arrangements with the mining companies. His closing words are carefully selected for maximum iconic and emotive effect. They hark back to his use, earlier in the documentary, of a clip of René Lévesque as Minister of Natural Resources in 1962 impressing on Quebecers the urgency of effective government control over business corporations. "It's about time," says Desjardins, reprising the famous slogan of the Quiet Revolution, "that we become masters in our own house."

Trou Story: Reception and Impact

Despite its compelling narrative and visuals, the impact of *Trou Story* is in many ways less direct and less personal than that of *L'erreur boréale*, the substantial emphasis on historical material creating a more academic and distant effect. Compounding this impression, the lunar devastation of abandoned mining sites, though certainly shocking, lacks the immediate poignancy of the tree as a living being, whose abrupt dispatch is readily apprehended anthropomorphically as an image of human vulnerability and mortality. Nevertheless, *Trou Story* generated immediate controversy and debate—a tribute, it seems, to the high profile achieved by Desjardins with *L'erreur boréale*.[34] In the event, the emphasis on history came as a considerable relief to a nervous mining sector, which was quick to argue that irresponsible mining was a thing of the past.Even so, in advance of the film's release, the mining companies seem to have been less sanguine, attempting, according to Desjardins, to stifle the impact of the initial Abitibi showing by trying—unsuccessfully, as it turned out—to buy up large numbers of the tickets. At the same time, the television channels were full of advertisements by Osisko and by the mining sector's public relations arm, Minalliance. The Osisko publicity focused on job opportunities and featured three bronzed and smiling employees, male and female, kitted out in their mining gear against a background of blue sky and sunshine, with a short piece of dialogue from each in which they enthusiastically outlined their involvement in the company. The same publicity campaign ran a full-page, full-colour advertisement in the newspapers emblazoned with the words: "Nous sommes des employés, nous sommes des actionnaires, nous sommes Osisko [*We are the employees, we are the shareholders, we are Osisko*]." Minalliance, taking a different line, attempted to emphasize the quasi-magical nature of the metals and minerals themselves.[35] An excellent sense of their television advertisement, a version of which was reproduced in newspapers, is provided by Nathalie Petrowski in her scathing criticism in *La Presse*:

> Cette pub présente une énorme et scintillante roche sur un fond noir qui rappelle un écrin de velours. [The rock in question was in the shape of Quebec.] Une musique vaguement disco joue en sourdine pendant que la voix suave de chambre à coucher d'un acteur payé très cher pour faire le Gino nous susurre à l'oreille: «Cette roche est une roche sexy. Partout dans le monde on se l'arrache. On en fait des puces électroniques, de la fibre optique, des voitures hybrides et tout ce qui reste à imaginer. Et comme cette roche est québécoise, elle est encore plus sexxxyyy! L'industrie minérale québécoise, bâtie sur du solide.»

> [*This ad shows an enormous, scintillating chunk of rock against a black background resembling a velvet jewel case. Some vaguely disco music plays softly while the suave bedroom voice of an actor highly paid to play the gigolo, murmurs in our ear: This rock is a sexy rock. All over the world people can't get enough of it. They make electronic chips with it, optical fibres, hybrid cars and everything that still has to be imagined. And as that rock is Quebec rock, it's even more sexxxyyy! The Quebec mineral industry, a winner through and through.*]

Many newspapers extended the pun in the documentary's title when crafting headlines for their articles and reviews: "Grise mine" and "Pour que le Québec ait meilleure mine," or changing language and metaphor: "Digging up the dirt," or, with an eye to the broader political horizon: "Les Québécois perdront-ils leur Nord?"[36] These articles introduced a variety of opposing viewpoints, many of them determinedly and explicitly partisan. Thus André Duchesne's article, "Les Abitibiens divisés," focused on the pro-industry views of politicians and business people: Serge Simard, the Quebec Minister of Natural Resources and Wildlife, PQ deputy, François Gendron; and Oskisko's human resources director, Mario Paquin. It concluded, however, in apparent counterbalance, with a comment from Jacques Matte, director of the Abitibi-Témiscamingue Film Festival (FCIAT), that the mining companies sponsoring the event had in no way sought to have Desjardins's film excluded. But the objectivity of this declaration was somewhat compromised by the mention in bold following the article: "Les frais de ce reportage ont été payés par le FCIAT" (which was hardly, it would seem, a disinterested, self-supporting entity). A subsequent article, also in *La Presse*, continued to promote the industry's case; in it, Valérie Fillion, Dominique Dionne, and Claudine Renauld, respectively identified as managing director of L'Association de l'exploration minière du Québec, president of the Conseil d'administration de l'Association minière du Quebec, and managing director of Minalliance, insisted that the film showed mining as it used to be in the bad old days, but that things had now greatly changed.[37]

In contrast to these aggressively positive statements, Ugo Lapointe, identified as co-founder and spokesman for the Coalition pour que le Québec ait meilleure mine, writing in *La Presse* (3 November 2011), considered the film "plus actuel que jamais [*more topical than ever*]," in that it showed for the first time elected representatives, former elected representatives, former civil servants, and sons and daughters of miners denouncing current practices in mining, as anxieties mounted regarding the much debated Bill 14 *On the mines* and Jean Charest's Plan Nord for the development of northern Quebec and the many mining operations it envisaged. The human suffering involved in the displacement of some Malartic residents, stressed by Natalie Petrowski in her critique in *La Presse* of the Minalliance publicity, was brought to the fore in an emotional open letter addressed to Osisko shareholders by the displaced Malartic residents Mario Gagnon, Alain Lahaie, and Carl-Hugues Leblanc, representing le Regroupement des citoyens du quartier sud de Malartic and printed in *Le Devoir* on 11 November 2011. Interestingly, though, as with Odile Tremblay's articles of 29 and 31 October, *Le Devoir* made a point of presenting both sides of the argument, placing this letter in the section "Idées," and setting its three columns of text and accompanying photo in parallel with a two-column text "Pour en finir avec le cas Malartic" [*Malartic: to put the record straight*]" by the well-known Quebec economist, businessman, and political adviser Marcel Côté, "originaire de Malartic ..., fondateur de SECOR[38] et administrateur d'Osisko depuis 2010." Côté's text, again from an interested party, presented an account in measured terms of Osisko's activities in Malartic. It stressed the town's sharp decline as all its industries disappeared, the last being the Domtar sawmill in 2005, the consequent enthusiasm of the majority of its few remaining residents for the renewal of mining, the concomitant regional investment, the new employment opportunities, immediate and secondary, and the resultant social revival of the town. He accepted—with, it could be argued, some significantly disingenous glossing over, since only the transitory nuisances of noise and dust were mentioned—that there were inevitable environmental impacts. He also accepted that the life of the new mine would probably not exceed twenty years. But he also pointed out that a dying Québécois town was being given a chance to get back on its feet and to plan properly for that future, by a company founded and developed by Quebeckers. While Côté's argument skated over long-term environmental concerns such as the permanent scarring of the landscape and the short- and long-term impacts of toxic wastes on the land, lakes, and rivers, as graphically and disturbingly explored by Desjardins and Monderie, the filmmakers had in fact acknowledged some of Côté's points, and had given some weight to the economic needs of the Abitibi region, thus escaping the charge of simplistic nimbyism. In this, their film differed sharply from the films of Simon Plouffe and Nicholas Paquet, which focus very specifically, indeed more or less exclusively, on the unhappiness of a small number of long-term residents of Malartic.[39]

WHAT HAS CHANGED SINCE THE MAKING OF *TROU STORY*?

In April 2011 the Malartic mine poured its first gold bar; on 17 June 2011, it began operating on a commercial basis. Meanwhile, an early report on the impacts of the mine, commissioned by a follow-up committee, the Comité du suivi du projet de la compagnie minière Osisko, produced inconclusive results regarding the benefits and disadvantages, and consequential stress levels, of Osisko's operations.[40] Then in early autumn of 2012, the full environmental impacts of noise and dust, summarily dismissed in Marcel Côté's 2011 article, were headline news on several occasions as Osisko was forced to wait for formal one-off government authorization for some exceptionally large-scale and lengthy blasting needed to demolish some of the town's old mine tunnels. Since then, however, according to an article in the *Northern Miner* of 13 November 2013, community relations have improved, with the Malartic mine (according to its owner) "probably the quietest in the world at this point." In counterpoint to *Trou Story*, and building on its 2011 advertisements, the Osisko website now offers its own highly polished version of the company's inception, development, and achievements and the benefits it has brought and continues to bring to Malartic and its residents. At the same time, though, stills from *Trou Story* (and also from Desjardins and Monderie's 2007 documentary *Le peuple invisible*) have been on open-air display at the Place Émilie Gamelin in the centre of Montreal, under the auspices of the Mouvement Art Public, ensuring the continuing presence of the debate in the public eye.

On the political front, the Quebec general elections in September 2012 saw the defeat of Charest's Liberals and the installation of a minority Parti Québécois government. In a campaign speech of 25 August 2012, the PQ leader, Pauline Marois, proposed a substantial increase in mining royalties and soon after signalled a revised approach to a "Plan Nord pour tous." In autumn 2012, the PQ involved itself with one element of the old Plan Nord, renegotiating with the diamond miner Stornoway Diamond the extension of Route 167 to the Monts Otish, and thereby incurring the disfavour of both its Liberal opponents and dissident regional interests.[41] In 2013 it nevertheless attempted to go ahead with reform, issuing a draft regulation on mining site restoration (13 February 2013), tabling a Plan Nord consultation paper on its proposed new mining royalty regime (March 2013), and following this in autumn 2013 with a draft bill, Bill 43, intended to replace the 1988 Mining Act. Again, however, no one was satisfied. The proposed assignment to the Minister of Natural Resources of a veto power over all mining projects was disliked both by mining companies and by environmentalists, each side seeing it as a doorway for lobbying. The mining companies, facing a more difficult world market than in 2011, feared for their profit margins under the proposed new royalty regime; the Liberals, whose own two attempts to reform the Mining Act had been scuppered by the PQ when it was in opposition, were only too ready in their turn to vote down the PQ government's proposal. As a result, the draft bill was thrown out by the Quebec National Assembly on 30 October 2013. As the title of a *Globe and Mail* article by Sophie Cousineau neatly summarized it on 13 November 2013: "Quebec mining reforms mired in the bottomless pit of politics."[42]

The mining corporations and their investors were relieved that the bill failed but also aware that the issues it raised have not gone away and that Quebec may become a less attractive and less competitive option for future investment.

Meanwhile, increasing public concerns about environmental pollution and climate change, intensified by the potential encroachment of mineral and energy exploration on more populated areas, is stimulating more proactive local approaches to proposed corporate activities. The rejection of shale gas exploration in the St. Lawrence Valley, the debate over the suggested reversal of oil flow in Enbridge's Pipeline 9 between Montreal and Sarnia, Ontario, continuing unease around the Alberta Oil Sands, and concerns about the transportation of oil following the 2013 Lac Mégantic disaster[43] are all significant examples of this trend. Academic studies of these problems geared to a broad audience have encouraged a more inquiring public mindset. Recent examples include Alain Deneault and William Sacher's *Paradis sous terre. Comment le Canada est devenu la plaque tournante de l'industrie minière mondiale* (Montréal, 2012) and two books by Normand Mousseau: *La révolution des gaz de schiste* (2010) and *Le défi des ressources minières* (2012).[44]

CONCLUSION

Environment, Government, and Business

The broader environmental and political context for the militant approach of Desjardins and Monderie in their two documentaries is a perceived lack of government and public control over Quebec's natural resources to the advantage of corporate business and to the detriment of all Quebecers.[45] With regard to *L'erreur boréale*, some improvement has clearly been achieved, but management of the forest as a sustainable resource remains a significant matter of concern. As for mining, the central issues for Desjardins and Monderie in *Trou Story* are still the unprotected nature of public land, its vulnerability to unsupervised claims, private appropriation and environmental contamination, and the absence of an effective regulatory framework to ensure responsible corporate behaviour and appropriate royalties and infrastructure contributions. On the federal level, the Harper government's refusal to sign up to post-Kyoto objectives highlighted around the globe Canada's dismal environmental record, and the 27 March 2012 federal budget (Economic Action Plan 2012) of Jim Flaherty, the Conservative finance minister, under the debatable heading "Responsible Resource Development," promised "to streamline the review process for major economic projects, support consultation with the aboriginal peoples, and to strength pipeline and marine life safety"—a proposal seen by many as designed to facilitate the contentious building of the planned pipeline from Alberta to the West Coast and the export of Albertan oil to Asia.

Public Interest, the Documentary, and the Media

Government-supported documentaries in Canada have for decades played a major role in the construction of citizenship and in the building of national, regional, and group identities. But that support may come with strings attached. In the case of *L'erreur boréale*, Desjardins's original idea, evaluated by and agreed to by the National Film Board of Canada (NFB), was a film about the world's boreal forests. But the contract, when it finally arrived a few days before the start of filming, included a clause reserving the right for final editing, in the case of disagreement between filmmaker and producer, to the federally funded NFB. Rejecting this as infringing his artist's integrity and freedom of speech, Desjardins agreed with the NFB to make the film with his own resources and then to offer it to the NFB on a "take it or leave it" basis. Desjardins was able to complete a truncated version of the project in coproduction with the Association coopérative de production audio-visuelle (ACPAV)[46] and the documentary turned out to be all the more effective for being restricted to the boreal forest of Quebec. His experience highlights, however, the difficulties and conflicts of interest that can so easily confront documentary filmmakers, especially if their films are of a polemical nature.

Investigative reporting, when not commissioned in advance, is an expensive and highly speculative activity, and the makers of documentaries need to take careful account of who will buy and distribute their films and how and to whom they will be shown. If public funding channelled through a public agency may present difficulties of the type just described, how much more may this be the case with private finance? As Desjardins points out, Québécor's *Journal de Montréal* could never have supported investigative work about the wood or paper sector.[47] Similarly, the mining companies and the mining industry seem prepared to go to inordinate lengths to counter any negative publicity. In the case of *Trou Story*, Desjardin's celebratory profile was arguably a particular trigger. Barrack Gold's three-and-a-half-year $6-million lawsuit against the small publishing company Ecosociété for its publication of *Noir Canada* (2008), an analysis of the role of Canadian companies in Africa, is a further indication of the mining sector's sensitivity to negative coverage and a telling example of its readiness to use its financial clout to suppress adverse comment.[48]

The digital revolution is of course opening up huge new documentary opportunities, offering important alternative avenues in the making and distribution of documentary material.[49] Even back in 1999, although some sequences of *L'erreur boréale* were shot on 16mm film—including, notably, the final scene showing the logging machines working in winter with their headlights on—much of it was filmed with a variety of video cameras, creating not necessarily the absolute best in visual and sound effects (as might be required for a big-screen or art-house movie) but ones which, according to-Desjardins, were "good enough" and "fit for [their documentary] purpose" (*24 Images*, 96 [printemps 1999]).

Meanwhile, on the professional and commercial side, private media companies and public corporations alike are notably open to the appeal of celebrity as a hook for programs and audiences. Celebrity endorsement—and, even more importantly, celebrity spearheading of a cause—can provide an important boost to the documentary genre with guaranteed public interest and guaranteed viewing figures. As Desjardins wryly and cynically put it with regard to *L'erreur boréale*: «si je n'avais pas été un chanteur populaire, les télédiffuseurs ne se seraient pas intéressés au projet.... Pour faire un documentaire aujourd'hui, il faut être chanteur, ou joueur de hockey» [*if I hadn't been a popular singer, the television companies would not have been interested in the project.... To make a documentary today, you need to be a singer or to an ice-hockey star*]" (*24 Images*, 1999, pp. 34, 38).[50] In line with this perception, a decade later with *Trou Story*, it was Desjardins's public profile as an artist and celebrity that again carried the day, over the much more limited media exposure achieved by the films of Plouffe and Paquet. ∎

NOTES

1 [*I no longer believe the businessmen and the politicians when they say they are following normal practice and my feeling now is that I have the right to mount a legitimate challenge against them with such weapons as I have at my disposal.... It's war.*] Desjardins in a 1993 televised interview with Michel Desautels (quoted in Couture, *Richard Desjardins*, 166). All translations into English are my own, and are given in italics.

2 I was fortunate in being able to see both the Desjardins and the Plouffe films. According to Natalie Petrowski ("La Roche Sexy"), Paquet's film was due to have a preliminary showing to the *indignés* of Victoria Square on the evening of 5 November 2011, prior to subsequent screening by TéléQuébec later on in winter 2011–12. The two Desjardins films discussed in this chapter are distributed in both French and English with either a French or an English title. The English titles in square brackets for the Plouffe and Paquet films are my suggested versions of the French titles of these two francophone documentaries.

3 «Quand j'étais petit, je vendais *La Frontière* le jeudi à la porte de la *punch-clock* de la mine. Je les voyais sortir, un à un, les mineurs, les fondeurs, leurs visages de déterrés, silencieux. Ça me frappait: personne ne se parlait. Même pas heureux d'être remontés à la surface, d'être sortis des chambres à gaz. Comme si leurs vies s'étaient arrêtées à la Noranda.» Desjardins, «Autochtones et blancs.» [*As a small boy I sold 'La Frontière' on Thursdays by the clocking-off*

door of the mine. I would see the miners coming out, one by one, from the depths of the pit, their faces all black with dust, in total silence. That was what struck me: there was no talking to each other. Not even any sense of happiness at being back on the surface, and out of the gas chamber. As if they had no life beyond the Noranda mine.]

4 In 1991, Desjardins commented: «À la radio, c'est toute une mafia. Il n'y a que quatre réseaux. Quatre majeurs, disons quatre importants. Quatre réseaux de diffusion de musique commerciale. Parce que pour toute une chaîne qui va jusqu'à Chibougamau, jusqu'à Rouyn, jusqu'à Gaspé, la programmation est établie à Montréal et est suivie à la lettre jusqu'au bout du Québec. Y sont quatre yuppies qui décident du son que le monde va écouter. 'te jure, c'est comme ça. [...] C'est vraiment une tyrannie [...]. J'suis pas le seul à en parler ouvertement.» M.H. Bergeron and G. Perron, «La musique, sa nature, la poésie, sa culture,» *Québec français* 82 (1991), 189, quoted in Couture, *Richard Desjardins*, 34. [*The radio is a whole mafia. There are only four networks. Four majors, that is, four important ones. Four commercial music networks. Because for a whole channel that transmits as far as Chibougamau, Rouyn, or Gaspé, the programming is all done in Montreal and followed to the letter through the whole of Quebec. There are just four yuppies deciding what people will hear. I'm telling you, that's how it is. It's an out-and-out tyranny.... I'm not the only one saying that publicly.*]

5 Couture, *Richard Desjardins*, 65–67. In this new context, Desjardins' hand-to-mouth experiences of the 1970s and 1980s «devenaient autant de péripéties d'une légende, celle d'un Desjardins Richard-Coeur-de Lion contreculturel, chevalier à la triste figure dressée contre les moulins à tendances de l'industrie [musicale].» Julien, *Richard Desjardins*, 80–81). [*took on a legendary hue, that of a countercultural Richard the Lionheart Desjardins, knight of the sad countenance, tilting against the windmills fixed by the [music] industry.*]

6 At this concert inside the jail on 13 January 1968, Cash sang "Greystone Chapel" by inmate Glen Sherley. Julien, *Richard Desjardins*, 67. "Le Screw" is reproduced in Desjardins, *Paroles de chansons*, 24–25.

7 Ferland, in Couture, *Richard Desjardins*, 162.

8 Couture, *Richard Desjardins*, 162.

9 Julien, *Richard Desjardins*, 56, 58, stresses the importance of Desjardins' open-air concert on the Plains of Abraham at the 1990 Festival international d'été de Québec in making him known to a broad public. This performance brought him two prizes, the Prix de la chanson d'expression française and the Prix Miroir de la chanson francophone. Julien (162–63) lists twenty-one prizes received by Desjardins between 1989 and 2006 for his songs and for his films. See also Julien, *Richard Desjardins*, 51.

10 Literally *Like dogs in pasture*. Possible translations, taking up the tethering implication of "en pacage," might be *At the end of their tether* or *Fit to be tied*. Alternatively, with the mining context to the fore, the ambiguities of *Blasted* might, perhaps, better capture the devastating ironies of a dual celebration of fifty years of workers' toil and fifty years of company profits in a company mining town. The Internet offers as an English title *A raging disaster*.

11 «J'ai vécu vingt-cinq ans dans une petite ville de vingt-cinq mille habitants, et c'est le genre de ville où tu vois tous les pouvoirs, tu les vois de visu. Je pars de là. J'ai beaucoup de souvenirs, je traite tout à partir de ce que j'ai vécu là.» Quoted Couture, *Richard Desjardins*, 159. [*I spent twenty-five years in a small town of twenty-five thousand people, and it's the type of town where you see exactly who's running things. It's blatant. That's my starting point. I have lots of memories and I approach everything from my experiences there.*]

12 «*Comme des chiens en pacage* était un poème populaire, [*L'erreur boréale*] est une arme, une arme utile»; «J'ai voulu construire le «gun». Mais, en ce qui concerne le recrutement de l'armée, je suis moins spécialiste. Libre aux gens de s'emparer du film et de le montrer, de s'en servir.» «Entretien,» *24 Images* 96 (1999), 38, 34. [*"Comme des chiens en pacage" was a popular poem. ["L'erreur boréale"] is a weapon, a useful weapon'; "I wanted to make the 'gun.' But I'm no army recruiting sergeant. People are free to take over the film, to show it, to use it."*]

13 "Le pays d'Arthur Lamothe," a useful dossier of seven short articles, compiled by Simon Galiero, can be found in *24 Images* 132 (juin–juillet 2007). Writing on *Les Bûcherons de la Manouane*, Gilles Marsolais notes: «Il n'est pas anodin que ce film ait été réalisé par un Français qui avait quitté sa Gascoigne natale à peine dix ans plus tôt pour émigrer au Québec, et qui avait lui-même manié la hache dans les forêts de l'Abitibi dès son arrivée au pays.... En filmant à hauteur d'homme les dures conditions de vie et de travail dans un camp de bûcherons perdu dans les forêts enneigées du Haut-Saint-Maurice, ... en donnant à voir cette réalité de l'intérieur, du point de vue des travailleurs exploités, contraints de s'exécuter par 54 degrés sous zéro, ... le film, avec son commentaire informatif, factuel, qui relaie une imagerie déjà forte pour en faire un cas exemplaire, devient une dénonciation implacable du système d'exploitation de type colonial, tiers-mondiste, dont les Québécois (francophones) faisaient les frais depuis des lustres au profit de l'establishment anglophone et des multi-nationales» (Ibid., 27). [*It's no accident that this film was made by a Frenchman who had left his native Gascony scarcely ten years earlier to emigrate to Quebec and who had himself worked as a lumberjack in the Abitibi forests as his first job here.... Giving a direct insight into the harsh working and living conditions of a logging camp in the remote snow-bound forests of Haut-Saint-Maurice, ... showing that reality from within, from the point of view of the exploited workers, forced to function in temperatures of 54 degrees below, ... the film, with its informative, factual commentary, that builds on the impressive visuals to make an exemplary case, becomes an implacable denunciation of a longstanding colonialist, third-world type of exploitation of (francophone) Quebeckers by the anglophone establishment and the multinationals.*]

14 Even before *L'erreur boréale*, Desjardins was addressing these themes on the album *Chaude était la nuit* (1994), where the song "Les grands remous" tells of "quelqu'un qui fait du pouce à Grands-Remous, près de Val d'Or, comme ça m'est déjà arrivé" [*someone hitchhiking at Grands-Remous, near Val d'Or, as has happened to me*] and who encounters "un Algonquin du lac Barrière ... Il vient avertir le Blanc qu'il n'y a plus de bois. C'est tout." [*an Alonquin from Lake Barrière ... He's come to tell the white man that the forest is gone. That's it.*] Richard Desjardins in conversation with Hélène Pedneault, *Elle-Québec* 52 (décembre 1993), quoted in

Couture, *Richard Desjardins*, 85, n166. The monologue "L'embaumeur forestier," recorded by Desjardins for *Abbittibbi Live* (1995), offers an ironic treatment of the same problem from the opposite point of view: "Mon nom c'est Rondin, / embaumeur forestier pour la Domtar" [*My name is Log, / forestry embalmer for Domtar* [the giant wood and paper company]]. Quoted in Couture, *Richard Desjardins*, 148–49; Couture at 98–100 offers further extracts.

15   Desjardins, «Entretien,» *24 Images*, 96 (1999), 35.

16   In interview, Desjardins states that his own preference was for the free dialogue format of *Comme des chiens en pacage*, but that the producers insisted on Desjardins as the dominant voice. «Entretien,» *24 Images*, 96 (1999), 35.

17   "La berceuse aux étoiles" (1942), words by Albert Viau, music by François Brunet, has as its refrain: "Pendant que les heureux / Les riches et les grands / Reposent dans la soie / Ou dans les fines toiles / Nous autres les parias / Nous autres les errants / Nous écoutons chanter / La berceuse aux étoiles' [*While the happy, the rich and the mighty / Sleep in silk / Or in fine linens / The rest of us the outcasts / The rest of us the vagabonds / We listen to / The lullaby of the stars.*]

18   Kilmer, born 6 December 1884, was an American poet, writer, and journalist. Apart from a few poems such as "Trees," his work is now largely unknown. He was killed by a sniper's bullet at the battle of the Marne on 30 July 1918. It is noteworthy that for Desjardins, environmental concerns take precedence over Quebec language issues: «Mon patriotisme à moi, c'est la conservation de l'eau et des forêts…. Ça se fait, nettoyer les rivières, y ont nettoyé la Tamise …! Alors, quand on me parle de l'indépendance du Québec, si c'est pour scrapper les rivières en français plutôt qu'en anglais, je peux attendre encore 1000 ans» [*What I'm patriotic about is the conservation of water and the forests. So, when people talk about independence for Quebec, if that means scrapping the rivers in French rather than in English, I can wait indefinitely*]. Desjardins to Michèle Laferrière, «Un poste d'essence sur l'autoroute du bonheur,» *Le Soleil* (1er juillet 1995), quoted in Couture, *Richard Desjardins*, 100.

19   Like Arthur Lamothe before him, Desjardins has specifically highlighted in both song and film the difficulties of the First Nations—notably the Innu, in the 2007 documentary *Le peuple invisible / The Invisible Nation*. See André Dudemaine's review, «Le rideau déchiré,» *24 Images* 134 (2007): 62–63.

20   Why are rights needed—he disingenuously inquires—if consultation takes place?

21   Reviewers, such as Philippe Gajan, highlighted its multifacetted impact: «[un] film d'une beauté révélée, à ceci près qu'il emprunte la forme d'un monument funéraire à la forêt défunte … [un film] aussi acéré que la lame aiguisée d'un couteau … un grand film de société … une ample geste épique, une geste du réel ancré dans une problématique actuelle» [*[a] film of such manifest beauty that it takes on the form of a funerary monument to the lost forest … [a] film as sharply honed as the blade of a knife, a film of impressive social import … an epic tale of ample proportions, a real-life epic, anchored in an issue of the here and now*] Gajan, *24 Images* 96 (1999) : 36–37.

22 Desjardins insisted, among other things, that his 2003–4 album *Kanasuta* include, as part of its box set, the DVD of *L'erreur boréale* and carry on its sleeve the following statement: «Ressources naturelles bloque systématiquement les suggestions du rapport Coulombe sur la protection des forêts, contrairement à la volonté de son propre gouvernement. Il faut mettre un maximum de pression pour qu'on se dote d'une vision. Il faut arrêter d'envoyer nos arbres en deux par quatre aux États-Unis. Il faut les travailler ici. L'arbre le plus payant est celui dans lequel tu fais des violons» [*The Ministry of Natural Resources is systematically blocking the suggestions of the Coulombe report on the protection of the forests, contrary to the wishes of its own government. Maximum pressure needs to be brought to achieve a vision for the future. We must stop exporting our trees in two by four planks to the US. We need to process them here. The most profitable tree is the one that is used for violins*]. Quoted in Julien, *Richard Desjardins*, 64. Kanasuta is the name of a river, a lake, and a region in the Abitibi–Témiscamangue region of Quebec.

23 As Desjardins stresses in his film, Canadians have, especially in the last few years, spectacularly lost control of their mining resources to international corporations, whose primary aim is to dominate global trading markets and whose acquaintance with, and commitment to, the localities in which they conduct their on-the-ground operations is even weaker than that of the previous Canadian miners. The Canadian Copper Company, based in Sudbury, Ontario, had already by 1902 been absorbed into the American-dominated International Nickel Company (INCO), which itself was taken over a century later (2006) by the Brazilian miner Vale. Noranda, incorporated in 1922 to exploit the Rouyn copper reef identified by Edmond van Horne, merged with Toronto-based Falconbridge in 2005 and almost immediately afterwards was taken over by Swiss miner Xstrata in 2006. Xstrata has itself now been taken over (December 2012) by the general commodities corporation Glencore, weakening yet further the connection between local mining and the international boardroom of company directors and management executives.

24 In an interview, Desjardins explains: «Je travaille depuis dix ans pour l'Action boréale, dont l'un des mandats est de créer des aires protégées autour des communautés en Abitibi. Continuellement, on se casse les dents sur des terrains sous claim, sous emprise minière. À un moment donné, je me suis dit: crisse ça va faire! Le plan de développement de ces minières a préséance sur toute forme d'aménagement. C'est abusif, ça» [*I've been working for ten years for Action boréale, one of whose aims is the creation of protected areas around communities in Abitibi. We're continually coming up against land claims under mining control. Finally I said to myself: Enough is enough! The development plans of these mining companies take precedence over any kind of conservation or protection. That's an abuse of power*]. Malavoy-Racine, «Grise mine», 41.

25 Desjardins's feelings, apparent in his film commentary on the despoiling of Timmins, were expressed even more strongly in an interview with Pierre Maisonneuve in the 27 November 1996 edition of the RDI program *Maisonneuve à l'écoute*: «[On déploie] une énergie incroyable pour aller chercher, aller extraire l'or qui est dans le ventre de la terre, et puis

on le ramène à la surface, y faut utiliser le cyanure pour le détacher de la roche, le cyanure, c'est pas du marshmallow ça, ça fait des dommages épouvantables dans l'environnement, ça revient en lingot et ça retourne dans des voûtes, dans la noirceur et ça reste là. La seule utilisation qu'on connaît de l'or, les dents, quelques instruments de chirurgie, quelques bijoux, mais quatre-vingt-dix pour cent de l'or ne sert absolument à rien et le système économique repose là-dessus» [*An incredible amount of effort is expended looking for and extracting gold from the bowels of the earth, then it's brought to the surface, cyanide has to be used to detach it from the rock, cyanide, that's no soft option, it does terrible things to the environment, the ingots come back and off they go to the vaults, back into the dark, and there they stay. Gold is used for teeth, some surgical instruments, some jewellery, but ninety percent of it is totally useless and the economic system rests on that*]. Quoted in Couture, *Richard Desjardins*, 168.

26 It should be pointed out that the Quebec government's approval for the Osisko project came with several conditions, including the establishment of a local milling plant, the recycling of 90 percent of the treatment water, the reuse of an existing waste disposal site, measures to attenuate noise, dust, and vibrations, and, at the end of mining operations, restoration and revegetation of the mining site.

27 Desjardins includes a clip of Laurier speaking in Cobalt, the Union Jack behind him, enjoining the listening miners with their miserable life expectancy of 45 years: "Tout ce que nous vous demandons, c'est de donner le meilleur de votre humanité" [*All that we ask of you is that you give the best of yourselves*].

28 Slurry, the mining engineer stresses, is non-toxic crushed rock and water, but Desjardins queries the effect of pumping that slurry onto a contaminated site and the possibility of leakage as a result of the disturbing of the toxins it already contains.

29 Desjardins's interviewees include a middle-aged third-generation miner reflecting sadly on the declining employment opportunities in an industry in which his family has had so much personal investment; as well as a small group of miners on a protracted strike in 2009 on a Vale picket line, who stress the loss of power for their cause brought about by the legal restrictions now placed upon them: no more than eight pickets at any one time, no detaining beyond eight minutes of other workers crossing the picket line.

30 The refrain and first verse run as follow: "For we'll sing a little song of Cobalt / If you don't live there it's your own fault / Oh you Cobalt / Where the wintry breezes blow. / Where all the silver comes from / And you live a life and then some / Oh you Cobalt / You're the best old town I know. // You may talk about your cities / And all the towns you know / With trolley cars and pavements hard / And theatres where you go. / You can have your little auto / And carriages so fine / But it's hobnail boots and a flannel shirt / In Cobalt town for mine."

31 Founded in 1985 as a street-busking group, Grievous Angels has since produced many songs related to the mining and smelting towns of the Canadian Shield.

32 The hole made by the mine will be 2 kilometres long and 1,500 metres wide, and deep enough to more than absorb the height of the Eiffel Tower. The mill will crush 155,000 tons of rock per day to extract 55,000 tons of ore-bearing mineral, using 25 million litres of water.

33 A different slant on this image, echoing what appears in the film as a cynical observation on the part of Malartic's mayor, emerges in a CTV.ca report of the Canadian Press of August 4, 2010. According to this, the "ramshackle" house, which had been the childhood home of Ken Masse, the solitary resister, was owned not by him but by his mother, Mary Elizabeth Wilczynski, and only occupied part-time by family members. Osisko had offered them $350,000 for the property, otherwise valued at $14,000, but they were attempting to hold out for $1 million from the mining company. "Quebec man loses fight to keep home above gold mine," http://www.ctv.ca/servlet/ArticleNews/print/CTVNews/20100804/man-must-leave-house (26 March 2012).

34 Reporting respectively in *Le Devoir* (A3) and *La Presse* (Arts, 5) of 31 October 2011, Odile Tremblay ("Controverse autour du lancement de Trou Story à Rouyn-Noranda") and André Duchesne ("Les Abitibiens divisés") provide a first taste of the sharp differences of opinion.

35 *Trou Story* includes some similar earlier publicity with a set of poster images featuring 1920s or 1930s transport vehicles and consumer white goods superimposed on a background array of sparkling mineral specimens.

36 "Faire grise mine": to look gloomy; "avoir meilleure mine": to look better; "perdre le Nord": to lose one's bearings, but referring also here to the Charest government's Plan Nord for the economic development of Northern Quebec (including, notably, mineral extraction).

37 «Le jour et la nuit. Avec sa conscience environnementale, l'industrie minière n'est plus celle décrite dans le film *Trou Story*» [*Day and night. With its environmental awareness, the mining industry is no longer the one described in the film The Hole Story.*] *La Presse* 5 novembre 2011, A35. Highlighted in bold, as an insertion in the body of the article, is this statement: «Aucune mine ne peut plus être construite au Québec sans que son propriétaire ne soit tenu d'élaborer un plan de réhabilitation approuvé par le gouvernement» [*No mine can now be constructed in Quebec without its owner having developed a restoration plan approved by the government*]. Jeff Heinrich, for the anglophone *Gazette* (Montreal) of 4 November 2011, gives significant space to the remarks by representatives of the mining companies and the mining industry and their political supporters. Furthermore, although noting the "trenchant" nature of the documentary and accepting the authoritative personal acquaintance with corporate greed, experienced by Desjardins and Monderie as native sons of Rouyn-Noranda, he still contends that "[their] choice of talking heads is numbingly monotone. Only one mining executive appears on screen; the filmmakers prefer underdogs, people like themselves. Though there are veins of truth running through this movie…, *Trou Story* never hits the motherlode of truth. The whole story of the 'hole story' has yet to be told." Desjardins and Monderie, it is true, never comment, for example, on the huge upfront costs and risks of exploratory mining, nor are they interested in the volatility of the commodities market.

38   Founded in 1975 and with offices in Montreal, Quebec City, Toronto, and Vancouver, SECOR was one of Canada's leading management consultants. It was acquired by KPMG in July 2012. Marcel Côté ran subsequently as a candidate in the 2013 mayoral election in Montreal but was defeated by Denis Coderre. He died suddenly of a heart attack on 25 May 2014, aged 71.

39   The spectator cannot but be touched by the very real emotional distress of the individuals concerned; at the same time, s/he may also be led to ponder the difficult balance between conservation and economic and social revival and development. Simon Plouffe, in his Malartic documentary, *L'or des autres*, is much more victim-oriented, focusing on the sadness of the few in leaving and losing a place they have always known. According to Natalie Petrowski («La roche sexy»), Nicholas Paquet pursues a similar line: «[*La règle d'or*] n'est pas un film coup-de-poing et ouvertement militant comme l'est *Trou Story*. C'est un film tout en nuances qui réussit néanmoins à soutirer du maire de Malartic, le plus gros entrepreneur du coin et l'heureux propriétaire d'un rutilant garage Ultramar, une affirmation qui fera époque pour son ironie involontaire. Ici à Malartic, dit le maire, on voit la vie en rose même si tout autour est gris. La vie est rose en effet» [*"The rule of gold] is not an in-your-face, openly militant film like "The Hole Story." It's a nuanced film that nevertheless manages to winkle out of Malartic's mayor, the biggest entrepreneur in the place and the happy owner of a shiny Ultramar garage, a claim to be remembered for its involuntary irony. Here in Malartic, says the mayor, we see life through rose-coloured spectacles even if everything around us is grey. Life is indeed a bed of roses*].

40   The committee is an independent group of local residents and businessmen, established at the recommendation of the Bureau d'audiences publiques sur l'environnement (BAPE) and selected through the Chaire Desjardins en développement des petites collectivités of the Université du Québec en Abitibi-Témiscamangue (UQAT), from whom the report was also commissioned.

41   See Fontaine, «Les élus espéraient plus»; Journet and Fontaine, «La facture baisse pour Québec,» 2; Lévesque, «Prolongement de la route 167» ; and Nadeau, «Mines».

42   Nadeau, in «Le projet de loi sur les mines renaît», reported that Martine Ouellet, the PQ Minister of Natural Resources, would attempt to reintroduce an amended version of the bill. Meanwhile on the facing page, a full-page advertisement by La coalition pour que le Québec ait meilleure mine presented photos of the four political leaders, Pauline Marois (Parti québécois), Philippe Couillard (Parti liberal du Québec), François Legault (Coalition Avenir Québec) and Françoise David (Québec solidaire), over the message «A nos élus: redéposez rapidement une réforme minière» [*To our elected representatives: put in a rapid proposal for mining reform*], supported by twenty signatories and their statements, including one by Desjardins: «nous ne sommes pas contre l'industrie minière. Mais l'emprise totale qu'ont les compagnies minières sur le développement des régions, on est contre» [*We are not against the mining industry. But we are against the total control over the mining companies on the development of our regions*].

43 Lapierre in "Le pétrole albertain: du toc retro [Albertan oil: retro rubbish]" links the shale gas issue with the oil sands exploitation in Alberta, labelling both as environmentally damaging and inappropriate old-style energy "solutions."

44 Since this chapter was completed in 2013, the global downturn has continued, with significant economic slowdown, most notably in China, and with a concomitant fall in demand for raw materials. This situation amply illustrates the vulnerability of industries such as mining, with their high up-front investment costs in exploration and development; it also explains their desire to keep restoration costs to a minimum. Meanwhile the 19 October 2015 federal election of a Liberal government under Justin Trudeau and the appointment of lawyer Catherine McKenna as Minister of Environment *and* Climate Change has signalled a new commitment to environmental and climate change issues—a position strongly reaffirmed by Trudeau at the UN's December 2015 Climate Change conference in Paris. However, precise emission targets and details remain to be worked out, and the global economic outlook remains unclear.

45 The Quebec situation, for Desjardins, is but one example of a worldwide problem, as he explained to Pierre Maisonneuve in his November 1996 interview on *Maisonneuve à l'écoute*, during which he denounced "la monarchie industrielle," constituted "au niveau mondial" [*on the global level*] by "357 personnes qui contrôlent 45% du revenu mondial brut" [*357 people who control 45% of global gross income*], with the result that "Les gouvernements locaux obéissent aux ordres de ces fonds monétaires internationaux" [*national (and provincial) governments are in thrall to the orders of those international monetary funds*] (quoted in Couture, *Richard Desjardins*, 92). Desjardins's introduction to his song "Les Yankees" on his album *Live* presents the same idea with many of the same words: "Au-dessus des gouvernements nationaux" [*Above national governments*], there exists "[une] espèce de super-puissance, une gang de money-junkies, ... les organismes [comme] le Fonds monétaire international ou la Banque mondiale. C'te gang-là ... oblige chacun des gouvernements nationaux à privatiser les profits et à socialiser les déficits. J'les entends dire tout' les jours: «On veut vot'bien, pis on va l'avoir»' [*a sort of superpower, a gang of money junkies, ... entities like the IMF or the World Bank. That gang ... forces each national government to privatize profits and to socialize deficits. I hear them saying all the time: "we have your best interests at heart and will treat your money as our own"*].

46 Founded in 1971 by a group of young filmmakers, including among others Mireille Dansereau and Roger Frappier, ACPAV provides flexible production support and pooling of administrative and technical resources and expertise to independent filmmakers.

47 Desjardins, in *24 Images* 96 (printemps 1999), 34 and 36: «Pensez-vous que *Le Journal de Montréal* commandera une enquête sur les opérations forestières de Donohue, qui appartient à 50% à Québécor? Un exemple: le moulin de Matane en Gaspésie appartient à Donohue. Ils ont reçu 200 millions de subventions du gouvernement, c'est-à-dire de nous. Péladeau avait obtenu le moulin pour trois fois rien. Ils l'ont rouvert et aujourd'hui ils s'approvisionnent dans l'île d'Anticosti. Qu'est-ce que ça veut dire? Simplement qu'il n'y a plus de bois derrière! Et évidemment ce n'est pas un journaliste du *Journal de Montréal* qui ira voir où se situe le problème»} [*Do you seriously think that «Le Journal de Montréal» could*

commission an inquiry into Donohue's forestry operations, which are 50% owned by Québécor? One example: the Matane paper mill in Gaspésie belongs to Donohue. They received 200 millions in subsidies from the government, that is, from us. Péladeau bought the mill for almost nothing. They reopened it and today they're getting their wood from the island of Anticosti. What does that mean? Simply that all the wood is gone. And of course, no journalist from the "Journal de Montreal" will go out to see what the problem is]. Pierre Karl Péladeau, former CEO of Québécor, was elected leader of the independantist Parti québécois and thus Leader of the Opposition in Quebec's National Assembly on 12 May 2015. He resigned from this position on 2 May 2016.

48 *Noir Canada* by Alain Deneault, with Delphine Abadie and William Sacher, has as its polemical subtitle "Pillage, corruption et criminalité en Afrique." Spiralling legal costs finally obliged Écosociéte to agree to an out-of-court settlement, and to withdraw the book in October 2012. Coincidentally, Barrack Gold was the last Malartic miner before Osisko.

49 *Fort McMoney,* an interactive Web documentary in three languages (French, English, and German) is a recent stunning example featuring all of the paradoxes of Fort McMurray, the boomtown of the Albertan oil sands. Made by David Dufresne, in conjunction with the Montreal game developer Toxa with support from the NFB, Arte, Radio-Canada, the *Globe and Mail*, the French newspaper *Le Monde*, and the German *Süddeutsche Zeitung*, it premiered at the Montreal International Documentary Film Festival on 19 November 2013 and went online on 25 November 2013. Visit www.fortmcmoney.com.

50 Earlier in the same issue of *24 Images*, Jean Chabot («Rue Rachel», 14, 15) provides a sober assessment of the poor outlook for the vast majority of the year's documentaries: «Il vient d'avoir tout près de cent documentaires cette année, au Québec. On imagine le nombre d'images, de jours de tournage, les problèmes de financement, de montage, les conflits, les espoirs, les audaces. Mais la plupart de ces films passeront inaperçus des médias à quelques exceptions près» [Nearly a hundred documentaries have been made in Quebec this year. Think of the number of images, days of filming, problems of financing, of editing, the conflicts, the hopes, the risk-taking. But the majority of these films, with just a few exceptions, will have passed unnoticed by the media].

WORKS CITED

Côté, Marcel. «Pour en finir avec le cas Malartic». *Le Devoir*, 9 novembre 2011, A9.

Cousineau, Sophie. "Quebec mining reforms mired in the bottomless pit of politics." *Globe and Mail*, 13 November 2013, B2.

Couture, Carole. *Richard Desjardins. La parole est mine d'or*. Montréal: Triptyque, 1998.

CTV. "Quebec man loses fight to keep home above gold mine" (26 March 2012), http://www.ctv.ca/servlet/ArticleNews/print/CTVNews/20100804/man-must-leave-house

Deneault, Alain, and William Sacher. *Paradis sous terre. Comment le Canada est devenu la plaque tournante de l'industrie minière mondiale*. Montréal: Les Éditions Écosociété, 2012.

Desjardins, Richard. *Paroles de chansons*. Montréal: VLB, 1991.

———. «Autochtones et blancs, nous sommes tous les serviteurs de la compagnie». *Le Devoir*, 13–14 mars 2004, B5.

———. «Entretien avec Richard Desjardins». *24 Images* 96 (printemps 1999) : 32–38.

———. «Environnement: un ministère édenté». *Le Devoir*, 20 novembre 2012), A7.

Desjardins, Richard, and Robert Monderie. *Comme des chiens en pacage* [1977]. Abbitibbi Blue Print. Montréal: Cinéma Libre, 1989.

———. *Mouche à feu*. Abbitibbi Blue Print, 1982.

———. *L'erreur boréale / Forest Alert*. Association coopérative de productions audio-visuelles (ACPAV) and ONF/NFB, 1999.

———. *Le peuple invisible / The Invisible Nation*. ONF/NFB, 2009.

———. *Trou Story / The Hole Story*. ONF/NFB, 2011.

———. *Trou Story / Dossier de presse*. onf.ca/Troustory.

Duchesne, André. «*Trou Story*. Les Abitibiens divisés». *La Presse*, 31 octobre 2011.

Dudemaine, André, «Le rideau déchiré». *24 Images* 134 (octobre-novembre 2007) : 62–63.

Ferland, Jolin. *Anatomie du succès de trois noms récents de la chanson québécoise: Daniel Bélanger, Les Colocs et Richard Desjardins*. Mémoire présentée à l'Université Laval, 1996.

Fillion, Valérie, Dominique Dionne, and Claudine Renauld. «Le jour et la nuit. Avec sa conscience environmentale, l'industrie minière n'est plus celle décrite dans le film *Trou Story*». *La Presse*, 5 novembre 2011, A35.

Fontaine, Hugo. «Les élus espéraient plus qu'une moitié de route». *La Presse*, 16 novembre 2011, Affaires, 3.

Francoeur, Louis-Gilles. «Les Québécois perdront-ils leur Nord?» *Le Devoir*, 20 novembre 2011, B8.

Gagnon, Mario, Alain Lahaie, et Carl-Hugues Leblanc. «Lettre aux actionnaires de la minière Osisko. Notre quotidien, cet enfer». *Le Devoir*, 9 novembre 2011, A9.

Gajan, Philippe. «Alerte rouge. L'erreur boréale de Richard Desjardins et Robert Monderie». *24 Images* 96 (1999) : 36–37.

Galiero, Simon, ed. «Le pays d'Arthur Lamothe». *24 Images* 132 (juin-juillet 2007), 12–37.

Gouvernement du Québec. *Forests: Building a Future for Québec*. Quebec City: 2008.

Heinrich, Jeff. "*Trou Story*. Digging Up Dirt." *The Gazette* (Montreal), 4 November 2011.

Journet, Paul, and Hugo Fontaine. «La facture baisse pour Québec. Nouvelle entente pour la route des Monts Otish». *La Presse*, 16 novembre 2012, Affaires, 2.

Julien, Jacques. *Richard Desjardins. L'activiste enchanteur*. Montréal: Triptyque, 2007.

Lapierre, Michel. «Le pétrole albertain: du toc rétro». *Le Devoir*, 27–28 novembre 2010, A3.

Lapointe, Ugo. «Plus actuel que jamais. Le film *Trou Story* ouvre un «panier de crabes» pour l'industrie minière et le gouvernement Charest». *La Presse*, 3 novembre 2011, A25.

Lévesque, Kathleen. «Prolongement de la route 167. Des Cris mettent le Québec en garde». *Le Devoir*, 12–13 novembre 2011, A3.

Malavoy-Racine, Tristan. «Grise mine». *Voir*, novembre 2011, 41.

Marsolais, Gilles. «*Bûcherons de la Manouane* d'Arthur Lamothe». *24 Images* 132 (juin–juillet 2007), 27.

Mousseau, Normand. *Le défi des ressources minières*. Québec: Éditions Multimondes, 2012.

———. *La révolution des gaz de schiste*. Québec: Éditions Multimondes, 2010.

Nadeau, Jessica. «Mines: le PLQ veut déposer son projet de loi». *Le Devoir*, 27 novembre 2012, A3.

———. «Le projet de loi sur les mines renaît». *Le Devoir*, 13 November 2013, A3.

Petrowski, Nathalie. «La roche sexy». *La Presse*, 5 novembre 2011, Arts, 13.

Tremblay, Odile. «Petit train va loin. 30 ans de miracle avec Jacques Matte». *Le Devoir*, 29–30 octobre 2011, E9.

———. «Controverse autour du lancement de *Trou Story* à Rouyn-Noranda». *Le Devoir*, 31 octobre 2011.

Wright, Ronald. *A Short History of Progress*. Toronto: Anansi, 2004.

TEN

Postcolonial Territorial Landmarks within Canada's Multiculturalism:
The Myth of Virility

Édith-Anne Pageot
Translated from French by Guy Laverdure

INTRODUCTION

It is a **well-established fact** that territorial references and myths associated with the Canadian "North" and the Canadian "wilderness" have strongly influenced the collective imagination and significantly contributed to the identification of Canadian national landmarks. This has played a fundamental role in defining Canada's national identity. For example, the landscapes painted by the Group of Seven idealized territorial representations and defined a presumably "virile and pan-Canadian" nationalism. These territorial representations actively participated in defining social perceptions, not just as a collective reservoir of images, but through performativity, while ignoring the human condition, cultural specificities, and geographic disparities.

In the first quarter of the twentieth century, the modern state sought to establish the idea of a collective national unity. The federal government—pushed by a wind of protectionism—undertook the exploration of the North while the growing tourist industry tended to promote a so-called national specificity embodied in pristine nature.[1] In this political and social climate, the vision presented by the Group of Seven quickly became a national proposal. As a result, the inherent value of the Canadian Shield and the Canadian North's magnificence was rapidly identified as a unifying "national" image,[2] even though this image ignored social division.

In contrast to these idealized modern landscapes, denuded of all human presence and associated with a strong imperialist territorial impulse and with an all-inclusive national narrative, several contemporary art projects give the territory a more fragmented, pluralistic, sensitive, and, in some cases, sexual vision. For the past few decades, several Canadian artists have sought to challenge or to invalidate a national identity or reference based on uniform reductionist national landmarks. Some excellent examples of this are Michael Snow's now notorious video *The Central Region* (1971), the inverted and ironic images of Rodney Graham's *Upside Down Trees*, and Jin-me Yoon's photographic work *A Group of Sixty-Seven* (1996), to name just a few. Other artists' works, such as Nadia Myre's video *Rethinking Anthem* (2008) and Jaime Black's ongoing *REDress project* (2010–), challenge the lack of Indigenous cultural references and renew forgotten Indigenous narratives. These artists offer a sensitive approach to the concept of territory, exploring space from a more personal, meditative, ritual, mnemonic, spiritual, or ontological experience. They participate in an approach to space mediated by the senses and analyze the influence of space on the body and affects.

Furthermore, these contemporary representations of nature are intimately associated with discourses on sexuality and gender. In fact, our understanding of nature and of a given territory influences discourses on sexuality. Conversely, discourses on sexual identity affect our understanding of territory and nature. This rapport shapes our perception of what is natural, healthy, normal, degenerate, or perverse. As a historical example of this correlation, Isenberg points out that the rapid urbanization of the United States at the turn of the twentieth century caused a form of border closure anxiety. However, border conquest is, let us recall, a founding American myth. Moreover, at the beginning of the century, the city represented, for many, a confined captive space in which men were physically less active, and therefore their virility was threatened or weakened. In this context, William Temple Hornaday's passion for hunting trips in Montana, accompanied by the photographer L.A. Huffman, produced images of a physical conquering masculinity and, in so doing, acted as a means of protection against the menace of urban feminization. In that sense, the proliferation of adventure stories and the increasing interest and participation in outdoor sports and activities was associated with virility and constituted a form of reparation for the perceived urban threat to virility.[3]

In short, representations of nature and the wild define the elements that are associated with feminine and masculine sexual normality. Images of nature participate, therefore, in the sexual economy. Moreover, as explained previously, our understanding of sexuality and gender shapes our perceptions of nature. As a result, various contemporary artists bind not only the body and race to the territory, but also the concept of gender and discourses on sexuality. The works of Lori Blondeau, Shana Dempsey and Lori Millan, Kent Monkman, and Adrian Stimson clearly demonstrate this concept. For example, Shawna Dempsey and Lorri Millan conducted *queer* performances in iconic tourist sites as a part of their project, *Lesbian National Parks and Services,* started in Banff during their residency in 1997. By opting for aesthetics and deliberately provocative themes, Lori Blondeau, Kent Monkman, and Adrian Stimson, artists of Aboriginal ancestry, have developed a unique vision of territory, body, race, and identity. Their specificity lies with the staging and "denaturing" of traditional romantic or modern canonical "landscapes" through the presence of marginal, hypersexual, or *queer* characters. These projects force us to consider the possibility that Canadian history has a blind spot with respect to the symbolic and real-life links between culture, territory, and gender. This provokes a fundamental paradigm shift, and two questions immediately come to mind. First, how does this paradigm shift drive a symbolic requalification of cultural spaces and the Canadian territory? Second, in light of the relatively recent resounding recognition both nationally and internationally of Kent Monkman's work, which conditions, which political and symbolic issues explain the favourable support for these contemporary aesthetics?

This chapter presents pertinent and convincing examples of work from the artists Monkman, Blondeau, and Stimson that provide essential information for reflection and possible answers to these questions. It emphasizes the logic of emancipatory resistance and subversion proposed by these narratives. Analyses of strategies involving the *performative* function of painting, photography, and the diorama support these examples. In other words, using specific theoretical approaches to *visual culture studies,* this chapter presents the historicity of the gaze as well as the *social construction of the gaze.*[4] Finally, this chapter focuses on the paradigm shift elicited by these projects as well as the value of the symbolic and political support garnered, in particular, for Monkman's work.

QUEER TERRITORIES

By borrowing from popular culture, from camp sensitivity, drag, *queer*, kitsch, or even rococo aesthetics, Blondeau, Monkman, and Stimson renew the "berdache" image, or more appropriately the "two-spirits." Flamboyant alter egos often evolve in landscapes explicitly evoking canonical images borrowed from painting or photography. Belle Sauvage (Blondeau), Miss Chief Eagle Testickle (Monkman), and Buffalo Boy (Stimson) all have in common a taste for excess, exuberance, exaggeration, self-deprecation, artifice, and outrageous theatricality. Multifaceted satires, hybrid and variable, these alter egos borrow the elusive identity of the *trickster*, which is simultaneously the hero of the fable and the deceiver. Just as the *trickster* "lends itself to 'crazy and erotic adventures'" (Désy, 1999, 11), the alter egos,[5] disguised as a man or woman, cowboy, Indian, or "squaw," depending on their appetite, violate taboos. In so doing, they pervert and satirically defy the myths of the colonial founders and, at the same time, the preconceptions of postcolonial criticism related to sexuality, gender, race, and the territory. The characters created by these artists have elusive and marginal identities. Through their elusive nature, their relationship with the narratives of other characters of European descent sheds light on a complex and contradictory rapport marked by desire, connivance, tension, and resistance. As pointed out by several authors,[6] by adopting specific attitudes related to satire, irony, masquerade, or desire, these alter egos convey a subversive ideology and are an effective and proven protest tool that can only be welcomed.

Kent Monkman, born 1965 in St. Marys, Ontario, is of Cree origin on his paternal side and of English–Irish origin on his maternal side. His paintings stem from North American and European nineteenth-century and early-twentieth-century pictorial landscape traditions. Among them, he uses the iconic works of the Group of Seven. For example, *Superior* (2001) is a reference to Lawren Harris's canonical work titled *North Shore, Lake Superior* (1926). Influenced by theosophy, a philosophical anti-materialistic and esoteric position, Harris's work began as a spiritual quest. He conceived territory as a source of vibrations and the North as having spiritual significance.[7] As Eva MacKay recalls, Harris's quest for purity began as a highly gendered, manly, individualistic, colonial, and conquering notion of territory; he associated Canadian wilderness with the feminine and therefore as in need of taming.[8] Monkman keeps only the word *Superior* in the title of the source work and, in doing so, unveils the outright sexist and racist ideological underpinnings of the vision of Canadian territory proposed by Harris. Monkman somehow contaminates Harris's quest for purity and the heteronormality associated with it.

Here, as noted by Jonathan D. Katz, homosexual desire, "directed between two subjects rendered equal due to sexual orientation, if not in other areas, [he] makes it possible to equalize, through sex, the asymmetrical distribution of power."[9] On a background of garish colours and a text depicting violent passages from westerns and gay pornographic stories found on the Internet that demonstrate a fetish for Aboriginal men, the sexual antics of the "Indian" and the cowboy are barely veiled.

Monkman's *Superior* (2001) is a continuation of his earlier work, including *The Prayer Language* series (2000),[10] where he uses text merged with the landscape to underscore the role of writing in performance and spatial imagination in the creation of identity. These images reveal a deep Western bias that favours a phonetic writing model as the only form of language. As Derrida explains, Western thought assumes a radical separation between language and writing.[11] This separation introduced a dualistic and hierarchical rapport between consciousness and body, interior and exterior, identity and otherness, own and foreign, and so on, by placing at the centre the first terms of these oppositions and marginalizing the latter. The text in Monkman's work envelops the scene in the manner of a palimpsest, and words and body merge in a kind of rhizomic epidermis that escapes dualistic thought. Through the written word, power relations within sexual games border on rhetoric that is complex and intensifies the conditions of exclusion and exploitation caused by colonialism and Christianity.

The character *Miss Chief Eagle Testickle* (a play on the word mischief) gradually appears in painting, performance, film, and, recently, diorama. This character emerged shortly after Monkman abandoned the use of text in his works. Miss Chief stars in a film directed in collaboration with Gisèle Gordon (2005) titled *Group of Seven Inches*, which satirizes the travelogues of the American artist George Catlin (1796–1872) and Irish-born Canadian painter Paul Kane (1810–1871). In her/his performance, Miss Chief intoxicates young European men and makes them don outlandish clothes, which supposedly better correspond with their "true nature" and, hence, produce a more "authentic" vision of reality. The film was shot at the site of the McMichael Canadian Art Collection, located north of Toronto in the middle of a protected hundred acres of land where Tom Thomson's cabin sits. As the depositary of a national treasure, this site is a "sacred" space with strong heritage value. In the words of Anne Cauquelin, its spatiality is a *site*, meaning that it resides within and possesses the characteristics of a spatial map, geo-localized, positioned, and orderly. It is thereby "committed to the present" and, at the same time, serves as a spatial memory and as a national heritage identity.[12] Overthrowing the traditional colonial position, Miss Chief profanes a dedicated "site" and leads the copying and falsification operations historically used in the manufacture of the "Indian."[13] The appearance of Miss Chief also results in a decrease in operations involving hybridization, copying, and falsification. "Half-Breed," the number-one song on the charts in 1973 by pop singer Cherilyn Sarkisian La Pierre—better known as Cher—proclaims her mixed origins: Cherokee and Armenian on her paternal side and French and Irish through her mother. Inspired by the costume worn in "Half-Breed" by Cher, and by accessories, such as shoes and quiver, borrowed either from name brands, like Louis Vuitton, or from modern quasi-"heritage" colours of the Hudson's Bay Company, Miss Chief succeeds in thwarting the Hollywood clichés. Sometimes embodying the role of the "Indian" object in old ethnographic photography, and sometimes the colonizing director in the film, Miss Chief simultaneously occupies the position of the subject photographing, and that of the object being photographed. David McIntosh also notes: "she moves from object of photographic representation to simultaneous subject and object of her own photographic gaze."[14]

Miss Chief continues to evoke these male–female or "two-spirit" beings found in almost all Indigenous cultures. The Ojibwa language had a word for this *third gender*—*agokwa*—meaning "like a woman." As explained by Pierrette Désy, *agokwa* evokes the idea of «passage d'un statut à un autre, après qu'une vision, des rêves, des révélations ou des signes eurent mis en évidence le caractère irrévocable d'une destinée beaucoup plus que d'une fatalité» (passing from one status to another, after a vision, dreams, revelations or signs highlighted the irrevocable characteristics of destiny rather than one of fate)" (translated by the author).[15] Most Native cultures traditionally placed humans with "two spirits" surrounded by a mysterious, spiritual aura, immediately beyond a specifically feminine or masculine status.[16] These beings were believed to have a destiny thought to be trans-biological and often shamanic. In most Native American cultures, this hybrid identity, as well as same-sex practices «s'inscrivaient à l'intérieur d'un modèle culturel global et cohérent, d'où était exclue toute référence au registre du pathologique» (were inside a global and coherent cultural template, and hence any reference to being pathological was excluded) (translated by the author).[17] European explorers understood these practices differently. The English translation of the French "berdache" is catamite, a word that French and Canadian travellers use incorrectly when referring to "homosexual" Aboriginal North Americans. We know that European explorers strongly disapproved of sodomy. In *Sex and Conquest*, Richard Trexler demonstrates how the practice was associated with bestiality, which was severely condemned. The presence and inclusion of men/women in Amerindian communities fascinated the painter George

Catlin, but only rarely did he represent them in his work. These representations were accompanied by the following disdainful comment: «Voici bien l'une des coutumes les plus dégoûtantes et les plus bizarres que j'aie jamais rencontrées dans les territoires indiens, et qui, autant que je sache, appartient seulement aux Sioux, aux Sauk et aux Fox» (This may well be one of the grossest and most bizarre customs I've ever encountered in the Indian territories, and which, to the best of my knowledge, belongs only to the Sioux, the Sauk and the Fox) (translated by the author).[18] European explorers quickly interpreted the practices of human beings with "two spirits" as evidence of bestiality. The term *berdache* reflects this tendency to bestialize the other. Moreover, the widespread tendency to debase others by comparing them to the animal world also affects other Amerindian practices. Worried about the decline of the bison population in the Missouri Valley, Catlin recommended, as early as 1832, the creation of a large national park where nomadic Aboriginal hunters, in the same way as the bison, could be seen and preserved "in their pristine beauty and wilderness in a magnificent park."[19] In this context, nomadic Aboriginal hunter-gatherers were perceived as wild beasts. The intimate association between the "Indian" and the bison, and between the savage and brute naked masculinity, is conveyed by the painted images, prints, and photographs of Louis Maurer and Felix O.C. Darley, who were themselves inspired by the works of Catlin and German-born American artist Albert Bierstadt. On a conceptual and cultural level dating back to ancient tradition, the bestializing of another is used to justify their destruction.[20]

Miss Chief highlights the falsification campaigns that have transformed human beings with "two spirits" into *berdache* through the use of exaggeration. In the work titled *Artist and Model* (2003), Miss Chief is standing firmly before an easel style tipi. She/he holds in one hand a quiver and arrows, and in the other hand the tools of the painter. An effigy of his/her model, a cowboy with a traditional French Canadian sash, painted on birchbark, evokes Saint Sebastian, the unofficial patron saint of homosexuals. At the feet of the model lies a camera recalling the museum-like role of the photographic process and the colonial gaze. It also highlights heteronormality and the modern passion for possession, collection, and classification of both territory and Aboriginal cultures. When the work is flipped from left to right, it also recaptures the background of Miss Chiefs' *Fort Edmonton* (2003), which is itself a reversal of the foreground and the background of Paul Kane's images of Fort Edmonton (1849–1956). Kane is considered one of the first tourist-explorers. He led two large expeditions to Canada, taking the Great Lakes fur trade route to the Pacific. This pilgrimage was an opportunity for him to observe Aboriginal customs and culture and to "document" aspects of the territory and border areas from a supposedly objective perspective.[21] Following his observations of mainland reality, he put forth a set of personal views and presented romanticized writings.[22] This is notably the case with his bestselling book *Wanderings of an Artist among the Indians of North America,* published in London in 1859. Kane's works, like those of Catlin and Albert Bierstadt, played a prominent role in the exhibition and merchandising of territory and its occupants.

The work of Lori Blondeau questions stereotypes associated with Aboriginal women—specifically, the notions of the "Indian Princess" and the "squaw." Historically, there has been an association between the female "savage" and a perverse or even deviant[23] female sexuality. For example, in the photograph titled *The Lonely Surfer Squaw* (1997) the artist is wearing a bikini sewn from a beaver pelt. Her pink oval surfboard, whose size is obviously disproportionate, evokes a vaginal and, at the same time, a monumental phallic shape owing to its vertical position. Blondeau appropriates and parodies, simultaneously, the aesthetics of the classic pin-up, with the "squaw" embodying a licentious sexuality, and of Princess Pocahontas's idealized virginal beauty. As we know, the life of Pocahontas has given rise to many infamous legends built around stereotype clichés. Pocahontas embodies a young, beautiful, resourceful princess, always willing to lend a helping hand to the Europeans.[24] In metaphorical terms, images of manipulable and *penetrable* Indigenous women provided colonizers with a justification for appropriating land. Betty Daybird, another of Blondeau's alter egos, shakes the imperialist and patriarchal values that underlie the stereotyped vision of Native women. This character was inspired by the artist's family biography[25] as well as by elements of her artistic performances. In fact, Daybird is the name of the artist's great-grandfather. According to Blondeau, Betty was born on a Cree reserve in the shadow of St. Anne's steeple. In the summer, Betty spent her time travelling with her grandmother, Belle Sauvage, to participate in the country's only *gay* Wild West Show (pure fiction).[26] A sexy, neglected, and fallen Hollywood diva, Daybird has an Indian Princess tattoo that reads: "Falls to pieces." The different attitudes adopted by Betty Daybird, the falsified references to a glamorous diva, the Indian Princess, the stripper, and the cabaret-type atmosphere together parody the exoticism, the eroticism, and the threatening yet seductive sexuality inspired by the stereotypical image of the "squaw." In essence, Betty Daybird, like Surf Squaw and Belle Sauvage, is a caricature of the clichés that historically were used to rationalize the forced servitude of Aboriginal women.[27] In the dioramas, Belle Sauvage takes its inspiration from Native actors who played in the Wild West shows of the early twentieth century. She also mimics *Calamity Jane* (1953), a film in which Doris Day portrayed a vaguely androgynous personality.

Finally, Stimson's Buffalo Boy is a satire of the legendary William Frederick Cody, otherwise known as Buffalo Bill (1846–1917). Buffalo Bill was a bison hunter and the director of a popular theatre troupe, as well as a mythical figure representing the conquest of the West. The first of his theatre troupe's Wild West shows, which became the prototype for that genre, was devoted principally to the famous Buffalo Bill. These shows played to large audiences. Several of them depicted a number of legendary figures of the Wild West and presented a romanticized version of the Indian and the American West. Using a parody of the peep show, Buffalo Boy's performance makes clear the association between games of power and those of sexuality: "I create my own world in these peep shows—playing on how sex and conquest go hand-in-hand."[28] Knowingly embodying the "energy" of the vast herds of bison by then eradicated from the plains territory, Buffalo Boy was created in 2005 for Saskatchewan's hundredth-anniversary celebrations. The goal was to introduce a drag, *queer* geography within the colonial, patriarchal, and heteronormative version of the province's official history.[29] By transgressing the categories of male and female for the benefit of a body that escapes the symbolic logic of gender, these alter egos certainly interest the "transitive dimension" of sexual identity.[30] In contradiction to Manichean and heteronormative Western linear thought, they violate the masculine/feminine, man/woman, nature/culture, savage/civilized categories in favour of a more dynamic hybridization and exchange. The body escapes the fantasies of authenticity that characterize race and gender. These figures evolve in an environment rife with heterogeneous references and open up an ineffable, indefinable zone that rejects fixed descriptions. One can certainly view these *queer* spaces as an alternate "location"—an expression borrowed from the now famous text *The Location of Culture* by Homi Bhabha, which designates an ever changing time-space in-between, an interstitial space: between the sign and the referent, between proposal and action, between the production of a statement and the subject of the statement. Quoting Walter Benjamin's remarks concerning Berthold Brecht, Bhabha proposes that strategies such as slowdown, standstill, and time lag reveal "everything that is involved in the act of staging per se."[31] Contrary to modernity's linear drive, an empowering perspective of marginality requires something like a "projective past" or "time lag."[32] Monkman, Blondeau, and Stimson definitely use the strategy involved in overlapping temporal and spatial boundaries and, thus, staging the act of staging. "In splitting open those 'welds' of modernity, a postcolonial contramodernity becomes visible."[33] This political space defuses discourses based on authenticity and firmly defined binary positions (Aboriginal/European, inside/outside, subject/object, signifier/signified, past/present, male/

female). This "alternate location," where the notion of desire is firmly anchored, forces us to consider the territory and to seize space from an incarnate experience of interpenetration between its constituent elements. This is a fundamental difference beyond Western thinking involving an ontological anteriority of human beings with respect to the world and to the territory. Thus, these alter egos question and undermine stereotypes that have historically served to refute the definition of self-colonizer. They fail voluntarily to provide permanent structures to myths that would annul the possibility of conflict, overcome disparities, and obscure social divides. As such, it is the unifying potential of large landscapes that is disarmed (those of Catlin, Kane, Bierstadt, or the Group of Seven).

STAGING THE "INDIAN": PAINTING, PHOTOGRAPHY, AND DIORAMA

The media used in these projects by Monkman, Blondeau, and Stimson are interesting in themselves due to their *performative* function—in other words, because of the processes through which these media devices participate in the shaping of the body and the territory. We know how photography, lithography, and painting had a concrete and decisive impact on the management decisions regarding North American territories, and in particular on the establishment of reserved areas that were turned into national parks. Photography, which was first used to document, played a major role in the mapping of the territory. After the end of the nineteenth century, vast territorial observation campaigns converted the landscape—and the Indian—into a spectacle. The painted works of Kane, Bierstadt, and Catlin also played a major role in this process.

Figurative documentary painting based on photography and the Euclidian perspective has historically objectified the environment and rendered it seemingly neutral. The examples provided here demonstrate that the objectification processes of writing, painting, photography, and film build identity mythologies. For example, the camera's fixed point of view, and the frame and its perspective—assimilated by the painter—organize, structure, and circumscribe space by giving structure to the distance between the subject and the object. Rosalind Krauss recalls that photography, ever since its invention, indeed offered the possibility of *contemplating* "views."[34] This distance contributes to the *spectacle* of what is represented. Monkman's work suggests that campaigns involving copying, falsification, miscegenation, tampering, manipulation of the media, and temporality and the narrative are invariably subversive and deliberately ambivalent, making it impossible to suggest a real space, or one perceived as such. These restrictive interwoven effects cause a compression of space and time that resembles the new globalized culture's configuration of space-time. Using a large number of citations, and highlighting the effects of interwoven processes and *mise en abîme*, Monkman brings the constructed image to the fore, along with the false characterizations and mythical stereotypes surrounding both the colonized and the colonizer.

The diorama was first designed by Louis Daguerre in 1822 for theatrical entertainment purposes; to lure spectators into believing they were in the presence of nature or a particular political event.[35] The diorama was historically a political space within which narrated stories were often used to glamorize military leaders. This was the case, for example, with the diorama titled *The Battle of Sedan* (1895). The effect produced by the medium was one of perfect illusion, obtained by using large paintings painted on both sides of a translucent canvas and animated by lights and transparency effects. These monumental scenes were painted with transparent pigments on the front and opaque colours on the back. Changes in the lighting projected onto the canvas provided the illusion of changes in the weather. The objective was to give the spectator the impression of being part of a palpable universe—to provide a strong sense of immediacy.[36] Dioramas immersed their spectators, eliminating their distance from what actually was an objective, static, and structuring documentary image. Obviously, the spectators knew it was an illusion. Yet when they were immersed in darkness within the rotunda, there were no visual cues whereby they could identify the device's workings.[37] At this point, the experience of the diorama (like that of cinema later on) allowed the spectator to internalize the experience and to assimilate and strengthen the stereotypes conveyed by paintings and photography. Similarly, as noted by Hans Belting regarding the cinematic experience, "an imaginary relationship is established between the author and his audience in that personal imaginations are brought into contact and eventually overlap in the spectator's process of autosuggestion."[38]

Between 2006 and 2008, Adrian Stimson and Lori Blondeau produced dioramas titled *Putting the Wild Back into the West*. These dioramas, presented in several Canadian cities, imitated the travelling vaudeville Wild West shows. Against backgrounds of sublime landscapes, the artists embodied their respective alter egos, Belle Sauvage and Buffalo Boy, to present their installations-performances. Spectators could take part, with a signature (an x) and a modest sum of money, in a Polaroid 665 photo session. Ironically, the obsolete, positive/negative, black-and-white Polaroid 665 provides a snapshot thirty seconds after exposure of the fixed position of the subject, thus exaggerating the stereotype. If the diorama is based on a feeling of immersion and involves a subjective dimension of a sensitive experience of nature, the derisory nature and openly artificial character of Blondeau and Stimson's installation-performance illustrates the misleading and false power of the illusionist's device. Moreover, by signing an "x" and accepting the financial transaction, the spectators consciously lend themselves to the game. They act, that is, as lucid accomplices introducing *de facto* a critical distance incompatible with the goal of the illusionists and the immersive effect of the diorama. The exhibition process and the media used reveal the techniques of staging.

CANADIAN MULTICULTURALISM AND *QUEER* GEOGRAPHIES

These projects, both narrative and iconographic, propose a symbolic requalification of Canadian cultural spaces in several ways. They raise compelling questions with respect to the way in which the nature of a place and of a space has allowed limited and constructed activities and sexual identities, most notably the *queer* identity. In terms of historiography, the embodied and sexual experiences of territory, as proposed by Monkman, Blondeau, and Stimson, integrate and highlight the relationships between the body, the social, and the territory, which have been given, paradoxically, little consideration even though they are fundamental aspects of colonial history. In fact, the body was an important vector in encounters between Europeans and Aboriginal peoples. After all, the individuation of the self-colonizer was achieved through self-corporeality and the redefinition of the "Other." The body is obviously a geopolitical territory. The restrictions and integration imposed through obligatory boarding schools and reservations, and the legal dictates for marriage and dances under the *Indian Act* (1876), are just some examples of the "bio-power" that was exerted. In this context, the stereotypical images of the bodies of the "Indian," the cowboy, and the "squaw" were constructed into myths that fully participated in the colonization process. These artistic projects highlight the techniques for—and the media's historical contribution towards—the development of a number of stereotypes and myths related to images of the body, race, sexuality, and territory. They participate in the dismantling of these systems of representation. In other words, they are combatting these representations, using the same media devices, technologies, aesthetic conditioning, and emotional control.

Moreover, these projects endorse the political dimension of art in that they formulate a radical critique of racism and homophobia. Both of these contradict Canadian multiculturalism. Canada is one of the few countries to have laws dating back to the early 1970s supporting multiculturalism. Despite this fact, Canada's cultural diversity is often perceived as a threat to the traditional way of life, and although political and public discourse reveals a certain faith in Canadian pluralism, Canadians too often resist requests for equality, inclusion, and empowerment of minorities—notably First Nations. Canadian anthropologist Frances Henry writes that "the Multiculturalism Act is mainly passive, non-coercive, and non-threatening.... It focuses on limiting diversity to symbolic rather than political and transformative kinds of changes."[39] Canadian multiculturalism is experienced essentially as "tolerance" and as the "participation" of marginal cultures within the dominant culture. But clearly, tolerance is a minimal form of recognition because it is based on the maintenance of positions of superiority and inferiority between individuals and/or groups and does not challenge the status quo, nor does it require institutional structural reconfigurations.

This brings me to the last part of my question concerning the political and symbolic issues related to the critical reception reserved for *queer* geographies. From the outset, I have pointed out an obvious rupture with modern work, including the Group of Seven—historically perceived to be manly, pioneering, heterosexual artists—who were supposedly confronted by a savage land (female) in need of taming. Furthermore, this interpretation of the Group of Seven's work has been used as a symbol to federate cultural disparities and geographical territories around an idealistic Eden. For Blondeau, Monkman, and Stimson, the modernist model finally gives way to a postmodern referent mediatized identity, one whose icons come from vaudeville, *queer* culture, and American popular culture through the characters of Cher, Buffalo Bill, Pocahontas, and Calamity Jane. This shift is important. It involves abandoning the foundations of an enchanting Canadian territorial fantasy and refers to a rather more continental, American cultural reality, experienced within and through media space. The ideal of media visibility in the contemporary world culture is bound, most certainly, to this logic. The diva or drag queen personifies the stimulation of desire, which is connected to the imperatives of the contemporary celebrity culture. Certainly, the coincidental adherence to the consumer *and* celebrity cultures explains, in part at least, the resounding success of these artists' productions and specifically those of Kent Monkman. Signature clothing in Monkman's work can still be associated with a merchant, and with gay and urban culture.

Of course, the relatively favourable reception of these artistic projects is also a result of actions taken to recognize contemporary Aboriginal art in Canada, especially since the 1990s. On the international scene, the support became a reality at the Venice Biennale in 1995, and more recently with the presentation of Sakahàn at the Canadian Museum of Fine Arts (2013). Although recent (not to say late), the recognition currently enjoyed by Monkman, Blondeau, and Stimson is, therefore, not an isolated phenomenon. In the same way, issues touching transgender, feminist, gay, and sexual identities have garnered some support in the art world in recent years. Indeed, there has been a proliferation of funding allocated to *queer* artists since the 1980s and increasingly since the early 1990s. Reaping the rewards of this wind of change, artists like Monkman, Blondeau, and Stimson are today attaining a certain amount of success on the Canadian cultural scene.

One should probably also take into account that on a symbolic level, this support counterbalances the reaffirmation of Canada's commitment to the British Crown. In 2011, Ottawa made a number of symbolic gestures intended to restore Canada's sense of belonging to the monarchy. For example, during Prince William and his wife Kate's visit, Canada's foreign affairs minister, John Baird replaced two 1944 paintings by Quebec artist Alfred Pellan—a canonical work of modernity—with the portrait of Queen Elizabeth II painted during the Queen's visit to Canada for her Golden Jubilee in 2002. The two Pellan paintings, *Coast to Coast*, commissioned for the opening in 1944 of the first Canadian mission to Rio de Janeiro, represent and embody the ideals of the collective homogenization of the eastern and western territories of Canada while respecting local particularities. One of the paintings has totem poles and coastal mountains; the other has anglers, moose, and sailboats. After 1973, with the Queen's inauguration of a parliament building, the two works hung side by side above the reception counter. The replacement of Pellan's paintings by the portrait of Elizabeth II was a strong reaffirmation of Canada's symbolic allegiance to the British Crown and revived the now secular belief that because of its affinity with British political institutions, Canada is different from the United States. These two paintings have been recently put back in place by the Liberal government elected in October 2015. Nevertheless, Gérard Bouchard, as early as the beginning of the nineteenth century, analyzed this specific aspect of the Canadian imagination from a continental perspective: «une grande partie des élites a été capable de conjuguer d'une manière relativement harmonieuse le désir d'émancipation nationale (rupture) et le maintien prolongé du rapport colonial de la dépendance à l'endroit de la Grande-Bretagne (continuité)» [A large number of the elite have been able to deal relatively harmoniously with the desire for national emancipation (rupture) and the prolonged maintenance of colonial dependency with respect to Great Britain (continuity)].[40] Falling back on strong, unifying conservative and imperialist values allows the acceptance of this contradiction and unifies a Canadian federalism based on multiculturalism, which symbolically admits the other but remains in fact a fragile and constantly negotiated concept. The apparent acceptance of the subversive and of marginality projects an image of a liberal and progressive state that allows or "tolerates" otherness, thereby providing a democratic ideal that, although fragile, theoretically embodies a Canadian multiculturalism.

But at the same time, it is clear that the celebration of humour, of the celebrity, of the "star" (Cher, Calamity Jane, Buffalo Bill, the *drag queen*) and Monkman's use of Louis Vuitton's signature fashion—associated with a consumerist, gay and urban culture—has become a part of the "brand" fetishism in our "hypermodern" culture.[41]

These factors explain, at least in part, the informed and elitist contemporary art milieu, as well as the wider, more general audience's fascination with these artistic projects. In some measure, one may wonder whether the celebrity cult, the sense of attachment to images, and the endogenous quality of these images do not, unintentionally, mask the issues surrounding Canadian multiculturalism with respect to the relationship between the discourses of the body, sexual identity, politics, and representations of territory.

CONCLUSION

Blondeau, Monkman, and Stimson question and undermine the stereotypes of the Indian, the "squaw," and the cowboy as well as the value of a "savage and sublime landscape" as a national unifying reference. These works occupy a *queer* interstitial and transitional space. Polysemous and plural, they present an elusive identity. Just as with their appropriation of sublime, gorgeous, romantic, and modern landscapes in which they "live," Miss Chief, Belle Sauvage, and Buffalo Boy exist as pure simulacra. As a result, the seemingly permanent constructions and unifying identity narratives of the founding stories, based on mythical and landscape representations of the territory, which obscure social division and defuse racial, social, and cultural disparities ... fail.

It is not just that the "true nature" of the crystallized narrative stories (associated with the cowboy, the Indian, and the "squaw") is revealed; the visual performance process by which speech, gestures, and attitudes are incorporated and internalized and become "natural" is updated. That is to say, that deconstruction takes place on both the thematic and iconographic planes as well as in terms of the images' function as created by various technical media (painting, photography, film, diorama) that have historically shaped the intimate relationship between the body and territory, national identity cues, and gender. The overlapping time frame, and the techniques and mechanical processes used to create the mirage (i.e., the Euclidean perspective, the camera frame, the immersiveness of the diorama or cinematic experience) become obvious. Before the appearance of Miss Chief, Monkman's work specifically explores the power games that define the relationships between the body, territory, and writing—relationships used in the shaping of identity. His work also increases our comprehension of the relationship between the terms *race*, *gender*, and *territory*. Blondeau, Monkman, and Stimson's alter egos expose the so-called objective documentary, the constricting interwoven logic, the layers of falsehoods of the respective proposals of painted and photographic images historically perceived as true and neutral. These alter egos also place the media's role and the continental and American popular culture's role in the construction of myths surrounding identity under the magnifying glass of the subversive experience.

The exaltation of the star, humour, and fashion becomes knowingly part of the "brand" fetishism culture of today's global and transcontinental culture. The apparent acceptance of the subversive and of marginality projects an image of a liberal and progressive state that allows or "tolerates" otherness, thereby succeeding in providing the democratic ideal that, although fragile, theoretically embodies a Canadian multiculturalism. As a result, the privileged position of Kent Monkman's work in both major exhibitions *Sakahàn: International Indigenous Art* (National Gallery of Canada, 17 May–9 September 2013) and *Beat Nation: Art, Hip-Hop and Aboriginal Culture* (Vancouver Art Gallery, 25 February—3 June 2012, and Montreal Contemporary Art Museum, 17 October–5 Januuary 2014) and the symptomatic absence of any other proposal that would have involved an Aboriginal *queer* ecology should not come as a surprise. ■

NOTES

1. As explained by MacCannell, the tourist experience corresponds to a search for a certain authenticity, the quest for a unified experience in a social fabric which remains, in fact, deeply fragmented (*The Tourist*, 13).
2. Zemans, "Establishing the Canon"; Tobby, *The True North*, 42.
3. Isenberg, *The Destruction of the Bison*, 170.
4. Bryson, *Vision and Painting*; Mitchell, *Iconologie*.
5. Similarly, Blondeau's Cosmosquaw and Stimson's Shaman Terminator are also alter egos. http://adrianstimson.com/home.html.

6   Anderson, *Contemporary Canadian Women's Performance Art*; McMaster, *The Geography of Hope*; Lee, *The production of Racialized Masculinities*; Katz, «Miss Chief»; Hill, "Kent Monkman"; Porterfield, "History Painting."
7   This philosophical position will eventually lead him to paint more stylized and abstract representations of territory.
8   MacKay, *Picturing the Land*, 41.
9   Katz, «Miss Chief», 41.
10 In 2000, Monkman designed a series of paintings titled *The Prayer Language*, which juxtaposed images of gay erotic scenes and the system of Cree syllabic writing collected by Christian missionaries in the nineteenth century. http://www.kentmonkman.com.
11 Derrida, *De la grammatologie*, 176.
12 Cauquelin, *Le site et le paysage*, 85.
13 Francis, *The Imaginary Indian*; Crosby, «The Construction of the Imaginary Indian.»
14 McIntosh, "Miss Chief Eagle Testickle," 37.
15 Désy, «L'homme-femme», 7.
16 Ibid., 13.
17 Ibid., 9.
18 Ibid., 14.
19 Quoted in Isenberg, *The Destruction of the Bison*, 164.
20 Trexler, *Sex and Conquest*, 17.
21 Harper, *Paul Kane*.
22 Smith, *Le Sauvage pendant la période héroïque*.
23 The stereotype appears to continue today in the marketing of certain signature clothing that combines ethnic references, trash, punk, and urban influences with a bestial sexuality. See, for example, the Virginia Ferreira and Chris Neuman creations of the Belle Sauvage line of clothing. http://www.belle-sauvage.co.uk.
24 Valaskakis, *Indian Country*, 133–34.
25 It is a recurring strategy for Blondeau. Several other individual performances, like *Minding the Motherland* (1997), *Sisters* (2000), and *Are You My Mother?* (2000), integrate family stories, especially those related to residential schools experiences.
26 Anderson, *Contemporary Canadian Women's Performance Art*, 82.
27 Stevenson, «Colonialism and First Nation Women in Canada,» 57.
28 Quoted in Bell, "Buffalo Boy at Burning Man Camp."
29 Stimson, *Buffalo Boy's Heart On*, 14.
30 Braidotti, *Metamorphoses*.

31 Bhabha, *The Location of Culture*, 364.

32 Ibid., 360–67.

33 Ibid., 361.

34 Krauss, "Photography's Discursive Spaces," 28.

35 Monkman also uses the diorama in recent extremely political works. See the exhibition *My Treaty Is with the Crown*, Leonard & Bina Art Gallery, 2011, and Porterfield, "History Painting."

36 Crary, *Techniques of the Observer*, 112–13.

37 Grau, *Virtual Art*, 127.

38 Belting, *Pour une anthropologie des images*, 105.

39 Henry, "Canada's Contribution," 236.

40 Bouchard, qtd. in Vigneault, Espace Artistique, 52.

41 Lipovetsky and Juvin, *L'occident mondialisé*, 48.

WORKS CITED

Anderson, Heather Marie. *Contemporary Canadian Women's Performance Art: Reading Postfeminism and Third Wave Feminism*. Mémoire de maîtrise. Women's Studies, Joint program. Halifax: Mount St. Vincent University, Dalhousie University, and Saint Mary's University, 2003.

Bell, Lynne. "Buffalo Boy at Burning Man Camp: Mourning and the Forgiving of History in the Work of Adrian Stimson." *Canadian Art* (Summer 2007): 44–48.

Belting, Hans. *Pour une anthropologie des images*. Paris: Gallimard, 2004.

Bhabha, Homi. *The Location of Culture*. London and New York: Routledge, 1994.

Braidotti, Rosi. *Metamorphoses: Towards a Materialist Theory of Becoming*. Cambridge and Malden: Polity Press, 2002.

Bryson, Norman. *Vision and Painting: The Logic of the Gaze*. New Haven: Yale University Press, 1983.

Cauquelin, Anne. *Le site et le paysage*. Paris: Presses universitaires de France, 2002.

Crary, Jonathan. *Techniques of the Observer: On Vision and Modernity in the Nineteenth Century*. Cambridge, MA: MIT Press, [1990]1995.

Crosby, Marcia. «The Construction of the Imaginary Indian.» In *Vancouver Anthology: The Institutional Politics of Art*, ed. Stan Douglas. Vancouver: Talon Books, 1991.

Derrida, Jacques. *De la grammatologie*. Paris: Éditions de Minuit, 1967.

Désy, Pierrette. «L'homme-femme. Les berdaches en Amérique du Nord, Libre». *Politique, anthropologie, philosophie* 78, no. 3 (1978): 57–102.

Désy, Pierrette. *Amérique du Nord. Mythes et rites amérindiens. Dictionnaire des mythologies et des religions des sociétés traditionnelles et du monde antique*, sous la direction d'Yves Bonnefoy, tome 1, 18–31 et 514–20; tome 2, 1999–2003. Paris: Flammarion, 1999.

Didi-Huberman, Georges. *Devant l'image: question posée aux fins d'une histoire de l'art*. Paris: Les Éditions de Minuit, 1990.

Francis, Daniel. *The Imaginary Indian: The Image of the Indian in Canadian Culture* Vancouver: Arsenal Pulp Press, 1992.

Grau, Oliver. *Virtual Art: From Illusion to Immersion.* Cambridge, MA: MIT Press, 2003.

Harper, John Russell. *Paul Kane, 1810–1871.* Forth Worth: Amon Carter Museum of Western Art; Ottawa: National Gallery of Canada, 1971.

Henry, Frances. "Canada's Contribution to the Management of Ethno-Cultural Diversity." *Canadian Journal of Communication* 27 (2002): 231–42.

Hill, Richard W. «Kent Monkman's Constitutional Amendments : Time and Uncanny Objects». In *Interpellations: Three Essays on Kent Monkman / Trois essais sur Kent Monkman*, edited by Michèle Thériault, 49–84. Montreal: Galerie Leonard & Bina Ellen Art Gallery, Concordia University, 2012.

Isenberg. Andrew. *The Destruction of the Bison.* Cambridge: Cambridge University Press, 2000.

Katz, Jonathan D. «Miss Chief ne manque jamais de s'intéresser aux dernières tendances de la mode européenne.» In *Interpellations: Three Essays on Kent Monkman / Trois essais sur Kent Monkman*, ed. Michèle Thériault, 37–72. Montreal: Galerie Leonard & Bina Ellen Art Gallery, Concordia University, 2012.

Krauss, Rosalind. "Photography's Discursive Spaces." In *The Contest of Meaning: Critical Histories of Photography*, ed. R. Bolton. Cambridge, MA: MIT Press, 1989.

Lee, Ruthan. *The Production of Racialized Masculinities in Contemporary North American Popular Culture.* PhD diss., Department of Sociology, York University, 2011.

Lipovetsky, Gilles, et Hervé Juvin. *L'occident mondialisé. Controverse sur la culture planétaire.* Paris: Éditions Grasset, 2010.

MacCannell, Dean. *The Tourist: A New Theory of the Leisure Class.* New York: Schocken Books, [1976]1989.

MacKay, Marylin J. *Picturing the Land: Narrating Territories in Canadian Landscape Art, 1500–1950.* Montreal and Kingston: McGill–Queen's University Press, 2011.

McIntosh, David. "Miss Chief Eagle Testickle, Postindian Diva Warrior, in the Shadowy Hall of Mirrors." In *The Triumph of Mischief*, 31–46. Hamilton: Hamilton Art Gallery, 2007.

McMaster, Gerald. "The Geography of Hope." In *The Triumph of Mischief*. Catalogue exposition, co-commissaires, David Liss and Shirley J. Madill. Hamilton: Hamilton Art Gallery, 2007.

Mitchell, W.J.T. *Iconologie: image, texte, idéologie.* Traduit de l'anglais par Maxime Boidy et Stéphane Roth. Paris: Les Prairies ordinaires, 2009.

Porterfield, Todd. "History Painting and the Insoluble Question of Sovereignty." In *Interpellation: Three Essays on Kent Monkman / Trois essais sur Kent Monkman*, ed. Michèle Thériault, 85–93. Montreal: Leonard & Bina Ellen Gallery, Concordia University, 2012.

Smith, Donald B. *Le Sauvage pendant la période héroïque de la Nouvelle-France (1534–1663), d'après les historiens canadiens-français des XIXe et XXe siècles.* Montréal: Hurtubise HMH, coll. «Cahiers du Québec» 1974.

Stevenson, Winona. «Colonialism and First Nation Women in Canada.» In *Scratching the Surface: Canadian Anti-Racist Feminist Thought*, ed. Enakshi Dua and Angela Robertson, 49–80. Toronto: Women's Press, 1999.

Stimson, Adrian A. *Buffalo Boy's Heart On: Buffalo Boy's 100 Years of Wearing His Heart on His Sleeve*. MA thesis, Departmentof Art and Art History, University of Saskatchewan, Saskatoon, 2005.

Thériault, Michèle, ed. *Interpellations: Three Essays on Kent Monkman / Trois essais sur Kent Monkman*. Montreal: Galerie Leonard & Bina Ellen Art Gallery, Concordia University, 2012.

Tobby, Michael. *The True North: Canadian Landscape Painting 1896–1939*. London: Lund Humphries, Barbican Art Gallery, 1991.

Trexler, Richard C. *Sex and Conquest: Gendered Violence. Political Order, and European Conquest of the Americas*. Ithaca: Cornell University Press, 1995.

Valaskakis, Gail Guthrie. *Indian Country: Essays on Contemporary Native Culture*. Waterloo: Wilfrid Laurier University Press, 2005.

Vigneault, Louise. *Espace artistique et modèle pionnier. Tom Thomson et Jean-Paul Riopelle*. Montréal : Éditions Hurtubise, 2011.

Zemans, Joyce. «Establishing the Canon: Nationhood, Identity, and the National Gallery's First Reproduction Program of Canadian Art.» *Journal of Canadian Art History* 16, no. 2 (1995): 6–39.

BIBLIOGRAPHY

Anderson, Heather, and Helen Yeomans. *Wilderness Acts: Lori Blondeau, Rita McKeough, Janet Morton*. Halifax: Eyelevel Gallery, 2007.

Basaldu, Christopher Robert. *Hopi Hova: Anthropological Assumptions of Gendered Otherness in Native American Societies*. MA thesis, American Studies, University of Arizona, 1999.

Bishop-Stall, Reilley. "Re-Imaging and Re-Imagining the Colonial Legend: Photographic Manipulation and Queer Performance in the Work of Kent Monkman and Miss Chief Share Eagle Testickle." *Journal* 12, no. 1 (2011). http://gnovisjournal.org/2011/11/21/reilley-bishop-stall-journal

Bell, Lynne, and Janice Williamson. «High-Tech Story Teller: A Conversation with Performance Artist Lori Blondeau.» *Fuse* 24, no. 4 (2001): 27–34.

Cameron, Michelle. Two-Spirited Aboriginal People: Continuing Cultural Appropriation by Non-Aboriginal Society." *Canadian Women Studies* 24, nos. 2–3 (2005): 123–27.

Cauquelin, Anne. *L'invention du paysage*. Paris: Quadrige Presses universitaires de France, 2000.

Crowston, Catherine, et al. *Face the Nation: KC Adams, Lori Blondeau, Dana Claxton, Terrance Houle, Maria Hupfield, Kent Monkman, Adrian Stimson, Jeff Thomas*. Edmonton: Art Gallery of Alberta, 2008.

Dion, François, et Marie-Josée Lafortune (éd.). *Abus mutuel : négocier la survivance ; actes du colloque*. Montréal: Optica, un centre d'art contemporain, 2005.

Elkins, James. *Visual Studies: A Skeptical Introduction*. New York: Routledge, 2003.

Henry, Frances. "Canada's Contribution to the Management of Ethno-Cultural Diversity." *Canadian Journal of Communication* 27 (2002): 231–42.

Jacobs, Sue-Ellen, Wesley Thomas, and Sabine Lang, eds. *Two-Spirit People: Native American Gender Identity, Sexuality, and Spirituality*. Urbana: University of Illinois Press, 1997.

Kane, Paul. *Wanderings of an Artist among the Indians of North America: from Canada to Vancouver's Island and Oregon through the Hudson's Bay Company's territory and back again*. London: Longman, Brown, Green, Longmans, and Roberts, 1859.

Harper, John Russell. *Paul Kane, 1810–1871*. Forth Worth: Amon Carter Museum of Western Art; Ottawa: National Gallery of Canada, 1971.

Heinich, Nathalie. *De la visibilité. Excellence et singularité en régime médiatique*. Paris: Éditions Gallimard, 2012.

Herald, Sherbert Garry, Annie Gérin, and Sheila Petty. *Canadian Cultural Poesis: Essays on Canadian Culture*. Waterloo: Wilfrid Laurier University Press, 2006.

Hoolboom, Michael. *Practical Dreamers: Conversations with Movie Artists*. Toronto: Coach House Books, 2008.

Lee, Ruthan. *The Production of Racialized Masculinities in Contemporary North American Popular Culture*. PhD diss., Department of Sociology, York University, Toronto, 2011.

Lefebvre, Henri. *La production de l'espace*. Paris: Anthropos, [1974]1986.

MacDonald, Megan L. *Indigenous American Two-Spirit Women and Urban Citizenship in the Late Twentieth Century*. PhD diss., Purdue University, West Lafayette, 2009.

Maurice, Rolland. *The Otherings of Miss Chief: Kent Monkman's Portrait of the Artist as Hunter*. MA thesis, Departmentof Art History, Carleton University, 2007.

MacKay, Marylin J. *Picturing the Land: Narrating Territories in Canadian Landscape Art, 1500–1950*. Montreal and Kingston: McGill–Queen's University Press, 2011.

McIntosh, David. "Miss Chief Eagle Testickle, Postindian Diva Warrior, in the Shadowy Hall of Mirrors." In *The Triumph of Mischief*. Catalogue exposition, co-commissaires, David Liss and Shirley J. Madill, 31–46. Hamilton: Hamilton Art Gallery, 2007.

———. "Kent Monkman's Postindian Diva Warrior. From Simulacral Historian to Embodied Liberator." *Fuse Magazine* 29, no. 3 (2006): 13–23.

Mitchell, W.J.T. *Iconologie: image, texte, idéologie*. Traduit de l'anglais par Maxime Boidy et Stéphane Roth. Paris: Les Prairies ordinaires, Coll. «Penser/Croiser». 2009. Print.

Monkman, William Kent. *The Prayer Language: Kent Monkman*. Hull: Centre d'art indien, 2001.

Olwig, Kenneth Robert. *Landscape, Nature, and the Body Politic: From Britain's Renaissance to America's New World*. Madison: University of Wisconsin Press, 2002.

Portis, Benjamin. *Who Is Creating Waves in the Canadian Art Scene?* Calgary: Trépanier Baer, 2010.

Racette, Sherry Farrell, et al. *Close Encounters: The Next 500 Years*. Winnipeg: Plug In Editions, 2011.

Ryan, Allan. *The Trickster Shift: Humour and Irony in Contemporary Native Art*. Vancouver: UBC Press, 1999.

Saad, Sandy. *Purloined Stories*. Toronto: Doris McCarthy Gallery, University of Toronto, 2011.

Slater, Sandra Dale. *My God Was Called Conqueror on Man: Constructions and Contestations of Masculinities in the New World, 1480–1640*. PhD diss., College of Arts and Sciences, University of Kentucky, 2009.

Smith, Donald B. *Le Sauvage pendant la période héroïque de la Nouvelle-France (1534–1663), d'après les historiens canadiens-français des XIX*ᵉ *et XX*ᵉ *siècles*. Montréal: Hurtubise HMH, coll. «Cahiers du Québec», 1974.

Stimson, Adrian A. *Articulation: Conex-us, Express, Joined*. Saskatoon: Mendel Art Gallery, 2008.

Sullivan, Garrett A., Jr. *The Drama of Landscape: Land, Property, and Social Relations on the Early Modern Stage*. Redwood City: Stanford University Press, 1998.

Thériault, Michèle, ed. *Interpellations: Three Essays on Kent Monkman / Trois essais sur Kent Monkman*, Montreal: Galerie Leonard & Bina Ellen Art Gallery, Concordia University, 2012.

Tilton, Robert. *Pocahontas: The Evolution of an American Narrative*. Cambridge: Cambridge University Press, 1994.

VanDeCar, Katryn Lynn. *Killing the Berdache and Raising the Two-Spirit: Continuing and Emerging Roles of American Indian Two Spirits*. Master's thesis, Department of Anthropology, Michigan State University, 2002.

Warren, Louis S. *Buffalo Bill's America: William Cody and the Wild West Shows*. New York: Alfred A. Knopf, 2005.

Wark, Jayne. "Dressed to Thrill: Costume, Body and Dress in Canadian Performative Art." In *Caught in the Act: An Anthology of Performance Art by Canadian Women*, ed. Tanya Mars and Johanna Householder. Toronto: YYZ, 2004.

ELEVEN

Mapping the Migrant Mindscape in Gabrielle Roy: A Macro Definition of *écriture migrante*

Julie Rodgers

dentified as a new current in Québécois literature in the 1980s, the term *écriture migrante*[1] is one that has incited much academic debate as to how it should be defined and, indeed, to whom the label can be applied.[2] *Écriture migrante* became emblematic of the end of the twentieth century in Canada, especially in Quebec with the influx of multicultural immigrants following the *Révolution tranquille*. In its original sense, it refers to an emerging group of writers largely identified by their having a foreign geographical birthplace and/or mother tongue and for whom the personal experience of having left behind the original homeland is a common preoccupation of their literary output.[3] Often their writing reflects on and negotiates their position of alterity and liminality within a new world that is not yet fully theirs (and may never be) in circumstances where a return to the old world is no longer possible. When one thinks of prominent writers representative of *écriture migrante* in Quebec today (and this is reflected in university courses and academic texts on *écriture migrante*), key names that come to mind include Ying Chen (Chinese Québécoise), Abla Farhoud (Lebanese Québécoise), Naïm Kattan (Iraqi Québécois), Dany Laferrière (Haitian Québécois), Marco Micone (Italian Québécois), and Régine Robin (Polish Québécoise). What all of the above writers share is their obvious minority ethnic status, or, rather, their "otherness" in the face of a Quebec society that for a long time sought to maintain a homogenous vision of its identity based on French ancestry and the French language. Studies of *écriture migrante*, therefore, often focus on the ambiguous place of migrant writers in Quebec and their contributions to a canon of Quebec literature whose parameters are constantly being forced to become more fluid and open.

Without denying the validity of this approach to *écriture migrante*, this chapter argues for a more abstract definition of the term and demonstrates how the concept of *écriture migrante* can be applied to Quebec writers from a much earlier epoch, whose work would normally be located firmly within the established canon. By examining the case of Gabrielle Roy (1909–1983), an author whose name has become almost synonymous internationally with "traditional" Quebec literature, this chapter will contend that a definition of *écriture migrante* should not be limited to contemporary, multicultural Quebec, nor should it necessarily entail ethnic "otherness." In fact, one could even argue that *écriture migrante* has been a constant undercurrent flowing through Quebec literature right from its inception, when the first French pioneers recorded their encounters with an unfamiliar land in the seventeenth and eighteenth centuries in what are now known as the writings of New France.

To demonstrate the migrant tendencies of Roy's writing and to expand the term so that it can be rendered more inclusive, this chapter focuses on the aesthetics involved in *écriture migrante* instead of limiting it to the ethnic origins of the writer. In adopting such an approach, it follows up on and contributes to earlier critical interventions by Nepveu and Carrière and Khordoc.[4] Nepveu's discussion of the term in *L'Écologie du réel: Mort et naissance de la littérature québécoise contemporaine* views *écriture migrante* as an artistic and stylistic practice. Similarly, Carrière and Khordoc, in their "Introduction" to *Migrance comparée*, raise questions as to what is actually meant by *écriture migrante* and whether it only refers to authors who have immigrated. It is perhaps more fruitful, then, to conceive of *écriture migrante* as a poetics of movement "involving a series of antithetical notions—belonging and exile, roots and uprooting, centre and periphery,"[5] rather than as a rigidly delineated cultural and social position, that of immigrant. At the heart of this poetics of movement is a subject who is indeed caught between two worlds, but not necessarily two countries or nationalities, and who experiences feelings of loss, marginalization, dislocation, and hybridization as a result of his or her "in-betweenness." In Den Toonder, it is possible to draw up what could be deemed a list of the key recurring tropes of a migrant aesthetics.[6] These include a dispossession of origins; a worrying or stressful sense of strangeness; a confusion between "here" and "there"; an experience of exile; an exploration of space; and an encounter with the "other." Den Toonder also draws attention to the trope of journeys in *écriture migrante*, journeys both real and imaginary but always part of an arduous identity quest. It is not unusual to find in works labelled as *écriture migrante* a desire to leave and reinvent oneself, contradicted by a constant need to return to and reaffirm one's origins.

It is with this more abstract vision of *écriture migrante* in mind that this chapter will interrogate the writings of Gabrielle Roy with the goal of demonstrating how this particular artistic practice can be detected in authors who are not usually associated with the genre. It will examine the presence of a migrant aesthetics—or, rather, mindscape—in her work that is often more metaphorical than literal in its composition but one in which issues of conflicted identity and a complex relationship to space nonetheless remain at the fore. Morgan defines "mindscapes" as "imaginary geographies" and highlights the important role they play in people's understanding of the world.[7] The interpretation of mindscape I adopt in this chapter will expand on Morgan's "imaginary geographies" and employ the term to refer to a landscape of ideas or a mapping of thoughts, placing more emphasis on the conceptual than on the physical. In the case of Gabrielle Roy, this chapter will argue that a very particular type of mindscape characterizes her writing (and, indeed, the writer herself), one that can be qualified as "migrant" in that it is imbued with many of the features that have already been identified as pertaining to the phenomenon of *écriture migrante*, in particular, the tropes of otherness, movement, and liminality. The chapter will demonstrate how a "migrant mindscape" can be applied to the way in which Roy "looks out" onto the world as well as the way in which the reader "looks into" the Royan universe.

VOICES FROM THE OUTSIDE

A key feature of *écriture migrante* lies in its ability to question and destabilize the centre from the periphery.[8] How this relates to Gabrielle Roy is in the transgressive potential of her writing and its capacity to overturn established norms. Roy's first appearance on the Quebec literary stage occurred in 1945 with the publication of the immensely successful *Bonheur d'occasion*, a text that could in itself be seen as outsider or "immigrant" in terms of its dramatic impact on the Quebec literary canon, given that until then, that canon had been characterized mainly by a strong focus on the rural aspect of Quebec identity. With *Bonheur d'occasion*, Gabrielle Roy faisait entrer donc, d'un seul coup, dans notre littérature, la ville avec ses destins problématiques, ses mentalités jamais encore décrites, ses stagnations sociales engendrées par la Crise, et une référence aux conflits mondiaux les plus actuels qui auraient des résonances jusqu'en France et aux Etats-Unis, portant ainsi notre imaginaire sur une scène beaucoup plus vaste que l'étroite scène sociale.[9]

introduced to our literature, therefore, in one fell swoop, the city with all its problematic destinies, its mentalities which had not yet been described, its various social stagnations brought on by the Economic Crisis, and a reference to current world conflicts which would resonate as far as France and the United States of America, thus guiding our imagination on to a much wider platform than the narrow social scene to which we were accustomed.[10]

Roy has been seen by many critics as a key player in the dismantling of the very rigid parameters of the canon of Quebec literature in that she forced it to embrace a new reality, the urban space, and redefine itself afresh. The effect of *Bonheur d'occasion* on the Quebec literary scene is comparable to the effect produced by immigrant writers in Quebec whose creative output has similarly led to "une modification profonde, substantielle de la cartographie littéraire" (a profound and substantial modification of the literary map).[11] However, while the innovative nature of Roy's urban realism was instantly recognized by critics, it took longer for other transgressive aspects of her writing to be noticed—namely, the feminist potential of her work. Agnès Whitfield (1990), in her essay "Relire Gabrielle Roy, Ecrivaine," comments on the traditional and patriarchal tone that dominated critical engagement with Roy's texts for a long time and that prevented the feminist perspective present in her writing from coming to the fore: "on a passé sous silence la portée féminine voire féministe" (the feminine, or, rather, feminist impact was silenced).[12] Mary Jean Green (2003), in her essay "Reading Gabrielle Roy: Confessions of an American Feminist," makes an observation similar to Whitfield's.[13] She reveals having been confused as a young academic by what the established critics had to say about *Bonheur d'occasion*. For her, the novel clearly centred on the mother–daughter relationship between Rose-Anna and Florentine Lacasse, whom she viewed as the principal characters. Yet it seemed that most scholarship had thus far been directed to the less developed male characters, especially Azarius Lacasse, who was held up as a tragic hero:

After all my years of literary training, how had I managed to so badly misread this narrative? A novel that for me had focused on the tragic struggle of a young woman, emblematically placed at the centre of the novel's opening and closing scenes, was according to the "experts," really about other things: the conversations about the war among the men at the *Deux Records* and, perhaps most important, the demise of the Quebec hero.[14]

Until recently, Gabrielle Roy was predominantly read from a traditional angle and her representations of women were considered to adhere to the accepted social outlook of her era. Rose-Anne Lacasse, therefore, who epitomizes the Christian mythical figure of the "mater dolorosa," was seen as promoting the worthiness of motherhood and as justifying the suffering it entailed. By readers and critics alike, Roy was applauded for upholding the natural vocation of women and protecting the religious (and patriarchal) values of Quebec. The irony of such praise, however, is that Roy was actually attempting to deconstruct the masculine myth of motherhood by denouncing it as a life of thankless servitude, one in which one's personal identity and freedom were sacrificed to the interests of the family. Roy's interest in the female condition and feminism passed unnoticed, yet there are many instances when the author holds a mirror to women's lives, highlighting and criticizing their narrow range of life choices and the constraints placed on them by society's expectations. Thanks to the work of feminist scholars such as Whitfield, Green, and also Saint-Martin,[15] a feminist reading of Roy has now been firmly established. The point to be made here, in relation to the subject of this article, is that Gabrielle Roy, as is typical of *écriture migrante*, paved the way for "other" voices in Quebec literature, allowing those who had previously been deprived of subjectivity and relegated to the periphery the opportunity to be represented. If *écriture migrante* is associated with facilitating the voice of the "other" (Den Toonder 2008),[16] with challenging the majority culture/the centre and carving out a space for the minority subject, then this is exactly what Roy does with her female characters. The majority culture that is called into question in Roy's writing is patriarchal society; the minority culture that seeks to dismantle this hegemony is her community of women. To relate this to the concept of the "migrant mindscape," the emphasis here is on the very particular way that Roy envisages the world as one in which old structures need to be challenged and alternative perspectives considered. The examples offered here are only two instances of the emergence of "otherness" in Roy's writing. Numerous examples are scattered throughout her fiction; a number of her works present immigrant characters and communities (*Rue Deschambault, Un jardin au bout du monde, Ces enfants de ma ma vie*), as do even more of her journalistic reports published in the *Bulletin des Agriculteurs* (which pre-date her fiction), in which the traditions of a wide range of ethnic minorities in Canada (such as the Mennonities, the Hutterites, and the Doukhobors) are recounted.[17]

IN-BETWEENNESS

Gabrielle Roy, a "pure" French Canadian, whose mother tongue was French, does not at first appear to be an obvious example of what we tend to understand as a Quebec migrant writer today—that is, someone of mixed nationality who is forced to deal with language and culture clashes in a unfamiliar environment, having left an old world, the place of their ancestral roots, to carve out a new life and a new identity. Yet as I have begun to demonstrate, many of the issues associated with the migrant condition are a constant motif throughout Roy's corpus, fictional and non-fictional. This is a view supported by Rosemary Chapman,[18] who notes that "Roy's case exposes a whole network of tensions between competing notions of identity and culture"[19] that are comparable to those encountered in *écriture migrante*. Whether it be the sense of dislocation experienced by the first generation of rural folk to take up residence in the city of Montreal (*Bonheur d'occasion*); the solitude and individual displacement characteristic of the modern human condition (*Alexandre Chenevert*); the call of the unknown that haunts the writer and artist (*Rue Deschambault, La Route d'Altamont, La Montagne Secrète*); an attempt to understand the perspective of the immigrant (*Fragile Lumières de la Terre*); an internal marginalization felt by the French Canadian in his/her own land vis-à-vis the English presence (*La Détresse et L'enchantement*); or, indeed, Roy's own desire to break free from her mother and her roots contradicted by a need to return to them through writing (her autobiographies), it is clear that Roy's texts are crosscut with the particular conflict that lies at the heart of almost all migrant writing and that, therefore, can been seen as intrinsic to the "migrant mindscape"—namely, the frictional pull between "here" and "there."[20] In fact, such is the centrality of this paradox in the Royan universe that François Ricard, critic and biographer of Gabrielle Roy, has divided the author's early work into two distinct cycles: the cycle of exile and the cycle of return. According to Ricard, *Bonheur d'occasion* (1945) and *Alexandre Chenevert* (1954) constitute the exile dialectic while *Rue Deschambault* (1955) and *La Route d'Altamont* (1966) represent the return to one's origins.[21] Interestingly, however, the existence of two separate cycles in the trajectory of Roy's writing is not quite so clear-cut, for Ricard also points out that in the middle of each cycle (in terms of publication dates) is a text that would appear to belong to the opposite cycle, thus highlighting the difficulty in reconciling two opposing desires, to separate from or to reunite with one's origins, which is a common feature of migrant writing. Consequently, *La Petite Poule d'Eau* (1950), a novel charting a return to the author's roots, is situated between the two novels of exile (*Bonheur d'occasion* and *Alexandre Chenevert*), and *La Montagne Secrète*, a novel of displacement (1961), is enveloped by *Rue Deschambault* and *La Route d'Altamont*, which make up the cycle of return.

Ricard is not the only critic to have noted this persistent paradox throughout the work of Gabrielle Roy, this "affrontement de deux tendances également pressantes mais ennemies, l'une allant à la solitude et à l'absence, l'autre à la possession du monde et au rassemblement" (confrontation of two tendencies, equally pressing but antithetical to one another, one moving towards solitude and absence, the other towards belonging in the world and togetherness).[22] Albert le Grand, in his 1965 essay "Gabrielle Roy ou l'être partagé," was perhaps one of the first to truly highlight the pull between "here" and "there" that was felt so fiercely by Roy's characters.[23]

> L'oeuvre de Gabrielle Roy renvoie sans cesse l'image d'un être double, tiraillé entre le besoin d'être ici en sécurité et là en liberté, ici à l'ombre et là dans la lumière.[24]

> The work of Gabrielle Roy forever presents us with the image of the double-self, torn between the need to be here in a state of security and there in a position of freedom, here in the shade, there in the light.

Paula Gilbert Lewis pursues a similar argument in her 1980 article "The Incessant Call of the Open Road," describing Roy's characters as longing "for the security of the home, the warmth of a small interior space. At the same time, they are dissatisfied with their present structured lives and dream of escapes, either in a distant past or in an ambitious future of total freedom."[25] Gilbert Lewis reiterates this image in her 1986 book *The Literary Vision of Gabrielle Roy*. She summarizes Roy's characters as "antithetical creatures, equally divided between their obsessive need for freedom, for travel on the open road, and for the security of the protective home, with its links of solidarity."[26]

MIGRANT INSTINCT

Many of the characters in Roy's texts seem to be imbued with what could be termed a migrant instinct. From Roy's first novel *Bonheur d'occasion* right through to posthumous publications such as *De quoi t'ennuies-tu Eveline*, travel and exploration form a central part of the Royan narrative.[27] Indeed the omnipresence of the theme of migrancy in Roy's oeuvre has led critic Jean Morency to remark that:

> il appert en effet que, pour la romancière du Manitoba, l'état du migrant constitue ce qui symbolise le mieux la condition humaine. Pour Gabrielle Roy, du point de vue philosophique, l'expérience humaine fondamentale est justement celle de la migration, de l'être jeté dans le monde.[28]

> it appears, in fact, that for the Manitoban novelist, the state of migrancy is the one that best symbolizes the human condition. For Gabrielle Roy, from a philosophical point of view, the fundamental human experience is essentially that of migration and the self being thrown into the world.

Similarly, Dominique Fortier in *Gabrielle Roy Réécrite* remarks on a to-ing and fro-ing between the real in the imaginary, the familiar, and the unfamiliar in Roy:

> La figure principale, le motif essentiel qui caractérise l'écriture de Gabrielle Roy est sans contredit le paradoxe.... La romancière qui s'efforce, d'une part, de 'consolider' le monde existant, de le réaffirmer en le dépeignant tel qu'il est, travaille également, d'autre part, à nier cette réalité donnée pour lui en substituer une autre.[29]

> The key figure, the core motif that characterizes Gabrielle Roy's writing is, without doubt, paradox.... The novelist who, on the one hand, forces herself to "consolidate" the existing world and to reaffirm it by depicting it as it is, also works, on the other hand, to deny this given reality and replace it with another.

In Roy's own words, her characters, both male and female, are incorrigible nomads (*La Rivière sans repos*, 240), "ces pauvres gens qui glissent pour ainsi dire à la surface de l'existence ... à la derive, au fil de la vie" (these poor people who slide, so to speak, on the surface of existence ... drifting throughout the course of life) (*La Route d'Altamont*, 97). In *Le Pays de Bonheur d'occasion* (published posthumously in 2000), Roy herself perhaps summarizes best the ambiguous desire for the unknown contradicted by our need to belong somewhere that haunts not only her work but human existence itself as she sees it:

> Je cherchais déjà, je cherche encore à concilier le besoin de liberté dont nous ne pouvons pas passer avec l'affection qui attache, la tendresse qui retient, les liens de solidarité qui ne doivent pas se défaire. Et voilà notre vie! Nous voulons les opposés, les inconciliables. Et arrange-toi comme tu peux entre tes désirs qui s'entre déchirent. (96)

> I was already trying, I am still trying to reconcile this need for freedom that we cannot do without with an affection that attaches us, a tenderness that holds us back and the bonds of solidarity that must not be undone. This is our life! We want opposing, irreconcilable things. So manage as best you can between your desires that divide each other.

In a discussion of the migrant nature of the writings of Gabrielle Roy, it is not irrelevant to look at the experiences of the author herself. It would seem that within her own family, Roy was something of an "outsider," struggling to find her place, deeply attached to her home but eager to explore the world beyond it at the same time. In his biography, Ricard describes the young Roy in terms of her alterity, as "dans la maison de ses parents, une étrangère" (an outsider in her parents' home).[30] In addition, there is the back story of her family's own migration westward from Quebec to Manitoba—a journey that, along with this innate sense of "otherness" on the part of the author, comes to play an important role in the mapping out of a migrant mindscape in Roy's work. This need to be constantly on the move, this "instinct migrateur" (migrant instinct) (*La Route d'Altamont*, 131), penetrates Roy's oeuvre almost as if it were a genetic condition passed down from one generation to the next. Roy's maternal family history (the Landry side) is one of adventure and geographic displacement that starts in Acadia and then moves to Connecticut and Quebec before finishing up in Manitoba. Gabrielle Roy is a veritable "filles des pionniers" (pioneers' daughter), as Ricard puts it, her maternal grandparents having made the brave decision to leave behind family and home in Quebec in favour of moving westwards.[31] Granted, this is a type of internal movement, moving from one Canadian province to another, but one should not underestimate the courage and initiative that was required to undertake such a mission. Ricard remarks :

> Il fallait quand même, à ces paysans illettrés, une bonne dose d'audace – et d'ambition – pour se lancer ainsi à l'aventure, c'est-à-dire abandonner leurs maisons, leurs voisins, leur parenté, pour aller recommencer leur vie à deux mille cinq cents kilomètres de chez eux, autant dire, à l'autre bout du monde. On oublie trop souvent, quand on évoque l'immobilisme et le conservatisme de la société rurale du Québec de cette époque, l'élan et l'esprit d'initiative qui animaient ces immigrants et que la nécessité seule ne saurait expliquer.[32]

> Even so, these illiterate country folk needed a good dose of audacity and ambition to embrace adventure in the way that they did, that is, abandoning their homes, their neighbours and their family to start their lives afresh 2,500 kilometres away, practically the other side of the world for them. Too often we forget, when evoking the immobility and conservatism of rural society in Quebec at this time, the vigour and spirit of initiative that ignited these immigrants and for which necessity alone cannot account.

This *instinct migrateur* was not confined to the mother's side of Roy's family. Roy's father, Léon Roy, left his hometown of Saint-Isidore-de-Dorchester at the age of thirteen, never to return. As an adult, his career as a colonizing agent for the Canadian government required him to spend long periods away from his wife and children among unfamiliar cultures. Léon expressed no nostalgia for lost origins; his wife Mélina, by contrast, harboured a burning desire throughout her life to return to her homeland in Quebec. Given this family background, it is not surprising that Gabrielle and her fictional double, Christine, manifested from a very young age this *instinct migrateur*. But hers was an ambiguous urge comprising a fascination with new worlds (shared with her father and maternal grandfather) alongside a yearning to return to one's source (shared with her mother). Jean Morency sums this up:

> La mémoire de la tragédie initiale, dont la mère de Gabrielle Roy a retenu des bribes transmises de génération en génération, en arrive à constituer la face sombre de l'expérience migratoire et à mettre un bémol sur l'esprit des pionniers qui caractérise l'imaginaire de Gabrielle Roy. C'est pourquoi les persepectives infinies ouvertes par les grands espaces de l'Ouest—foi en l'avenir, optimisme multiculturel—seront toujours mises en balance, dans les écrits de Gabrielle Roy, avec la nostalgie des pays perdus.[33]

The memory of the initial tragedy of which Gabrielle Roy's mother retained details which were transmitted from generation to generation, comes to constitute the sombre face of the migrant experience and diminish the pioneering spirit that characterizes Gabrielle Roy's imaginary universe. That is why the infinite and open perspectives brought on by the vast expanses of the West—faith in the future and multicultural optimism—will always be counterbalanced, in the writings of Gabrielle Roy, by a nostalgia for the lost country.

THE OUTSIDER AT HOME

What is interesting to note in an examination of the migrant experience in Roy is that one does not necessarily have to travel to a far-off place to feel like an outsider. Such a feeling of exile, "cette sensation de dépaysement, de pénétrer, à deux pas seulement de chez nous, dans le lointain" (this sensation of uprootedness, of entering into, at only two steps away from our home, a far off land) (*La Détresse et l'enchantement*, 11) can arise even when one is firmly "at home." In *Bonheur d'occasion*, the extreme poverty in which the people of Saint-Henri live has deprived them of a fixed sense of home or of belonging in a city that, theoretically speaking, should be theirs. Financial hardship has forced them into the position of "outsiders within," and as a result, they experience the same feelings of dislocation and liminality that are commonly found in *écriture migrante*:

> Chez nous, c'était un mot élastique et, à certaines heures, incompréhensible, parce qu'il évoquait non pas un seul lieu, mais une vingtaine d'abris éparpillés dans le faubourg. Il contenait des regrets, des nostalgies et, toujours, une parcelle d'incertitude. Il s'apparentait à la migration annuelle. (*Bonheur d'occasion*, 289)

> Home was an elastic word and, at certain moments, incomprehensible because it did not evoke one single place, but, rather, around twenty different places spread out all over the neighbourhood. It contained regret, nostalgia and, always, a lot of uncertainty. It was a word aligned with annual migration.

If dispossession[34] and uprootedness[35] are what define *écriture migrante*, then it is undeniable that this is the experience of the impoverished francophones of Saint-Henri as depicted in *Bonheur d'occasion*. Similar feelings of being an outsider at home can be detected in Roy's *La Détresse et l'enchantement*. Roy opens her autobiography with the following question: "Quand donc ai-je pris conscience pour la première fois que j'étais, dans mon pays, une espèce destinée à être traitée en inférieure?" (When did I realize for the first time that I was, in my own country, part of a race destined to be treated as inferior?) (11). Roy recounts how each time she and her mother travelled into Winnipeg on shopping expeditions, to "cette ville qui nous traitait en étrangers" (this city that treated us as foreigners) (14), they became ashamed of their "différence," felt threatened by the presence of English, and began lowering their voices when they spoke in French. They did not feel that they belonged, even though Winnipeg was just as much their city as it was for any other Manitoban. It was not until they are back within the confines of Saint-Boniface, "notre milieu naturel" (our natural environment) (16), that they felt comfortable speaking aloud in French once more. Roy describes the state of being a French Canadian as "un malheur irremediable" (an irremediable unhappiness) (15) due to a constant sense of displacement and dispersal, which her mother traced back to the fall of New France: "Tout vient ... de ce vol de nos terres là-bas, dans notre premier pays, quand nous en avions un, que les Anglais nous ont pris lorsqu'ils l'ont découvert si avantageux" (Everything stems from ... the theft of our former lands, those of our first country, when we had one, and that the English took when they discovered their potential" (25). This, in turn, leads Roy to reflect on the status of French Canadian patrimony: «J'ai commencé à me tracasser au sujet de la notion de patrie, de ce qu'elle signifiait au juste ... si nous autres en avions une patrie» (I began to fret about questions of homeland and what exactly the term meant) (25). Later on in *La Détresse et l'Enchantement*, she reaches this conclusion:

> C'est alors que j'ai compris que nous, Canadiens français, n'avons peut-être pas le sentiment du sang. Celui de la nationalité, oui, mais pas du Cœur, comme les Juifs, comme d'autres dispersés.... J'ai beaucoup souffert de cette distance que les Québécois mettaient alors et mettent encore entre eux et leurs frères du Canada français. (140)

> That's when I understood that we, French Canadians, do not, perhaps, have a sense of kinship. Nationality, yes, but not from within, in their hearts, like the Jews or other diasporic peoples.... This distance that Quebecers placed and continue to place between themselves and their French Canadian countrymen has caused me much anxiety.

These feelings of inferiority stemming from her origins, and the problem of belonging they give rise to, are intertwined with the concept of a migrant mindscape in the work of Gabrielle Roy. They translate as the questioning of place and identity that is frequently encountered in *écriture migrante*.

THE EXILE'S DESIRE TO RETURN

If the desire to leave and explore elsewhere is an integral aspect of the migrant mindscape, this is problematized by the sense of loss for what is left behind and by the nostalgia that surrounds the home place. The latter, having been abandoned, re-emerges in the migrant mindscape as a kind of lost paradise and as a place where the original self can be recuperated, even if this was not the case to begin with. Thus in *La Route d'Altamont*, Eveline, the mother figure, longs to return to her birthplace in her old age (a stage of life associated with erosion of the self, both physical and mental), and when she does, thanks to an outing with her daughter, she is instantly rejuvenated. It is the same for Rose-Anna in *Bonheur d'occasion*, who travels back from Saint-Henri to the countryside where she grew up and bathes in its nourishing qualities while there. However, it must also be pointed out that these glorious returns are short-lived for both: after the trip to the countryside, Rose-Anna's saga takes a turn for the worse; and in *La Route d'Altamont*, mother and daughter, despite their best efforts, are unable to find the correct road the next time they attempt this return. Thus, the home place is not always as stable or as accessible as it may first appear, and returning home, although it may prove beneficial in the short term, is not always so in the long term.

In the writings of Gabrielle Roy, the actual house itself (not just one's birthplace) takes on symbolic dimensions and comes to represent security, shelter, stability, and belonging, all that the migrant experience is not. Alongside this, the mother, because of her strong association with the home, emerges as a protector of the family's identity and of each member's sense of self. Each time the young Christine runs away in *La Route d'Altamont* and *La Rue Deschambault*, although she has enjoyed her adventures, she is glad to be welcomed back in the bosom of a familiar environment. In Roy's writing, having to move house is depicted as a soul-destroying upheaval that threatens the cohesiveness of the family unit. In *La Montagne Secrète*, the artist Pierre Cadorai takes inspiration from the expansiveness of his surroundings, and he needs access to this space to work, yet his cabin is depicted as equally essential as a place of respite and is just as necessary to him as his periods of nomadism. In *Bonheur d'occasion*, the notion of home is the least stable as a result of the Lacasse family's economic difficulties, and most of the Lacasse family members dream of escaping it, yet in moments of distress, this prison lights up "comme un phare" (like a lighthouse) and becomes a place of shelter and healing (268).

With regard to Roy herself, there appear to have been two key voyages in her life, one physical and the other metaphorical. Having grown restless in Canada, and no longer satisfied with teaching, Roy embarked on a voyage to Europe in her early thirties, prior to commencing her career as a writer. The first leg of this journey involved Paris—or, speaking more broadly, the French Canadian's ultimate bid to return to the mother country. Ironically, however, it was in Paris that Roy felt most displaced: «Parmi les flots dépaysés que Paris reçoit tous les jours, en vit-il jamais arriver de plus égaré que moi, à l'automne 1937?» (Among the streams of disoriented people that Paris welcomes every day, had it ever seen one as lost as me in the autumn of 1937?) (*La Détresse et l'enchantement*, 247). The French and the French Canadians may share a mother tongue, but language was perhaps the key isolating factor in Roy's Parisian experience: "Il me paraissait aussi difficile de me faire entendre à Paris que si j'avais été transportée au coeur de la Chine" (It seemed to me to be just as difficult to make myself understood in Paris as it would have had I been transported to the heart of China) (248). Rather than improve, Roy's experience in Paris deteriorated further despite her best efforts to fit in:

> Je me sentais de moins en moins à ma place à Paris. J'y perdais pied. Je croyais voir que je n'y arriverais à rien de bon. Je commençais à me dire que je n'y arriverais à rien de bon. Je commençais à me dire que je m'étais trompée de destination. (298)
>
> I felt less and less at home in Paris. I was losing my way. I believed I could foresee that I would come to nothing there. I started to tell myself that I would come to nothing there. I started to tell myself that I had picked the wrong destination.

The destination she should have opted for in the first place ironically turned out to be London, home to the enemy language, English: "Cher Londres et chère isle" (Dear London and dear island) (334); "Je me suis trouvée en sécurité" (I felt secure) (393). In England, Roy was less of an exile than she had been in France. The irony continues: it was during her stay in England that she managed to reconcile herself with her origins:

Pour moi qui avait parfois pensé que j'aurais intérêt à écrire en anglais, qui m'y étais essayée avec un certain succès, qui avais tergiversé, tout à coup il n'y avait plus d'hésitation possible: les mots qui me venaient aux lèvres, au bout de ma plume, étaient de ma lignée, de ma solidarité ancestral. Ils me remontaient à l'âme comme une eau pure qui trouve son chemin entre les épaisseurs de roc et d'obscurs écueils. (392)

Je ne m'étonnais pas d'ailleurs que ce fût en Angleterre, dans un hameau perdu de l'Essex, chez des gens hier inconnus de moi, que je naissais enfin peut-être à ma destination, mais sûrement en tout cas à ma propre identité que jamais plus je ne remettrais en question. (Ibid.)

For me who had sometimes thought that I should write in English, who had tried it with a certain amount of success, who had procrastinated, suddenly there was no more hesitation possible: the words that came to my lips, to the nib of my pen, were those of my lineage, of ancestral solidarity. They rose up from my soul like pure water finding its way among the thick layers of rock and dark reefs.

I wasn't surprised, moreover, that it had been in England, in a forgotten hamlet in Essex, staying with people whom I hadn't known until very recently, that I finally discovered, perhaps, my destination, but certainly, in any case, my identity, which I would never call into question again.

It would seem, therefore, that abandoning one's home and migrating elsewhere is what paves the way for a successful and willing return. The metaphorical journey mentioned, which many critics might argue is actually at the heart of Roy's migrant mindscape, refers to the constant to-ing and fro-ing between mother and daughter in Roy's writing, the daughter's need to separate from the mother in order to locate her own voice, followed by feelings of guilt for having abandoned the mother and thus an attempt to reunite with her. Indeed, Roy's writing itself, described by Ricard as "une longue entreprise de rachat" (a long task of redemption),[36] could be interpreted as a bid to return to the mother via the text and to repair the trauma[37] of their rupture. It is well known that Roy was haunted until her death by the thought that she had abandoned her mother, her source, in favour of her writing career, hence the maternal omnipresence in the vast majority of Roy's texts, which could be seen as constituting a pseudo-reconciliation with her matrilineal origins.[38]

THE WRITER AS THE QUINTESSENTIAL MIGRANT

Having examined the various ways in which a migrant mindscape manifests itself in the writing of Gabrielle Roy, from feelings of displacement to the desire to belong, accompanied by an incessant need on the part of Royan characters to travel and explore, I would now like to consider, in the conclusion of this chapter, the figure of the writer as the quintessential migrant: "ni enraciné, ni déraciné, habitant d'ici et d'ailleurs, voyageur et sédentaire, recherchant tout ensemble le désert et l'étroite compagnie de ses semblables" (neither rooted nor rootless, living here and there, traveller and sedentary, seeking both the desert and the close company of others).[39] In the Royan universe it is the writer who perhaps best sums up the push and pull between here and there that is so characteristic *écriture migrante*. The writer for Roy is the liminal figure par excellence, caught up in needing solitude, freedom, and adventure but at the same time seeking to return to his or her origins through writing, just like the author herself in her own personal trajectory. It is the writer who tries to reconcile the irreconcilable, the new world with the old, to find a place where both the familiar and the unfamiliar can meet, to belong but to also be apart.

> Je veux «tout avoir» ...; le temps de marcher et le temps de m'arrêter pour comprendre; le temps de m'isoler un peu sur la route et puis de rattraper les autres, de les rejoindre. (Christine, in *Rue Deschambault*, 220)
>
> I want "to have everything" ...; the time to walk and the time to stop and understand; the time to isolate myself a little along the way and then catch up with others again, rejoin them.

Thus it is perhaps the figure of the writer in whom the migrant mindscape evoked in this article is most present. Writing, for Roy, necessitates a constant to-ing and fro-ing, existing in a state of in-betweenness, uprooting oneself and leaving behind loved ones in order to encounter new experiences, while never fully being able to renounce one's past (as is evident in the trope of "returning home" in Roy). As we have seen in the case of Roy, this to-ing and fro-ing quality of the writer's existence infiltrates the very body of the narrative (its themes, its characters, and also the overall structure of Roy's oeuvre), and it is in the figure of the wandering writer that a fusion, of sorts, of all the migrant traits of Roy's writing seems to occur. As has been demonstrated in this chapter, it is less important whether or not the writer has actually physically and culturally experienced immigration, and more of a question of aethetics or *pratique scripturale*.⁴⁰ By adopting a more fluid interpretation of *écriture migrante*, it is possible to appreciate the migrant verve of writers in whom such a quality might otherwise be overlooked. In this respect, Roy truly emerges as visionary, laying down the landmarks of a mindscape that would come to characterize a whole wave of writing in Quebec in the closing decades of the twentieth century. ∎

NOTES

1. Robert Berrouet-Oriol (1986/1987), himself from Haïti, is credited with coining the term and defining the notion of *écriture migrante* in Quebec literature. The term translates into English as "migrant writing."
2. Harel, *Les passages obligés*.
3. Chartier, «Les originies de l'écriture migrante».
4. Nepveu, *L'écologie du réel*; Carrière and Khordoc, *Migrance comparée*.
5. Ireland and Proulx, "Negotiating New Identities," 37.
6. Den Toonder, in Carrière and Khordoc, *Migrance comparée*, 19–37.
7. Morgan, *Mindscapes of Montreal*, 1.
8. Ireland and Proulx, "Negotiating New Identities."
9. Brochu, *Bonheur d'Occasion: Une étude*, 18.
10. All translations from French to English in this article are my own.
11. Harel, *Les passages obligés*, 15.
12. Whitfield, «Relire Gabrielle Roy», 55.
13. Green, "Reading Gabrielle Roy."
14. Ibid., 90.
15. Saint-Martin, *La Voyageuse et la Prisonnière*.
16. Den Toonder, in Carrière and Khordoc, *Migrance comparée*..
17. For a detailed discussion of the treatment of the immigrant subject in Roy's journalistic writings, refer to Morency, "Récits de l'immigration».
18. Chapman, *Between Languages and Cultures*. Chapman's text offers an illuminating discussion of Roy herself as a non-unified, bicultural subject, traits that are often associated with the figure of the migrant. In particular, Chapman draws attention to Roy's bilingualism and how difficult it was for her to choose between French and English when it came to writing. This linguistic conflict experienced by Roy can be seen as a further factor contributing to her "migrant mindscape."

19 Ibid., 8.
20 Den Toonder, in Carrière and Khordoc, *Migrance comparée*.
21 Ricard, *Introduction à l'oeuvre de Gabrielle Roy*.
22 Ibid., 127.
23 Le Grand, «Gabrielle Roy ou l'être partagé».
24 Ibid., 39.
25 Lewis, "The Incessant Call," 818.
26 Lewis, *The Literary Vision of Gabrielle Roy*, 202.
27 Examples of journeys that come to mind include those that mother and daughter embark on in *Rue Deschambault* and *La Route d'Altamont* as well as the individual adventures of the daughter figure Christine in the same two texts.
28 Morency, «Récits de l'immigration», 37.
29 Fortier, in Everett and Ricard, *Gabrielle Roy réécrite*, 35.
30 Ricard, *Gabrielle Roy, une vie*, 109.
31 Ibid.
32 Ibid., 20.
33 Morency, «Récits de l'immigration», 42.
34 Den Toonder, in Carrière and Khordoc *Migrance comparée*.
35 Ibid.
36 Ricard, *Introduction à l'oeuvre de Gabrielle Roy*, 167.
37 Harel, in *Les passages obligés*, views trauma as inherent to *écriture migrante* (44). This trope can be extended to the "migrant mindscape."
38 *Bonheur d'occasion* was dedicated to her mother, and much of Roy's unpublished work (for example, *La Saga d'Eveline*) can be said to constitute a desire to rewrite the mother into existence.
39 Ricard, *Introduction à l'oeuvre de Gabrielle Roy*, 178.
40 Bessy and Khordoc, «Plaidoyer pour l'analyse des pratiques scripturales», 1.

WORKS CITED

Texts by Gabriel Roy (in order of original publication date)

[1993] 1945. *Bonheur d'occasion*. Montreal: Boréal.
[1993] 1950. *La Petite Poule d'Eau*. Montréal: Boréal. [1995]1954. *Alexandre Chenevert*. Montreal: Boréal.

[1993] 1955. *Rue Deschambault*. Montreal: Boréal.
[1995] 1961. *La Montagne secrète*. Montreal: Boréal.
[1993] 1966. *La Route d'Altamont*. Montreal: Boréal.
[1995] 1970. *La Rivière sans repos*. Montreal: Boréal.
[1995] 1975. *Un jardin au bout du monde*. Montreal: Boréal.
[1995] 1977. *Ces enfants de ma vie,* Montreal: Boreál.
[1996] 1978. *Fragiles lumières de la terre*. Montreal: Boréal.
[1988] 1984. *De quoi t'ennuies-tu, Eveline? Ely! Ely! Ely!* Montreal: Boréal.
1984. *La Détresse et l'enchantement*. Montreal: Boréal.
2000. *Le pays de Bonheur d'occasion*. Quebec: Boréal.

Secondary Texts

Berrouet-Oriol, Robert. «L'effet d'exil». *Vice versa* 17 (1986–87): 20–21.
Bessy, Marianne, and Khordoc Catherine, 2012. «Plaidoyer pour l'analyse des pratiques scripturales de la migrance dans les littératures contemporaines en français». *Nouvelles Études Francophones* 27, no. 1 (2012): 1–18.
Brochu, André. *Bonheur d'Occasion: Une étude*. Montreal: Boréal, 1998.
Carrière, Marie, and Catherine Khordoc, eds. *Migrance comparée* Bern: Peter Lang, 2008.
Chapman, Rosemary. *Between Languages and Cultures: Colonial and Postcolonial Readings of Gabrielle Roy*. Montreal and Kingston: McGill–Queen's University Press, 2009.
Chartier, Daniel. «Les originies de l'écriture migrante. L'immigration au Québec au cours des deux derniers siècles». *Voix et Images* 27, no. 2 (2002): 303–316.
Den Toonder, Jeanette. In *Migrance comparée*, ed. Marie Carrière and Catherine Khordoc, 19–37. Bern: Peter Lang, 2008.
Fortier, Dominique. «La Route d'Altamont comme réécriture de Rue Deschambault». In *Gabrielle Roy réécrite*, ed. Jane Everett and François Ricard, 35–55. Quebec: Nota Bene, 2003.
Green, Mary Jane. (2003). Reading Gabrielle Roy: Confessions of an American Feminist." In *Gabrielle Roy aujourd'hui*, ed. Paul Socken, 87–96. Saint-Boniface: Plaines, 2003.
Harel, Simon. *Les passages obligés de l'écriture migrante*. Montreal: XYZ, 2005.
Den Toonder, Jeanette. In *Migrance comparée*, ed. Marie Carrière and Catherine Khordoc, 19–37. Bern: Peter Lang, 2008.
Le Grand, Albert. «Gabrielle Roy ou l'être partagé». *Etudes Françaises* 1, no. 2 (1965): 39–65.
Lewis, Paula Gilbert. "The Incessant Call of the Open Road." *French Review* 53, no. 6 (1980): 816–25.
———. *The Literary Vision of Gabrielle Roy*. Birmingham: Summa, 1984.
Morgan, Ceri. *Mindscapes of Montreal: Quebec's Urban Novel, 1960–2005*. Cardiff: University of Wales Press, 2012.
Morency, Jean. «Récits de l'immigration. L'expérience migratoire dans l'oeuvre de Gabrielle Roy». In *Prendre la route. L'expérience migratoire en Europe et en Amérique du Nord du XIVe au XXe siècle*, ed. Andrée Courtemanche and Martin Pâquet, 37–51. Hull: Vent d'Ouest, 2001.

Nepveu, Pierre. *L'écologie du réel. Mort et naissance de la littérature québécoise contemporaine.* Montréal: Boréal, 1988.
Ricard, François. *Gabrielle Roy, une vie.* Montréal: Boréal, 2000.
———. *Introduction à l'oeuvre de Gabrielle Roy.* Quebéc: Nota Bene, 2001.
Saint-Martin, Lori. *La Voyageuse et la Prisonnière.* Montréal: Boréal, 2002.
Whitfield, Agnès. «Relire Gabrielle Roy, écrivaine». *Queen's Quarterly* 97, no. 1 (1990): 53–66.

TWELVE

The Green Fields of Canada—Forgotten! A Reappraisal of Irish Traditional Music History in Canada

Gearóid Ó hAllmhuráin

When analyzed through the prism of diaspora, the transmission of Irish music across the Atlantic encapsulates critical non-textual forms of cultural memory that have taken root in North America over the course of four centuries. Hitherto neglected by Irish cultural historians, the transplantation and adaptation of Irish traditional music is especially significant in the construction of Canadian Irish identities. The historic trajectory of Irish traditional music from colonial Ireland to the rural fringes and urban centres of Canada is marked by several interlocking narratives, among them, the complex and diffuse process of transculturation that brought it into contact with Scottish, French, English, and First Nation soundscapes. Sharing a frontier with Old World pioneers and New World hosts, Irish musicians in Canada, like their Scots-Irish cohorts farther down the Appalachian chain, were guardians of ethnic tradition and keepers of cultural memory. In this respect, their contribution to historic, symbolic, and translocal expressions of Irish identity in Canada is as significant as those of lauded writers, political leaders, and diplomatic figures whose chronicles have dominated the annals of Irish history in Canada.

The cultural history of Irish traditional music in Canada is inextricably linked to centuries of Irish immigration and settlement stretching from Newfoundland to Yukon, from Hudson Bay to the Great Lakes, and that continues to echo through the heteroglossic soundscape shared by Irish, Scottish, French, English, and First Nation communities throughout Canada today. Unlike the settlement of Irish people in urban America in the wake of the Great Famine, Irish settlement in Canada reached its apex by the middle decades of the nineteenth century. By then, many of the key ingredients of what we know today as *Irish traditional music*—the reel, for example, was the latest rising fad, and the quadrille had ousted the minuet as the most popular court dance in Europe—were being absorbed into various vernacular music traditions in oceanic and mainland Europe, and were being exported by their pioneer communities to the New World.[1]

Irish immigration to Canada began in the late 1600s. Like their counterparts who settled in the American colonies and the Caribbean, the earliest Irish who settled in Canada were emigrating in search of new opportunities or cheap land, or in response to "political and socioeconomic dislocations caused by wars, rebellions, and the increasing commercialization of Irish life."[2] By the mid-1700s, New France had received a quota of Wild Geese soldiers from the Irish brigades that were employed by the Bourbon kings, as well as other *hibernois*—deserters from the English colonies to the south, pioneer farmers, servants, merchants, lumbermen, and tradesman, whose numbers remain indeterminate.[3] This cohort grew after France ceded Quebec to Britain in 1763. Newfoundland attracted thousands of immigrants from the south Ireland in the 1700s. By the 1830s, they accounted for half the island's population. Halifax, Nova Scotia, as well as Cape Breton Island, Prince Edward Island, and New Brunswick, all had significant numbers of Irish by the early nineteenth century. Large-scale Irish immigration to British North America began in earnest after the Napoleonic Wars.[4] In all, 450,000 Irish immigrated to Canada (as opposed to the 400,000 who passed through American ports) between 1825 and 1845. This accounted for 60 percent of all new arrivals. By 1881, immigrants of Gaelic origin from Ireland and Scotland—both places were victims of internal colonialism—made up one-third of the population of Canada, which was now in excess of 4.5 million.[5]

The principal ports of entry for the Irish were Saint John, New Brunswick, which had trading links to Derry, as well as Montreal and Quebec City, the latter being one of the cheapest routes across the Atlantic. Many Irish immigrants followed a traditional pattern of chain migration. Although most of this settlement was unassisted, there were several assisted schemes, the most notable being those organized by Peter Robinson, brother of the Attorney General of Upper Canada, who settled 2,500 immigrants from Cork, Limerick, Tipperary, and Waterford in the Ottawa Valley and Peterborough between 1822 and 1825.[6] Unlike their post-famine cohorts in the United States, who chose to settle in urban centres, the

Irish who immigrated to Canada settled predominantly in rural communities. In these often isolated and self-contained rural milieux, they maintained their material and artistic cultures much longer that their Irish American homologues, who were quickly absorbed into the all-subsuming American melting pot. This pattern of Irish rural settlement in Canada was by no means exclusive, however. Larger urban centres like Toronto, Montreal, and Quebec City all had sizable Irish communities, both Catholic and Protestant, throughout the nineteenth and twentieth centuries, and many of their members contributed to an eclectic tapestry of Irish music, song, and dance. A distinct sense of regionalism and regional music dialects is one of the defining features of Irish music history in Canada. This can be gleaned from a brief exploration of Irish music communities in Newfoundland, the Maritime provinces, Quebec, Ontario, and small pockets of western Canada, all of which continue to bear the imprints of Irish musical culture today.

TALAMH AN ÉISC—IRISH MUSIC IN NEWFOUNDLAND

Historical geographer E. Estyn Evans noted that Ireland, which had been "on the edge of the known world found itself, in the sixteenth century, near the center of the new world."[7] The globalization of cod and sugar cane, and the corresponding scramble for New World colonies, had a direct impact on the exodus of Irish people to Canada. Newfoundland cod had been a Basque secret for centuries, but by 1600, fleets from France, Portugal, and England were all competing for the bounty of the Grand Banks. Throughout the seventeenth century, as England challenged Holland for economic hegemony, the West Country ports of Southampton and Bristol became the hubs of the British North Atlantic fishing industry. Every spring, fleets arrived to fish the Grand Banks and jostled for shore space to dry cod in the makeshift outports of Newfoundland. After fishing throughout the summer, fleets headed for home on the fall westerlies, often leaving caretakers in their wake to maintain the fishing rooms until their return the following spring.[8]

The West Country fleets that arrived in Newfoundland every spring usually called at Waterford in the south of Ireland to stock up with provisions (beef, pork, butter, bread, etc.) before heading west across the Atlantic. Spurred by the rising demand for seasonal labour on the Grand Banks, these ships took on Irish fishery workers, who were recruited from within a fifty-mile radius of the ports of Waterford, Youghal, and Dungarvan. As early as 1696, Abbé Jean Beaudoin, recalling a French raid on the English fisheries in Newfoundland, described Irish fishery workers as "slaves to their English masters."⁹ While the majority of these workers signed on with English fleets, others opted to work with the French fisheries in Newfoundland and Acadia (Nova Scotia), through existing networks that linked Waterford with St-Malo, Nantes, and Bordeaux.¹⁰ Irish fishery workers usually signed on for two summers, which involved staying on during the intervening winter in the brutal cold of Newfoundland. Hence, the term "wintermen" by which they were known when they returned home to Ireland. In 1776, the English geographer Arthur Young noted that five thousand migrant workers were sailing from Waterford to Newfoundland every year.

Many wintermen chose to settle permanently in Newfoundland. By 1720, just seven years after France ceded Acadia to Britain under the terms of the Treaty of Utrecht, small Irish outport settlements were emerging in Carbonear, Bay Bulls, Harbor Grace, and Placentia.¹¹ By 1784, the Irish comprised seven-eighths of the population of St. John's. Irish was the language spoken by the majority of these immigrants, and they dubbed their new home *Talamh an Éisc*—the land of the fish. By the 1780s, Irish speakers were so numerous that they were requesting Irish-speaking priests from Ireland. One of the most celebrated figures to spend time in Newfoundland during the eighteenth century was the poet Donncha Rua Mac Conmara (1716–1810). Born in Cratloe, Co. Clare, in 1716 during the Penal period, Mac Conmara was a talismanic figure for the Gaelic world of his time. Like many of his contemporaries marginalized by political and public life in Ireland, he hoisted his sails for Europe and its exiled Irish Catholic nation-in-waiting. As a young man, he was educated for the priesthood in Rome but was expelled for wildness. He returned to Ireland in 1740 and found work as a schoolmaster in Co. Waterford. Chronic penury, however, forced him to take the boat for Newfoundland in 1745. Humorous, precise, and allegorical details of his eleven-year sojourn in Talamh an Éisc colour his verse, especially his nostalgic poem *Eachtra Ghiolla an Amaráin* (Adventures of a Luckless Fellow), in which he parodies Virgil's *Aeneid*.¹² Although Mac Conmara took full advantage of the macaronic song form (to praise King George in English and the Young Pretender in Irish), his classic *Bánchnoic Éireann Ó* (The Fair Hills of Ireland), in which he described the isolation of the outport communities, is one of the earliest anthems of exile composed in Irish and has withstood the test of time relatively well since the eighteenth century. Two centuries after the settlement of wintermen in Newfoundland, the island still boasts a sizable Irish population, complete with Waterford surnames and accents that have defied the melting pot of time. Lancer sets are still danced in some outport and island communities where, until recently, Christmas mummering continued an ancient tradition of music, song, dance, and folk verse that their ancestors brought from insular Europe over two centuries ago.[13]

Distinguished by rare dialects of accordion and fiddle tunes that have grown out of a polymorphic matrix of Irish, French, English, and Scottish dance music and a colossal storehouse of ballads and songs from the same ethnic sources, Newfoundland is a unique laboratory for the study of folk music culture.[14] This ethnographic cornucopia has been unveiled in the seminal work of historical geographers and architects John Mannion, Gerald Pocius, and Robert Mellin, historians C.W. Doody, Cyril Byrne, and Kildare Dobbs, and folklorists and musicologists Kenny Goldstein, Neil Rosenberg, Anita Best, Evelyn Osborne, and Colin Quigley, whose monograph *Close to the Floor: Folk Dance in Newfoundland* is a milestone in ethnochoreographical studies.[15] Since its inception in 1968, the Memorial University Folklore and Language Archive (MUNFLA) has accumulated one of the largest reserves of folk music and song in North America, including a formidable corpus of Irish dance music, vernacular ballads, and trace elements of the Irish language that survived in Newfoundland until the end of the First World War.

REFUGEES, LOYALISTS, AND HIGHLANDERS— IRISH MUSIC IN THE MARITIMES

In his seminal collection of short stories *The Lost Salt Gift of Blood*, Cape Breton writer Alistair MacLeod delivered an astute and discerning epitaph of early Nova Scotian culture. Appraising the ethnic and religious tensions of his native place, he noted that "the houses and their people, like those of the neighboring towns and villages, were the result of Ireland's discontent, Scotland's Highland Clearances, and America's War of Independence. Impulsive Catholic Celts who could not bear to live with England and shrewd determined Protestant Puritans who, in the years after 1776, could not bear to live without."[16] While the political psyche of the Maritime provinces—New Brunswick, Nova Scotia, and Prince Edward Island—was shaped largely by French and British colonialism, their cultural psyche has been enriched by traditional music from Scotland, Ireland, and France. What is interesting from an ethnomusicological perspective is the manner in which First Nation Canadians, such as the Mi'kmaq, have adopted these musical traditions, which they now share with "the white man" in a vibrant nexus of cross-cultural creativity.

The ethnic tapestry of Nova Scotia still bears the imprint of its perplexed colonial past, however. During the seventeenth century, Acadia became embroiled in the conflict between France and England for political supremacy in Canada. The Treaty of Utrecht in 1713 transferred control of the area to England, and it became known as Nova Scotia because of its likeness to Scotland. Cape Breton Island—a separate province until 1820—remained French for a short time afterwards. The incumbent Acadians struggled to maintain their settlements in Nova Scotia. In 1755, their loyalty was deemed suspect and thousands were forcefully expelled. Some escaped to Quebec, Prince Edward Island, and Cape Breton. Others returned to France, while more headed south to Louisiana, where their descendants became known as Cajuns—a corruption of *Acadians*.[17] The land left by Acadians was settled in the 1770s by United Empire Loyalists who crossed the Bay of Fundy from New England to escape the American Revolution. In all, about 250,000 loyal colonists migrated to Nova Scotia to escape the perils of independence. The final influx of Puritan loyalists to southern Nova Scotia paralleled the arrival of Highland Scots on the barren eastern uplands of the province. These Gaelic-speaking settlers arrived in Atlantic Canada in the wake of the Highland Clearances in Scotland.[18] Driven from their crofts to make way for sheep less than a generation after the abortive Jacobite rebellion of 1745, their diaspora to the New World was a callous consequence of economic determinism, which led ultimately to the punctilious dismemberment of Highland society. By the 1820s, more than 50,000 Highland Scots had settled in Pictou and Antigonish counties, as well as on Cape Breton Island.

Small enclaves of Irish settlement were also part of this cultural mosaic. While some Irish arrived as part of the Loyalist flight from New England, others were sponsored immigrants who settled in rural Nova Scotia. There were three main clusters of Irish settlement: rural settlers from the north of Ireland at the head of the Bay of Fundy; Irish-speaking rural Catholics from the south of Ireland on Cape Breton Island—among them refugees from the 1798 rebellion, like Mogue Doyle, as well as Laurence Kavanagh, the first Irish Catholic elected to an English assembly; and a Catholic urban population in Halifax, which reached maturity by the 1860s.[19] New Brunswick and Prince Edward Island also featured strongly in Irish immigration. The beginning of the timber trade brought Irish lumbermen to New Brunswick in large numbers, especially to the Kennebecasis Valley, the Gulf Shore, and the Miramichi, which today hosts one of the oldest Irish music festivals in Canada.[20] The largest single influx of Irish came during the Great Famine, when hordes of destitute victims passed through the port of Saint John. Although never a stable group, some Irish followed the work in lumber camps across the province, while others opted to settle down and farm. They constituted about 35 percent of the population of New Brunswick by 1871.[21] The rolling hills and green fields of Prince Edward Island, by contrast, offered the prospect of good land and a solid future. Between 1767 and 1850, about 10,000 immigrants from twenty-five Irish counties had settled on Prince Edward Island. According to historian Brendan O'Grady, they constituted one-quarter of the founding communities of the island.[22] The place names on PEI still bear witness to these first settlers from Ireland.

The potent iconography of piping and tartanism—much of it engineered as a tourist incentive by Angus L. Macdonald when he was premier of Nova Scotia—has created a near ubiquitous sense of Scottish music in the Canadian Maritimes.[23] On closer examination, however, other musical traditions also become apparent, not least, Irish and Acadian. Irish uilleann pipers, for example, were being cited in Nova Scotian records shortly after uilleann pipes reached maturity in the early nineteenth century. Local church records, for example, indicate that in 1824, John Ceasy from Kilkenny, a "professor" of the uilleann pipes, died in Halifax.[24] Likewise, the abundant store of Irish ballads and songs collected by Helen Creighton, Edward D. Ives, and Edith Fowke throughout the Maritimes is an ample testament to the presence of Irish songs and singers in the region over the past two centuries.[25] What are referred to simplistically as *Irish tunes* also enjoy prominence in the powerful current of Highland Scottish music in the Maritimes. Some of this repertoire can be traced to the popularity of commercial recordings issued by Irish fiddlers Michael Coleman and Seán McGuire, especially, in Cape Breton, as well as to musical contacts between Irish and Cape Breton immigrants in the "Boston States" and in the Detroit–Windsor industrial region between 1930 and 1980. In more recent times, touring performers from Ireland and Cape Breton—among them Natalie MacMaster, Sharon Shannon, Dougie MacDonald, and Antóin MacGabhann—have started to share repertoires from both traditions. Irish American as well as Scottish American performers have also explored these repertoires in recent years.

The interface between Irish and Cape Breton music also speaks to an older cultural milieu.[26] Ever since the Scots became the first Irish diaspora after Colmcille's exile to Iona in 563, Ireland and Highland Scotland have shared a common Gaelic heritage.[27] Buttressed by a vernacular language, bardic poets and harpers found patrons on both sides of the North Channel up until the eighteenth century, despite the vicissitudes of political and sectarian upheaval. An extensive repertoire of airs and dance tunes index these centuries of exchange: "Port Gordon," composed by Rory Dall Ó Catháin (c. 1570–c. 1650) during his sojourn in

Scotland; "Killiecrankie," by Sligo-born Thomas Connellan (c. 1640–c. 1700), in memory of the Jacobite battle fought in 1689; and Myles O'Reilly's "Marbhna Luimní," which became "Lochaber No More" in Scotland. By the late 1700s, the printed collections of William Marshall, Neil Gow, and other Golden Age composers were finding their way to Ireland, where the new Scottish reel genre found avid patrons. Despite the amnesia that often marks discourse on Cape Breton stepdancing, Ireland and Cape Breton also share common dance antecedents.[28] The pan-European dispersal of quadrille sets in the eighteenth century and the intense traffic of dancing masters in and out of Ancien Régime France spawned innumerable variants of these group dances and their solo cognates. The ethnochoreographical symbiosis between Irish *sean nós* dancing, Cape Breton stepdancing, the Québécois *gigue*, Newfoundland lancers, and a host of other clogging traditions all over North America still bear witness to these once ubiquitous dance fashions in the Old World. Cape Breton dancing is a dialectal outgrowth of a macrohistorical process and, as such, shares links with a complex tapestry of archaic European dances that survive in Ireland and Scotland and throughout North America.

Until recently, Irish traditional music played by second and third generation performers enjoyed a healthy presence in industrial Cape Breton. These Northside Irish, as they were known, were descendants of shipyard workers and miners who had arrived in North Sydney, Centerville, and Sydney Mines from Newfoundland. Many of these transient workers took up residence along the Gannon Road, the main street running from the Newfoundland ferry terminal to Bras d'Or, and as they integrated with the host population, they began to infuse the region with Irish dance music. The key performers in this enclave beginning in the late 1800s were fiddlers Billy and Henry Fortune (the latter born around 1870), Joe Confiant, Johnny Wilmot, Robert Stubbert, flute player Tony Whelan, and mouth organ player Tommy Basker.[29] The doyen of this syncretic Scottish–Irish dialect, however, was Winston "Scotty" Fitzgerald (1914–1987) from White Point in north Cape Breton. Fitzgerald, whose background was Irish and French Acadian, was one of the stars of Canadian fiddling in the 1960s and 1970s and hosted numerous shows on CBC radio during his formative years. In more recent times, the Northside Irish style has found a new voice in the fiddling of Cape Breton composer Brenda Stubbert from Point Aconi.

GROSSE ÎLE AND BEYOND: IRISH MUSIC IN QUEBEC

The Irish presence in Quebec has been documented by diverse official sources since the early seventeenth century.[30] During the cosmopolitan French period (1608–1763), Irish surnames appeared in military, municipal, and trade records; after the transfer of power to Britain in 1763, Irish Protestant bureaucrats became prominent in the life of the province.[31] In 1765, Irish Protestant officers garrisoned in Quebec City began celebrating St. Patrick's Day (as did their cohorts in Boston), a practice that continues throughout the province today.[32] In 1844, Irish immigrants accounted for 6.3 per cent of the population of Lower Canada, and they remained the most numerous immigrant group in the region for the remainder of the nineteenth century.[33] The position of Quebec City at the head of a deepwater navigational system made it a natural entrepôt for Irish and other immigrants to Lower Canada. Because large ocean vessels could not navigate the upper reaches of the St. Lawrence River, most immigrants travelled in converted timber ships that were intended to transport timber back to England. This trade flourished in the wake of Napoleon's blockade of Baltic trade in 1807.[34] This river traffic and, especially, the quarantine station at Grosse Île, 50 kilometres downriver from Quebec, became a focal point of Ireland's Great Famine tragedy in 1847.[35] Official estimates tell us that 5,424 famine victims were buried at Grosse Île; unofficial estimates suggest a far higher number.[36] The proverb *bíonn súil le muir ach ní bhíonn súil le huaigh* (one looks forward to the sea, but does not expect to find a grave) proved more than telling for so many who braved the Atlantic in coffin ships only to die within sight of the New World.[37]

Deprived of audiences in Ireland, Irish musicians followed their bedraggled patrons into exile, some to struggle as anonymous street players, others to thrive in an emergent nexus of professional music. Uilleann piper William Connolly, for example, took advantage of the professional opportunities available to Irish music makers in Quebec. Born in Miltown, Co. Galway, in 1839, Connolly played the professional circuit in the United States in the 1850s before crossing the border to find work on the steam packets plying the St. Lawrence.[38] A half-century later, Irish Québécois society produced one of its most celebrated professional performers in Mary Travers, otherwise known as La Bolduc, Canada's iconic *chansonnière* of the 1920s and 1930s. Born in 1894 in the Gaspé to an Irish father and a French mother, Travers grew up hearing Irish songs and dance tunes. As a child, she learned the accordion, fiddle, and harmonica, as well as Acadian mouth music, or *turlutes*.[39] One of the first Québécois women to work as a professional singer, she began her career in 1927 and recorded more than three hundred songs during the

Great Depression, producing a record a month by 1930. Her songs enjoyed tremendous popularity during a time of intense poverty and social anomie in Canada.

While Québécois sources provide some of the earliest accounts of music among the First Nations, as well as the earliest field collections of European folk songs in North America, research on the fusion between French, Scottish, and Irish genres that gives Québécois music its distinct character has been somewhat sporadic.[40] Since the 1980s, however, Carmelle Begin, Myriam Laflamme, Simonne Voyer, and Lisa Ornstein have shed new light on the historical alchemy of *gigues* and *quadrilles,* fiddles and diatonic accordions, foot percussion and *chansons à repondre,* that have shaped Québec's musical ethnoscape.[41]

Although Quebec City and its environs (which included Valcartier, Stoneham, and Shannon) were older centres of Irish settlement—and, hence, older storehouses of Irish music and dance—by the mid-nineteenth century, Montreal had replaced Quebec City as Canada's economic hub.[42] Home to a historic underclass of Irish ship labourers and cove men, domestic servants, and railway workers, who lived in the hovels of Griffintown, as well as a bourgeois coterie of businessmen, journalists, and politicians, who lived in more stylish quarters "above the hill," Montreal has long been a port of entry for Irish immigrants to Canada.[43] In musical terms, it is a vibrant forum for Irish and Québécois performers, who continue to share repertoires and styles and to explore the sources of their respective ethnic traditions. Among the most illustrious performers to highlight this common ground was Montreal cab driver Ti-Jean Carignan (1916–1988), who was influenced by the fiddling of James Scott Skinner, Michael Coleman, James Morrison, and Seán McGuire. Diatonic accordionist Philippe Bruneau, a *confrère* of Carignan, also explored the multiple layers of Irish and Scottish music embedded in Quebec's traditional soundscape.

Montreal today is a transnational crossroads of Irish music, in its generic as well as its hybrid forms. Artists like Robert Leonard, Brad Hurley, Aindriú MacGabhann, Paul Legrand, Jocelyn Goerner, and Emily Andrews have all added greatly to the city's Irish music scene. Likewise, the city's myriad Irish societies, music and dance associations, and Irish language circles have created a warm and eclectic milieu for musicians to congregate and perform. One of Montreal's key nurseries is the Siamsa School of Irish Music, which began in 1991 with teachers David Papazian, Nancy Lyon, and Philippe Longval. Likewise, the School of Canadian Irish Studies at Concordia University acts as a major forum for Irish ethnomusicological studies. While professional ensembles like La Bottine Souriante, Ad Vielle Que Pourra, and Le Vent du Nord have all dipped into the Irish-Scottish–Québecois wellspring over the years, few ensembles have managed to discerningly revisit the Irish and Scottish sources of this wellspring like the Montréal ensemble Phenigma. Focusing on Donegal dance music and songs in Scots Gaedhlig, Phenigma included Scottish Canadian singer, Sine McKenna, Austrian guitarist Reinhard "Golo" Goerner, English fiddler Steve Jones, Canadian pianist Lynda Kathan, and Québécois flautist and composer Jean Duval.[44]

RURAL TOWNSHIPS AND URBAN COUNTRYMEN—
IRISH MUSIC IN ONTARIO

In the wake of the *Constitution Act* of 1791, Quebec was divided into the provinces of Lower and Upper Canada. Lower Canada with its largely French-speaking population was governed according to French civil law and the existing seigneurial system of land tenancy. Upper Canada, which was settled mainly by English-speaking Loyalists who had fled across the border after the American War of Independence, adopted English common law and a system of freehold tenure.[45] The period between 1815 and 1855 saw a strong influx of both Irish Catholics and Protestants to Upper Canada in pursuit of land and opportunity. Assisted emigration schemes (James Buchanan's in 1817, Richard Talbot's in 1818, Peter Robinson's in 1823–25) were followed by subsequent periods of chain migration to a number of core areas in the province. According to the 1871 census, expatriate and Canadian-born Irish made up 35 percent of Ontario's population. Using statistical evidence and comparative data on migration and settlement patterns, Donald Akenson posits that Protestant and Catholic immigrants from Ireland were relatively successful in transforming forested countryside into productive farms and small towns into affluent centres of commerce.[46] According to Cecil J. Houston and William J. Smyth, the pattern of Irish settlement "exemplified in Ontario and Québec highlights the relationship between of arrival of the Irish and other groups. The Irish settled in behind the loyalist and American settlements and were able, especially, in Ontario and along the Ottawa Valley, to create extensive communities. Where there was little settlement before 1820, the Irish became the primary group."[47]

While traditional Canadian fiddling enjoys a ubiquitous presence throughout Ontario—as a result of the popularization of "Down Home" fiddling by media stars like Don Messer (a native of New Brunswick) in the 1950s and 1960s, the emergence of national fiddling competitions, and the widespread growth of musical literacy among traditional players—the heartland of Irish traditional music in that province is among the older Irish communities in the Ottawa Valley, as well as among newer Irish immigrant communities in Toronto and, to a lesser extent, Ottawa. The Ottawa Valley is one of the best-kept secrets in the Irish traditional music world. A heterogeneous conflation of Irish, Scottish, and French traditions, this remote musical community developed in relative isolation from other Irish music and dance communities in North America, has largely eschewed commercial music-making, and has received precious little attention or affirmation from music historians in the homeland that spawned it almost two centuries ago.

Settled initially by Scottish loyalists and later by Clearance Highlanders (in Glengarry County), the Ottawa Valley became a focal point of rural Irish settlement in Canada during the pre-famine decades. Tipperary Protestants settled in Carleton County between 1815 and 1855.[48] In 1823 and 1825, Peter Robinson's southern Catholics (mainly from Cork, Tipperary, and Limerick) settled in Lanark County. In the wake of Daniel O'Connell's *Catholic Emancipation Act* of 1829, a large wave of Irish Protestants from Wexford and Wicklow settled in farms along the Rideau River and in Lanark County. These were followed by famine immigrants in the 1840s and 1850s, who settled in new townships in remote parts of the valley. A century and a half after these settlements were established, the Ottawa Valley still contains evidence of an older Irish rural milieu, not least in its material culture and in the transplanted Irish place names that are scattered throughout the valley (for example, Killaloe, Westmeath, and Calabogie, the latter a corruption of *Na Cealla Beaga*, the Irish name for Killybegs, Co. Donegal). This older world is echoed in the music and dance gatherings of the region and in the communal *habitus* that sustains them.

Reflecting an archaic but by no means fossilized nexus of the house *cuaird* (visit), the *seanchaí* (storyteller), the *meitheal* (communal workforce), and the village gathering, townships in the Ottawa Valley host an annual calendar of old-time community dances, music festivals, and fiddle contests, as well as informal house sessions and seasonal parties. Church halls, Orange halls, community centres, hotels, and even hockey arenas all serve as venues for community dances.[49] The fiddle and piano are the standard instruments, and repertoires include a polyglot mix of Irish, Scottish, French Canadian, Cape Breton, and old-time Canadian tunes. Most fiddlers play a variety of locally sourced valley tunes, American rags, and German and Polish polkas and waltzes. Tune types include reels (often referred to as *breakdowns*, or *deux-quatre* in French), hornpipes (usually played at reel speed), clogs (in 4/4 and 4/2 time), jigs (*six huit*), and waltz-clogs (in 3/4 time).[50] In Scottish communities like Glengarry, the march, strathspey, reel format still holds sway. One of the biblical sources of dance tunes in the valley is Cole's *One Thousand Fiddle Tunes*, which is a reprint of William Bradbury Ryan's *Ryan's Mammoth Collection*, published in Boston in 1883. The ubiquitous Sears

Roebuck catalogue was the primary conduit of Cole's collection into isolated rural communities throughout North America.[51] The same catalogue was used to source musical instruments and various items of household furniture.

Stepdancing has enjoyed a long history in the Ottawa Valley and has been maintained over the years by dancing masters like Donnie Gilchrist (1925–1984), who learned much of his dancing in lumber camps in the 1930s, where stepdancing and fiddling provided a welcome respite from hard physical work.[52] Unlike formal Irish competitive dancing, stepdancing in the Ottawa Valley (which also has a competitive element) was largely unaffected by the *kulturkampf* of prescribed and invented dance traditions unleashed by the Gaelic League in the early 1900s, and, later, by An Coimisiún le Rincí Gaelacha.[53] Absent are the airborne acrobatics, the ringlet wigs, and costumes bespeckled with motifs from the *Book of Kells*. Absent too are the rows of *feis* medals worn by competitive Irish dancers in the ostentatious style of retired field marshals. In its place is a looser, "close to the floor" genre more in keeping with Irish *sean nós* and Cape Breton stepdancing.

The building of the railway in the 1850s linked Toronto to New York and Montreal, as well as to Detroit and Chicago. By then, the lakeside city had become a centre of banking, wholesaling, and entrepreneurship. After Confederation in 1867, Toronto was chosen as the new provincial capital; a decade later, it was the thriving industrial hub of Upper Canada.[54] After receiving an inordinate number of Irish famine immigrants in the 1840s, Toronto became an entrepôt for Irish Catholic and Protestant immigrants to North America throughout the latter half of the nineteenth century.[55] While some immigrants chose to stay, others used Toronto as a stepping stone to gain entry to the United States, a practice that has proven to be particularly resilient in Irish immigration patterns to North America.[56] Among the Irish immigrants who chose to stay was Dublin uilleann piper Chris Langan (1915–1992) who immigrated to Toronto in 1958. Over the next three decades, Langan became a pivotal influence on the Irish traditional music community in Toronto and its environs.[57] A teacher, pipe maker, performer, and music historian, he is remembered in the *tionól* that convenes in his honour every spring in Toronto. Other immigrant musicians followed in Langan's footsteps, among them piper Debbie Quigley from Newtownards, Co. Down, flute player Daithí Connaughton from Dublin, and pianist Éamonn O'Loughlin from Ennistymon, Co. Clare. The city today boasts a thriving community of expatriate Irish and Canadian born musicians. A key figure in this coterie is East Galway accordionist Ena O'Brien, who has sustained the rich musical dialect of her native Sliabh Aughty in exile. The Irish song tradition also enjoys a strong presence in Toronto. Canadian-born singer Catherine Crowe, whose family immigrated from Limerick to Toronto in the 1940s, is regarded as one of the foremost traditional ballad singers in Canada. Her albums have brought renewed attention to the rich corpus of Irish songs that continue to enjoy patronage in Ontario.[58]

Ottawa too has its coterie of Irish immigrant performers. Among them are Dublin harmonica player Don Kavanagh, Offaly whistle player and composer Frank Cassidy, and Dublin string player Eugene Deery.[59] Home to one of the oldest Comhaltas Ceoltóirí Éireann chapters in North America (founded in 1975), Ottawa, as the nation's capital, is an artistic hub for visiting and local performers, whose traditions straddle Irish, Scottish, Québécois, and Cape Breton genres. Musicians who exemplify this transnational milieu include Highland piper Duncan Gillis, fiddler James Stephens, guitarist Ian Clark, and pianist Denis Lanctôt. While Ottawa's creative ambiance has brought some seminal experiments to fruition—among them, composer Frank Cassidy's original tribute to Thomas D'Arcy McGee—Ottawa is also a performance forum for some of Ontario's most celebrated performers, not least, Canadian Grand Master fiddler Pierre Schryer.[60]

ALL THE WAY TO YUKON—IRISH MUSIC IN WESTERN CANADA

From time to time, historians have made reference to Métis leader Louis Riel's Irish ancestry and the various Irish subplots and characters who featured in his ill-fated Red River Rebellion in the 1870s.[61] Other, less spurious Irishmen also feature in the economic and cultural history of Canada's western provinces. The Canadian prairies were settled mainly by internal waves of settlers moving west as the frontier expanded and as the Canadian Pacific Railway opened up access to new land after 1885. Canadian-born people of English, Irish, and Scottish descent were among the first waves to move west, followed by German, Ukrainian, and Russian communities in the late nineteenth and early twentieth centuries. The Irish who moved west were especially influential in pioneer communities, not least in Manitoba, which was home to 150 Orange Lodges by 1900.[62] The gold rushes in British Columbia (1862) and Yukon (1896) also proved key enticements for young Irishmen heading west in search of fame and fortune. The Irish-language memoir of Donegal gold miner Mící MacGabhann, *Rotha Mór an tSaoil*, is a vivid testament to the hundreds of Irishmen who braved the elements in search of Klondike gold.[63] That the Irish left a musical trail to mark their ill-documented peregrinations out west, there is little doubt. Ethnomusicological research among First Nation communities in Manitoba and Yukon bear witness to these musical artifacts and their continued presence in western Canada today.

Although Irish music has found a forum in folk festivals from Winnipeg to Edmonton, as well as in the folk clubs of British Columbia, the random treads of Irish dance music that are speckled throughout the repertoires of Canada's First Nations—from the Mi'kmaq fiddling of Lee Cremo and Will Prosper in Cape Breton, to the Athapaskan fiddling of Charlie Crow and Bill Stevens in Yukon—tell a more intriguing story of transmission, one that has been largely ignored by Irish ethnomusicologists. In documenting First Nation and Métis fiddling in Manitoba, Anne Lederman has demonstrated linkages between old-time Métis fiddling, Saulteaux fiddle music, and various French Canadian, Scottish, Irish, and American traditions.[64] She notes that "the structure of fiddle tunes in this area have much in common with old Native song traditions, especially those of Ojibwa and Plains groups. This observation has led me to conclude that Native fiddlers in this area, and perhaps throughout the Canadian northwest, have created a syncretic music, one which combines features of two separate traditions to form a new style."[65] A striking example of this are the "devil tunes" collected from Métis fiddler Grandy Fagnan of Camperville, Manitoba, who "spoke ten languages and played old Scotch reels."[66] Played in *scordatura* tuning (with the strings retuned to AEAE), Fagnan's "sinful" pieces were reminiscent of the obscure repertoires of "dark" or haunted fiddlers cited in folklore collections in the west of Ireland.[67]

By the end of the nineteenth century, Orcadian fiddling, a composite of Norse and Scottish fiddling from the Orkney Islands, was enjoying widespread popularity among the Athapaskan people in Yukon and Alaska. This genre had been dispersed by Orcadians, who by the late eighteenth century made up three quarters of all Hudson's Bay Company employees in Canada. These clerks, who had been assigned to a network of trading posts stretching across the Canadian tundra, shared their music and square dances with Canada's First Nations for generations.[68] This isolated tradition was augmented by Irish miners during the Klondike Gold Rush. Irish musicians who went to Yukon in search of gold played for their fellow miners in Dawson City, Fort Yukon, and Fairbanks. They also shared tunes, dances, and playing styles with native Athapaskans. A century later, striking similarities persist between Irish and Athapaskan dance music. Both genres are played for set dancing—quadrilles (in extended permutations and patterns) and contra dances are popular in Athapaskan communities—and both are still passed on through oral transmission. While favouring slides and double-stops to ornament their music, Athapaskans use lilting techniques to memorize tunes (not unlike Irish players) before transferring them to instruments. Like older set dancers in Ireland, Athapaskan dancers favour "close to the floor" stepping styles. Several recent Athapaskan performers have paid homage to Irish musical sources. Fiddler Arthur Kennedy, for example, who lived in the Koyukon village of Galena, regarded himself as an "Irish" Athapaskan.[69] His repertoire included Irish dance tunes as well as American old-time music. Athapaskan fiddler Bill Stevens, who has been a guest performer with the Chieftains, readily acknowledges localized Irish dance tunes in his repertoire.[70]

RECLAIMING IRISH MUSIC HISTORY IN CANADA

Canadian history today is still coming to terms with the ethnocentricities of its two official founding nations—as opposed to its fifty-five First Nations and countless other nations inscribed in its collective psyche by immigrants from around the globe. Irish cultural history in Canada, however diffuse and fragmented, is slowly being reclaimed from the country's colonial meta-narratives and is being reappraised through the wide-angle lenses of Canadian multiculturalism. Like the cultural history of the Highland Scots, French Acadians, and other "unofficial" founding cultures, Canadian-Irish culture is buttressed by vast reserves of oral history, folklore, spiritual history, and material culture, as well as by a polysemic store of Irish music, song, and dance that has criss-crossed the country from coast to coast over the past three centuries. While attracting the attention of a growing coterie of music historians and ethnomusicologists in Canada, this soundscape has eluded the attention of academics and media networks in Ireland and in other parts of North America—not least, of those who profess an interest in the music of the Irish diaspora.

Most published work on Irish traditional and popular music in North America has eschewed broad cultural narratives for more focused regional studies, many focusing on Irish music communities along the East Coast industrial corridor in the United States, with the key entrepôts of New York and Boston dominating epistemological and ontological agendas.[71] While few would dispute the fact that some of the most significant changes in the recent history of Irish traditional music took place in the United States, it is equally difficult to deny the fact that large centres of Irish immigration have claimed the lion's share of academic and media attention. One such pantheon is New York City and its presiding trinity of Sligo fiddlers Michael Coleman, James Morrison, and Paddy Killoran, who left an indelible imprint on Irish American music in the 1920s and whose recordings determined the course of Irish traditional music for most of the last century. While by no means suggesting that this trinity be dethroned from its hagiographical perch, it is worth reminding Irish music scholars, nonetheless, that there *is* Irish musical life beyond the Hudson—in the midwestern and southern states, on the American West Coast, and most certainly north of the Canadian border. The same message could be delivered to the makers of Irish television history. A classic example of gross indifference towards Irish music history in Canada was the BBC documentary on the transatlantic journey of Irish music *Bringing It All Back Home* that was aired in 1991. Lavish in its use of commercially successful performers in the American market and skewed in its choice of ethnomusicological and historiographical data, the best it could muster for the presence of Irish traditional music in Canada were a few subordinate clauses. In the myopic vistas of television history, it seemed that there was nothing much to bring back home from Canada. Ironically, nothing could have been further from the truth. Now, twenty years later, with Irish world music loquaciously coming of age in the Irish academy, it is high time to explore the *world* of Irish music—across the vast expanses of Canada and elsewhere throughout the world, where the rhizomorphic soundscape of the Irish diaspora continues to grow and flourish. ■

NOTES

1. Raviart, «Danse irlandaise traditionnelle». See also Szwed and Marks, '"The Afro-American Transformation"; and De Garmo, *The Dance of Society*.

2. Miller, *Emigrants and Exiles*, 137–38. By the 1620s, ships carrying provisions, textiles, and servants were sailing from Cork and Kinsale and returning home with West Indian sugar and Chesapeake tobacco. In Virginia and Maryland, whole tracts of land were set aside explicitly for Irish settlers. Likewise, younger sons of Galway's mercantile tribes—Old English gentry like the Blakes, Darcys, and Kirwins—were establishing sugar plantations and counting houses on the Caribbean islands of Barbados and Montserrat in an attempt to recoup their family losses in the wake of the Cromwellian confiscations of the mid-seventeenth century. See ibid., 141. Similar transatlantic networks, resulting from the globalization of cod in the eighteenth century, linked southern Irish ports with the Newfoundland, Gaspé, and New England fisheries.

3. Grace, *The Irish in Québec*, 21–25. See also Vaillancourt, «Les Québécois des Irlandais qui s'ignorent?»

4. Canada as we know it today did not exist until 1867. Prior to this, British North America consisted of Upper Canada (Ontario), Lower Canada (Quebec), the Maritimes, and a huge tract of trading land running west to the Pacific Ocean that was controlled by the privately owned Hudson's Bay Company.

5   O'Driscoll and Reynolds, "Introduction," xiii–xiv.

6   Elliott, "Regionalized Migration and Settlement Patterns."

7   Evans, *The Personality of Ireland*, 18.

8   Kurlansky, *Cod*, 72.

9   Byrne, "The First Irish Foothold in North America," 171.

10 Ibid., 171.

11 Ibid., 172.

12 Byrne, "Donnchadh Ruadh Mac Conmara." See also de Blácam, *Gaelic Literature Surveyed*, 332–33.

13 Mellin, "The Material Culture of Tilting."

14 Mannion, *Irish Settlements in Eastern Canada*; Mannion, *The Peopling of Newfoundland*.

15 Quigley, *Close to the Floor*. See also Kenneally, "Reconfiguring Irish Studies in Canada."

16 MacLeod, *The Lost Salt Gift of Blood*, 108.

17 See Daigle, *The Acadians of the Maritimes*.

18 See Devine, *Clanship to Crofter's War*. See also Campbell and MacLean, *Beyond the Atlantic Roar*.

19 See Punch, "Gentle as the Snow on a Rooftop." See also MacKenzie, *The Irish in Cape Breton*, 20–21.

20 Toner, "Another 'New Ireland' Lost," 231.

21 Ibid., 232.

22 O'Grady, "A 'New Ireland' Lost," 203.

23 Tartanism was largely "constructed" by the state (in the province of Nova Scotia) from 1933 until 1954 during the tenure of Nova Scotia premier Angus L. Macdonald. Up until 1952, it was still possible to see a Highland piper at the border with New Brunswick, piping summer visitors into the province of Nova Scotia. See McKay, "Tartanism Triumphant."

24 Punch, "Gentle as the Snow on a Rooftop," 227.

25 See Creighton, *Songs and Ballads from Nova Scotia*; Ives, *Folksongs of New Brunswick*; and Fowke, *The Penguin Book of Canadian Folk Songs*.

26 Irish musicians Antóin Mac Gabhann and James Kelly are frequent visitors to Cape Breton, whereas Cape Breton fiddler Natalie MacMaster, as well as the late Dougie MacDonald and Jerry Holland, all made trips to Ireland and absorbed some of its traditional repertoire. In 1928, for example, Cape Breton fiddlers Charlie MacKinnon and Big Dan Hugh MacEachern joined Boston's celebrated Dan Sullivan on the Columbia 78-rpm recording *The Columbia Scotch Band*. Later on, in the 1950s, Cape Breton fiddler Johnny Wilmot collaborated with Boston accordionist Joe Derrane.

27 See Hughes, *Early Christian Ireland*, 222–26. See also Ó hÓgáin, *Myth, Legend and Romance*, 93.

28 See MacInnes, *A Journey in Celtic Music*, 76–79. See also MacGillivray, *A Cape Breton Ceilidh*, 24–25. The sustained popularity of quadrille set dances like the Caledonian and the Lancers (or its cognate, the Saratoga Lancers) in Ireland as well as in Canada (where they were carried by Irish and Scottish diasporas) is a convincing indicator of vernacular dance traditions being grafted onto particular regional idioms and being sustained in dialectal isolation over long periods. The historiographical task of unravelling these surviving variants presents a formidable challenge to Celtic dance historians.

29 Paul MacDonald, "Irish Music in Cape Breton."

30 Robert Grace, *The Irish in Québec*.

31 O'Gallagher, "The Irish in Québec," 255.

32 See Schmitz, *Irish for a Day*, 1991. Apart from large municipal centres like Montreal and Quebec City, other key centres of Irish settlement were Saint Sylvestre and Saint Patrice in Beaurivage, Valcartier, Shannon, the eastern end of the Gaspé Peninsula, the Eastern Townships, and Pontiac County, which contained the highest density of Irish in the province. See Brochet, "The Celtic Family in Feudal Gaspé"; and McQuillan, "Beaurivage."

33 Ibid., 263.

34 O'Gallagher, "The Irish in Québec," 255.

35 See Ó Laighin, "Grosse Île." See also Charbonneau and Sévigny, *1847, Grosse Île*; and MacKay, *Flight from Famine*.

36 Ó Laighin, "Grosse Île," 89. See also O'Gallagher and Dompièrre, *Eyewitness Grosse Isle 1847*. Montreal too bears testimony to Ireland's Great Famine. A prominent black rock on a traffic island at the entrance to Victoria Bridge in Pointe Saint-Charles marks the final resting place of 6,000 famine victims who were tended to by Les Soeurs Grises de Montréal. See Ó Laighin, "Grosse Île," 90.

37 The arrival of the *Urania* from Cork on 8 May 1847 signalled the first of eighty-four plague-ridden ships filled with Irish immigrants that sailed up the St. Lawrence in a single month. See Fallows, *Irish Americans*, 24.

38 O'Neill, *Irish Minstrels and Musicians*, 226.

39 See Lonergan, *La Bolduc*.

40 Jacques Cartier, in his first and second voyages (1534, 1535–36), was one of the first Europeans to describe music among the First Nations. Several musicological treatises and travelogues were produced in New France in the seventeenth and eighteenth centuries. Similarly, song collectors F.A. Hubert LaRue, Ernest Gagnon, and Ernest Myrand were active in Quebec in the nineteenth century, as was Marius Barbeau (father of Canadian ethnomusicology) a century afterwards. See Robbins, "Canada."

41 Bégin, *La musique traditionnelle pour violon*; Ornstein «Instrumental Folk Music of Québec». The quadrille arrived in Quebec after the Napoleonic Wars and was influenced by the French *contredance* (or *cotillion*) from the late eighteenth century. At that time, the term *quadrille* referred to a group of dancers from the opera and suites of contredanses sometimes included as many as nine different dances. See Voyer, *La danse traditionnelle dans l'Est du Canada*.

42 Grace, *The Irish in Québec*, 63–96. For a detailed account of music and dance in the small rural community of Shannon, 30 kilometres northwest of Quebec City, see Schmitz, *Irish for a Day*, 211–45. Among the guardians of these older traditions were melodeon player Keith Corrigan, accordionist Allan King, and fiddlers Eric Corrigan and Jimmy Kelly. See Ornstein, *L'Irlande au Québec*.

43 Grace, *The Irish in Québec*, 169–73. The Lachine Canal (the first works program in Canada: 1815–26), which bisected Griffintown, attracted an unprecedented density of industries to Montreal after it was opened. The canal provided work for newly arrived Irish immigrants who lacked the skills to find work as tradesmen or skilled labourers. The back-breaking conditions and horrid humidity of Montreal's summers were not unlike the conditions portrayed by Charles Dickens during his visit to Canada in 1842. See Burns, *The Shamrock and the Shield*. See also David O'Keefe, "The Ghosts of Griffintown" (2002), 15 April 2007, http://www.bytown.net/griffin.htm.

44 Goerner et al., *Phenigma*.

45 Akenson, *The Irish in Ontario*, Cited in Kenneally, "Reconfiguring Irish Studies in Canada," 29.

46 Houston and Smyth, *Irish Emigration and Canadian Settlement*, 215–17.

47 See Elliott, *Irish Emigrants in Canada*.

48 Trew, *Music, Place and Community*, 161.

49 Ibid., 147–48.

50 Sky, *Ryan's Mammoth* Collection, 15. See also Cole, *One Thousand Fiddle Tunes*.

51 Trew, *Music, Place and Community*, 153.

52 Ó hAllmhuráin, *A Pocket History of Irish Traditional Music*, 125–26.

53 See Whelan, "The Cultural Effects of the Famine," 145.

54 See Kealey, "The Orange Order in Toronto."

55 Ó hAllmhuráin, "Old Age Pipers and New Age Punters," 121.

56 See Cranford, Hutchinson, and Papazian, *Move Your Fingers*.

57 Crowe, Gould, and Goodfellow, *Dark Is the Colour*.

58 Kavanagh, *A Dubliner and His Harmonica*.

59 Cassidy and Stephens, *Present Original Music*.

60 See Pierre Schryer's *Canadian Celtic Celebration*, http://www.canadiancelticcelebration.com (accessed May 1, 2016).

61 Davis, "Irish Nationalism in Manitoba." Having left France during a time of religious and political turbulence, Riel's ancestors, the Rielsons, settled in Limerick for a brief period in the mid-seventeenth century. They left for Canada after the Treaty of Limerick. In Canadian sources, the family is referred to as Riels d'Irlande. The trial of Louis Riel in 1885 was arguably the most famous in Canadian history. He was a leader of the resistance movement organized by the Métis and First Nations in what is now Saskatchewan. The Riel Rebellion was violently suppressed by the Canadian military, and Riel was arrested and charged with treason. His trial lasted five days in July 1885 and returned a guilty verdict. He was hanged on 18 September 1885. The episode had a lasting impact on relations between francophone and anglophone Canadians. See Collins, *The Story of Louis Riel*.

61 See Houston and Smyth, *Irish Emigration and Canadian Settlement*.

62 MacGabhann, *Rotha Mór an tSaoil*.

63 See Lederman, "Old Indian and Métis Fiddling in Manitoba."

64 Ibid., 205.

65 Lederman, *7 Cats*.

66 See Ó Rócháin and Hughes, "Talking with Martin Rochford."

67 See Mishler, *The Crooked Stovepipe*. The Athapaskans referred to the quadrille sets they learned from the Orcadians as "dancing in English" (113).

68 Ó hAllmhuráin, *A Pocket History of Irish Traditional Music*, 108.

69 Stevens, *Gwich'in Athabascan Fiddle Music*.

70 L.E. McCullough's doctoral thesis *Irish Music in Chicago: An Ethnomusicological Study* (University of Pittsburgh, 1978) was among the first dissertation-level analyses of Irish traditional music conducted in the United States. More recent publications include Patrick Mullins, Rebecca Miller, and Marion R. Casey, *From Shore to Shore: Irish Traditional Music in New York City—A Video Documentary* (Ramsey; Cherry Lane, 1993); and Susan Gedutis, *See You at the Hall: Boston's Golden Era of Irish Music and Dance* (Boston: Northeastern University Press, 2004).

71 Lane (1993); and Susan Gedutis, *See You at the Hall: Boston's Golden Era of Irish Music and Dance* (Boston: Northeastern University Press, 2004).

WORKS CITED

Akenson, Donald. *The Irish in Ontario: A Study in Rural History*. Montreal: McGill–Queen's University Press, 1999.

Bégin, Carmelle. *La musique traditionnelle pour violon: Jean Carignan*, Coll. «Mercure». Ottawa: Musées nationaux du Canada, 1981.

Brochet, Aldo. «The Celtic Family in Feudal Gaspé». In *The Untold Story*, ed. O'Driscoll and Reynolds, 271–79.

Burns, Patricia. *The Shamrock and the Shield: An Oral History of the Irish in Montréal*. Montreal: Véhicule Press, 1998.

Byrne, Cyril. "Donnchadh Ruadh Mac Conmara: Poet at the Edge of the Old Gaelic World and the Edge of the New World." *An Násc* 16 (Summer 2004): 13–18.

———. "The First Irish Foothold in North America." In *The Untold Story*, ed. O'Driscoll and Reynolds, 171–74.

Campbell, D., and R.A. MacLean. *Beyond the Atlantic Roar: A Study of the Nova Scotia Scots*. Toronto: McClelland and Stewart, 1974.

Cassidy, Frank, and James Stephens. *Original Music in Traditional Style in Honour of the Life and Times of Thomas D'Arcy McGee*. Ottawa: McGee Music, 2005.

Charbonneau, André, and André Sévigny. *1847, Grosse Île: A Record of Daily Events*. Ottawa: Canadian Heritage Parks Canada, 1997.

Cole, M.M. *One Thousand Fiddle Tunes*. New York: M.M. Cole, 1940.

Collins, John Edmond. *The Story of Louis Riel the Rebel Chief*. Whitefish: Kessinger Publishing, 2004.

Cranford, Paul, Patrick Hutchinson, and David Papazian. *Move Your Fingers: The Life and Music of Chris Langan*. Cape Breton: Cranford Publications, 2002.

Creighton, Helen. *Songs and Ballads from Nova Scotia*. New York: Dover, 1966.

Crowe, Catherine, Martin Gould, and Ian Goodfellow. *Dark Is the Colour* Toronto: CGG, 1994.

Daigle, Jean. *The Acadians of the Maritimes: Thematic Studies*. Moncton: Centre d'études acadiennes, 1982.

Davis, Richard. "Irish Nationalism in Manitoba, 1870–1922." In *The Untold Story*, ed. O'Driscoll and Reynolds, 393–416.

de Blácam, Aodh. *Gaelic Literature Surveyed*. Dublin: Talbot Press, 1929.

De Garmo, William B. *The Dance of Society: A Critical Analysis*. New York: WA Pond, 1875.

Devine, T.M. *Clanship to Crofter's War: The Social Transformation of the Scottish Highlands*. Manchester: Manchester University Press, 1994.

Elliott, Bruce S. *Irish Emigrants in Canada: A New Approach*. Montreal and Kingston: McGill–Queen's University Press, 1988.

———. "Regionalized Migration and Settlement Patterns of the Irish in Upper Canada." In *The Untold Story*, ed. O'Driscoll and Reynolds, 309–18.

Evans, E. Estyn. *The Personality of Ireland: Habitat, Heritage and History*. Belfast: Blackstaff Press, 1981.

Fallows, Marjorie R. *Irish Americans: Identity and Assimilation.* Ethnic Groups in American Life Series. Englewood Cliffs: Prentice Hall, 1979.

Fowke, Edith. *The Penguin Book of Canadian Folk Songs.* London: Penguin, 1973.

Goerner, Reinhard, Steve Jones, Lynda Kathan, Sine McKenna, and Jean Duval. *Phenigma.* Montreal: Phenigma Productions, 1995.

Grace, Robert. *The Irish in Québec: An Introduction to the Historiography.* Instruments de Travail 12. Québec: Institut Québécois de la Recherche sur la Culture, 1993.

Houston, Cecil J., and William J. Smyth. *Irish Emigration and Canadian Settlement: Links, Patterns, and Letters* Toronto: University of Toronto Press, 1990.

Hughes, Kathleen. *Early Christian Ireland: Introduction to the Sources.* Cambridge: Cambridge University Press, 1972.

Ives, Edward D. *Folksongs of New Brunswick.* Fredericton: Goose Lane, 1989.

Kavanagh, Don. *A Dubliner and His Harmonica.* Alymer: Kavanagh Productions, 1998.

Kealey, Gregory S. "The Orange Order in Toronto: Religious Riot and the Working Class." In *The Untold Story*, ed. O'Driscoll and Reynolds, 829–51.

Kenneally, Michael. "Reconfiguring Irish Studies in Canada: Writing Back to the Centre." In *Ireland Beyond Boundaries: Mapping Irish Studies in the Twenty-first Century*, ed. Liam Harte and Yvonne Whelan, 28–38. London: Pluto, 2007.

Kurlansky, Mark. *Cod: A Biography of the Fish That Changed the World.* New York: Penguin, 1998.

Lederman, Anne. *7 Cats.* Toronto: Falcon Productions, 2000.

———. "Old Indian and Métis Fiddling in Manitoba: Origins, Structure and Questions of Syncretism." *Canadian Journal of Native Studies* 7, no. 2 (1988): 205–30.

Lonergan, David. *La Bolduc: La Vie de Mary Travers.* Gaspé: Musée de la Gaspésie, Isaac-Pion, 1992.

MacDonald, Paul. "Irish Music in Cape Breton," in A.A. MacKenzie, *The Irish in Cape Breton*, 119–29. Wreck Cove: Breton Books, [1979]1999.

MacGabhann, Micí. *Rotha Mór an tSaoil.* Indreabhán: Cló Iar-Chonnachta, [1959]1996.

MacGillivray, Allister. *A Cape Breton Ceilidh.* Sydney: Sea Cape, 1988.

MacInnes, Sheldon. *A Journey in Celtic Music—Cape Breton Style.* Sydney: University College of Cape Breton Press, 1997.

MacKay, Donald. *Flight from Famine: The Coming of the Irish to Canada.* Toronto: McClelland and Stewart, 1990.

MacKenzie, A.A. *The Irish in Cape Breton.* Wreck Cove: Breton Books, [1979]1999.

MacLeod, Alistair. *The Lost Salt Gift of Blood.* Toronto: McClelland and Stewart, 1976.

Mannion, John. *Irish Settlements in Eastern Canada: A Study of Cultural Transfer and Adaptation.* Toronto: University of Toronto Press, 1974.

———, ed. *The Peopling of Newfoundland: Essays in Historical Geography.* Social and Economic Papers No. 8, Institute of Social and Economic Research. St. John's: Memorial University of Newfoundland, 1986.

McKay, Ian. "Tartanism Triumphant: The Construction of Scottishness in Nova Scotia, 1933–1954." *Acadiensis: Journal of the History of the Atlantic Region / Revue d'Histoire de la Region Atlantique* 21, no. 1 (Fall 1991): 5–47.

McQuillan, D. Aidan. "Beaurivage: The Development of an Irish Ethnic Identity in Rural Québec, 1820–1860." In *The Untold Story*, ed. O'Driscoll and Reynolds, 263–70.

Mellin, Robert. "The Material Culture of Tilting, Fogo Island, Newfoundland." *Canadian Journal of Irish Studies / Revue canadienne d'études irlandaises* 26, no. 2 (Fall 2000) / 27, no. 1 (Spring 2001): 49–73.

Miller, Kerby A. *Emigrants and Exiles: Ireland and the Irish Exodus to North America*. Oxford: Oxford University Press, 1985.

Mishler, Craig. *The Crooked Stovepipe: Athapaskan Fiddle Music and Square Dancing in Northeast Alaska and Northwest Canada*. Urbana: University of Illinois Press, 1993.

O'Driscoll, Robert, and Lorna Reynolds, eds. *The Untold Story: The Irish in Canada*. Toronto: Celtic Arts of Canada, 1988.

O'Gallagher, Marianna. "The Irish in Québec." In *The Untold Story*, ed. O'Driscoll and Reynolds, 253–61.

O'Gallagher, Marianna, and Rose Masson Dompièrre. *Eyewitness Grosse Isle 1847*. Quebec City: Carraig Books, 1995.

O'Grady, Brendan. "A 'New Ireland' Lost: The Irish Presence in Prince Edward Island." In *The Untold Story*, ed. O'Driscoll and Reynolds, 203–10.

Ó hAllmhuráin, Gearóid. "Old Age Pipers and New Age Punters: Irish Traditional Music and Musicians in San Francisco, 1850–2000." In *The Irish in the San Francisco Bay Area: Essays on Good Fortune*, ed. Donald Jordan and Timothy J. O'Keefe. San Francisco: Irish Literary and Historical Society, 2005.

———. *A Pocket History of Irish Traditional Music*. Dublin: O'Brien Press, 1998.

Ó hÓgáin, Dáithí. *Myth, Legend, and Romance: An Encyclopedia of the Irish Folk Tradition*. New York: Prentice Hall, 1991.

Ó Laighin, Pádraig Breandán. "Grosse Île: The Holocaust Revisited." In *The Untold Story*, ed. O'Driscoll and Reynolds, 75–101.

O'Neill, Captain Francis. *Irish Minstrels and Musicians*. Chicago: Regan Printing House, 1913.

Ó Rócháin, Muiris, and Harry Hughes. "Talking with Martin Rochford." *Dal gCais: Journal of Clare* 4 (1978): 112–117.

Ornstein, Lisa. "Instrumental Folk Music of Québec." *Canadian Journal for Traditional Music* 1 (1982): 3–11.

———. *L'Irlande au Québec: Musique et chansons traditionnelles de Keith Corrigan et Jimmy Kelly avec Lisa Ornstein, André Marchand, Nick Hawes*. Portland: Talencourt Music, 2008.

Punch, Terrence M. "Gentle as the Snow on a Rooftop: The Irish in Nova Scotia to 1830." In *The Untold Story*, ed. O'Driscoll and Reynolds, 215–29.

Quigley, Colin. *Close to the Floor: Folk Dance in Newfoundland*. Folklore and Language Publications, Monograph Series no. 3. St. John's: Department of Folklore, Memorial University of Newfoundland, 1985.

Raviart, Naïk. «Danse irlandaise traditionnelle et dance française ancienne: Histoire en deçà, ethnologie au delà». *Tradition et histoire dans la culture populaire*, Doc. d'Ethn. Rég. n° 11, C.A.R.E., 1990, 53–70.

Robbins, James. "Canada." In *Ethnomusicology: Historical and Regional Studies*, ed. Helen Myers, 63–77. New York: W.W. Norton, 1993.

Schmitz, Nancy. *Irish for a Day: St. Patrick's Day Celebrations in Québec City 1765–1990*. Quebec City: Carraig Books, 1991.

Sky, Patrick. *Ryan's Mammoth Collection: 1050 Reel and Jigs, Hornpipes, Clogs, Walk-arounds, Essences, Strathspeys, Highland Flings and Contra Dances, with Figures and How to Play Them*. Pacific: Mel Bay, 1995.

Stevens, Bill. *Gwich'in Athabascan Fiddle Music*. Fairbanks: Bill Stevens Music, 1999.

Szwed, John F., and Morton Marks. "The Afro-American Transformation of European Set Dances and Dance Suites." *Dance Research Journal* 20, no. 1 (Summer 1988): 29–36.

Toner, P.M. "Another 'New Ireland' Lost: The Irish of New Brunswick." In Robert O'Driscoll and Lorna Reynolds, 'Introduction,' in *The Untold Story*, ed. O'Driscoll and Reynolds, 231–35,

Trew, Johanne. *Music, Place, and Community: Culture and Irish Heritage in the Ottawa Valley*. PhD diss., Limerick, University of Limerick, 2000.

Vaillancourt, Madeleine. «Les Québécois des Irlandais qui s'ignorent? Pour partir à la recherche de l'Irlandais perdu parmi nos ancêtres». *Québec Science* 14, no. 12 (août 1976): 18–21.

Voyer, Simonne. *La danse traditionnelle dans l'Est du Canada, quadrilles et cotillons*. Québec: Presses de l'Université Laval, 1986.

Whelan, Kevin. "The Cultural Effects of the Famine." In *The Cambridge Companion to Modern Irish Culture*, ed. Joe Cleary and Claire Connolly, 137–54. Cambridge: Cambridge University Press, 2005.

Wynn, Graeme. "On the Margins of Empire (1760–1840)." In *The Illustrated History of Canada*, ed. Craig Brown, 191–278. Toronto: Lester Publishing, 1991.

THIRTEEN

The Contemporary Powwow in Eastern Canada:
A Practice of Gathering

Dalie Giroux and Amélie-Anne Mailhot
Translated from the French by Carmen Grillo

Present-day powwows in Indian Country offer an unparalleled experience of sight and sound: the dancers moving in colour through the circles, voices soft and loud telling stories, praying, and honouring ancestors, the old and the young standing side by side, learning from one other and celebrating their living culture—and all to the drum's never-ending beat, resounding deeply in everyone's hearts. This rhythm, it is said, embodies the spirit of the powwow: that which brings people together. In this chapter, we offer an interpretation of how this spirit is expressed in the material practices of the powwow. More specifically, we present a preliminary analysis of data gathered through an ethnographic and philosophical inquiry conducted between 2009 and 2013 at summer traditional dance meetings (called "powwows") in several Aboriginal communities in southern Quebec and Ontario. The fieldwork was done by a small, interdisciplinary team comprised of researchers in arts and social sciences, which visited Anishnabe (Ojibway and Algonquin), Atikamekw, Innu (Montagnais), and Haudenosaunee (Mohawk) communities in the Great Lakes region, on the Niagara Peninsula, in Haute-Mauricie, and in the Saint Lawrence Valley.[1]

The results presented here are drawn from the analysis of twelve instances of participant observation over a three-year period (2009–12) in nine communities, where we conducted twenty semi-directed interviews with traditional powwow dancers, professional Aboriginal dancers, powwow organizers, drummers, and craftspeople. The data, analyzed through an auto-historical approach as outlined by Georges Sioui in *For an Amerindian Auto-History*, were interpreted in the context of existing literature on the history of powwows (see Berbaum; Browner; Diamond; Ellis, Lassiter, and Dunham). This auto-historical method consists of receiving and using the words of the participants, as well as the epistemologies they express and propose. We were therefore often required, as best as we were able, to take to the road, to camp, to eat by the fire and have coffee with our camp mates, to travel the concentric circles of powwow places, to forge links, and to endeavour to know the powwow through experience and through mutual and attentive interaction. This body of gathered speech and observations comprises the base material of our analysis.

We seek to understand the symbolic politics of place and the lived experience of Aboriginal dwelling on the continent through the particular aesthetic and social practice of the powwow. This phenomenological theorization of continental dwelling is based on an Indigenous geographical and political conception of the "Indian Country," taken up by the Ojibway researcher Gail Valaskasis in an important essay in her book *Indian Country: Essays on Contemporary Native Culture*:

> Indian Country is recognized by Indians as a place that gathers Native North Americans together, wherever—on any reservation, at any powwow or Native conference, in any Indian bar or Native center, at any Native ceremony, feast, or communal event. Indian country signifies both a shared sense of cultural and historical experience and a consciousness of what in Ojibway is called pimatiziwin, or "living in a good way"—in physical, social and spiritual health and harmony; a mixture of meanings that is intertwined with land. In Indian country, the struggle over the land is not only experienced, it is told and retold in the stories of dominance and survival that reconstruct, imagine and, most of all, assert Indian spirituality and empowerment in the memoried past and the politicized future.[2]

What Valaskakis offers here is a performative, political, and (post)traditional definition, according to which Indian Country consists of a multitude of gatherings that organize a system of specific places and that define a consistent form of material and symbolic dwelling (a form of life).

By contextualizing the powwow as a social and spiritual event territorialized by the dancers' movements, the body of literary, graphic, and narrative data gathered through the study allows for an evocation of specific forms, a specific makeup of this Indian Country of contemporary Indigenous thought and life. In this regard, our findings suggest that the Indian Country is created and re-created through the North American powwows. This process can be observed in the community practices since 1980 that we have studied in southeastern Canada. To illustrate, we offer the following:

1. A brief definition of the powwow form as a framework or structure organized by an ensemble of social, cultural, and spatial practices.
2. Some remarks on the continental origins of the powwow form in eastern Canada, particularly regarding how Indigenous cultural transfers allowed it to spread in different directions across the American continent.
3. A description of the geocultural composition of eastern powwows that distinguishes between the different nations and groups of nations therein, and that sketches an image of the social relations that underlie and organize this form of life.
4. A description of the powwow as a practice comprised of three dimensions: storytelling, gathering, and moving.

1. DEFINITION OF THE POWWOW AS AN ENSEMBLE OF SOCIAL, CULTURAL, AND SPATIAL PRACTICES

The powwow can be approached as a nexus of material, artistic, and social forms that intertwine and intersect to produce a particular notion of dwelling in Indian Country. First, as a social practice, the powwow is a popular and intertribal gathering. It is also organized and financed locally, which makes it an almost entirely community-based event. We find this form of gathering in numerous Aboriginal communities in North America, predominantly in the plains cultures, in both the south and the north of the continent. Powwow events happen generally over two to four days, usually outdoors in the summer. There are some exceptions—for example, there are large, competitive powwows held indoors, in Hamilton, Ontario, every fall, and there are other types of powwows organized throughout the year everywhere on the continent. As for its demographic makeup, the powwow brings together dancers from the host and surrounding communities. The powwows we attended in eastern Canada typically brought together between fifty and five hundred dancers and anywhere between one hundred and a few thousand other participants; the precise numbers depended on the importance, type, and location of each event.

Second, a number of intersecting material and cultural practices underlie the powwow as a social form. For example, while the heart and primary cultural vector of the powwow is the drum,[3] the corresponding cultural practice is the traditional dance, whether in competitive, social (recreational), or spiritual form.[4] In a similar vein, the dance itself is linked with another cultural form; the garments worn by the dancers, "regalias," are artisanal and family-made, and in addition to being tied to particular dances (some categories of which are jingle, grass, traditional male, traditional female, shawl, fancy, and smoke), are also vectors in a particular symbolic economy. Each has a unique narrative of how it came to be, of who made it and in what circumstances. Thus, we see that these kinds of complex relationships between social practices and material and cultural objects and practices characterize the form of the powwow as a way of meaning-making.

Third, corresponding to the social and cultural practices of the powwow is a particular spatial and topographical orientation, one that can be understood as being concentric and ex-centric. Spatially and topographically, the powwow is organized systematically in concentric circles that serve to reinforce community and create solidarity within. The big drums, which set the beat from the beginning to the end of the event and whose sound is inseparable from the powwow experience, are placed in the inner circle of the powwow or on the edges of the dancers' field.[5] Around the physical centre of the space dedicated to the powwow, where there are sometimes drums or a strip of cedar surrounded by stones called the "grandfathers," are the dancers and the dance field. Next, forming a circle around the dance field, are the platforms with spots reserved for the master of ceremonies, the elderly, and sometimes the drummers and drums. Next, there are the food kiosks and the vendors, interspersed with meandering participants who eat and chat. Finally there are the tents and the people circulating among the improvised camps around the periphery.[6] These concentric circles are fluid and permeable to the people who circulate from one to another. For this reason, every person can be called a "participant" in the powwow; it would be incorrect to speak of a divide between dancers and singers and spectators (an exception here would be at ceremonial events, which we will not be discussing in this article).[7] In this way, the powwow is open in many ways to the entire community.

In addition to the internal, concentric structure of the powwow, there is another spatial aspect that is at its heart: the ex-centric journey of the powwow trail. Although the powwow is about reinforcing community solidarity, another of its most important aspects relates to how it is used to establish ties outside of the community while simultaneously strengthening relationships among people who are already acquainted and who travel together from place to place. For example, many of the dancers and their families, as well as the artisans, the cooks, the organizers, and the merchants, along with the friends of all the aforementioned move themselves every year from community to community to participate in different powwows, taking part in what we call the "powwow trail." So it is not uncommon to meet, in community after community, week after week, entire families as well as dancers and musicians for whom collective time and seasonal territorial movement are harmonized in the practice of the powwow as *pimatiziwin* (good life). We return to this spatial orientation later in the article.

2. THE CONTINENTAL ORIGINS OF THE POWWOW

To understand the powwow as a cultural, spatial, and—most importantly, political—practice means to understand its historical and geographic specificity as well. The North American powwow is sometimes thought of as a pan-Indian practice, one that has remained more or less constant over time, when actually it has emerged through particular regional interactions and cultural and social ties among specific Aboriginal communities. The contemporary powwow form[8] in eastern Canada is the result of north–south and west–east cultural transfers originating in the Great Plains Warrior ceremonies.

The forms of the powwow are multiple, contested, and varied; that said, the principal influences for all of its forms can be found in the rituals of the southern Great Plains warrior societies (such as the Omaha, the Ponca, and the Shawnee). Over the course of the nineteenth century, the powwow was brought west by the Dakota, then north and east by the Cree and the Ojibway. The contemporary practice was thus well established in the Great Lakes region by the end of the 1950s, where it came under the influence of the rituals of the Big Drum Society practised since the turn of the twentieth century by the Ojibway in the southern Great Lakes.[9]

Based on the historical context just described, we hypothesize two aspects of the origins of powwows in eastern Canada:

1. It is mainly through the Ojibway powwow that the contemporary form of gathering developed in Indigenous nations in southern Ontario and Quebec, most notably amongst the Haudenosaunee, Atikamewk, and Innu.[10]
2. In this context, it becomes clear that the transmission of the powwow form happened through continuous continental cultural exchanges, which followed both a south–north trajectory (from south of the Great Lakes towards

the north, and from the Saint Lawrence Valley towards Haute-Mauricie and the north coast) and a west–east trajectory (from the Ojibway communities to the Haudenausonee, Algonquin, Attikamekw, and Innu).

Given these two hypotheses, it is important to clarify this article's title: if this article situates the powwow in a Western concept of territory—eastern Canada—it is primarily to orient our readers, not to suggest that the actual history of the powwow unfolded along these lines. It is essential to understand that the territoriality of the powwow is more continental than state-based: like other aspects of the traditional Indigenous way of thinking, it tends to disregard the strictly delimited border between Canada and the United States. In this case, if the "country" that is performed through the powwow form intersects with a territory called Canada, this is not the same as the one produced around the political, cultural, or economic parameters of the Canadian state.

This continental movement of Aboriginal cultural and social life across North America culminated in the cultural ensemble of eastern powwows. This allows us to offer a preliminary portrait of the nations in that group:

1. We find first of all in the eastern powwow culture the Anishinabe world (particularly the group of nations known as the "Three Fires Confederacy": Odawa, Ojibway, and Potawatomi), which constitutes a social, cultural, and political network spanning from the north to the south of the Great Lakes (notably between Ontario and Michigan) despite the border that divides this region.
2. Next, the eastern powwow ensemble includes the Haudenosaunee communities (mostly Mohawk) of the Saint Lawrence Valley, which maintain strong ties with their sister communities situated in what is today known as New York State.
3. Finally, the Algonquin of Ontario and Quebec—the Atikamekw, the Abenaki, and the Innu, who also maintain ties with the Anishinabe of the Great Lakes and the Haudenosaunee—are also part of this cultural ensemble.

The powwow form is transmitted across these worlds through exchanges of expertise, through mutual aid between communities, and by the dancers, musicians, and organizers who frequent multiple powwows. It is out of this cultural exchange of the powwow between those three worlds (the Ojibway world, the Algonquin, Attikamek, Abenaki, and Innu world, and the Haudenosaunee world), that intensive social and cultural exchanges emerged or grew stronger through the last three decades of the twentieth century.

3. THE GEOCULTURAL COMPOSITION OF THE EASTERN POWWOWS

We are able to establish that of the Eastern powwows, those in the Ojibway world are the oldest. These came from historical contact between the Ojibway cultures and the Plains peoples (the great powwow of Wikwemikong is more than fifty years old).

The Haudenosaunee powwows are much more recent: the "Champion of Champions" of the Six Nations in southern Ontario was born only in 1979, while the powwows in the Mohawk communities of the Saint Lawrence Valley developed in the 1990s. In the case of Kahnawake, it was only in 1991, after the political turmoil around the "Oka Crisis," that the community decided to have a powwow.[11]

The Atikamekw and Innu communities of Quebec developed their powwows after the mid-1990s. These powwows benefited from participant exchanges with the Haudenosaunee powwows, in particular attendance at Kahnawake. The communities integrate Anishinabe rituals with other cultural elements through regular and sustained exchanges. The Wemotaci powwow, established in the mid-1990s, was the first, followed by the Manawan, Mashteuiatsh and Opiticwan, all three of which it inspired.

Figure 13.1 Eastern powwow communities

The emergence of a powwow trail makes it clear that more or less durable exchanges and alliances have developed among the eastern powwow groups, despite the sometimes long distances between them. As we will discuss later in the chapter, powwow dancers participate in a fairly large number of powwows over the course of a single summer. Proximity encourages cultural exchanges between communities; that said, distance does not seem to be a barrier to the formation of ties, even though hitting the powwow trail often involves long-distance travel. For example, the 1,000-kilometre trip from Manawan to Wikwemikong takes fifteen hours, the trip from Mashteuiatsh to Kahnawake seven hours or 500 kilometers, and the trip from Six Nations to Wikwemikong takes another seven hours or 400 kilometers. Furthermore, since the legs of the powwow trail are almost always covered by car, the journey comes with significant costs, mainly for gas. Despite these challenges to intercommunity travel and exchange, a clear powwow trail has emerged.

Another important aspect of the powwow trail is that movement along it happens in groups. Families, friends, the old, and the young: although the nomadic social networks that form around the powwow are diverse, all contribute to establishing a particular way of moving together and of meeting others in a congenial spirit. The dancers choose the communities they visit by applying diverse criteria (to see family and friends, to meet new people, for special occasions), but for many of the ones who live off-reserve—and this is a fundamental aspect—the powwow is a chance to "return home," to reconnect by spending time with family, with friends, and with the community at large. It is also a chance to expand one's social networks and make new acquaintances. There are therefore two principal topographical orientations to the powwow: the powwow as concentric, where the community reunites and reinforces its solidarity around dance; and the powwow as ex-centric, where people weave together new networks by going outside their communities to find new friends and meet different people.

It is through the powwow that people host one another, accompany one another, and meet one another. Within their communities and without, people stake out a special territory—with dance—on which they found ties and, most of all, through which they remind themselves that they share a life in common. In this way, operating through a common structure of cultural exchanges tied to the powwow, relationships and exchanges between participants are constantly shaped around multiple and diverse varieties of the powwow trail and around the specific practices of host communities.

4. STORYTELLING, GATHERING, MOVING

Having described the eastern powwow's origins, we now return to the social, cultural, and spatial practices of the powwow. Since the material and symbolic complex of the powwow is activated, sustained, and reiterated around a series of gestures, practices, and relationships, there are many ways of approaching its material and symbolic makeup; that being said, the powwow can be understood primarily as a way of gathering, one whose practices feature a particular epistemology. So in this section, we turn to three moments or specific movements in the articulation between knowledge and the political that occur in the powwow, with the goal of understanding its political and symbolic economy. These three moments are (1) the dance, which can be called the act of storytelling, (2) the gathering, as the place where storytelling happens and where communities recentre the centripetal axis around which their lives in common revolve, and (3) the "gift," meant specifically here as the exchange that activates a particular way of moving—in other words, a movement that re-creates spaces where people tell and transmit stories, spaces tied together by a network of practices and relationships that develop and are sustained and nourished in the particular place of the powwow. Even if we present these as three conceptually distinct moments, they are not empirically separable; as we discuss in the following sections, they activate and sustain one another.

Storytelling (the Dance)

There are many types of dances, and each has its own unique history and meaning. For our purposes, however, we understand the dance primarily as a deed, understood as a moment in the powwow complex in which one can witness the activation of multiple nodes of meaning. While it can be said that the dancers had their own individual and political motives for participating in the powwow, it was possible for us to trace out some commonalities or constants in the interviews. Thus, we can sketch out the dance according to seven elements. Dancing is simultaneously:

1. a prayer
2. a retelling of histories or stories
3. a way of expressing oneself
4. a way of healing

5. a way of keeping traditions alive
6. a way of knowing
7. a symbolic act of recognition and giving, where one dances "for others"

What is most interesting about these different elements is how they relate to one another in certain moments of the gathering. Below, we offer three examples.

One dancer, thinking back to the dances at the summer gatherings in her community, insisted that the dance was a kind of prayer—above all, a prayer for what *one could give*, a prayer *for others*:

> It was a prayer. That was when you held each other, and you gave one to the other. And the prayer was always for each other. Not only for what you wanted, but for what you could give. What you had to share, and for the blessing to be on your neighbours, your friends.

In the same spirit, a Wikwemikong traditional dancer spoke—shortly after speaking at length about the first powwow in her community—of the dance as a symbolic act of recognizing others, one that was important in the transmission of meaning between generations:

> Then, sometimes at the powwow we're reminded of this, that you're not only dancing for yourself, you're dancing for … think of all of the elders, those that cannot dance, or even those that you know can't walk. Think about those people that cannot dance, and you're dancing for them too. Or even in memory of those people too. And that's what came to me, the memory of my grandmother. I didn't personally see her dance but my mother told me that her mother danced.

She continued, mentioning a particular article of clothing that belonged to her grandmother:

> This year I had a feeling to wear it. Like in honour of her, like especially for the grand entry. Which is what I did, I had my buckskin dress and I wore her shirt underneath … and it just brought a special like close feeling [of] what it must have been like for her to dance there too. Then to see my mother … she was in the elders; just to see her dancing ahead; and then me, the next generation.

We see here that to dance is to dance *for others*, for those who cannot dance, in memory of the elders. It is to take part in the transmission of practices. If the first example demonstrates the link between praying and the symbolic act of giving where the dance is "for others," and if the second demonstrates the link between the dance and intergenerational transmission, the third allows us to draw out new threads in the powwow fabric, particularly the links between storytelling, knowledge, and healing.

First of all, one hoop dancer from Wikwemikong told us that storytelling—which she defined as encompassing the oral tradition, songs, dance, and the arts—is the primary medium of traditional teaching. This echoes the academic literature on the subject. Another dancer, who had already suggested to us that the dance is a prayer *to give to others*, added in the negative that to dance is to retell with one's body. "In the negative," in the sense that she recounted moments in her career in the 1940s as a traditional dancer when her audiences failed to understand the meaning of the dances:

> They didn't understand that Native dancing told a story. Each different suggestion, each different gesture of hand, of, touching ... the way you use your hands and the way your feet move was a story. And you, and only you know the story, but you told it to them.

To tell a story with each gesture of the body and put it in relation to the other part of the dancer's account, to at the same time pray to give to others, to share—this is the dancer's purpose. There is therefore a creating and sharing of knowledge in the dance.

The maintenance of tradition is also at the heart of the dancer's concerns. Asked about the importance of transmitting knowledge about the dance to future generations, an Ojibway dancer said, "If we don't, then, we're gonna get assimilated into the mainstream society. And ... participating in this ... that makes ... our culture live." To dance, then, is to take part, to keep Aboriginal culture alive and to refuse assimilation into dominant society. One organizer of the Wikwemikong Cultural Festival (powwow) mentioned that at the powwow, people tend to talk about the return or renaissance of traditional culture (in this case, Ojibway culture); thus the powwow is not just a space where practices are transmitted, it is not just part of the renaissance—it is itself a yearly celebration of that cultural revival:

> One of the words we use in our offices a lot, right now, is ... resurgence, revitalization of our culture, rebirthing of our culture. Because it does seem to get lost sometimes, for some people. But then there's always this time of the year where it's right back again, it's like it never left.

We now turn briefly to the role of knowledge in the examples discussed above. The many allusions to knowledge of the dance and the powwow ceremonies and the imperative to "do it yourself" and to "understand by living it" demonstrate that knowledge here happens through the body, through movement in space, and through experience.

When the time came for dancers to discuss how they learned to dance or to participate in powwows, the central and indeed almost exclusive theme was a kind of mutual apprenticeship. There were three ways for dancers to learn: "by themselves," "with others," and "thanks to the elders." These three are actually simultaneous, since learning by oneself entails asking for help from the elders and from other dancers, watching others, and doing research. First, many of the dancers repeatedly insisted that learning had to happen on a voluntary basis ("you can't force anyone," "people have to choose for themselves," "it's up to you," etc.). Second, the dancers insisted that the sharing of powwow knowledge was a mutual and horizontal affair. One musician stated: "We go to the powwow we all help each other sing songs and that's how we keep our culture alive and ... our traditions alive ... you know we're learning from each other." Third, the elders' knowledge is solicited throughout the learning process, and they are always thought to be at the heart of the cultural resurgence. One of the Manawan powwow organizers said in this regard: "The elders ... they gave us something marvelous: they remembered" (our translation). The elders thus occupy a central place in the history of the founding or resurgence of each of the Manawan, Wikwemikong, and Kahnawake powwows, not only in the examples we mentioned, but in others as well. These three moments of knowledge and of mutual learning seem to constitute the act of the dance of the powwow. There will be other examples of this later in the chapter. What is important to notice here is how a particular gesture, the dance, activates a whole system of knowledge and social relations around this knowledge.

Gathering

The act of gathering in a common space, a space that becomes the focal point of daily life for the span of many days, makes the powwow possible. The powwow itself becomes a place of transmission: people go there first of all—according to our informants—to meet, to be together, and to share. As one of the Kahnawake organizers said: "Powwows are of bringing people together, sharing our food. And to dance, and to dance all day and to dance at night ... and share your food." These two elements, being together and sharing, are central to the powwow.

The accounts of our interviewees all converge around this intertwining of gathering and sharing knowledge and food, which happens through the relationships that have formed at the powwow. We turn now to three accounts. First of all, for one woman from Wikwemikong, the powwow allowed her to meet people, make new friends, see old ones, share food, share knowledge, and share experiences. Next, for an Innu dancer of Mashteuiatsh, the powwow was about "living our culture," keeping in touch with the earth, dancing and praying, meeting people from other communities, making friends, and sharing. For a Haudonosaunee dancer it meant socializing, gathering, dancing, singing, meeting people (old friends), keeping up with the news, and eating together. So what do people do at powwows? They maintain their existing relationships, they make new friends, they keep themselves abreast of the news, they "live their culture," they share knowledge, joy and experiences, they dance, they sing, and they eat together.

Moving

Another important aspect of the powwow is the practice of gifting or exchange. Although the symbolic gift—given through special dances (people dance for those who have passed on throughout the year, for the survivors of residential schools, etc.) and other ceremonies—is important, we focus here on an example of the material gift, which is central in the political economy of the powwow and in the modality of sharing and recognition. One could even say that in this way, the material gift enables the kind of hospitality that facilitates gathering: it activates networks of hospitality and alliances.

The accounts we compiled indicate that powwows are generally managed and financed locally; more specifically, the money that community members give to the dancers actually makes it possible for the latter to participate. As we mentioned earlier, it is generally understood that coming to the powwow means travelling a long distance by car and paying for gas. As one of the Innu dancers said: "A bit of money, generally that covers expenses. It's ... to encourage ... people to come and participate at the powwow" (our translation).

In a similar vein, giveaways were another important part of the traditional powwows we attended. They could be organized by community members wanting to thank everyone else for their support over the course of the year, or by powwow organizers as a means to show their gratitude to the singers and dancers or to honour a specific dancer. The reasons for having giveaways and the opportunities to do so are thus multiple. The practice itself is simple: it consists most of the time of distributing money or goods to certain community members, dancers, singers, and other participants, and takes place during the day of the dance. Again, "participants" can be almost anyone. As a Haudonosaunee dancer said: "Powwow people are a family. And you don't have to be dressed to be part of the family." The community members who come to the powwow and join its concentric circles on weekends are not simply spectators—the life on the platforms where the audience sits, in the vendors' aisles, and in other places is just as much part of the mutual act of community recognition as the dance.

Nevertheless, it takes more time and money to travel the powwow trail for a whole season than it does to occasionally attend. Some dancers only participate in the annual summer powwows in their communities, or return to their own communities specifically for the powwow; many other dancers follow a busy and carefully organized schedule that takes them all the long way down the powwow trail.[12] As we mentioned earlier, people usually travel in groups, for different reasons. A Manawan dancer told us: "Like, in the month of July ... we haven't stopped yet.... It continues, one place to another.... [It's] true that it's pretty tiring to travel. It's pretty tiring but I have to follow these young people here. They need guiding" (our translation).

Money, time, knowledge, gifts ... all of this is reinvested in the community, with the aim of creating a certain presence and group of practices on a territory. Giveaways thus serve a symbolic purpose: besides serving a material function of welcoming and sharing, they recognize the community and the participants in the powwow, including those coming from elsewhere. In this way, the many acts of giving and of recognition activate a network of hospitality in a mode of celebration around traditional practices that consist of maintaining certain bodies of knowledge, in particular an epistemology articulated around the political and symbolic economy of the community. Remember that in the dance, our interlocutors recognized a system of mutual, corporeal, and experiential knowledge that went beyond the particular personal motivations of each of the dancers. The same structure seems to be active in the gestures of gathering and moving: people meet, reconnect, show gratitude, and transmit experience, all in varying ways and with different levels of intensity.

In this way, people move: life is resumed, people settle, they remake friendships, they eat, they dance, and most of all, they ensure the perpetuation of traditional practices: they retell their stories. After that, they move, they gather, they retell—and they move again, gather again, and retell once more, living the concentric circles of the powwow trail. These are three distinct moments, but when juxtaposed, they cannot be disentangled from one another, especially as they share the common political thread of that corporeal, experiential, and mutual knowledge. In other words, the powwow features the interplay of a complex political articulation, of knowledge of place, of the body and movement, of the deeds, of the symbolic and material exchanges that give consistency to a certain way of knowing and living. All of this activates a system of the relations that comprise the continental Indigenous dwelling.

CONCLUSION

These observations of the contemporary powwow in eastern Canada allow us to offer, based on the picture we have painted and the accounts we heard, a phenomenological description of this cultural and artistic practice as a kind of dwelling oriented towards a particular use of symbolic and material place. The powwow, a grassroots gathering of dancing and singing—practices that have been perpetuated and transmitted despite governmental repression—thus emerges as the vector of new regional and continental exchanges and forms of solidarity. The idea of continental dwelling through song and dance, and the form of gathering in the powwow, in its political and geographic effects, is evidently fed by different discourses, histories, and gestures. Three performative trajectories unfold in the powwow. The first manifests itself in the gestures, the dances, the songs, and the regalias (ceremonial dress) worn by the dancers, and in the personal histories and political motives of all participants. The second, community trajectory, emerges out of the powwow as gathering. The third and final one is the powwow form as a practice of continental dwelling. In reality, these three trajectories cannot be separated from one another. This dwelling constitutes itself as a material and symbolic occupation of territory lived and practised through the intertwining of political, geographic, artistic, spiritual, and ceremonial practices of gathering. The persistence and constancy of these intensive community exchanges actuated in the powwow allow us to take in the landscape of a home constructed through art—of a country, a uniquely "Indian Country," crafted through song, through dance, and most of all, through the sound of the big, ever-beating drum. ∎

NOTES

1 This work was a collaborative effort between the Observatoire des nouvelles pratiques symboliques (ONOUPS) of the Faculty of Social Sciences at the University of Ottawa and the Ethnoscenology Laboratory at the Department of Theatre of the University of Paris-8. Over the years, a number of people in addition to the authors contributed directly and indirectly to this project: Jérome Dubois, Darren O'Toole, Georges Sioui, Aurore Martinez, Christian Desmeules, Julie Perreault, David Welch, Jade Bourdages and Sylvain Flamand, the communities and powwow organizers who welcomed us continuously over three years—in particular Gordie Odjig and Réginald Flamand—and the participants (especially Sylvie Berbaum) of the Symposium sur les arts performatifs et spectaculaires des Premières nations du Canada held 1–2 June in Paris.

2 Valaskakis, *Indian Country*, 103.

3 Also called "the Big Drum" or the "Ojibway Drum."

4 For more information on the different types of powwows, see Albers and Medicine, "Some Reflections."

5 According to Browner, *Heartbeat of the People*, the Ojibway powwow supposedly accords a central place to the drums, referring to the "sacred fire," while Lakota powwows have the drums in the circle around the dancers for protection, referring instead to a "sacred hoop." It is difficult in the framework of this research to infer cultural exchanges based on this hypothesis, but this could be an area for further research.

6 The circular layout of the powwow evidently corresponds with the circular vision of the world that is present elsewhere in the Indigenous way of thinking, and a number of participants and authors have noted the spiritual parallels that underlie this similarity (see Berbaum *Ojibway Powwow World*; Browner, *Heart Beat of the People*; and Young Bear and Theisz, *Standing in the Light*).

7 The events that mark the powwow proceedings, other than the regular dance program, are comprised of special dances and community ceremonies, particularly in traditional powwows. The meaning and unfolding of these ceremonies in the powwow context—and the idea that the powwow itself is a ceremony—will not be covered in this article, even if these elements are a part of the continental Indigenous dwelling we are outlining here.

8 The literature distinguishes in general two types of powwows: "Southern style," associated with communities in the American Southwest, and "Northern style," associated with communities in the Northern Plains region of the United States, in the Cree and Assiniboine regions

of the Canadian West, and even in the Ojibway communities of the southern Great Lakes region. The eastern form (Diamond) studied in this research is derived from the "Northern style" in the southern Great Lakes region.

9   See Vennum, *The Ojibwe Dance Drum*. It is important to note that the development of the contemporary powwow form was marked by various legal instances of prohibition of Aboriginal cultural and artistic practices by the American and Canadian governments from 1880 until 1950. The "Round House" that sheltered the dances of the "Big Drum Society" is thus an architectural expression tied to these restrictions, particularly since the Plains dances that inspired the Big Drum Society normally took place outdoors (Nabokov and Easton, *Native American Architecture*). That prohibition in fact fundamentally affected the history of Aboriginal dances across the continent. It was the lifting of those restrictions that largely contributed to a renaissance of Aboriginal cultures in the second half of the twentieth century. For the specifics of that prohibition, see Shea Murphy, *The People Have Never Stopped Dancing*. The perpetuation of dance practices must be understood in the context of struggles to keep Aboriginal ways of life alive (articulated in terms of territory) against the colonial structure; the nexus of political, geographical, and artistic articulations of these practices is thus situated in a circular rather than linear history, which has been marked—but not co-opted—by colonialism.

10 That being said, these nations have their own dance, song, and gathering traditions rooted in the North American history of the powwow, sometimes in ways that distinguish them from the Ojibway traditions. For example, the Haudenosaunee probably came into contact more directly with the Plains powwow form through geographic proximity and through the Indigenous renaissance in North America between 1960 and 1970.

11 It should be noted that that unlike for the Ojibways, powwows are not a part of Haudenosaunee tradition. For more on the "Champion of Champions," see Cavanagh, Cronk, and von Rosen, "Vivre ses traditions."

12 There is of course a network of competition dancers who work the powwow circuit to make money and who choose the powwows they attend to maximize their prize earnings. In this research, though, we have chosen to focus on traditional powwows and on the social and spiritual motivations of the dancers and other participants.

BIBLIOGRAPHY

Albers, Patricia C., and Beatrice Medicine. "Some Reflections on Nearly Forty Years on the Northern Plains Powwow Circuit." In *Powwow*, ed. Clyde Ellis, Luke Eric Lassister, and Gary H. Dunham, 26–45. Lincoln: University of Nebraska Press, 2005.

Berbaum, Sylvie. *Ojibwa Powwow World*. Thunder Bay: Lakehead University of Northern Studies, 2002.

Browner, Tara. *Heartbeat of the People: Music and Dance of the Northern Powwow*. Champaign: University of Illinois Press, 2002.

Cavanagh, Beverley, M. Sam Cronk, and Franziska von Rosen. "Vivre ses traditions: Fêtes intertribales chez les Amérindiens de l'Est du Canada." In *Recherches Amérindiennes au Québec* 28, no. 4 (1988): 5–22.

Diamond, Beverly. *Native American Music in Eastern North America*. New York and Oxford: Oxford University Press, 2008.

Ellis, Clyde, Luke Lassiter, and Gary Dunham, eds. *Powwow*. Lincoln: University of Nebraska Press, 2005.

Nabokov, Peter, and Robert Easton. *Native American Architecture*. New York and Oxford: Oxford University Press, 1989.

Sioui, Georges E. *For an Amerindian Autohistory*. Montreal and Kingston: McGill–Queen's University Press, 1992.

Shea Murphy, Jacqueline. *The People Have Never Stopped Dancing: Native American Modern Dance Histories*. Minneapolis: University of Minnesota Press, 2007.

Valaskakis, Gail. *Indian Country: Essays on Contemporary Native Culture*. Waterloo: Wilfrid Laurier University Press, 2005.

Vennum, Thomas. *The Ojibwe Dance Drum: Its History and Construction*. Saint-Paul: Minnesota Historical Society Press, [1982]2009.

Young Bear, Severt, and R.D. Theisz. *Standing in the Light: A Lakota Way of Seeing*, Lincoln: University of Nebraska Press, 1994.

ABOUT THE AUTHORS

Maeve Conrick is Professor and former Principal of the UCD College of Arts and Humanities, University College Dublin, Ireland. She has published extensively in books and journals in the areas of Sociolinguistics and Applied Linguistics, with particular reference to French and English in Canada, France, and Ireland. Among her publications are *French in Canada: Language Issues* (Peter Lang, 2007, co-authored with V. Regan) and *Multiculturalism and Integration: Canadian and Irish Experiences* (University of Ottawa Press, 2010, co-edited). She is a former President of the Association for Canadian Studies in Ireland, a recipient of the Prix du Québec, and a Trustee of the Ireland–Canada University Foundation (ICUF).

Olivier Craig-Dupont is in the final stage of a PhD at the Université de Montréal. His dissertation focuses on the political history of the land trust movement in Quebec. It looks at how this devolution and privatization of nature has affected land dynamics, especially in terms of land values, access to property, and rural gentrification. His work is based on the theoretical framework of recent environmental history, specifically on the use of scientific rationality in the construction of ideas of nature, a theme explored in this present contribution on the social— and physical—construction of the Canadian national park wilderness.

Munroe Eagles is Director of the Canadian Studies Academic Program and Professor of Political Science at the University at Buffalo–SUNY, where he has taught since 1989. His main research interests are Canadian politics and political geography. He is currently serving as President of the Association of Canadian Studies in the United States (ACSUS).

Dalie Giroux has taught political theory at the University of Ottawa since 2003. Her research explores the many ways in which space, language, and power interact. She has published several articles (referred and otherwise) on language, post-industrial spaces, university, theatre, America, Indigenous questions, Quebec, methodological anarchism, emancipation, state violence, Nietzsche, Deleuze, Agamben, and Sloterdijk. She is a member of the editorial board for *Les Cahiers de l'Idiotie*.

Rachel Killick is Emeritus Professor of Quebec Studies and Nineteenth-Century French Studies and Visiting Research Fellow at the University of Leeds, UK, and also Adjunct Professor at University College Dublin. Her research highlights the crucial role of writers, dramatists, and filmmakers in defining and shaping the socio-cultural landscape of twentieth- and twenty-first-century Quebec. It has focused in particular on Michel Tremblay, portraitist of Montreal's Plateau Mont-Royal and father of modern Quebec theatre, but has also included work on the poetics of landscape in the cinema of Léa Pool and on consumerism and landscape in North America as critiqued by the novelists Noël Audet and Catherine Mavrikakis.

Jane Koustas served as the Craig Dobbin Professor of Canadian Studies at University College Dublin for several mandates. She is a Professor in the Department of Modern Languages and Literatures at Brock University, St. Catharines, Ontario, where she also directed Canadian Studies. Professor Koustas's research interests include English-Canadian literature in translation, translation theory and practice, translation history in Canada, Quebec theatre, and theatre translation. She is the co-editor of five books: *Plurilinguisme et pluriculturalisme : Des modèles officiels dans le monde*, with Gillian Lane-Mercier and Denise Merkle; *Canadian Studies: Past, Present, Praxis*, with Christl Verduyn; *Translating from the Margins : Traduire depuis les marges*, with Denise Merkle et al.; *Théâtre sans frontières: Essays on the Dramatic Universe of Robert Lepage*, with Joe Donohoe; and *Vision/Division Théâtre : l'oeuvre de Nancy Huston*, with Marta Dvorak. Professor Koustas published *Les belles étrangères : Canadians in Paris*. She recently published *Robert Lepage on the Toronto Stage: Language, Identity, Nation*.

Amélie-Anne Mailhot, a PhD candidate at the University of Ottawa, specializes in Indigenous politics in Canada and critical theory. Her current research inquires into and conceptualizes materialist dimensions of Indigenous and feminist political thought, using literary criticism, ethnography, and creative non-fiction.

Jane Moss is a Visiting Scholar at Duke University, where she directed the Center for Canadian Studies (2007–15). She was the Robert E. Diamond Professor at Colby College (Maine), where she taught French and Francophone Studies for thirty years. A past president of the American Council for Quebec Studies, she is the editor of its bilingual, interdisciplinary journal, *Québec Studies*. For her scholarship and promotion of the study of French Canada, the Government of Quebec awarded her the Prix du Québec in 2002 and the International Council for Canadian Studies awarded her a Certificate of Merit in 2015.

Caitríona Ní Chasaide is a lecturer at the Limerick Institute of Technology. Her research interests include sociolinguistics, immersion education, language learning in a study-abroad context, and technology-enhanced learning. She is a former secretary of the Association of Canadian Studies in Ireland and former committee member of ALFIT, AFA and AFLS.

Tim Nieguth is Associate Professor of Political Science at Laurentian University. His research centres on nationalism, secession, and everyday culture. His recent publications include the edited volume *The Politics of Popular Culture: Negotiating Power, Identity, and Place* (McGill–Queen's University Press, 2015).

Professor **Gearóid Ó hAllmhuráin** is an award-winning Irish musician, ethnomusicologist, and cultural historian. Formerly Jefferson Smurfit Professor of Irish Studies and Professor of Music at the University of Missouri–St. Louis, he holds the bilingual Johnson Chair in Quebec and Canadian Irish Studies at Concordia University, Montreal. Funded by the Quebec government, his research focuses on cultural memory and Irish soundscapes in Quebec and Canada since the fall of New France. He is the author of *A Pocket History of Irish Traditional Music*, as well as recordings, chapters, and articles on Irish music and culture. His *Flowing Tides: History and Memory in an Irish Soundscape* was published by Oxford University Press in 2016.

Pádraig Breandán Ó Laighin is a Research Associate at the Social Science Research Centre, University College Dublin. Previously, he was Professor of Sociology and Coordinator of Social Sciences at Vanier College, Montreal. He has published articles on the social history of the Irish in Quebec, especially the catastrophic events at Grosse Île during the Great Famine. He holds an MA in Psychology from McGill University and a PhD in Sociology from University College Dublin.

Édith-Anne Pageot is a Professor of Art History at the Université du Québec à Montréal. Her research pertains to art practices and critical discourses related to the politics and the negotiation of identity from the perspective of sustainable development in modern and contemporary visual culture in Canada. Working with both Aboriginal and non-Aboriginal subjects, her interests include notions of gender, intersubjectivity, community, and territory. She is a member of l'Institut de recherches et d'études féministes (IREF-UQÀM).

Tracey Raney is an Associate Professor in the Department of Politics and Public Administration at Ryerson University in Toronto, Ontario. Her research interests include national identity in Canada, politics and popular culture, and women and politics. Her publications on national identity have appeared in international and Canadian journals such as *Nations and Nationalism*, *Journal of Canadian Studies*, *Critique Internationale*, and *Canadian Journal of Political Science*.

Julie Rodgers is lecturer in French at Maynooth University, Ireland. She holds a PhD on the topic of Quebec Women's Writing from Trinity College Dublin. She has published various articles and chapters in the field of Quebec literature but predominantly relating to the work of Gabrielle Roy, Francine Noël, and Ying Chen. She is the incoming president of the Association for Canadian Studies in Ireland (ACSI) for 2016–18.

Stephen A. Royle is Emeritus Professor of Island Geography at Queen's University Belfast, where he taught for almost forty years. He was Director of the university's Centre of Canadian Studies. The most significant of his publications on Canada is *Company, Crown, and Colony: The Hudson's Bay Company and Territorial Endeavour in Western Canada* (2011). He was an Eccles Centre Visiting Fellow in North American Studies at the British Library in 2007 and a winner of the Prix du Québec in 2010. He is a Member of the Royal Irish Academy.

David A. Wilson is a Professor in the Department of History and the Celtic Studies Program at the University of Toronto, and is the General Editor of the *Dictionary of Canadian Biography*. A Fellow of the Royal Society of Canada, he has written widely on the Atlantic world and on the Irish in North America. His books include a two-volume biography of Thomas D'Arcy McGee, as well a study of the United Irishmen in the United States. He has also edited books on Irish nationalism in Canada, the Orange Order in Canada, Ulster Presbyterianism, and Scottish and Irish encounters with Indigenous peoples.

Shauna Wilton is as Associate Professor of Political Studies at the Augustana Campus of the University of Alberta, Canada. Her research focuses on the politics of inclusion and exclusion, gender and ethnicity, in Canada and Europe. She has published articles and book chapters on immigration, national identity, gender, media, popular culture, and pedagogy. Her current research focuses on the political construction of national identity and on the politics of mothering.

INDEX

Aataentsic creation story (Wendat), 12–13
Aboriginal peoples. *See* First Nations peoples
Acadia: colonial history, 18–20, 222; Treaty of Paris, 18; and United Empire Loyalists, 222
Acadian deportation: art depicting, 103–4; and British imperialism, 101; British motivation for, 92; commemorative monuments, 105; English depictions of Acadians, 96; as ethnic cleansing, 92; "Evangeline" and reappropriation of collective memory, 5–6; Evangeline as foundational myth of Cadiens, 96–99; flight/migration, 94; and folklorization of culture, 103; historical accounts of, 93, 95, 104; loyalty oath, 92, 222; official apology, 104–5; oral literature, pre-deportation, 96; 1750 population, 93; St. Martinville (Louisiana), as site of false memory, 97–98; and *survivance*, 96; tourism, and Evangeline story, 100–101. *See also* Grand Pré National Historic Site
Acadian Historical Museum, 103
Acadian Reminiscences (Voorhies), 97
actant: as source of action, 67–68
Action from Ireland (AfrI), 132
Action Grosse Île, 133, 136
activist *chansonniers*, 146–47, 164n5
actor-network theory, 67
Ad Vielle Que Pourra, 226
Afghanistan: "Operation Enduring Freedom," 47, 57; public response to war deaths, 54
Agricultural Rehabilitation and Development Act (ARDA), 31
Air Canada, 20
air travel: and continentalization of Canada, 20
Akenson, Donald, 227
Akins, Thomas, 93, 100

alter egos: and objective documentary, 190; queer territories of, 178–84, 190n5; in refutation of self-colonizer, 184
Amundsen, Roald, 21, 23
Ancelet, Barry Jean (Jean Arceneaux), 104
Ancient Order of Hibernians, 131, 137
Anderson, Benedict, 1, 63
Andrews, Emily, 226
Angel Island (US), 17
Anglo-American Convention, 15
Anishnabe (Ojibway/Algonquin) peoples, 243; powwow origins in eastern Canada, 247, 259n10; Three Fires Confederacy, 248
Arceneaux, Jean (Barry Jean Ancelet), 104
Arsenault, Samuel, 104
arts: and Canadian identity, 66; challenge to stereotypes, 6–7; contemporary Aboriginal art, recognition of, 187–88; "denaturing" of landscapes, 177; depictions of land/landscape, 77, 79; as emancipatory resistance, 177; funding allocations to queer artists, 188; and identity mythologies, 184–85; performative function of, 184; photography, in figurative documentary painting, 184–85; and political dimension of multiculturalism, 186–89
Asia: immigration from, 124
Assemblée générale des associations irlandaises, 131
Association Coopérative de production audio-visuelle (ACPAV), 162, 171n46
Atikamekw peoples, 243, 248; powwow development, 249; powwow origins in eastern Canada, 247, 259n10
Atlantic Canada: colonial history, 18–20. *See also provinces by name*
Atwood, Margaret, 77
auto-historical approach to data analysis, 244
"A Very Fine Class of Immigrants" (Campey), 19
Azaryahu, Maoz, 68

Baffin Island, 22
Baird, John, 188
Bancroft, George, 95
Banff National Park, 32; commercial mandate of, 29
Barrack Gold, 162
Bar-Tal, Daniel, 50
Basker, Tommy, 224
Basque, Maurice, 104
Beaudoin, Abbé Jean, 219–20
Begin, Carmelle, 226
Behaim's Globe, 13
Belcher, Jonathan, 99, 102
belonging: and citizenship, 2, 49–50, 51–52; and literary migration, 7
Belting, Hans, 185
Benjamin, Walter, 183
berdache image, 178; and homosexuality, 180–81
Bermuda, 14
Best, Anita, 221
Bhabha, Homi: *The Location of Culture*, 183
Bierstadt, Albert, 181, 182, 184
Big Drum Society, 247, 259n9
Billig, Michael, 50, 78
Black, Jaime: *REDress project*, 176
Blanshard, Richard, 16, 17
blind patriotism, 49
Bloc Québécois (BQ): 2011 campaign spending, 82–83; attack ads, 83–84; landscape images in election advertising, 85
Blondeau, Lori, 177; Belle Sauvage, 178, 182, 185; Betty Daybird, 182, 191n25; and stereotypes of Aboriginal women, 182, 191n23
Blondeau, Lori: works: Cosmosquaw, 190n5; *The Lonely Surfer Squaw*, 182; *Putting the Wild Back into the West*, 185–86
Bonheur d'Occasion (Roy): mother–daughter relationship, 200–201, 214n27; nostalgia for home place, 209; sense of dislocation, 202; travel

and exploration, 204, 214n27; urban
realism of, 199–201
borders: establishment of in western
North America, 15; murals as border
demarcations, 68
Bouchard, Gérard, 188
Boudreau, Jules, 104
boundaries: perceptions of, 3
Boundary Peak 187 (Yukon), 3
Bourassa, Napoléon: *Jacques et Marie*, 95
Bourque, Denis, 104
Boyer, Christine, 103
Brasseaux, Carl, 104
Brecht, Berthold, 183
Breuilly, John, 78
Britain: colonial relationship with Canada, 111
British Columbia: *British Columbia Act*
(1866), 17; and Confederation, 20; gold
rushes, 230; as New Caledonia, 17;
Vancouver Island Colony, 15–17
British North America: Irish colonization
project, 112
Brubaker, Rogers, 63, 65, 66, 73
Bruneau, Philippe, 226
Buchanan, Alexander Carlisle, 128
Buchanan, James, 227
built environment: cultural landscape of
"things," 4; and national identity,
2; transformation of landscape into
landmark, 2
Bureau d'aménagement de l'Est-du-Québec
(BAEQ): tourism initiatives, 31
Burke, Edmund, 110
Bush, George H.W.: Gulf War media ban, 55
Byrne, Cyril, 221

Cabot, John, 18
Cadiens (Cajuns): Americanization of, 97;
bonds with Maritime Acadians, 103;
Evangeline as foundational myth
of, 96–99; memorialization of the
imagined past, 91–92

Cambrosio, Alberto, 29, 40
Campey, Lucille: *"A Very Fine Class of
Immigrants,"* 19
Canada: Canadian Irish culture, reclamation
of, 232–33; colonial history, Atlantic
Canada, 18–20; colonial history,
British Columbia, 15–17; commitment
to monarchy, 188; confederation
arrangement with Prince Edward
Island, 19–20; *Constitution Act* (1791),
227; continental articulation of,
12–13, 18; 49th parallel as border,
15; ideological representation of, 11;
Intercolonial Conference, 113; Irish
immigration, 112, 218–19; island
image of, 3, 11–12; "land" and nature,
conceptual tropes of, 2; language,
use of in definition of public spaces,
69–70; Lower Canada, 227; military
history, importance of, 56; motto,
3, 4, 28; national anthem, 3, 4–5, 11;
national identity, and the "North,"
175–76; Northwest Passage sovereignty
issues, 23; peacekeeping images of,
53–54; Protestant–Catholic conflict,
64–65; resource-based economy of, 80;
role of islands in colonization, 14; in
"Shield of Achilles" speech, 109–11; as
storied landscape, 5–6; Upper Canada,
227. *See also* Acadian deportation;
individual provinces
Canada: 2011 federal election: attack ads,
83–84, 86; campaign materials, analysis
methods, 80–82; campaign spending
by party, 82–83; land/landscape
as political tool, 77–78; landscape
images in election advertising, 4–5,
77–78, 83, 84–85, 86–87; negative
campaigning, 83–84, 86; positive
advertising messages, 84–85, 86; social
construction of landscapes, 78–80
Canada Land Inventory, 31

Canadian Forest Service, 33
Canadian Irish identity: traditional music in construction of, 217–18
Canadian National Parks conference (1968), 31
Canadian National Railways, 20
Canadian Pacific Railway, 20, 230; Evangeline, marketing of, 100–101
Cape Breton Island: colonial history, 18, 92, 222; and Confederation, 20; as Île Royale, 18; Northside Irish, 224. *See also* Irish traditional music
Cape Columbia, 3, 11
Cape Spear (Nfld.), 3, 11
Careless, J.M.S., 125
Carewe, Edward: *Evangeline* (film), 98
Carignan, Ti-Jean, 226
Carrière, Marie, 198
Cartier, Jacques, 235n40
Casgrain, Abbé Henri-Raymond, 93, 95
Cassidy, Frank, 230
Catholic Church: and French Catholic nationalism, 65; and Irish Catholicism in Canada, 119–20; position of in Canadian life, 112–13
Catlin, George, 179, 180–81, 182, 184
Cauquelin, Anne, 179
Ceasy, John, 223
CFB Trenton, 4; repatriation ceremonies, 47–48, 51
Chapman, Rosemary, 202, 213n18
Charest, Jean, 134, 160; Plan Nord, 158, 169n36
Chen, Ying, 197
Cher, 180, 187
Chiasson, Herménégilde, 104
Chiasson, Zénon, 104
cholera epidemic: deaths at Grosse Île, 128–31; Grosse Île quarantine, 127–28; spread of in Canada, 127–31
Chrétien, Jean: on parks research policy, 35; support of national parks, 31–32
citizenship: national identity, and sense of belonging, 2, 49–50, 51–52; role of documentary films in construction of, 162
civic rituals, role of in national identity, 49, 50
Clark, Ian, 230
Claudel, Paul, 97
climate change. *See* environmental concerns
Coalition pour que le Québec ait meilleure mine, 158
coasts: role of in definition of space and place, 3
Coates, Colin, 8
Cobalt (Ont.), 153, 168n30
code switching, 6
Cody, William Frederick (Buffalo Bill), 183, 187
Cole, M.M.: *One Thousand Fiddle Tunes*, 228–29
Coleman, Michael, 223, 226, 232
collective forgetting, 102
collective identities: in construction of ethnic diversity, 64–67; malleability of, 64–65; state role in identity construction, 65–67
collective memory: and collective forgetting, 102; in commemoration of dislocation, 103; and Grosse Île and the Irish Memorial National Historic Site, 136–38; and historical consciousness, 2; and imagined community, 1–2; of Irish Canadians, 6, 131, 138–41; and national identity, 92; of oral history, 93, 95; permanent evolution of, 8; reappropriation of, 5–6; usability of, 5
colonial history: Acadia, 18–20, 222; British Columbia, 15–17; and sexual experiences of territory, 186–89
colonization: role of islands in, 14
Comhdháil na nEagras Éireannach, 131
Comité du suivi du projet de la compagnie minière Osisko, 159
Comité Québec–Irlande, 131
Commission de l'Odyssée acadienne, 105

communication systems: and national unity, 113
Comparative Manifesto Coding Database (Manifesto Project), 80–81
Concordia University: School of Canadian Irish Studies, 226
Confederation: and Atlantic Canada, 18–20; and continentalization of Canada, 20–22; "Shield of Achilles" speech, 109–11
Confiant, Joe, 224
Connaughton, Daithí, 229
Connellan, Thomas, "Killecrankie," 224
Connolly, William, 225
Conseil d'administration de l'Association minière du Quebec, 158
Conservative Party: 2011 campaign spending, 82–83; attack ads, 83–84; landscape images in election advertising, 84–85
Consolidated-Bathurst: in the Mauricie, 33, 36
constructed authenticity, 101
constructive patriotism, 49
Copps, Sheila, 136
Corrigan, Eric, 236n42
Corrigan, Keith, 236n42
Corvec, Daniel, *Noranda*, 147, 152
Costello, Lisa, 100
Côté, Marcel, 159
Cousineau, Sophie, 160
Craig-Dupont, Olivier, 3–4, 27–46
Creighton, Helen, 223
Cremo, Lee, 231
critical discourse analysis (CDA) of campaign materials, 81
Cronon, William, 28
Crooks, Harold: *Surviving Progress/Survivre au progrés* (film), 145
Crow, Charlie, 231
Crowe, Catherine, 229–30

cultural values and practices: maintenance of traditions, 7–8; role of in creation of national/historical identity, 3; and way of seeing, 6
Curtis, Bruce, 66

Dafford, Robert, 98
Daguerre, Louis, 185
Darley, Felix O.C., 181
David, Ohad, 50
Day, Gaston, 149
Deery, Eugene, 230
Del Rio, Dolores, 98
Dempsey, Shana, 177
Deneault, Alain: *Noir Canada*, 162, 172n48; *Paradis sous terre*, 161
Den Toonder, Jeanette, 198–99
Department of Indian Affairs and Northern Development, 31
Derrane, Joe, 234n26
Derrida, Jacques, 179
Désaulniers Club, 34
DesBrisay, Thomas, 19
Desjardins, Richard: narrative technique, 148–49; as singer/songwriter, 146–47, 164n4, 164n9, 165–66n14, 167n22; use of colour/black and white, 154–55; voice-over narration, 153–54
Desjardins, Richard: works: "16-03-48" (song), 152; *Comme des chiens en pacage*, 147, 148, 164n10, 165n11; *Le Party* (Falardeau), 147; *Le peuple invisible*, 160; *L'erreur boréale/Forest Alert*, 6, 146, 147–51, 161; "Le Screw" (song), 147, 164n6; "Les Fros" (song), 152; *Mouche à feu (Firefly)*, 147; *Noranda*, 147; *Paroles de chansons*, 147; *Trou Story/The Hole Story*, 146, 152–56, 156–59
Desmeules, Pierre, 35
Désy, Pierrette, 180
De Vere, Terence, 140

Dionne, Dominique, 158
dioramas: as political space, 185, 192n35; *Putting the Wild Back into the West* (Stimson/Blondeau), 185–86; spectator participation, 185–86
Dobbs, Kildare, 221
documentary films: *Bûcherons de la Manouane (Lumberjacks of the Manouane River)* (Lamothe), 147–48, 151, 165n13; *Comme des chiens en pacage* (Desjardins/Monderie), 147, 148, 164n10, 165n11; and the digital revolution, 162–63; *Fort McMoney* (Dufresne), 172n49; International Cinema Festival of Abitibi-Témiscamingue, 152, 158; and investigative reporting, 162; *La règle d'or [The rule of gold]* (Paquet), 146, 170n39; *Le peuple invisible* (Desjardins/Monderie), 160; *L'erreur boréale/Forest Alert* (Desjardins/Monderie), 6, 146, 147–52, 165n13, 165–66n14, 166n21; *L'or des autres [Other people's gold]* (Plouffe), 146, 170n39; Montreal International Documentary Film Festival, 145–46; *Mouche à feu (Firefly)* (Desjardins/Monderie), 147; *Noranda* (Monderie/Corvec), 147, 152; role in construction of citizenship, 162; *Surviving Progress/Survivre au progrès* (Crooks/Roy), 145; *Trou Story/The Hole Story* (Desjardins/Monderie), 6, 146, 152–56, 156–59
Dominion Atlantic Railway, 100–101
Domtar, 33
Doody, C.W., 221
Douglas, George Mellis, 128, 140
Douglas, James, 16
Doyle, Mogue, 222
Duceppe, Gilles, 85
Duchesne, André, 158
Dufresne, David: *Fort McMoney*, 172n49
Dupuy, Michel, 134
Duval, Jean, 227

écriture migrante: journeys, and quest for identity, 199, 211; literary immigration, 7; as outsiders within, 207–9; as poetics of movement, 198–99; of Quebec literature, 197–99; tensions of identity and culture, 202–3; trauma of, 211, 214n37; tropes of migrant aesthetics, 198–99
Elle et Lui (Léger), 96
Ellesmere Island, 3, 11
Ellis Island (US), 17
emancipatory resistance of art, 177
Emerson, Ralph Waldo, 28
Enbridge Pipeline 9, 161
environmental concerns: Alberta Oil Sands, 161, 171n43, 172n49; Enbridge Pipeline 9, 161; in Green Party advertising, 85–86; Kyoto Accord, 80; Lac Mégantic, 161; local approaches to corporate activities, 161; mining industry, 152–56, 159–61, 167–68n25, 168n28, 169n37; shale gas exploration, 161, 171n43; timber industry, 147–52; treatment of in documentary films, 147–51
ethnic diversity: alignment with bilingualism, 70; collective identities in construction of, 64–67; and new materialism, 72–73
ethnic identity: and "groupness," 65, 66–67; and material objects in construction of, 64, 72–73
ethnicity: and new materialism, 64, 72–73
Evangeline (film), 98
Evangeline (Longfellow): adaptations of, 95–101; *faux lieu de mémoire*, 92, 99; *lieux de mémoire*, 91, 100; memorialization of the imagined past, 91–92; reappropriation of collective memory, 5–6; as Romantic heroine, 95; and tourist industry, 100–101. *See also* Acadian deportation
Evangeline (Mullins), 98–99

Evangeline Oak, 97
Evans, E. Estyn, 219

Faëd, Thomas, 97
Fagnan, Grandy, 231
Falardeau, Pierre: *Le Party*, 147
Faragher, John Mack, 104
Farhoud, Abla, 197
faux lieu de mémoire of Evangeline, 92, 99
Ferguson, Samuel, 116
Ferrie, Adam, 140
figurative documentary painting, 184–85
Fillion, Valérie, 158
film. *See* documentary films
First Nations peoples: adoption of Irish/
    Scottish traditional music, 221,
    226, 230–31, 235n40; *agokwa*, 180;
    contemporary Aboriginal art,
    recognition of, 187–88; creation
    stories, 12–13; land as proof of
    nationhood, 78, 80; manufacture
    of the "Indian" as object, 180;
    powwows, 7–8; residential school
    system, 22; rights of, protests and
    demonstrations by, 22–23; treatment
    of in documentary films, 149, 150,
    166n19; two-spirit beings, 178, 180.
    See also powwows
Fitzgerald, Winston "Scotty," 224
Flaherty, Jim: Economic Action Plan 2012, 161
Fletcher, Joseph F., 51
folk music culture: studies of, 221
Forest, Leonard, 100
Forest Ontario: Highway of Heroes Tribute,
    55
forestry: in the Mauricie, 30
Fortier, Dominique: *Gabrielle Roy Réécrite*,
    204
Fortune, Billy, 224
Fortune, Henry, 224
Fowke, Edith, 223
France: Acadian colonies of, 18; traditional
    music of, 221

Franklin, Sir John, 13
Frobisher, Martin, 23
Fund for Rural Development (FRED), 31

Gadamer, Hans-Georg, 2
Gagnon, Mario, 158
Gallant, Melvin, 104
Gavan Duffy, Charles, 116
gaze: social construction of, 177, 180;
    and identity mythologies, 184–85
Gellner, Ernest, 78
gender: perceptions of nature as influence
    on, 176–77; and territoriality of
    sexuality, 176–77
Gendron, François, 158
General Assembly of Irish Organizations,
    136; campaign for Grosse Île and the
    Irish Memorial National Historic Site,
    131, 132, 133–34
geographic landscape: and national identity,
    11–12
geological surveys: in definition of the
    nation-state, 27
Gilbert Lewis, Paula: *The Literary Vision
    of Gabrielle Roy*, 203
Gilchrist, Donnie, 229
Gillis, Duncan, 230
Giroux, Dalie, 7–8, 243–59
Gleaner Tales (Sellar), 137
global warming. *See* environmental
    concerns
Goerner, Jocelyn, 226
Goerner, Reinhard "Golo," 227
Goldstein, Kenny, 221
Gordon, David, 1
Governors Island, 14
Gow, Neil, 224
Graham, Rodney: *Upside Down Trees*, 176
Grand Pré National Historic Site, 5–6;
    Acadian deportation, 91–92;
    Acadian Historical Museum, 103;
    as focus of politicized collective
    memory, 100–101; as *lieu de mémoire*,

102–3; memorialization of Acadian deportation, 101–4
grassroots patriotism: and Canadian neoliberalism, 54; as citizen-led, 50, 57; and Highway of Heroes, 48, 50, 51–52; as shared grief, 52; and state/institutional patriotism, 48, 52–54
Gray, R.C.: La Mauricie National Park master plan, 35–37
Green, Mary Jean, 200–201
Green Party: 2011 campaign spending, 82–83; attack ads, 83; environmental concerns, 80; landscape images in election advertising, 85–86
Grieve, Edward, 33
Grievous Angels: *Waiting for the Cage*, 155
Griffiths, Naomi, 104
Grosse Île: annual commemorations, 137, 138; built environment, and national identity, 2; Celtic cross, 126, 132, 137; Cholera Bay, 128; cholera mortality, 128–31; cholera quarantine, 127–31, 225; famine victims, 235nn36–37; historical documentation of immigrants health, 140–41; immigrant cemetery, 128, 130, 132, 225; as island gateway, 17; as "prohibited place," 137–38; typhus, 129
Grosse Île and the Irish Memorial National Historic Site, 6, 17, 123–44; Celtic cross, 126, 132, 137; cholera quarantine, 127–31; consultation process, 131, 132–34; final appeals, 135–36; and HSMBC recommendation for development, 123–24; ideological support for Irish dimension, 138–41; Irish Canadian response to proposals, 125, 131, 132–34; "Keegan diary," 136–37; marginalization of Irish experience, 125–27; naming of, 136; Parks Canada secret report, 134, 136; promotional orientation of development concept, 125–27; *Report on the Public Consultation Program* (Parks Canada), 133; thematic interpretations of, 123–24, 132; trilingual signage, 132
Groulx, Lionel, 93, 95–96
"groupness": ethnic identities, 65, 66–67
Group of Seven: and Canadian identity, 66, 77, 79, 175; Lawren Harris, 178, 191n7; portrayals of wilderness, 2, 6, 28, 187

Haida Gwaii (formerly Queen Charlotte Islands), 12
Haliburton, Thomas C., 93
Hannay, James, 93; *The Story of Acadia*, 101
Harkin, James B.: scenic beauty of national parks, 29
Harper, Stephen: conservative national identity, 56; environmental record, 161; images of in election advertising, 84–85; media ban from repatriation ceremonies, 55
Harris, Lawren: *North Shore, Lake Superior*, 178, 191n7
Haudenosaunee (Mohawk) peoples, 243, 248; Champion of Champions powwow, 249, 259n11; Kahnawake, 249; Manawan powwow, 249–50; Mashteuiatsh powwow, 249–50; Opiticwan powwow, 249–50; powwow origins in eastern Canada, 247, 259n10; Six Nations, 249; Wemotaci powwow, 249–50
Hayday, Matthew, 49
Heartland and Hinterland (McCann), 21
Hébert, Henri, 101
Hébert, Louis-Philippe, 101
Henry, Frances, 187
Highway of Heroes, 4; built environment, and national identity, 2; as challenge to state patriotism, 52–54; as demonstration of Canadianness, 53; and grassroots patriotism, 48, 50, 51–52; media coverage, 47, 52–53; memorial coin, 56; official renaming

of, 55; political responses to, 55–56; provincial governments recognition of, 55; Quebec response to, 52, 54; repatriation ceremonies, public response to, 47–48, 51–52
hip hop: and Aboriginal identity, 66
historical consciousness: and collective memory, 2
Historic Sites and Monuments Board of Canada (HSMBC): Grosse Île, development as national historic site, 123–24; political dimension of, 124
Hobsbawm, Eric, 49
Hodgins, Peter, 2, 3, 5
Hodson, Christopher, 104
Holland, Jerry, 234n26
homosexuality: attitudes of European explorers towards, 180–81
Hopson, Peregrine, 99
Hornaday, William Temple, 176
Houssaye, Sidoníe de la: *Pouponne et Balthazar*, 96
Houston, Cecil J., 227
Hove, Jennifer, 51
Hudson's Bay Company: Indian Trades Policy, 16; and northern Indigenous peoples, 21–22; and Vancouver Island Colony, 15–17
Huffman, L.A., 176
Huiskamp, Gerard, 51–52
Hurley, Brad, 226

identity. *See* national identity
Île Royale. *See* Cape Breton Island
Îles de la Madeleine. *See* Magdalen Islands (Îles de la Madeleine)
Île St-Jean. *See* Prince Edward Island
imagined community: and collective memory, 1–2
Imagining of a Canadian Archipelago (Vannini), 12, 18
immigrants and immigration: assisted emigration schemes, 218, 227; chain migration, 218, 227; disjunction with historical canon, 125, 127; Grosse Île and the Irish Memorial National Historic Site, 123–44; Highland Scots, 222, 228; sponsored immigrants, 222. *See also* Irish immigration
Innu (Montagnais) peoples, 243, 248; powwow development, 249; powwow origins in eastern Canada, 247, 259n10
insularity of islands, 12–13, 14
Intercolonial Conference, 113
Intercolonial Railway, 20, 113
International Cinema Festival of Abitibi-Témiscamingue, 152, 158
Inuit: postcolonial impact on traditional lifestyle, 21–22
Ireland: Fenianism, and parochialism, 119; Great Blasket Island, 13; Great Famine (*An Gorta Mór*), 17, 118, 136, 222; Henry VIII as king, 118; Irish sense of victimhood, 117–18; parochialism in, 6; railway development, and national unity, 113; Young Ireland movement, 116
Irish immigration: cholera mortality, 128–31; disjunction with historical canon, 125, 127; famine immigrants, 125, 127, 225, 228, 235nn36–37; Grosse Île quarantine station, 127–28, 225; to Quebec, 225; settlement patterns, 218–19, 227–29, 235n32
Irish Memorial National Historic Site. *See* Grosse Île and the Irish Memorial National Historic Site
Irish Protestant Benevolent Society, 131
Irish traditional music, 7; and Athapaskan dance music, 231–32; breakdowns, 228; *Bringing It All Back Home* (BBC documentary), 233; and Cape Breton music, 223–24, 234n26, 235n28; clogs, 228; An Coimisiún le Rincí Gaelacha, 229; Comhaltas Ceoltóirí Éireann, 230; cultural memory, transmission of, 217–18; dance traditions, 224, 235n28;

"devil tunes," 231; Donegal dance music, 227; fiddling competitions, 227; folk festivals, 231; Gaelic League, 229; and Highland Scottish music, 223–24; in history of Canada, 232–33; hornpipes, 228; jigs, 228; in the Maritimes, 221–24; in Newfoundland, 219–21; Northside Irish, 224; Orcadian fiddling, 231; quadrilles, 218, 224, 226, 231, 236n41; in Quebec, 225–27; reels, 218, 224, 228; regional music dialects, 219; stepdancing, 229; uilleann pipes, 223, 225; in western Canada, 230–32
Isenberg, Andrew, 176
islands: and colonization, 14, 18–20; as gateways, 15–17; geographic perceptions of, 12–13, 14; as immigration stations, 17; and international boundaries, 15; as "outlying," vs. gateways, 20; role of in definition of space and place, 3, 11–12
Island Studies Journal, 12
Ives, Edward D., 223

Jackson, Jim, 140
Jacques et Marie (Bourassa), 95
Jasper National Park, 32; commercial mandate of, 29
Jones, Steve, 227
Joseph, John, 129

Kane, Paul, 179, 184; as tourist-explorer, 181–82; *Wanderings of an Artist among the Indians of North America*, 182
Kathan, Lynda, 227
Kattan, Naïm, 197
Katz, Jonathan D., 179
Kavanagh, Don, 230
Kavanagh, Laurence, 222
Keane, Ellen, 128
Keane, John, 128
Kelly, James, 234n26
Kelly, Jimmy, 236n42

Kennedy, Arthur, 232
Kennedy, Liam, 117
Kerwin, Larkin, 135
Khordoc, Catherine, 198
Killick, Rachel, 6, 145–74
Killoran, Paddy, 232
Kilmer, Alfred Joyce: "Trees," 149, 166n18
King, Allan, 236n42
King William Island. *See* Nunavut
Kornblum, Jacqueline, 140
Krauss, Rosalind, 184

La Bolduc (Mary Travers), 225–26
La Bottine Souriante, 226
L'Action boréale, 152
Laferrière, Dany, 197
Laflamme, Myriam, 226
Lahaie, Alain, 158
La Laurentide pulp and paper company, 33
La Mauricie National Park: "Canadian Shield" region, 38; cleanup work, 33–34; folklorized presence of human history, 39; founding of, 27; Grand-Mère plantation, 37; inclusion in Parks Canada transnational grid, 37–40; industrial and recreational imprint, 33–34; Lake Wapizagonke, 33; as "Laurentian Heritage," 35, 37; master plan, 35–37; private hunting/fishing clubs, 33–34; proposal for, 32; restructuring of hybrid landscapes, 30; scientification of landscape, 39–40; scientific ecology in reinvention of wilderness, 34–37; thematic sections of, 39; zoning arrangements, 36–37
Lamothe, Arthur: *Bûcherons de la Manouane (Lumberjacks of the Manouane River)*, 147–48, 151, 165n13
Lanctôt, Denis, 230
land: and national identity, 78–80; political use of images, 78–80, 81; portrayals of, 2; as source of national identity,

77–78; themes of in art/literature, 77; trope of, 2
landmarks: as sites of memory, 3; transformation of landscape into, 2
landscape(s): dynamic/static interpretations of, 8; as measure of space and place, 3; and the "Other," 6; perception of as collective memory, 1–2; in political advertising, 83, 84–85, 86–87; political use of, 4–5, 77–78; scientification of, 39–40; in "Shield of Achilles" speech, 109–11; social construction of, 78–80; transformation of into landmark, 2
Langan, Chris, 229
L'Anse aux Meadows, 14
Lapointe, Ugo, 158
La règle d'or [The rule of gold] (Paquet), 146
L'Association de l'exploration minière du Québec, 158
Latour, Bruno: actant, as source of action, 67–68
Laurentian Club, 34
Laurier, Wilfrid, 153, 168n27
Lawrence, Charles, 99, 102
Layton, Jack, 84
LeBlanc, Barbara, 104
Leblanc, Carl-Hugues, 158
Leblanc, Robert, 105
LeBouthillier, Claude, 104
Le Carrefour Francophone, 70
Lederman, Anne, 231
Leduc, Jacques, 151
Lee, Charles, 14
Léger, Antoine-J.: Elle et Lui, 96
le Grand, Albert, 203
Legrand, Paul, 226
Le Grand Dérangement. See Acadian deportation
LeLoutre, Abbé, 92, 99, 100
Lemay, Pamphile, 95
Leonard, Robert, 226
L'erreur boréale/Forest Alert (Desjardins/Monderie), 6, 146, 147–51, 165n13, 165–66n14, 166n21; and National Film Board, 162; reception and impact, 151–52, 161
Les Acadiens à Philadelphie suivi de Accordailles de Gabriel et d'Évangeline (Poirier), 96
Lesbian National Parks and Services (Millan), 177
Le Vent du Nord, 226
Lévesque, René, 156
Liberal Party: 2011 campaign spending, 82–83; attack ads, 83–84
lieux de mémoire of Evangeline, 91, 100
Limoges, Camille, 29, 40
literature: adaptations of Evangeline story, 95–101; built environment, and national identity, 2; depictions of land/landscape, 77; landscape, and nationality, 114–16; landscape as way of seeing, 5; migration literature, 7. See also écriture migrante
logging: and lumber industry. See timber industry
Longfellow, Henry Wadsworth: commemorative monument of, 103; Evangeline, 91–92, 103
Longval, Philipe, 226
L'or des autres [Other people's gold] (Plouffe), 146
Louisbourg, 92
Louisiana: Evangeline, and tourist industry, 100; Evangeline as foundational myth of Cadiens, 96–99; St. Martinville, 92
Lyon, Nancy, 226

Mac Conmara, Donncha Rua: Bánchnoic Éireann Ó (The Fair Hills of Ireland), 220; Eachtra Ghiolla an Amaráin (Adventures of a Luckless Fellow), 220
Macdonald, Angus L., 223
MacDonald, Dougie, 223, 234n26
Macdonald, John A.: commercial mandate of park resources, 29; confederation arrangement with Prince Edward Island, 19–20
MacDonald, Monica, 100–101

Macdonald, Sandfield, 113
Macdonald–Cartier Freeway. *See* Highway of Heroes
MacEachern, Big Dan Hugh, 234n26
MacGabhann, Aindriú, 226
MacGabhann, Antóin, 223, 234n26
MacGabhann, Mící: *Rotha Mór an tSaoil*, 230
MacKay, Eva, 178
MacKinnon, Charlie, 234n26
Maclean's (magazine): Highway of Heroes media coverage, 53
MacLeod, Alistair: *The Lost Salt Gift of Blood*, 221
MacMaster, Natalie, 223, 234n26
Magdalen Islands (Îles de la Madeleine), 14
Mailhot, Amélie-Anne, 7–8, 243–59
Maillet, Antonine, 104
Malartic (Que.), 152–53, 155–56, 158, 159
Mangan, James, 140
Manhattan (New Amsterdam), 14
Manifesto Project, 80–81
Manning, Erin, 79
Mannion, John, 221
Marche, Stephen, 53
marginality: as projective past, 183–84
Marois, Pauline, 160
Marshall, William, 224
Martin, Paul, 135
material objects: agency of, 67–68; Belfast murals as border demarcations, 68; influence on social realities, 63–64; street names, 68–69
Matte, Jacques, 158
Maurer, Louis, 181
May, Elizabeth, 85
McCann, Larry: *Heartland and Hinterland*, 21
McCarthy, Dalton, 64–65
McGee, Thomas D'arcy, 230; and American continental imperialism, 111; and Canadian monarchy, 111, 114, 118; Fenianism, and parochialism, 119; Intercolonial Railway, 113; on landscape as literary theme, 114–15; preoccupation with Irish history, 116–18; "Shield of Achilles" speech, 109–11; "Shin Fane" colonization project, 112; and ultramontanism, 113, 117; and Young Ireland movement, 116
McGee, Thomas D'Arcy: literary works: *Canadian Ballads and Occasional Verses*, 114, 116; Celtic themes in, 116; "Jacques Cartier," 115; *Popular History of Ireland*, 117–18; "Sebastian Cabot to his Lady," 115; "Thomas Moore at St. Anne's," 115–16; "Time's Teachings," 116
McGuire, Seán, 223, 226
McHarg, Ian, 36
McIntosh, David, 180
McKenna, Sine, 227
McMichael Canadian Art Collection: and Miss Chief Eagle Testickle, 179–80
McNally, Bridget, 128
media: appeal of celebrity endorsement, 163; and Canadian identity, 66; election campaign ads, 77–78; investigative reporting, 162; performative function of, 184; repatriation ceremonies, coverage of, 47, 52–53; views on mining industry, 158–59
Mellin, Robert, 221
memorialization: in creation of historical identity, 1–2, 3
Memorial University Folklore and Language Archive (MUNFLA), 221
Merkle, Denise, 104
Messer, Don, 227
Micone, Marco, 197
Middle Island (Lake Erie), 3, 11
migration literature, 7
Mi'kmaq people: adoption of Irish/Scottish traditional music, 221, 231; relations with Acadians, 92, 96
Millan, Lori: *Lesbian National Parks and Services*, 177
Miller, David, 53

Minalliance, 157, 158
mindscapes: as imaginary geographies, 199
mining industry: in commercial mandate of park resources, 29; environmental concerns, 152–56, 167–68n25, 168n28, 169n37; international takeovers, 167n23; and investigative reporting, 162; in the Mauricie, 31; mining royalties, 160; *Noranda* (film, Monderie/Corvec), 147, 152; opencast gold mining, 152–53; shale gas exploration, 161; *Trou Story/The Hole Story* (film, Desjardins/Monderie), 6, 146, 152–56, 156–59; working/living conditions of miners, 153–54, 163–64n3, 168n27
Mitchel, John, 118
Mitchell, W.O., 77
Monderie, Robert: *Comme des chiens en pacage*, 147, 148, 164n10, 165n11; *Le peuple invisible*, 160; *Mouche à feu (Firefly)*, 147; *Noranda*, 147, 152; *Trou Story/The Hole Story*, 146, 152–56, 156–59
Monkman, Kent, 177, 190, 192n35; and manufacture of the "Indian" as object, 180; signature clothing, and "brand" fetishism, 187, 189, 190, 191n23
Monkman, Kent: works: *Artist and Model*, 181; *Beat Nation*, 190; *Fort Edmonton*, 181; *Group of Seven Inches*, 179; Miss Chief Eagle Testickle, 178, 179–82; *The Prayer Language* series, 179, 191n10; *Sakahàn*, 187, 190; *Superior*, 178–79, 191n10
Montreal, 236n42; cholera epidemic, 130; famine victims, 235nn36–37; as Irish port of entry, 218, 219, 226, 236n43; and Irish traditional music, 226–27; "le Camp des Indignés, Victoria Square occupation, 145; professional musical ensembles, 226; "Rue des Irlandais," 138; Victoria Bridge monument, 138, 139, 235n36

Montreal International Documentary Film Festival, 145–46
monuments: as mnemonic devices, 103
Moore, Thomas: "Canadian Boat Song," 115
Morency, Jean, 204, 206–7
Morgan, Cecilia, 8
Morgan, Ceri, 199
Mormons, 15
Morrison, James, 226, 232
Morton, Desmond, 127
Moss, Jane, 5–6
Mouche à feu (Firefly) (Desjardins/Monderie), 147
Mousseau, Normand, 161
Muir, John: Yellowstone Park, 28
Mullins, Richard F., 101–2; *Evangeline* (novel), 98–99
Mulroney, Brian, 133, 134
multiculturalism: and Canadian federalism, 188–89; and otherness, 190; in postwar identity, 56; and queer geographies, 186–89
multilateralism: and peacekeeping, 53–54
mummering, 220–21
murals: Aboriginal history, exclusion of, 71; as border demarcations, 68; ethnic diversity of, 70–71
Murdoch, Beamish, 93, 100
music. *See* Irish traditional music
Myre, Nadia: *Rethinking Anthem*, 176

Nash, Roderick, 28
national anthem: and ideological representation of Canada, 3, 4–5
National Film Board of Canada (NFB): and *L'erreur boréale/Forest Alert* (Desjardins/Monderie), 162
national identity: and "a-where-ness," 79; challenges to, 176; and collective memory, 92; conceptual tropes of, 2; conservative brand of, 56; and cultural practices, 3; and ethnic difference, 65–67; Evangeline, and French

heritage, 95; and geography, 11–12; and grassroots patriotism, 50, 57; ideological representation of Canada, 11; land as source of, 77–78; landscape, and nationality, 114–16; landscape as measure of space and place, 3–4; memorialization, in creation of historical identity, 1–2, 3; patriotism, and the national collective, 48–49; railway development, and national unity, 113; role of documentary films in construction of, 162; and sense of belonging, 49–50, 51–52, 78–80; social perceptions of the "North," 175–76; and territorial sovereignty, 78, 80
nationalism and nationalist movements: land, and national identity, 78–80, 85
national parks: *Canadian National Parks* conference (1968), 31; commercial mandate of, 29; and cultural identity, 27–28; as economic stimulation, 31–32; as "frontier-objects," 40; future park planning, themes in, 37–38; as historiographical productions, 40–41; official representations of as natural, 35; popularity of as potential curse, 31; recreational activities, 30; re-establishment of wildlife, 35; scientific ecology in preservation of wilderness, 27–30; as social/political construct, 3–4. *See also* La Mauricie National Park
National Parks Service (US), 37
national symbols: tropes of, 2, 3, 4–5
nation-state: and collective memory, 1–2; as imagined communities, 63; role of in identity construction, 65–67; role of science in definition of, 27
nature: trope of in national image, 2; wilderness as social/political construct, 3–4
Neatby, Nicole, 2, 3, 5
Nepveu, Pierre, 198
Nestsilik Inuit: HBC relationship with, 21–22

New Brunswick, 18; cholera epidemic, 130; Irish immigration, 222–23; and Irish traditional music, 221–23
New Caledonia. *See* British Columbia
New Democratic Party (NDP): 2011 campaign spending, 82–83; attack ads, 83–84; landscape images in election advertising, 84
Newfoundland, 3; Cape Spear, 3, 11; colonization of, 14; and Confederation, 18, 20; Grand Banks fishing fleets, 219–20; Irish traditional music in, 219–21; lancers, 224; Memorial University Folklore and Language Archive (MUNFLA), 221; mummering, 220–21; as *Talamh an Éisc*, 220; wintermen, 220
new materialism: and ethnic diversity, 72–73; and social constructivism, 63–64
Nicol, John I., 39
Nieguth, Tim, 4, 63–75
Noir Canada (Ecosociété), 162
Nora, Pierre, 3, 100
Noranda (Monderie/Corvec), 147, 152
North America: insularity of, 12–13, 14; as island in European views of, 13; national identity, and geography, 11; as "New Island," 13
Northwest Passage: and Amundsen, 21, 23; and Franklin, 13, 21; and global warming, 23; sovereignty issues, 23
Nova Scotia: and Acadian neutrality, 92; Cape Breton Island, 18; colonial history, 18, 222; and Confederation, 20; George's Island, 102; Highland Scots, arrival of, 222; and Irish traditional music, 221–24; Sable Island, 14; tartanism, 223, 234n23; Treaty of Paris, 18; Treaty of Utrecht, 222. *See also* Acadian deportation; Grand Pré National Historic Site
Nunavut, 11; home rule in, 22; King William Island, 21, 22

O'Brien, Ena, 229
O'Brien, William Edward, 64–65
Ó Catháin, Rory Dall: "Port Gordon," 223–24
The Ocean Plague (Whyte), 136
O'Connell, Daniel: *Catholic Emancipation Act*, 228
O'Driscoll, Robert: *The Untold Story*, 137
O'Grady, Brendan, 223
Ó hAllmhuráin, Gearóid, 7
Ó Laighin, Pádraig Breandán, 6, 123–44
Olivier, Alfred, 98
O'Loughlin, Éamonn, 229
Ontario: Irish settlement patterns, 227–29; and Irish traditional music, 227–30; Ottawa Valley Irish communities, 227–29; Scottish traditional music, 228; stepdancing, 229
"Operation Enduring Freedom," 47
oral history: of Acadian deportation, 93, 95
O'Reilly, Myles: "Marbhna Luimní" ("Lochaber No More"), 224
Ornstein, 226
Osborne, Brian, 1, 79, 82
Osborne, Evelyn, 221
Osisko mining corporation, 145–46, 152–53, 155–56, 159; environmental impacts, 159–60, 168n26, 169n33; publicity campaign, 157, 158
O'Sullivan, Maurice, 13
the Other: "otherness" of ethnic minorities, 197–99; as outsiders within, 207–9; and perceptions of place, 6; and the self-colonizer, 186; toleration of in multiculturalism, 190
Ottawa: and traditional Irish music, 230
Ouellette, Gilles, 39

Pageot, Édith-Anne, 6–7, 175–96
Papazian, David, 226
Paquet, Nicholas, 159; *La règle d'or* [*The rule of gold*], 146, 170n39
Paquin, Mario, 158

Parkman, Francis, 95
Parks Canada: evolution of mandate, 28–30; Grosse Île consultation process, 131, 132–34; Grosse Île and the Irish Memorial National Historic Site, 124, 125; Grosse Île secret report, 134, 136; *Guiding Principles*, 29; National Parks System Planning Manual (1972), 37–38, 41; parks as historiographical productions, 40–41; *Report on the Public Consultation Program*, 133; research policy, 35–37; wilderness as museum of natural history, 38–39; wilderness as social/political construct, 3–4
parochialism, 6; and Fenianism, 119; of Irish Catholicism, 117–18; and national unity, 113
Parti Québécois, 124, 160
patriotism, 4; blind patriotism, 49; constructive patriotism, 49; grassroots patriotism, 48, 50, 51–52; political research on, 48–50; and shared grief, 52; as socio-cultural phenomenon, 49; as state resource for nation-building, 48; symbolic resources of, 49; top-down vs. bottom-up process, 50. See also Highway of Heroes
peacekeeping: in Canadian postwar images, 53–54, 56
Pearson, Lester B., 31
Pellan, Alfred: *Coast to Coast*, 188
performative memorialization, 100
Petition Grosse Île, 133
Petrowski, Nathalie, 157, 158
Phenigma, 227
Picard, Claude, 103, 104
Plouffe, Simon, 159; *L'or des autres* [*Other people's gold*], 146, 170n39
Pocahontas: stereotype of, 182, 187
Pocius, Gerald, 221
Poirier, Pascal: *Les Acadiens à Philadelphie suivi de Accordailles de Gabriel et d'Évangeline*, 96

political parties: 2011 federal election, analysis methods, 80–82; attack ads, 83–84; campaign spending by party, 82–83; land and identity, manipulation of, 79–80; negative campaigning, 83–84; use of landscape images, 4–5, 77–78, 83, 84–85, 86–87
popular culture: and Canadian identity, 66
Pouponne et Balthazar (de la Houssaye), 96
power relations: of collective identities, 64; of colonialism, 179; of sexual identity, 183
powwows, 7–8; auto-historical approach to data analysis, 244; Big Drum Society, 247, 259n9; Champion of Champions powwow, 249, 259n11; circular layout, significance of, 246; competition dancers, 256, 259n12; competitive powwows, 245; contemporary practice, development of, 247–48, 259nn9–10; continental origins of, 247–48; continental territoriality of, 248; as cultural practice, 246; as cultural transfer from Great Plains Warrior ceremonies, 247; dance, as prayer, 252; data collection and analysis, 243–44; demographic makeup, 245; Diamond form, 258–59n8; drums, placement of, 246, 258n5; elders, role of, 254; financing of, 255–56; forms of, 247, 258–59n8; generational transmission of meaning, 252–53, 255; geocultural composition of, 249–50; gestures in storytelling, 253; gifting/exchange, practice of, 255–57; giveaways, 256–57; grandfather stones, 246; "Indian Country," geographical/political conception of, 244–45; as medium of traditional teaching, 253–54; movements of, 251–57; as mutual apprenticeship, 254; Northern style, 258–59n8; origins of in eastern Canada, 247–48, 259n10; reconnection with family, 250; as social practice, 245; Southern style, 258–59n8; spatial orientation of, 246, 258n5; special dances, 255, 258n7; storytelling (the dance), 251–54; as vector of regional/continental exchanges, 257–58; as way of gathering, 251; Wikwemikong Cultural Festival, 253
powwow trail: journey of, 246–47, 250; group travel, 255–57, 259n12
Prince Edward Island: colonial history, 18–20; Irish immigration, 222–23; and Irish traditional music, 221–23; leasehold tenure, and absentee landlords, 19; as St. John's Island, 19; Tenant League, 19; Treaty of Paris, 18
Princess Patricia's Canadian Light Infantry: "Operation Enduring Freedom," 47
Pronovost, Denyse, 29, 40
Prosper, Will, 231
Protestant–Catholic conflict: *Jesuit Estates Act*, 64–65

Qikiqtaaluk (formerly Baffin Island), 22
Quebec, 85; adoption of Irish orphans, 132; Bill 14 *On the mines*, 158, 170n42; Bureau d'aménagement de l'Est-du-Québec (BAEQ), 31; collective memory, maintenance of, 137; division into Upper/Lower Canada, 227; documentary films. *see* documentary films; ethnic diversity, accommodation of, 66; forest management, 149, 150, 161; *gigues*, 224, 226; and Irish traditional music, 225–27; *Jesuit Estates Act*, 64–65; mining industry, 146, 163–64n3; "otherness" of ethnic minorities, 197–99; patterns of Irish settlement, 235n32; Plan Nord, 158, 160, 169n36; Protestant–Catholic conflict, 64–65; Protestant Committee of Public Instruction, 64–65; public forest management policy, 150;

quadrilles, 226, 236n41; resource-based economy of, 31; role of in development of Canada, 124; sovereignty issues, 78; timber industry. *see* timber industry; tourism as economic stimulation, 31–32. See also *écriture migrante*; Grosse Île and the Irish Memorial National Historic Site; La Mauricie National Park

Quebec City: cholera epidemic, 127, 129, 130; as Irish port of entry, 218, 219, 225; St. Patrick's Day celebrations, 225; Taschereau Monument, 138, 139

Queen Charlotte Islands (now Haida Gwaii), 12

Quigley, Colin: *Close to the Floor*, 221

Quigley, Debbie, 229

railways: and continentalization of Canada, 20, 230; role in national unity, 113

Raney, Tracey, 4, 47–61

Raynal, Abbé, 93

religion and religious affiliation: as source of diversity, 65

Renauld, Claudine, 158

repatriation ceremonies: and grassroots patriotism, 51–52; media ban from, 55; national coverage of, 52–53; public response to, 47–48, 52

residential school system, 22

Ricard, François, 202–3, 205–6, 211

Richard, Zachary, 104

Riel, Louis: Irish ancestry of, 230, 237n61

Roanoke colony, 14

Roberts, Charles G.D., 93; *The Land of Evangeline and the Gateways Thither*, 101

Robertson, Ian Ross, 19

Robin, Régine, 197

Robinson, Mary, 134, 136

Robinson, Peter, 218, 227, 228

Roche, Marquis de la, 14

Rodgers, Julie, 7, 197–216

Roosevelt, Theodore, 28

Rosenberg, Neil, 221

Rossignol, Rino Morin, 104

Roussel, Claude, 103–4

Rouyn-Noranda (Que.), 153; environmental pollution, 154

Roy, Gabrielle, 7; cycle of exile and return, 202–3; and *écriture migrante* of Quebec literature, 197–99; feminist scholarship on, 200–201; as "filles des pionniers," 205–6; migrant instinct, 204–7; migrant mindscape of, 198–99, 212–13, 213n18; "otherness" of women in patriarchal society, 201–2; as outsider, 207–9; as quintessential migrant, 212–13; transgressive aspects of, 199–201

Roy, Gabrielle: works: *Alexandre Chenevert*, 202, 203; *Bonheur d'Occasion*, 199–201, 202, 203, 204, 207, 209, 214n27; *Bulletin des Agriculteurs*, 201–2; *De quoi t'ennuies-tu Eveline*, 204; *Fragile Lumières de la Terre*, 202; *La Détresse et L'enchantement*, 202, 207–8, 210; *La Montagne Secrète*, 202, 203, 209; *La Petite Poule d'Eau*, 203; *La Rivière sans repos*, 204; *La Route d'Altamont*, 202, 203, 204, 209; *La Rue Deschambault*, 202, 203, 209

Roy, Mathieu: *Surviving Progress/Survivre au progrés* (film), 145

Royal Canadian Mint: Highway of Heroes memorial coin, 56

Royle, Stephen, 3, 11–25

Runte, Hans, 104

Ryan, William Bradbury: *Ryan's Mammoth Collection*, 228

Sable Island (N.S.), 14

Sacher, William: *Noir Canada*, 172n48; *Paradis sous terre*, 161

Sadlier, Mary Ann, 116

Saint John (N.B.): as Irish port of entry, 218

Saint-Martin, Lori, 201

Sarkisian La Pierre, Cherilyn, 180

Schryer, Pierre, 230

scientific ecology: ecological planning approaches, 36; and institutional culture of national parks, 41; and parks research policy, 35–37; in reinvention of wilderness, 27–30, 34–35
Scotland: Highland Clearances, 222, 228
Scott, James: *Seeing Like a State*, 65–66
Scottish traditional music: in Maritime provinces, 221, 223
Secord, Laura, 8
Seeing Like a State (Scott), 65–66
Sellar, Robert: *Gleaner Tales*, 137; *The Summer of Sorrow*, 137, 140
sexuality: alter egos, queer territories of, 178–84, 190n5; berdache image, 178, 180–81; conquering masculinity vs. urban feminization, 176–77; and games of power, 183; perceptions of nature as influence on, 176–77; and queer geographies, 186–89; queer spaces as alternate location, 183–84; and territoriality of gender, 176–77; and the *trickster*, 178; two-spirit beings, 178, 180
Shannon, Sharon, 223
Shawinigan Club, 33, 34
"Shield of Achilles" speech (McGee), 109–11
Siamsa School of Irish Music, 226
Simard, Serge, 158
Sioui, Georges: *For an Amerindian Auto-History*, 244
Skinner, James Scott, 226
Smith, Anthony, 78
Smith-Lamothe, Terry, 103
Smyth, William J., 227
Snow, Michael: *The Central Region* (video), 176
social constructivism: *explanandum* vs. *explanans*, 65; "groupness," and ethnic identities, 65, 66; and new materialism, 63–64, 72–73
Société d'exploitation des ressources éducatives du Québec (SEREQ), 35–36
Société nationale de l'Acadie, 105

Sorlin, Sverker, 79
soundscapes, 7
sovereignty issues: First Nations peoples, 78, 80; Northwest Passage, 23; of Quebec, 78
speculative realism, 67
Stephens, James, 230
stereotypes: visual art as challenge to, 6–7, 178–84, 186, 189
Stevens, Bill, 231, 232
Stimson, Adrian, 177; Buffalo Boy, 178, 183, 185; sexuality, and games of power, 183
Stimson, Adrian: works: *Putting the Wild Back into the West*, 185–86; Shaman Terminator, 190n5
St. John's (Nfld.): Irish population, 220
St. Martinville (Louisiana): Acadian Memorial, 98; Evangeline Oak, 97; as false site of false memory, 97–98; as *faux lieu de mémoire*, 92; Longfellow-Evangeline State Historic Site, 97; memorialization of the imagined past, 91–92
Stornoway Diamond mining, 160
Story of Acadia (Hannay), 101
St. Patrick's Society, 131, 132, 135
street names: Aboriginal history, exclusion of, 69; British/French dualism of, 69–70; as reflection of social power relations, 68–69
Stubbert, Brenda, 224
Stubbert, Robert, 224
Sudbury (Ont.): Bridge of Nations, 71–72; and cultural landscape of "things," 4, 64, 73; mining industry, 153, 154; murals, 70–71; public signs, 69–70; street names, British/French dualism of, 69–70
Sullivan, Dan, 234n26
The Summer of Sorrow (Sellar), 137, 140
survivance, 96
Surviving Progress/Survivre au progrés (film, Crooks/Roy), 145

Tajfel, Henri, 51
Talbot, Richard, 227
tartanism, 223, 234n23
Taschereau, Elzéar-Alexandre, 138
Tenant League of PEI, 19
Thériault, Joseph-Yvon, 104
Thomson, Tom: *The Jack Pine*, 28
Thoreau, Henry David: *Walden*, 28
Thornham, Sue, 81
timber industry: *Bûcherons de la Manouane (Lumberjacks of the Manouane River)* (Lamothe), 147–48, 151, 165n13; in commercial mandate of park resources, 29; and deforestation of public land, 147–51, 165–66n14; Domtar annual general meeting, 149–50; forest management, 149, 150, 161; and investigative reporting, 162; *L'erreur boréale/Forest Alert* (Desjardins/Monderie), 147–52, 165n13, 165–66n14, 166n21; in the Mauricie, 31, 33–34
Timmins (Ont.), 153, 167–68n25; Hollinger Mine fire, 154
Toronto: cholera epidemic, 129; Irish communities in, 219, 228, 229
tourism: authenticity of wilderness, 175, 190n1; as economic stimulation, 31–32; Evangeline, marketing of, 100–101; in national park mandate, 29, 35
Trans-Canada Air Lines, 20
Trans-Canada Highway: and continentalization of Canada, 20
Travers, Mary (La Bolduc), 225–26
Treaty of Breda, 14
Treaty of Paris, 18
Treaty of Utrecht, 18, 220, 222
"Trees" (Kilmer), 149, 166n18
Tremblay, Odile, 158
Trenton Air Force Base. *See* CFB Trenton
Trexler, Richard: *Sex and Conquest*, 180
Trou Story/The Hole Story (Desjardins/Monderie), 152–56; environmental impacts, 159–60; reception and impact, 156–59, 161
Trudeau, Justin, 56
Turtle Island: creation stories, 12–13; First Nation founding myth of, 3

ultramontanism, 113, 117
United Irish Societies, 131
United Kingdom: Highway of Heroes media coverage, 53
United States: Angel Island, 17; border closure anxiety, 176; continental imperialism of, 111; Ellis Island, 17; 49th parallel as border, 15; Highway of Heroes media coverage, 53; and Irish traditional music, 232–33; Northwest Passage sovereignty issues, 23; "Support the Troops" campaign, 51–52; wilderness, and cultural identity, 27–28
unity. *See* national identity
urban landscape: cultural landscape of "things," 4

Valaskasis, Gail: *Indian Country*, 244
Vancouver Island: and British Columbia, 20
Vancouver Island Colony: *British Columbia Act* (1866), 17; European settlement of, 16–17; Fort Rupert, 16; Fort Victoria, 15; settlement of, 15–17
Vannini, Phillip: *The Imagining of a Canadian Archipelago*, 12, 18, 22
Venice Biennale, 187
Verchères, Madeleine de, 8
Vézeau, André, 156
Viau, Robert, 104
Vinland Map, 13
Viroli, Maurizio, 48
visual arts. *See* arts
vital materialism, 67
Voorhies, Felix: *Acadian Reminiscences*, 97
Voyer, Simonne, 226

Walden (Thoreau), 28
Wallingford, Ken, 147
war(s): and national identity, 49
Watkin, Edward, 113
Wendat (Huron): Aataentsic creation story, 12–13
Whelan, Tony, 224
Whitfield, Agnès, 200
Whyte, Robert: *The Ocean Plague*, 136, 140
wilderness: and cultural identity, 27–28; in documentary films, 6; as feminine, 178; national parks as museums of natural history, 38–39; reinvention of in the Mauricie, 34–37; and scientific ecology, 27–30, 34–37; social perceptions of the "North," 175–76; as social/political construct, 3–4, 29–30
Wilmot, Johnny, 224, 234n26
Wilson, David, 6
Wilton, Shauna, 4–5, 77–90
Winslow, John, 99; and Acadian deportation, 92
Woco Club, 34
Wright, Ronald: *A Short History of Progress* (film), 145
writing: role of performance in creation of identity, 179
Wylie, John, 5, 6; *Landscape*, 7

Yellowstone Park, 28
Yoon, Jin-me: *A Group of Sixty-Seven*, 176
Young, Arthur, 220
Young Ireland movement, 118
Yukon: gold rushes, 230, 231–32

Zeller, Suzanne, 27, 41

Books in the Cultural Studies Series
Published by Wilfrid Laurier University Press

Slippery Pastimes: Reading the Popular in Canadian Culture edited by Joan Nicks and Jeannette Sloniowski / 2002 / ISBN 0-88920-388-1

The Politics of Enchantment: Romanticism, Media and Cultural Studies by J. David Black / 2002 / ISBN 0-88920-400-4

Dancing Fear and Desire: Race, Sexuality, and Imperial Politics in Middle Eastern Dance by Stavros Stavrou Karayanni / 2004 / ISBN 0-88920-454-3

Auto/Biography in Canada: Critical Directions edited by Julie Rak / 2005 / ISBN 0-88920-478-0

Canadian Cultural Poesis: Essays on Canadian Culture edited by Garry Sherbert, Annie Gérin, and Sheila Petty / 2006 / ISBN 0-88920-486-1

Killing Women: The Visual Culture of Gender and Violence edited by Annette Burfoot and Susan Lord / 2006 / ISBN 978-0-88920-497-3

Canadian Cultural Exchange / Échanges culturels au Canada: Translation and Transculturation / traduction et transculturation edited by Norman Cheadle and Lucien Pelletier / 2007 / ISBN 978-0-88920-519-2

Animal Subjects: An Ethical Reader in a Posthuman World edited by Jodey Castricano / 2008 / ISBN 978-0-88920-512-3

Covering Niagara: Studies in Local Popular Culture edited by Joan Nicks and Barry Keith Grant / 2010 / ISBN 978-1-55458-221-1

Imagining Resistance: Visual Culture and Activism in Canada edited by J. Keri Cronin and Kirsty Robertson / 2011 / ISBN 978-1-55458-257-0

Making It Like a Man: Canadian Masculinities in Practice edited by Christine Ramsay / 2011 / ISBN 978-1-55458-327-0

When Technocultures Collide: Innovation from Below and the Struggle for Autonomy by Gary Genosko / 2013 / ISBN 978-155458-897-8

Parallel Encounters: Cultural at the Canada-US Border edited by Gillian Roberts and David Stirrup / 2013 / ISBN 978-1-55458-984-5

Europe in Its Own Eyes, Europe in the Eyes of the Other edited by David B. MacDonald and Mary-Michelle DeCoste / 2014 / ISBN 978-155458-840-4

Material Cultures in Canada edited by Thomas Allen and Jennifer Blair / 2015 / ISBN 978-1-77112-014-2

Reclaiming Canadian Bodies: Visual Media and Representation edited by Lynda Mannik and Karen McGarry / 2015 / ISBN 978-1-55458-983-8

Celebrity Cultures in Canada edited by Katja Lee and Lorraine York / 2016 / ISBN 978-1-77112-222-1

Landscapes and Landmarks of Canada: Real, Imagined, (Re)Viewed edited by Maeve Conrick, Munroe Eagles, Jane Koustas, and Caitríona Ní Chasaide / 2017 / ISBN 978-1-77112-201-6

www.ingramcontent.com/pod-product-compliance
Lightning Source LLC
Chambersburg PA
CBHW072146100526
44589CB00015B/2114